P9-DBY-060

The Big Board

The Big Board

A HISTORY OF THE
NEW YORK STOCK MARKET

Robert Sobel

FOREWORD BY BROADUS MITCHELL

THE FREE PRESS, *NEW YORK*
COLLIER-MACMILLAN LIMITED, *LONDON*

Copyright © 1965 by The Free Press, A Division of The Macmillan Company. *Printed in the United States of America.* All rights reserved. No part of this book may be reproduced or transmitted in any form or by any means, electronic or mechanical, including photocopying, recording, or by any information storage and retrieval system, without permission in writing from the Publisher. Collier-Macmillan Canada, Ltd., Toronto, Ontario. Library of Congress Catalog Card Number: 65-23023.

FIRST FREE PRESS PAPERBACK EDITION 1968

For Carole

Foreword

THE BIG SKY of American life has been reflected in the Wall Street pool of water. Perhaps my metaphor contains unfortunate reminders of collusive action and fraud which I do not intend at this point. A reflecting telescope may be a better figure, a polished bowl which collects light from every quarter and concentrates it. Or the stock market is a computer which selects, combines, and condenses from a vast store of data (without, however, possessing the comprehensive, accurate memory of the machine).

This book describes much more than the mechanism for trading in securities, though the operations of the exchange are skilfully explained. Beyond mere technical aspects, the author reports, through the medium of dealings in shares and bonds, the procession of developments in this country and, indeed in the world. Nothing of consequence has happened—political, military, economic, social, scientific—that has not been registered in quantitative terms. Of course, this does not mean that market estimates of imponderable forces have been accurate. The errors of bulls and bears have not canceled each other. Professor Sobel's story is full of extravagant hopes and fears that proved to be unfounded. At times fraud has contributed to miscalculations. At other junctures a worthy concern for the public good has overcome inducements to private advantage. The author's vivid language reenacts stressful hours on the floor and their gratifying or painful results. Historic crises in Wall Street have involved more than speculators and brokers, for government has frequently intervened to correct or support, and even clergymen have been rallied to exhort the public confidence.

In later chapters the oneness of the world is evident in financial appraisals of events all over the globe. It is ironic that no political, diplomatic, or cultural organization of peoples—League of Nations or United Nations—is so sensitive to human threats and promises as the money market.

The doings which Dr. Sobel recounts belong to the capitalistic economy. One may not better learn of its serviceable or mischievous motives than by reading these lively pages. In a constantly shifting scene, the intrusions of government responsibility, and of planning both in business and society generally, become prominent, and the end is not yet.

The author has drawn on a multiplicity of sources—reminiscences of the victorious and the defeated, contemporary newspaper accounts, official reports, and the comments of knowledgeable observers. He moves familiarly in this welter of materials, selecting with the candor of a scholar and the skill of a narrator. Though he scrupulously points us to his authorities, his friendly pages are not encumbered with research apparatus. His sketches of actors at dramatic moments form an engaging feature of his chronicle. These characters range from the noble to the base, from the wise to the foolish.

Whether the reader begins by thinking the stock market a sink of iniquity or a useful instrument in the prevailing society, he will be informed by this agreeable history.

BROADUS MITCHELL

May, 1965

Preface

AS FAR AS I KNOW, this is the first history of the New York Stock Market to be attempted. There have been several specialized studies of different periods in the history of Wall Street, many biographies of American financial leaders, and a handful of popular sketches of an anecdotal nature regarding the market. No one, however, has traced the development of the institution from its beginnings.

The present work is by no means a comprehensive one. Such a task would require the lifetimes of several researchers and result in a multivolume tome. Instead, I have tried to write a short history of the market, stressing different aspects at different times.

Carl Becker, the great American historian, once wrote that a man without history is the victim of amnesia. One of the more important tasks of history, he said, is to discover how we got to be what we are. This has been foremost in my mind while researching and writing this book, which is, primarily, an effort at explaining the origin and development of the financial district. I have tried to show how different pressures—political, social, locational, as well as economic and financial—have effected the New York money market.

In doing this, I have concentrated my attention on the New York Stock Exchange. Almost everyone who has an interest in American finance realizes that other markets handle a substantially greater proportion of trading than the Exchange—the government bond market alone is larger—and that the financial district is not centered on the Exchange Building. Still, the Big Board is and for a long while has been the natural leader on Wall Street, and because of this, it occupies the center of the stage.

I have also tried to tell the story of those individuals who were central to American investment banking and brokerage. One need offer no excuse for such an undertaking, for certainly men like Jay Cooke, Jay Gould, J. P. Morgan, E. H. Harriman, and Charles Merrill were far more important than many of the political figures of their times, who occupy space in textbooks unwarranted by their influence on the nation's destiny. The first decade of the present century was as much the Age of Morgan as it was that of Roosevelt and Wilson. Gould and Cooke were far more important to their period than any president from Grant to Roosevelt. It may be argued that Charles Merrill will one day be considered to have had greater impact on postwar capitalism than any economist of his day.

A final reason for this book involves the excitement of the financial district. Even to New Yorkers, Wall Street seems to have little in common with Times Square, and is almost a different city, unknown to most citizens of Manhattan Island. Still, the fascination of Wall Street rivals that of Broadway, and men like Jim Fisk, Daniel Drew, and Bet-A-Million Gates were more theatrical than any actor produced by the Forty-fifth Street showcases. In part, then, this book has been undertaken for the sheer joy of the task.

At the center of my drama is Wall Street. While it is true that the Street is only a small part of a larger financial district, it is, nonetheless, the symbol of finance capitalism. At the present time plans are being made to construct a new Exchange building at the south end of Broad Street. Even if trading does move there, it is difficult to imagine the Kremlin attacking "the plutocrats of Battery Park" rather than those of Wall Street.

A work of this magnitude is never done alone, especially when the author has academic and other duties to consider. I owe a large measure of gratitude to those in charge of the business divisions of the New York Public Library, the New York University Library, the Columbia University Library, and the New York Stock Exchange Library. The librarians and staff of the Hofstra University Library were most helpful in every stage of the work and with their aid, I was able to do most of my research there.

I have spoken to perhaps hundreds of brokers, analysts, and bankers about my undertaking, and have found all to be helpful. The gamut of talent in the financial district, as elsewhere, runs from utter incompetency to brilliance, and I have seen both extremes.

The late Burton Crane, one of the great financial writers and analysts of his day, was most generous in offering his time and advice, both of which were thankfully accepted. Gerald Kitay of Reynolds & Co. allowed me to try out many of my ideas on him before committing them to paper. My colleagues at Hofstra University were very helpful in this regard, as were dozens of brokers who, while giving advice on my interpretation of the market's history, spared me from tips on stocks.

I particularly wish to thank The Brookings Institution for permission to quote from Lester V. Chandler, *Benjamin Strong: Central Banker;* Harper & Row, Publishers for permission to reprint tabular matter from H. U. Faulkner, *American Economic History* and for permission to quote and to reprint tabular matter from John Sears, *The New Place of the Stockholder;* Simon Kuznets and Richard D. Irwin, Inc., for permission to reprint tabular material from the Revised Edition of Maurice W. Lee, *Economic Fluctuations: Growth and Stability;* The Johns Hopkins Press for permission to reprint tabular material from Joseph Hedges: *Commercial Banking and the Stock Market Before 1863;* Longmans, Green & Company, Ltd., and David McKay Company, Inc., for permission to quote and to reprint tabular material from George Edwards, *The Evolution of Finance Capitalism* (Longmans, Green & Company, 1938); Princeton University Press for permission to reprint tabular material from Ralph Nelson, *Merger Movements in American Industry;* and Vanguard Press, Inc., for permission to quote from Ferdinand Lundberg, *America's Sixty Families.*

The two most important people in the final preparation of this book were my wife and my mother. My wife read and reread every word of the manuscript with good grace and humor. My mother typed the various drafts, and gave freely of her time and effort. To them, and the many others who helped me with my task, my sincere appreciation.

Robert Sobel
Hofstra University
1965

Contents

FOREWORD *by Broadus Mitchell*   *vii*

Preface   *ix*

1. The European Background   *1*

2. Securities in Early America   *14*

3. Under English Domination: 1812–1837   *28*

4. The First Age of Rails: 1837–1857   *47*

5. The Fortunes of War: 1857–1865   *65*

6. Consolidation, Expansion, and Panic: 1865–1873   *81*

7. The Rise of Investment Banking: 1873–1884   *102*

8. All Roads Lead to Wall Street: 1884–1896   *124*

9. The Morganization of America: 1896–1903   *147*

10. The End of the Golden Age: 1903–1913   *174*

11. Genealogy of the Giant Bull: 1914–1924   *206*

12. The Triumphant Years of the Giant Bull: 1924–1929   *235*

13. Death of the Giant Bull: 1925–1933   *262*

14. Death and Transfiguration: 1933–1947   *293*

15. The Tardy Boom: 1947–1960   *321*

16. The New Wall Street: 1953–1965   *346*

Selected Bibliography   *376*

Index   *383*

The Big Board

1

The European Background

I think that it may be true that fortune is the ruler of half our actions, but she allows the other half or thereabouts to be governed by us.

Machiavelli

TWENTY-ONE MILLION AMERICANS—approximately one out of every seven adults—own common stocks. The others may have life insurance, annuities, or pension plans which, in part, are based on securities. Thus, the stock markets affect almost every citizen, not merely the "fat cats" of Wall Street. Those who never think to glance at the business section of their newspapers are more involved in the actions of the financial community than they may realize.

The purchase or sale of securities represents a speculation as to the shape of the future—although some would call it an investment, others a gamble. Man has always speculated in one way or another. Primitive farmers would not have planted their crops had they not had hope of harvesting them. Ancient nomads would pick up their belongings and move not through instinct, but rather because they knew what had happened in the past when they had failed to relocate. Today's businessman is constantly making speculations as to the condition of the economy and its future, the course of government actions, and the development of markets. Without this awareness of time and change, man could not have progressed to his present state.

Religion, a basic element of all civilizations, contains elements of speculation on the future. For example, today's Wall Streeter will recognize that Jacob in buying the birthright from Esau was a "bull," while his brother was a "bear."[1] The Pharaoh listened to Joseph's interpretations of his dreams as does today's investor scanning the predictions of his favorite financial analyst. Babylonian priests read meanings in sheep livers with as much seriousness—and perhaps as much rationality—as our chartists with their point-and-figure diagrams. In both cases, self-fulfilling prophecies are all-important. The oracles of Delphi told King Croesus of Lydia that if he crossed the Halys River to fight the Persians a great army would be destroyed. Croesus took his army across and found that the oracle was right. Unfortunately, the army was his. Oracular double-talk can be found in scores of stock market letters, which take many pages and charts to say that the averages will go up, unless they go down.

Ancient civilizations offer examples of practices developed and refined by modern finance capitalism. Mesopotamian merchants of the third millennium before Christ formed trading companies for specific projects. They would sell grain before it was harvested and merchandise it before payment, hedging in the manner of today's commodity trader. Greek "table merchants" helped finance missions to all shores of the Mediterranean. Homer tells how the Trojans would buy wine as a gamble on soldiers' thirst, and trade for large profits. The Greek philosopher Thales, who speculated on the nature of matter, also speculated on olive presses. One year he realized that the harvest would be especially bountiful, and he cornered the market in presses. He then sold them at a much higher price to the olive growers at harvest time.

Like ourselves, the Greeks were commercially inclined, but apparently they had a distaste for business as such. Xenophon, the historian, once proposed a joint-stock bank for Athens which in some respects resembled modern savings banks. This plan came to naught, and Xenophon's short career in commerce was ended. In Greece, the entrepreneur was often considered little better than a thief who stole from the farmer by buying his crops at too low a price, and then from the consumer by selling them at an exorbitant profit. It was believed that honest men would prefer work on the soil or service in the army to such rascality.

This disdain for the businessman often took the form of blaming him for the periodic depressions that occurred in most Greek trading states. Whenever a decline took place, legislation would be passed to curb business and confiscate the holdings of commercial classes. Solon, the famed lawgiver, came to power as archon of Athens in the sixth century B.C. on such a platform. He canceled debts, confiscated property, and in other ways relieved the distress of the poor at the expense of the wealthy. A member of one of Athens' most aristocratic families and a former merchant himself, Solon was decried by the businessmen as a traitor to his class.

Commerce was so vital to Rome that its disruption was an important cause of her decline. The Romans pioneered in corporate organization; they had cooperative industrial insurance and joint-stock companies formed for the primary object of bidding on government. contracts. Capital was raised by selling shares, called *partes,* to the public. The business class, known as *equites,* eventually became the most powerful force in the late Republic and during the Empire. Yet, Marcus Crassus, the wealthiest Roman of the first century B.C., could not gain political power, despite his many attempts to buy votes and senators. The Romans, like the Greeks, had a profound distrust of businessmen. Crassus had to participate in a triumvirate in order to gain the recognition that had eluded him. For a while he shared power with a soldier, Gnaeus Pompeius Maximus, and a politician, Julius Caesar. In all of Roman history not a single businessman was able to gain popularity on his own.

The Roman Catholic Church, the most important successor of the Empire, inveighed against the *avaritia* of those few businessmen who existed during the Middle Ages. To gain wealth from the sweat of fellow Christians was a sin, although a merchant might make a profit by risking his capital in a venture. In any case, the merchant was an unimportant part of medieval society, for landholding was the base of feudal life and the manor, not the city, was its center. Most businessmen were little more than traveling merchants, who carried their wares on their backs or in small carts from fair to fair. They would barter for cloth in one town and then exchange it for wine, salt, or other trading goods in another.

By 1000, some businessmen had formed associations resembling the old Roman companies. The *Mahona,* a share-holding firm engaged in piracy, was popular in northern Italy. During the Crusades this form was used by merchants who made fortunes by bringing crusaders to the Middle East and then returning with trading goods to Italy. Since capital was scarce and risks great, they existed to pool resources and divide losses.

Still, the most common form of business enterprise at this time was the sole proprietorship. The late medieval businessman was like the traveling merchant in some respects. He was his own banker and accountant, shipper and warehouser, correspondent and insurer. The major difference was that he was sedentary, engaging in his varied enterprises from a single location.

As commerce increased and became more complex, however, he was obliged to take on men and equipment. After a while the merchant found that it was more economical to hire shops than to buy them, using the capital he had accumulated for more profitable functions. Insurance soon became a separate business, as did banking. Motivated by a desire to share risks, some merchants also organized joint-stock companies with others in the same field. These firms were limited as to duration, purpose, and capital. A joint-stock enterprise in commerce for example would involve several ships sent on a specified voyage. After the trip, the profits and capital would be shared, and the company would be ended. Such enterprises were not popular, however, and were entered into rarely and with great reluctance. So long as business remained petty, the sole proprietorship predominated.

The Renaissance merchants built on these foundations, adding little although enlarging the scale. With the revival of trade during and after the Crusades, opportunities for profit abounded. A return of over 1000 per cent on a voyage to the Middle East was not unusual in the fifteenth century. Because of the increased demand for capital, the joint-stock companies became more common, creating a new problem: that of trust. Governments were weak, and no means of enforcement of contracts existed outside of personal policing. Thus, the entrepreneurs were obliged to develop a code of honor; to break faith meant to be expelled from the society of merchants forever. By the fifteenth century a merchant's word was his bond. While a corrupt Church and untrustworthy nobles and kings scraped for power, businessmen in Italy honored pledges of businessmen from England and Scandinavia. This trust (some have called it honor among thieves) is still a hallmark of modern brokerage.[2]

During this period the first brokers appeared.[3] Their original function was to bring together parties interested in a business transaction. The brokers would congregate in towns, which had revived and grown after the Crusades. Some of the new centers were little more than fairs that had developed into commercial and intellectual enclaves. In the late fifteenth century individuals interested in dabbling in commerce knew that they could hear of new enterprises in these market places. The Rialto Bridge of Venice, the most famous of the crude financial districts, was the business center for much of Europe during this period, although each part of the continent had its own capital markets.

The rising class of sedentary merchants and brokers was still snubbed by the nobility and the Church. Jacob Fugger, the wealthiest merchant of his time, was the grandson of a weaver; he was never allowed to forget this by those nobles with whom he dealt. Although he was able to buy himself the title of Count of the Empire, Fugger was sneered at as an *arriviste*. And if the great Fugger were held in such contempt, lesser merchants were more openly reviled.

A marked change took place with the Reformation. John Calvin claimed that salvation could not be earned; rather, it must be considered a gift from God to the elect. Some reasoned that God would give a sign to a chosen few, and that this sign might be in the form of worldly accomplishment. Many merchants snatched at this interpretation, and they became the bulwark of the Calvinist movement. Wealth, considered evil in itself by the Catholic Church, was viewed as a sign of divine grace by Calvinist congregations. Still, despite this theological change, the merchant was to be excluded from polite society in most of Europe until the late nineteenth century.

The commercial revolution of the sixteenth, seventeenth, and eighteenth centuries gave strong impetus to capitalism in general and to the merchant class in particular. Despite wars of religion and the dislocation within Europe, new opportunities in the Far East, Near East, and the Americas dazzled the middle class. Transportation and communication developed with nationalism, making possible larger trading areas and more internal tranquillity than had existed before. With larger markets came larger opportunities, and there are records of boom and bust in hundreds of joint-stock ventures of the period. In the sixteenth century German mining companies, usually made up of members of the same family, were in vogue. The Hochstetters and their allies tried unsuccessfully to corner the European supply of quicksilver, essential to the production of silver. The Rotts narrowly failed in their attempt to corner pepper. The Fuggers adapted to the new mania, and although their bid to monopolize tin was blocked, they did, for a short period, control most of Europe's copper.

The rapid expansion in trade, the increase in the amount of money in circulation, and the enlarged vision of the merchant-capitalists led to speculative orgies in the seventeenth and eighteenth centuries. Permanent joint-stock companies, such as the famed East India Company of England and the Dutch East India Company, were formed by favored merchants and nobles, and a lively trade in their shares took place. Smaller, less ambitious companies also appeared, and they solicited openly for the financial support of investors. In this area the Netherlands was far ahead of the rest of Europe. Small joint-stock companies, known as *rederijii,* were organized for every conceivable kind of venture. The *reders* (shareholders) might be interested in mill construction, the operation of a kiln, or a single voyage to the Orient. In most cases provision was made in the charter for dissolution after a given number of years. So long as the time factor was short, the original shareholders tended to keep their portions until dissolution. Later, when the ventures became permanent, the investors would often sell their shares when their prices went up or down. An active market developed, first in Antwerp, then in Amsterdam, the financial center of northern Europe during much of the seventeenth century. Brokers would mill in the streets of trading districts, buying and selling shares for their own accounts and those of customers. Since such business would not be sufficient to keep them busy, they tended to diversify into bills of exchange, commercial paper, and lottery tickets.

While the Netherlands controlled the seas, the *liefhebbers,* or bulls, ruled the markets, and stocks generally advanced. In the beginning of the seventeenth century some brokers began to realize that concentrated selling over a relatively short period of time might cause the less wary to offer their shares at low prices, in this way spreading and intensifying the decline. If prices could be beaten down artificially at first, frightened investors could be counted upon to join in and push prices still lower. Those who realized what was happening could then step in and buy shares at bargain prices. "Bear raids" of this nature were soon common in Amsterdam.

It was not long before some brokers developed a technique that further multiplied their profits: they sold shares they did not own just before depressing prices. After the market had collapsed, they bought the shares needed for delivery at prices lower than were specified in the first contract. Of course, if a broker had not actually delivered the shares he had sold, but had waited until the price had declined, he would have made this profit without having committed his capital. This method, known as the short sale, became a powerful weapon in the hands of the bears. It appeared later on in every major financial market, and was used extensively by Wall Street bears during and after the nineteenth century.

The most sensational market of the early seventeenth century was not in shares, however, but in tulip bulbs. The flowers had been introduced to the Netherlands from Turkey, and soon they had captured the imagination of the usually cautious Dutch burghers. In 1630 markets for bulbs opened in Amsterdam and Rotterdam, and from there spread to every urban center in the nation. Eventually each western European state had its own tulip exchange. Sober businessmen would obtain loans on their property in order to purchase a handful of very ordinary looking bulbs, whose only value lay in the fact that within a fortnight someone else would be willing to pay a higher price for them.[4] Bulbs became a form of currency, much like American cigarettes in Germany after World War II. By 1635, such species as the *Semper Augustus, Admiral Liefken,* and *Viceroy* brought fortunes on the market. *Viceroy,* an especially desirable variety, cost 2,500 florins on the Amsterdam Bourse at one time, when a yoke of oxen could be purchased for 250 florins and a suit of clothes for 80.

Toward the end of 1635, a few bulb merchants who began to realize that the craze could not continue forever entered into short contracts on the high-priced bulbs. Then, late in November, a sailor happened to visit the Amsterdam Bourse, where he picked up a *Semper Augustus,* and thinking it to be an onion, proceeded to eat it. The loss of the bulb, which cost the equivalent of $10,000 in the currency of the day, caused great consternation in the market. Some began to wonder whether the bulbs were worth the high prices they commanded. Panic erupted, and within a week the bulbs were almost worthless. The short sellers reaped new fortunes and others—especially the amateurs—lost their shirts.[5]

The Amsterdam market took a generation to recover from the tulip craze, but by the end of the century, commodity and security trading was again in full swing. So successful were some of the firms, that a new stock mania began. In addition, funds were exported to other countries, especially France and England.

The middle classes of these countries were less venturesome than the Dutch merchants. Nevertheless, trading was carried on in both nations as early as the fourteenth century, and financial districts appeared in the seventeenth century. Dutch, English, and French traders often entered into contracts together when their countries were at war with one another. Money was able to cross boundary lines when individuals found it difficult. During the Anglo-Dutch Naval Wars,

Dutch funds helped finance many English commercial schemes that promised vast profits.

In the early eighteenth century, during the great period of Anglo-French rivalry, a Scotch financier imprisoned for having murdered his mistress' husband escaped from England to the continent. This colorful rake, John Law, wandered from country to country, trying to interest different rulers in his plans for a central bank. The Dutch and the English already had banks that acted as depositories, issuing demand notes on the metal in their vaults. Theoretically, each note was based on 100 per cent gold backing. Many suspected, however, that the Dutch bank was investing the gold at a profit, realizing that so long as the public had confidence in the bank, they would transfer the certificates as though they were gold itself, and few would demand redemption. Law knew that the true backing for currency was trust in its purchasing power, and not in any special virtue of the yellow metal. He proposed an institution which would act as a depository, a central bank, and the prime investing medium of the nation. It would be so strong and respected that none would question the backing of its notes, thus enabling an almost unlimited expansion of the gold deposits. In this way, the money supply of the country could be expanded, invested wisely, and used in the interests of the state and the depositors.

In 1717, Law gained the ear of the Duke of Orleans, then Regent for King Louis XV. France was in dire financial condition, and the Duke was shown that the bank scheme could provide him with great quantities of money with which to pay debts. Orleans and his friends would receive more than enough funds to keep the ship of state on an even keel, Law would have power and prestige, and investors in bank stock would gain generous dividends.

The bank was established, and Law was soon able to take control of many companies through the use of the gold deposits. The most important of these, the Louisiana Company, had extensive rights in the Mississippi Valley. Once he had control, Law began issuing grandiose statements about the fantastic wealth of the New World. "There one sees mountains filled with gold, silver, copper, lead, quicksilver," he proclaimed.[6] "Since these metals are common there and the savages do not imagine their worth, they exchange them for a swallow of brandy."[7]

France was soon swept by a wave of speculation which in some ways resembled the tulip mania. The Rue de Quincamoix, home of the stockbrokers, was filled with eager speculators and brokers who had hopes of doubling their fortunes in weeks. Real estate in the area increased in value, and Paris soon had not only an Exchange Alley, but also a financial district of sorts. An illusion of prosperity blanketed the city, as messenger boys converted "confidential tips" into small purchases, then doubled their transactions and emerged millionaires. A wretched hunchback was able to make a good living by lending his back for use as a portable desk to the frantic brokers, who had no time to go to their offices. The Count d'Horn, a highly respected friend of the Duke, killed a broker in order to steal his shares; Law ordered him destroyed on the wheel for his crime.

The Louisiana Company had been pledged to pay dividends at the rate of 12 per cent. To accomplish this, Law would have had to show an annual profit of over 200 million livres, which was clearly impossible for a company whose only assets were raw wilderness and hope. Some speculators realized this, and they began to sell shares short. In order to prevent a panic, Law paraded a few thousand criminals through the streets of Paris, with picks and shovels in their hands, and then announced that they were about to leave for New Orleans to mine gold. Shares shot up again, as confidence was restored in Law's financial genius.

The inevitable fall of the Mississippi scheme came in 1720. The promises of wealth did not materialize, and after two years of illusion the market collapsed. Law was discredited, although his original plan for a bank of issue was recognized to have had merit. The Paris market was reorganized, and in 1726, the Bourse was chartered. But France never forgot its moment of insanity, and the new exchange was not destined to be of the first rank in Europe.

While the French were intoxicated with the "Mississippi Bubble," the English were imbibing a strong brew of their own. The London money market had begun along the old Roman wall of Londinium. Merchants from Lombardy settled in the city during the Renaissance and gave the name of Lombard Street to the center of English finance. By the early eighteenth century, the street was teeming with brokers who traded shares of joint-stock companies that went back to the time of Elizabeth.

In 1711, several businessmen and nobles received a charter for the South Sea Company, which was granted a monopoly of trade with South America. The venture prospered, and nine years later, while Law was in control of the Paris exchange, the company's directors

offered to take over the entire public debt of Great Britain in return
for certain concessions and grants. Those who held the government's
obligations would be permitted to exchange them for shares in the
South Sea Company, which would become the most powerful economic instrument in the state.

Parliament agreed, and at once the South Sea shares rose rapidly.
Dazzled by the French example, English investors began to plunge
into the market. Even as Parliament debated, shares went from 130 to
300. Members of both houses participated in the dealings, and were
granted "favors" by South Seas directors; they were doubtlessly influenced by their pocketbooks when it came time to vote. The Prime
Minister, Robert Walpole, later admitted to having owned shares
during this period.

By mid-year, South Sea shares were selling for over 1,000, and this
success led investors to look into other companies for similar profits.
Some of the new ventures, such as those which engaged in bridge
mending and wharf construction, were sound. Others, like one that
planned to make boards out of sawdust, may have been well inten-
tioned. But most were sheer frauds. Firms were proposed to manufacture perpetual motion machines, provide better funerals for mendi-
cants, cure sick horses, and transmute animals. One apparently
successful company, in terms of the rise in its stock price, was to
manufacture radish oil, which had no known use. Another, which
was oversubscribed, was "A company for Carrying on an Undertaking of Great Advantage, but Nobody to Know what it is." A
newspaper of the time wrote that the cry was "For God's sake, let
us subscribe to something; we don't care what it is."[8]

The bubble burst within a year, wrecking the fortunes of hundreds and discrediting an entire generation of British politicians. The
brokers and businessmen reaped their full share of blame. Parliament
passed a series of acts forbidding the issuance and trading of shares
without legal authority "either by act of Parliament or by Charter
from the Crown."[9] Another act, passed in 1734, prevented specific
abuses by stockbrokers, and forty years later, short selling was forbidden. For the most part these acts were ignored by the government
and the brokers. By the end of the century, the London market had
recovered, was loosely policed, and was prospering.

The rise of the London market, which took place as the Paris
Bourse stagnated, was due in part to the comparative lack of royal
power in England. The Bourbons controlled much of France's do-

mestic commerce and industry, as well as overseas ventures. The English rulers, with limited exchequers overseen by an increasingly powerful Parliament, had to allow private enterprise to develop trade and industry. Faced with opportunities and possibilities, English investors were encouraged to risk their capital on new ventures as well as established concerns.

At first, most of the shares traded were those of the older firms whose original owners had sold them to reap a profit or because their prospects had not been realized. Many of the newly chartered firms were formed by joint-stock subscriptions to "insiders." Even if they could have been traded, the fact that most had unlimited liability made them unattractive to all but the most wealthy and reckless. The brokers of Cornhill and Lombard Streets and Exchange and Sweeting Alleys would trade in old shares and securities of nonchartered companies, which were not sponsored by the Crown and therefore were considered quite risky. Government bills were to be more important to them than stock until the early nineteenth century.

A favorite gathering place for brokers was Jonathan's Coffee-House, where certain bills and stocks were traded regularly. The brokers in those days were far from specialists, however. An advertisement of the time read: "John Taylor, at his office next Jonathan's Coffee-house in Exchange Alley, buyeth and selleth New Lottery Tickets, Blank Tickets, Navy and Victualling Bills, East India Bonds, and other Publick Securities."[10] Jonathan's burned to the ground in 1748, but the brokers helped to construct New Jonathan's on the same site the following year.

The name of the Coffee-House was changed to "The Stock Exchange" in 1773, and a sign proclaiming the new designation was attached to the door. A list of members was drawn up, subscriptions were levied, and rules were laid down. Orderly trading, along the lines of an auction, was begun in selected securities. However, most of the business still took place in the streets and alleys by nonmembers who, if they wanted, could attend meetings for the price of sixpence a day.[11]

By the end of the century, the Stock Exchange had become too small, and a committee was named to look for a new location. In 1801, a building was erected for the Exchange near Capel Court, not far from the Bank of England. It was there that Nathan Rothschild operated as one of the first true stock market manipulators, although most of his business was on Lombard Street until after the Napoleonic Wars.

The market rose and fell with each new dispatch from the front, and foreign capital, fleeing from Napoleon's armies, added to the activity. Since most of the trading was still in government obligations, news of victories and defeats, not of industrial successes, sent the market up and down. Not until the first quarter of the nineteenth century did stock transactions assume primary importance for English investors. Then, they sent their funds all over the world, and the London bankers and brokers became the builders of England's Century in the Sun.

Notes

1. A "bull" believes that the market will go up and therefore buys in expectation of the rise. A "bear" thinks the opposite and sells. The terms may derive from the fact that a bull lifts and throws objects upward, while a bear presses down heavily. In the early nineteenth century a Wall Street bear was described as being like a hunter who sells a bear's skin before he had killed the beast, thus "selling short."

2. This trust did not extend to those outside the community, however. A fourteenth century merchant advised a protégé: "When you are in business, never cease to complain of taxes, saying that you should pay much less, pointing out your heavy losses, the poor harvest, and the bad times. Don't be afraid of lying, since you do no wrong to anybody thus; it is necessary to lie just enough to acquire a reputation for the truth." Miriam Beard, *A History of the Business Man* (New York, 1938), p. 151.

3. The Saxon word for misfortune is *broc,* and from this some scholars have deduced that a broker was originally a merchant who had to abandon trade through some commercial misfortune. Others hold that a broker was one who "broke down" large consignments into smaller ones for easier sales. John R. Dos Passos, *A Treatise on the Law of Stock-Brokers and Stock-Exchanges* (New York, 1882), p. 2.

4. A similar situation existed among the "glamour stocks" in America during the late 1950s. One broker developed "the other idiot principle," saying that a speculator would purchase a stock at an admittedly ridiculous figure, because he knew that some other idiot would buy it from him at a still higher price.

5. Charles Mackay, *Extraordinary Popular Delusions and the Madness of Crowds* (New York, 1932), gives an excellent description of the tulip craze and others.

6. *Ibid.,* p. 15 ff.

7. Beard, *History of the Business Man,* pp. 416–18.

8. *Ibid.,* pp. 437–38.

9. Joseph Stancliffe Davis, *Essays in the Earlier History of American Corporations* (Cambridge, 1917), p. 26.

10. Leland Hamilton Jenks, *The Migration of British Capital to 1875* (New York, 1938), pp. 14–15; E. L'Estrange Ewan, *Lotteries and Sweepstakes* (London, 1932), pp. 245–46.

11. Until the nineteenth century, transactions in public funds tended to be carried on in banks, which considered the traders shady characters. Francis W. Hirst, *The Stock Exchange* (London, 1911), pp. 43–44.

2

Securities in Early America

The Adventurers and Planters do agree that every person
that goeth, being sixteen years old and upwards, be rated
at ten pounds, and that ten pounds be accounted a
single share.

Conditions of Settlement, Plymouth Plantations

GEOGRAPHY WAS IMPORTANT in determining the types of business organizations and the roles of securities in England's North American
colonies. The American mainland had an abundance of good, cheap
land, that attracted yeoman farmers, not would-be miners and manufacturers. Given the land hunger of the colonial period, the distance
of America from Europe, and the virgin nature of the new continent,
it was natural that the colonies would become overwhelmingly agrarian. Those few persons who concerned themselves with business to the
exclusion of agriculture were rare indeed. Where mining and manufacturing existed, they were usually conducted as side interests by
wealthy farmers. Commerce was significant, but was controlled from
England, for the most part. On the eve of the Revolution, Jamaica
had a greater volume of trade with England than the future United
States.

What little business existed was handled by a struggling group of
traveling merchants. Thus, there was no need for joint-stock companies in America, and few appeared other than those engaged in
land speculation. Only six or seven chartered companies existed during the entire colonial period, and most of these had disappeared before the Revolution. Banking, a necessary precondition for business
development and the concomitant growth of securities markets, was
hamstrung by the Crown, and those few colonials who might have
been interested in starting businesses were prevented by lack of funds.[1]

Surplus earnings were usually reinvested in family enterprises, and what little was left went into land speculation or English bonds. George Washington, Patrick Henry, and others of the Founding Fathers lost heavily in the land market prior to the Revolution. John Watts, a petty New York merchant, made a small killing in English bonds during the 1760s. "I shall get something at last for my gaming in stocks, I see," he proudly wrote to his friend, Moses Franks, in 1762.[2] Such investments were unusual, however.

Southern investors lived on plantations, although they would go to cities on occasion. The few securities holders in the North were by and large urban people, living in Philadelphia, Boston, and New York. Each city had a business district of sorts, where sedentary merchants had set up their shops and from which commerce, factoring, and investing were conducted. In 1752 a group of New York merchants organized an exchange, or meeting place, for dealings in slaves and corn meal.[3] Gatherings were irregular and infrequent but the city's first formal market, located at the foot of Broad Street and later in Fraunces Tavern, had been established.[4]

Wall Street, today the world's foremost financial center, took its name from the 1,340-foot long wooden wall erected there by Governor Peter Stuyvesant in 1653.[5] The twelve-foot high structure replaced a picket fence that had served to keep the city's hogs and goats from straying into the *terra incognita* of what is now the lower East Side. The street was a colorful place during the colonial era. During the late seventeenth century it was a rendezvous for pirates; Captain Kidd took up residence at 56 Wall Street. Merchants moved to the street in the early eighteenth century. The city hall, slave market, town pillory, and city jail were located on Wall Street in this period, and cattle were driven to Murray's Wharf, located at the eastern end of the street. The corner of Wall and Pearl Streets was the usual site for the imported sport of bear-baiting—this, a century before the human bulls and bears would take over.[6]

Although most merchants conducted their business from shops, Wall Street was the scene of many auctions of merchandise and public subscriptions for loans, which were customarily held out of doors. These markets were quiet compared to those on Lombard Street, and not even so busy as those in Chestnut Street in Philadelphia. As the colonial economy matured, as demands for funds were made by local businesses, they increased in number. Coffee-houses proliferated and became the business centers of the city.

It would be incorrect to say that English attempts to stifle these and other similar businesses were a major cause of the Revolution, but they did play a part. Regulation of the currency, refusal to grant charters, and efforts to hamper commercial activities in America led many traders to oppose the English and support the Revolution. Some businessmen left New York and other cities for Canada and England, but most remained in the trading centers and tried to continue business as usual. Most of the coffee-houses were destroyed during the war, but in those that remained, bonds of the new Confederacy became a factor in speculation, their prices rising and falling with the news from Washington's army.[7] Beginning in 1777 and lasting with interruptions through most of 1791, a speculative frenzy appeared and reappeared on Wall Street and in other trading centers. The new country was, however, overwhelmingly agrarian, and did not note the activities of the small group of traders. Yet these almost-forgotten men participated in the first bull market in American history, the first speculative frenzy, and the first crash.

One typical trader, Thomas Eddy, came to New York in 1779 with a total capital of $96. He attended the small but exciting coffee-house auctions, and soon began to act as middleman between buyers and sellers. "I live by my wits," Eddy later wrote. In 1780 he was able to form the partnership of Eddy, Sykes & Co., which prospered until the crash of 1792.[8] Thomas Eddy is a shadowy figure, and little more is known of him. He is not mentioned in the newspapers of the period or in the letters and memoirs of famous New Yorkers. Because of this, we cannot assume that he was the lineal predecessor of the financial giants of a century later. Still, his career in finance, brief but meteoric, appears to resemble those of later years, and he is typical of the type of men who achieved prominence during bull markets.

Although the boom lacked solid underpinnings in the form of a sustained growth of the economy, certain institutional developments helped it along. In 1781 the Bank of North America was founded in Philadelphia, and three years later it was granted a national charter in return for making loans to the government and discounting its paper.[9] Wall Streeters responded by establishing the Bank of New York in 1787. During this period of uncertainty, New York, Boston, and Philadelphia each sought financial dominance over the others. This rivalry only added to the speculation, as the three cities vied with each other in bidding for securities. Speculation boomed until the brief panic of 1785, when depressed economic conditions finally caught up with the markets. Bankruptcies appeared in all parts of the nation, as the crisis that helped destroy the Confederation dried up the small stream of available capital.

For a variety of reasons, not the least of which was the desire to form a more stable business climate, the merchants and brokers favored a stronger government. Of the fifty-five members of the Constitutional Convention of 1787 only eleven were businessmen, but most of the rest were sympathetic to business's point of view. The document they drew up provided for the establishment of a government that would undertake to pay its debts through taxation and to promote business by the use of its police and other powers. Alexander Hamilton, a guiding force at the Convention, was attuned to the needs of the financial community. Among his other accomplishments, he had written the constitution of the Bank of New York and had been instrumental in the choice of William Maxwell, a Wall Street broker, as collector of its subscriptions. Hamilton was to champion the causes of businessmen for the rest of his life and to aid Wall Street against its rivals in Philadelphia and Boston.

New York was the temporary capital of the new government, and the old City Hall, renamed Federal Hall, became the seat of the first Congress. Hamilton, now Secretary of the Treasury, took up residence on the northwest corner of Wall and Water Streets. Aaron Burr, then a colleague at the Bank of New York, lived a few blocks away at the corner of Nassau and Pine. Senators and Congressmen sat with brokers and businessmen in the coffee-houses, and each learned the views of the other. In this way, an informal partnership between government and the financial community was developed.[10]

The Chestnut Street brokers in Philadelphia were not blind to the meanings of these partnerships, and their rivalry with New York was heightened. In 1790 the capital was shifted to Philadelphia, which still had the only nationally chartered bank in the nation, the Bank of North America. Hamilton was able to block an attempt on the part of Philadelphia interests to further increase its power, but when the Bank of the United States was formed in 1791, its headquarters were also located in Philadelphia. Philadelphia now was the banking center of the nation. Most of the new bank's public stock was held by residents of that city, and interest in securities turned from Wall Street to Chestnut Street. A stock exchange was organized, and Philadelphia quotations were the standards by which brokers in other cities set their prices.[11]

If Philadelphia was the nation's banking center, and hoped to become its economic and political capital as well, New York remained the home of the speculators and plungers. The nation's first bull market—born in New York, reinforced by the adoption of the Constitution and sustained by economic recovery after 1785—was also to crash in New York. As would be the case in almost every market crash in the nation's history, it was precipitated by an individual who came to symbolize the boom, extended himself beyond his resources, and then collapsed.

The man of 1792 was William Duer, a friend of Robert Morris, the financier of the Revolution. Duer was an adventurer cast in the mold of John Law. After receiving an Eton education, he went to India, where he served as aide to Lord Clive. Afterward, Duer came to New York and joined the city's financial community. As Assistant Secretary of the Treasury under Hamilton, he was one of Wall Street's luminaries.

In December of 1791, Duer organized what was called "The Six Per Cent Club," which was to speculate in debt securities issued by the federal government as part of Hamilton's financial program. The Club was successful from the first, and a buoyant Duer joined with Alexander Macomb and Benjamin Walker, two brokers, in an attempt to corner the stocks of the Bank of New York and the Bank of the United States. The three men, backed by the Club, formed a combine which was to be dissolved on the last day of 1792.

The combine's purchases of bank stock sustained the securities markets during most of the year. Toward the end of 1791 prices in New York, Philadelphia, and Boston rose sharply, attracting small investors to the financial centers. Writing to Thomas Jefferson, James Madison noted that "stocks and scrip are the sole domestic subjects of conversation." All the ingredients were present: a sharp, unexplained rise in prices, amateur investors in the markets, and a seemingly invulnerable, all-knowing combine operating with great mystery behind the scenes. The *New York Advertiser* of August 9 noted these factors, adding that "National Bank stock had risen so high, so enormously above its real value, that no two transactions in the annals of history can be found to equal it."[12]

Prices leveled off and declined moderately in early March of 1792. While disappointing to many bulls, the decline was not unexpected or unusual in the light of the sharp rise of the past year. But Duer and the Six Per Cent Club had overextended themselves in the expectation of a further rise, and were left with obligations that could not be met. Duer sold some of his holdings in order to gain cash, and in so acting forced prices lower. Rumors of his imminent failure were whispered along Wall Street, and other investors sold their holdings, causing further declines. Brokers offered to pay 1 per cent interest per day on loans, with no takers. Funds could not be raised on the best of collateral, as New York saw its first major bear market and panic. Finally Hamilton intervened, instructing his friends to buy $150,000 of debts at the going price. This buoyed the markets; the fact that Hamilton seemed bullish encouraged others to enter Wall Street. By the fall of the year the market was on its way up once more. As would be the case in all the crashes of the nineteenth century, the entry of a strong man halted a major decline. Another part of the pattern of the future was also taking shape: the ruin of Duer and his associates. In writing to a friend, Jefferson said that Duer was in trouble, but might rise out of it. "The stock buyers count him out, and the credit and fate of the nation seem to hang on the desperate throws and plunges of gambling scoundrels."[13] This was not really so, for the markets were not that important to American prosperity and liquidity. Duer was ruined, however. He declared bankruptcy and was taken to debtors' prison, never to reappear on Wall Street.[14]

By this time shares in the larger banks as well as state and federal debt issues were regularly traded on Wall Street. During the remainder of the decade, 295 chartered companies were formed, most of them banks, insurance companies, dock construction ventures, road companies, and mining firms. They would ordinarily begin operations with full subscription books. The stockholder was obliged to pay in a specified percentage of the par value, the remainder being on call when and if needed. These shares, often in questionable businesses, were the first "industrials" to be traded on Wall Street. The volume of trading in industrials was to mirror the economic development of the country in the years to come. In the agrarian America of 1800, weeks would pass before a trade in industrial shares would occur on Wall Street. Then, with the transportation revolution of the pre-Civil War era, more appeared. Not until well after the Civil War, however, would the industrial list come into its own.

After the recovery of mid-1792, the brokers returned to the coffee-houses, seeking buyers and sellers for stocks and bonds. During normal times, securities-holders in early America usually purchased stocks and bonds as investments, to be held for a lifetime or until the corporation was dissolved. As a result, there was little trading in these issues, and the major activity was in the marketing of new securities. In July, 1791, the firm of McEvers and Barclay floated a state issue of $180,000, and then held an auction to distribute the shares. Toward the end of the year auctions were held in other new issues. By early 1792, when Duer and others had to dump large amounts of securities, the first auctions for old securities were held. A pattern soon developed. In order to sell his holdings, the owner would contact an auctioneer and deposit the certificates with him for sale. Buyers, having been informed of the sale, would congregate at the auctioneer's table to bid on the securities. The auctioneer would call out the name of the security and its denomination, the terms of sale, and the date of delivery. Most dealings were on time, payments to be made within sixty days. While the transactions were taking place, other buyers and sellers would congregate in the back of the room, haggling over stocks not offered by the auctioneers.

The first auctions were scheduled irregularly, but generally speaking, two sessions—one in the morning, the other in the early afternoon—were held. In March, 1792, the first attempt to regularize this practice was made by a group of auctioneer-brokers. *Louden's Register* of that month carried the following announcement:

> The Stock Exchange Office is opened at No. 22 Wall Street for the accommodation of the dealers in Stock, and in which Public Sales will be held daily at noon as usual in rotation by A. L. Bleeker & Sons, J. Pintard, McEvers and Barclay, Cortlandt & Ferrers, and Jay & Sutton.[15]

From time to time the noon meeting was supplemented by one at seven in the evening. Newspapers carrying reports of the sales, along with stock lists and bid and ask prices, began to appear at this time. By early April the small room could not accommodate the brokers and their customers.

The crowded quarters and the coming of spring encouraged outdoor meetings. The brokers began to meet near a buttonwood tree in front of 68 Wall Street during balmy days, and to move indoors in case of rain. It should be noted that these brokers considered stocks and bonds only a minor part of their businesses. Almost all were more deeply involved in commercial factoring, insurance, and banking. Even the sale of lottery tickets was more important in this period than that of stocks and bonds. The competition was keen in all of these fields, and the business ethics were often strained.

Early in May of 1792, several leading brokers met in an attempt to end their rivalry in the field of securities. In addition, they hoped to unite against the auctioneeers, who they felt were gaining too much control over the market. On May 17 they gathered at Corre's Hotel and signed an agreement which, in effect, established a guild of brokers. In part, the agreement stated:

> We, the subscribers, brokers for the purchase and sale of public stocks, do hereby solemnly promise and pledge ourselves to each other that we will not buy or sell from this date, for any person whatsoever, any kind of public stocks at a less rate than one-quarter of one per cent. commission on the specie value, and that we will give preference to each other in our negotiations.[16]

Although the agreement was loosely written, and was soon found wanting in several important respects, the Corre's Hotel Pact organized the New York securities market as a definite institution.

The first meeting of the new market was held in the old Merchant's Coffee-House. During the winter of 1792, the brokers decided to construct a building of their own. A subscription for 203 shares of stock with a par value of $200 a share, only part of which was called, was taken up by the members. A lot was purchased at the corner of Wall and Water Streets, across the way from Hamilton's home, and there was erected the Tontine Coffee-House.

The Tontine was designed as a combination club and meeting room, the former open to the public while only members would trade at the auctions. According to the Act of Incorporation, the house was to be held by the corporation until the number of shareholders was reduced by death to seven, at which time the property would be sold and the assets divided among the survivors.[17]

The founders of the Tontine were all businessmen who had minor interests in brokerage of securities. Many were prominent in the social and intellectual life of the community, donating to charities, schools, relief funds, and the like. John Pintard, a leading figure at the Tontine, was also editor of the *New York Daily Advertiser,* an author of works on topography and medicine, an expert on Indian tribes and languages, a founder of New York's first savings bank, a charter member of the American Bible Society, and chairman of a dozen assorted charities. He even found time to help found the New York Historical Society.

Solomon Allen, another member, began his career as a broker in lottery tickets, and then became a dry goods king. Not until the 1820s did Allen's stock business become more important than the firm's other interests. Nathaniel Prime was an agent for British and French cotton importers. He dabbled in brokerage, and in 1808 organized the firm of Prime, Ward, and Sands, the largest and most prosperous brokerage of the time. Even then, the firm's major activities involved acting as agent for such British firms as Baring Brothers. Samuel Ward, a former London broker, handled the Baring account, while Joseph Sands acted as traveler for the firm.[18]

Men like Pintard, Allen, and Prime preferred to be known for their banking and commercial connections rather than their interests in brokerage. The Tontine was not the most conservative of addresses, for dealings in securities seemed less honest than other businesses. Men like Pintard and Prime would attend the auctions, exchange information, and then leave the coffee-house. Those who remained—the less respectable brokers—would make wagers on sporting events, elections, and anything else that was possible. "Mr. Walton bet me fifty dollars to twenty that if Barriere was delivered to the Revolutionary Tribunal by the French Convention on or before the 22nd of March last, that he w'd be Guillotined on or before the 3d April last," reported one broker.[19]

The brokers were Federalists in politics, following their mentor and leader, Hamilton. They provided a good deal of the money the party received from New York, and four of the Tontine's five trustees actively engaged in campaigning for the Federalists during the election of 1800. When Adams fell out with Hamilton, however, they followed their leader into opposition.

The Tontine bulletin board announced the duel between Hamilton and Burr on July 11, 1804. Business stopped and prayers were offered at Trinity Church for Hamilton's safety. Wall Street's protector died the following day, and almost all the brokers joined in his funeral procession and stood among the mourners. Hamilton was buried at the end of Wall Street, in Trinity Churchyard, just a few dozen yards from the site of the present stock exchange.

The brokerage business remained at a low level during the Tontine years. On the day prior to the duel, trading took place in four United States debt obligations, three banks, three insurance companies, and three bills of exchange. These kinds of security dominated trading until after the War of 1812. There were several reasons for this situation. The nation was primarily agrarian, importing most manufactured goods from Europe. Even when the Napoleonic wars hindered ocean transport, and Jefferson's embargo of 1807–1809 stopped all commerce, the new American manufacturing firms remained mostly partnerships or closed corporations, whose stocks were not available to the general public. In addition, the corporate form contained risks many were unwilling to take. Capital stock was issued at a percentage of par. The owner was responsible for the rest of the face value if needed, and this made long-range investment difficult. Even if and when the balance was called in, the stockholder's liability was not ended, for he was legally responsible for all actions taken by the corporation. Limited liability was not the rule during this period, and few were willing to risk their fortunes on the actions of a firm they did not directly oversee. Not until the eve of the War of 1812 did New York enact a general incorporation law, including provisions for limited liability. Other states followed, but it was only in 1850 that the limited liability corporation was accepted throughout the United States.[20]

Despite these discouraging drawbacks, corporations were formed with increasing frequency during the Federalist and Jeffersonian periods. Approximately two-thirds of the new companies were local in nature, providing for such needs as canals and roads. The par values of stocks were small, usually from twenty to fifty dollars, to enable local businessmen to invest in them. Although the stocks so floated were usually tightly held, or at most traded locally, some shares found their way to New York. On April 6, 1796, the following advertisement appeared in the *New York Daily Advertiser:*

CANAL SHARES
8 shares in the Western Lock Navigation Co., whereupon all the requisitions have been pd., for sale enquire of
Vos & Graves
58 Pearl St.

The fact that such a sale, which must have been for between one hundred and two hundred dollars, merited an advertisement, illustrates the low volume in New York at this time.

Stocks of banks and insurance companies were more actively traded. Gaining a charter was the key to success in these fields; without one, no institution could hope to grow. In the early years, the Federalists were able to dominate business by refusing charters to Republican banks and insurance companies. The Federalist company presidents and the Federalist brokers were on the best of terms, and Wall Street floated several issues of financial corporations in the late eighteenth century.

The banks were far more important than insurance companies. From 1792 to 1801, the number of chartered banks increased from three to twenty-three; at the turn of the century, their total capitalization exceeded $33 million. Seventeen years later more than a third of the issues traded in New York were those of banks.[21] This was to be expected, for while the new nation needed money for expansion, the amount of gold in the national and state treasuries was negligible. The Constitution forbade the states from issuing bills of credit, but each state could charter private banks which in turn could issue bank notes, thus inflating the currency. Naturally, the states encouraged the establishment of banks, hoping they would act to bolster the local economy and provide for capital expansion.

Insurance companies began more slowly, but by 1818 the number of issues eclipsed those of the banks; thirteen of the twenty-nine stocks traded in New York were those of marine, fire, and life companies. Like the banks, they were vital forces in the early development of American commerce and industry. At a time when all business was small business, risks of losses due to unexpected events had to be minimized. This was especially true for companies that did not enjoy limited liability. Thus, the discounting of risks became a prime consideration, and the insurance companies prospered. At times the insurance and bank firms would act together in ventures. The bank would lend money to a businessman, financing the loan through the private flotation of notes with an insurance company. A century later J. P. Morgan and others would use this technique to effect the great consolidation of American industry.

Next in importance were chartered firms engaged in local transportation and manufacturing. The canal, road, and dock companies were traded irregularly. Until the 1820s, only Boston dealt with manufacturing securities in any significant numbers.[22] Only one manufacturing stock was traded regularly in New York at this time, the New York Manufacturing Company. It was quoted at 105 in 1815, and appeared on the lists at around that price for the next two years. Then, in 1817, it left the list and trading.

Far more important than the securities of chartered companies were the government debt obligations, which were traded with the stocks and bonds at the auctions. Issues that had been used by Hamilton in raising funds for his financial programs were widely held in all parts of the country. The total volume of their sales exceeded the combined volume of all banks and insurance companies in New York, Philadelphia, and Boston. State issues were also important, although they were traded more locally. Governments were responsible for most internal improvements, primarily because private capital could not as yet shoulder the task, so special state issues provided funds for these ventures. The New York city and state governments floated bond issues each year from 1812 to 1817, and during this same period, federal obligations increased from $45 million to $123 million.[23]

At the same time, capital accumulation was taking place throughout the nation. These new accretions did not find their way to the markets, however. Each small merchant and farmer considered himself a capitalist; rather than invest his funds in companies he could not control, he would put them back into his farm or shop. Better a new piece of land and new tools than questionable pieces of paper. There was more confidence in the government than there had been in the Confederation, but Americans still distrusted all governments. Securities in 1800 were sounder than they had been before the Philadelphia convention, but it would be another half century until middle-class Americans would consider putting their earnings into stocks and bonds.

Accordingly, the exchanges were unimportant during the first quarter century of the nation's history. The traders on Philadelphia's Chestnut Street and those of New York's Tontine considered someone who dealt only in securities either an idler or a fool. Although records were not kept in those days, it can be reasonably assumed that most citizens, even those of wealth, did not view the brokers as a significant group. From time to time there would be speculative outbursts, but those who participated did so more in the spirit of gambling than investing. Not until the expansionist surge of the post-Napoleonic period, when American businesses attracted foreign capital in great amounts, did the nation's exchanges take on real importance. Then the Philadelphia and Boston brokers eclipsed the men of the Tontine.

The Philadelphia bank of Stephan Girard and the financial concerns manned by the Beacon Hill aristocrats became the main vehicles for the investment of British capital in America. Only Prime, Ward, and Sands and a few other New York brokers were able to participate in any important way. New York began its rise to domination after the War of 1812, when the British chose it as the best place to "dump" manufactures they had accumulated during the Napoleonic period. Only with the planning and financing of the Erie Canal did Wall Street successfully threaten the older centers. When the Big Ditch proved even more beneficial than had been expected, all of New York State and the old Northwest opened to the port. As the city grew, so Wall Street expanded its credit and banking operations. The brokers waxed strong, as New York became "the tip of the tongue that laps up the cream of the commerce of a continent."[24]

Notes

1. James Walker, *The Epic of American Industry* (New York, 1945), p. 26; Virginia D. Harrington, *The New York Merchant on the Eve of the Revolution* (New York, 1935), pp. 48–49.

2. *Ibid.*, p. 128.

3. Frederick L. Collins, *Money Town* (New York, 1946), p. 86 ff.

4. J. Edward Meeker, *The Work of the Stock Exchange* (New York, 1922), pp. 22–28.

5. Collins, *Money Town*, p. 64.

6. Leonard Lewis Levinson, *Wall Street: A Pictorial History* (New York, 1961), p. 13.

7. Collins, *Money Town*, p. 64.

8. Freeman Hunt, *Lives of American Merchants* (New York, 1958), p. 338.

9. Margaret Myers, *The New York Money Market* (New York, 1938), p. 3.

10. Matthew Smith, *Sunshine and Shadow in New York* (Hartford, 1883), pp. 43–48.

11. Davis, *American Corporations*, p. 200. The Bank of North America lost its charter in 1785, when it was blamed for having caused the panic of that year. It regained the charter two years later, however.

12. Earl Sparling, *Mystery Men of Wall Street* (New York, 1935), p. xv.

13. Davis, *American Corporations*, p. 289.

14. *Ibid.*, pp. 279, 334–35; Walker, *Epic of American Industry*, p. 53.

15. Davis, *American Corporations*, p. 198.

16. Henry Clews, *Fifty Years on Wall Street* (New York, 1908), p. 89.

17. The Tontine was named after an Italian banker of the seventeenth century, Tonti. He set up companies which paid their subscribers life annuities until all but a designated number of survivors were left. Then the company was dissolved, and its capital distributed among those who remained.

18. Martha Lamb and Mrs. Burton Harrison, *History of the City of New York* (New York, 1896), pp. 509–11; Humphrey Neill, *The Inside Story of the Stock Exchange* (New York, 1950), p. 30; John Ezell, *Fortune's Merry Wheel: The Lottery in America* (Cambridge, 1960), pp. 82–83; Hunt, *American Merchants*, pp. 187–88; Jenks, *Migration of British Capital*, p. 359.

19. Eames, *New York Stock Exchange*, pp. 16–17.

20. North Carolina passed an incorporation act in 1795, but this applied only to canal companies. Jenks, *Migration of British Capital*, pp. 234–35; Myers, *New York Money Market*, p. 14.

21. Sereno Pratt, *The Work of Wall Street* (New York, 1921), pp. 6–7; Joseph Hedges, *Commercial Banking and the Stock Market before 1863* (Baltimore, 1938), p. 32.

22. George Taylor, *The Transportation Revolution, 1815–1860* (New York, 1951), p. 320.

23. Schultz, *Securities Market*, p. 3. Of course, a major factor in this increase was the costs involved in fighting the War of 1812.

24. Oliver Wendell Holmes, Sr., writing in 1835, as quoted in Levinson, *Wall Street*, p. 6.

3

Under English Domination:
1812-1837

A man's learning dies with him; even his virtues fade
out of remembrance; but the *dividends* on the stocks he
bequeaths to his children live on and keep his memory
green.

Oliver Wendell Holmes, Sr.

MANY AMERICANS were not satisfied with the results of the War of
1812. The Peace of Paris restored the *status quo ante bellum*. The small
American navy, which had won several impressive victories in the
early stages of the war, was all but wrecked when the fighting ended.
The British, while engaged in a struggle for their existence against
Napoleon, were at the same time able to defeat the Americans in most
of the land battles. They were not dislodged from the Northwest or
Canada, and they had burned the new capital at Washington with
ease. The most dramatic American victory, that of Andrew Jackson at
New Orleans, came after the Peace had been signed.

But if one looks beyond the political and diplomatic developments,
the War of 1812 emerges as one of the more significant episodes in
American history. Before the war, imports from Europe totaled $54
million and exports $61 million; in 1814, the last year of the fighting,
these figures dropped to $13 million and $7 million. In addition to this
sharp decline in trade, what little European investment there had been
in America dried up. For the first time, the nation was thrown upon
its own resources.

Lacking funds with which to conduct the war, Congress had no
recourse but to borrow money. In March of 1812, the first of six war
loans, this one for $11 million, was floated by Congress. Three months

later the Treasury was authorized to issue $5 million in notes, the first of five such inflationary actions. The banks enlarged their facilities to accommodate this expansion, and 120 charters for new banks were issued. In Philadelphia, Stephan Girard turned all of his attention to his bank. New York fur millionaire John Jacob Astor increased his banking activities, as did Alexander Brown in Baltimore, the Legaré and Pettigrew families in Charleston, and many members of the Boston aristocracy. In 1816 the Second Bank of the United States was chartered. Capitalized at $35 million, it offered $28 million of stock to the public at $100 a share. Stephan Girard took $3 million of the issue and other American bankers subscribed for lesser amounts.[1] It was apparent to many that the nation was witnessing a return to Hamiltonian finance after a decade and a half of Jeffersonianism.[2]

Other areas of business expanded along with banking. Insurance companies prospered during the war, merchants being more interested than ever in protecting their cargoes. In 1812, the first pure life-insurance firm, the Pennsylvania Company for Insurance in Lives and Granting Annuities, was chartered, and dozens of others followed. Domestic manufactures were encouraged as English imports dropped. In 1800 there were fewer than twenty cotton mills in the nation, and by 1812 there were still fewer than ninety. But four years later the number had jumped to more than 200, and millions of dollars were invested in the New England mills alone.

This expansion was cut short during the early days of the peace. In 1817 exports exceeded the prewar level and imports also rose to new heights. The English goods dumped in New York's port forced many small firms into bankruptcy in 1816, but those that remained consolidated, expanded, and were able to meet British competition and still show large profits. Aided by the high tariff of 1816, the infant industries made the transition from war to peace, and shortened the 1819 depression, turning it into the precursor of a boom era.

The Tontine merchants had continued their meetings during the war, and continued their prosperity. The auctions were dull, but factoring and banking took up the slack. However, the Philadelphia brokers maintained their leadership and seemed destined to continue to do so. London houses interested in buying American securities after 1815 viewed that city, and not New York, as the financial center of the nation. Philadelphia banks were supreme; the Second Bank of the United States was situated in the city, as was the powerful Girard

Bank. The New York banks, while growing rapidly, could not compete with those in Philadelphia in assets or prestige.

Still, the rivalry between the two cities was fierce, each bidding for the same federal, state, and private bond issues, and both exchanges claiming leadership for the entire nation. Since news from Europe reached New York first, Manhattan brokers would often rush to Philadelphia in the hope of buying or selling securities whose prices might change when developments in London or Paris were made known. The appearance of a stagecoach full of New York brokers would cause consternation on Chestnut Street; the Wall Streeters' actions were viewed with suspicion and distrust.[3]

Some Wall Streeters thought that one major reason why their Philadelphia colleagues were getting so much of the European business was the inadequacy of the small Tontine auction. They had to admit that the Philadelphia auctions were better organized, more carefully policed, and less speculative than the wild Tontine sessions. It was decided, therefore, to form a new organization, patterned after that of Philadelphia, and in 1817, they sent William Lamb to that city to find out more about the operations there. Tradition has it that Lamb had just been married and was about to start on his honeymoon when he learned of his selection. A true Wall Streeter, he agreed to leave his bride and make the trip.[4] Lamb returned in mid-February, and gave his report. On the twenty-fifth the brokers met in "Mr. Beebe's office" to draw up a new constitution, which was almost an exact copy of the Philadelphia charter. It was probably the work of Nathanial Prime, Anthony Stockholm, Leonard Bleeker, and the host, Samuel Beebe. A new Board of Brokers, numbering twenty-eight individuals who belonged to seven firms, was formed, and an initiation fee was set at $25. This group of brokers was the beginning of the renamed New York Stock and Exchange Board.

The Constitution of 1817 provided for the selection of a president and a secretary, who were to be in charge of the auction; Nathanial Prime and Anthony Stockholm were named. New members were to be admitted by vote, and no one could join if three black balls were cast against him. Excluded from membership were those who had been in brokerage for less than one year. To prevent the wilder varieties of speculation that differentiated Wall Street from Chestnut Street, deliveries of securities were to be made on the day after their purchase "unless expressed to the contrary." "Wash sales"—the sale of a security by one broker to another who acted for him or his client, in order to give the impression of a transaction when one had not taken place—were forbidden. This device had been used to simulate a bull or bear market, when one actually did not exist. The brokers were required to be present at all sessions, and they were to be fined 12½¢ for each auction missed. If a member interrupted an auction, he could be fined 25¢, with the understanding that a limit of $10 a year would be placed for the total of all fines.[5] The Board rented a hall for meetings on the second floor of George Vaupell's property at 40 Wall Street, the site of the old Bank of Manhattan Building. Vaupell agreed to furnish the room with chairs, keep it clean, and provide heat in the winter, for a rent of $200 a year.[6]

The Stock and Exchange Board was a high-powered version of the Tontine. Gone was much of the easy informality of the coffee-house era. Although almost all the members had belonged to the Tontine, they seemed to settle down under the new Constitution. John Pintard attended meetings irregularly until his retirement in 1829 at the age of seventy. Bankers like Jacob Barker, insurance executives like Augustus Lawrence, and showman William Niblo became members of the Board. Still, as far as can be determined, there were no full-time stock brokers in the 1820s and 1830s.[7]

The Wall Street of this period did not seem much different from the narrow alley of the Washington Administration. Pigs, dogs, cats, and rats still inhabited the streets. There were fewer coffee-houses, as many of the part-time clubs moved uptown. But Baker's Tavern, A. Frumento's hairdressing establishment, Richard Carlow's tailor shop, and other small establishments had Wall Street addresses. There were six groceries between Hanover and Pearl Streets, and several stables. Manhattan Island had a population of some 135,000, of which 10,000 were free Negroes and 5,000 were foreigners. The city was booming in the context of Jacksonian America, but it still had the appearance of a small town in many respects.[8]

Boasting of a new exchange and noting that their city had more banks, if not larger ones, than Philadelphia, the Wall Street brokers hoped to lure foreign capital to their offices. Prior to the Napoleonic era there had been little demand for American securities in Europe, and during the wars, investors bought and speculated in continental and English issues rather than those of the United States. In 1803, only $32 million of American stocks and bonds—including government obligations—were held overseas. During the War of 1812 this figure dropped to $25 million. In the first year of peace, only government bonds and Bank of the United States stock seemed to interest the Europeans, although a few Dutch traders held stock in the New Jersey Manufacturing Company.[9]

Toward the end of the year, activity in American issues began to increase. Seeking higher returns than were available at home, and hoping for capital appreciation as well, London, Amsterdam, and Paris investors began to look into the exotic American stocks. The foreign exchanges often accepted questionable stocks in return for their gold. At first, the funds went to buy the familiar state bonds. Then, in 1817, European investors were caught up in the phenomenon known as the canal mania.

Canal building and operation were to be the glamour industries of the postwar period. For a decade and a half the entire nation appeared to go canal-crazy. Each district having two or more bodies of water seemed to want a ditch to connect them. The vast majority of these projects were financial and economic failures; nevertheless, they did act as a stimulus to the economy and encouraged American and foreign investment.

Although the canal mania began after the War of 1812, the ditches had been in use as early as the colonial period. The first truly important canal, the Santtee of South Carolina, was constructed at a cost of over one million dollars in 1800. Building was not on a large scale, however, first, because technology had not advanced to the stage where canals could be constructed with the ease and efficiency of the more familiar turnpikes, and second, because a canal could cost millions of dollars, while turnpikes usually were much cheaper. These problems could be seen in the case of the Western Inland Lock Navigation Company and the Northern Inland Lock Company, both of which were chartered in 1792 by the state of New York and charged with extending the Hudson River to Lakes Champlain and Ontario. These ventures failed. The canal walls collapsed, and the capital of $25,000 raised by stock sales in denominations of $100 a share plus $12,000 in state aid was insufficient.[10]

By the end of the war, the drawbacks had been overcome, at least in part. Canal technology, brought over from England, made it possible to construct efficient ditches. Then too, for the first time, there was an accumulation of American capital and an interest on the part of foreign investors, both of which were utilized in financing the new firms.

Most of the canal companies were set up along similar lines. The individual states would charter and operate the canal; even those under private control received financial aid and guidance from the states. Such sponsorship was necessary, for private companies could not hope to raise the enormous sums needed, and the federal government, under Presidents Madison and Monroe, considered that these undertakings were none of its concern.[11] The state would raise the money through increased taxes, and more usually, through the flotation of bonds. Private banks, such as Girard's and Astor's, would often buy up the entire issue and then offer it to investors. On some occasions they would take the bonds on consignment, hoping to sell them but able to return part of the issue if such sales were not forthcoming.[12] New York floated over $7 million worth of bonds in this fashion from 1817 to 1825. Other states followed suit, although not on so large a scale and often with considerably less success.

At first the funds for these enterprises tended to come from the Eastern financial districts, from those entrepreneurs who lived alongside the proposed canal, and more often than not, from European investors. In 1825, Ohio floated a loan of $400,000 with New York investment banks, which included Prime, Ward & Sands, John Jacob Astor, John Robins and John Hone. Similar transactions were made in Philadelphia and Boston, while Charleston and Baltimore acted as capital markets fo rthe southern and southwestern canals.[13]

Foreign funds came in from all over the world, but especially from England. French and Canadian investors were interested in American canals, as were those in the West Indies, Spain, and even one in China. But England remained supreme; in time, many American enterprises were controlled from bankers' offices in London, Birmingham, and Manchester.[14] Baring Brothers & Co. led the pack, becoming a major factor in American securities. Aware of the growing importance of foreign business, the Barings made sure that one or two of their partners were American.[15] The firm's agent, Thomas W. Ward, was one of the most astute observers of the commercial scene, traveling from one district to another for the Barings, and reporting back as to opportunities and pitfalls. With his help the Barings were able to invest wisely in American securities, both for their own account and those of their customers. Not all English firms were as fortunate. The Chesapeake and Ohio Canal Company, one of the more ballyhooed of the new ventures, was badly mismanaged from the start, but, nevertheless, the English firm of Peabody & Company invested in its stock. When the company failed, Peabody was in dire straits, and was almost forced to declare bankruptcy. Profits from American securities were large, and British investors were attracted to the new land. But the risks were also large, and for every European who made a fortune in American investments, dozens lost everything.[16]

By 1822 the canal mania overtook Lombard Street, and the demand for stocks was so great that there were not enough to supply English investors. Foreign banking houses instructed their agents to buy up older issues as well as those of newly chartered companies. The large overseas purchases caused several flurries in Philadelphia, New York, Boston, and Baltimore, and led to great optimism in American financial circles. The Barings had bought their first canal offering in 1823, and now they took the lead in bidding for older issues. By the end of the year, the firm had gained possession of $240,000 of various New York canal stocks; by the end of 1824, the Barings had increased their holdings by another $82,000.[17] In 1825, after a Lombard Street panic, London investors again turned to canal issues. The Blackstone Canal in Providence was capitalized at $500,000; bids for more than three times that amount were received. The Morris Canal and Banking Company, which hoped to raise one million dollars, could have had $20 million, much of which was offered from England.[18]

The new canal companies issued glowing reports of their plans and prospects. They promised to pay dividends in dollars, and convert them to foreign currency, at fixed rates. These reports were sent abroad, and although most were sheer fabrications of imaginative and often dishonest men, the supposedly sophisticated Europeans believed them. Even firms that refused to advertise did well. Although the New York Gas Light Company told its subscribers nothing of its plans, the new issue of stock was snapped up in 1824 by an eager public. In the following year, the Board asked the directors for information "so the public might be informed through us of the existing state of things in relation to the company." This first recorded request for such information was refused,[19] and the investors were obliged to trust the prospectus, listen to rumors, or have faith in the judgment of their brokers. Because of this last alternative, honest brokers who knew their business, such as Samuel Gurney of Philadelphia and Joshua Bates, a managing partner for the Barings, were able to attract customers without too much difficulty.[20]

We do not know what investments these men suggested to their British clients, although Ward's letters to the Barings indicate a preference for state securities and canal stocks. Some English investors refused to buy southern canal issues on the grounds that such purchases would be an encouragement to slavery. John C. Calhoun, who hoped that his section would become the industrial center of the nation, bemoaned this situation, but was unable to change it.

The demand for northern and western issues led some businessmen and adventurers to conclude that the investors were ready and willing to be bilked. Thus, Pennsylvania and Maryland paid high rates of interest and generous dividends—but out of new loans, not earnings. Such a condition would not continue indefinitely, and companies in these states and others with similar practices would regularly declare bankruptcy. The fact that New York insisted that funds be set aside for payments of dividends and interest, and forbade new loans for this purpose, made that state's issues attractive and was a factor in the rise of the Stock and Exchange Board.

Foreigners were amazed at how easy it was to go bankrupt in America, and how blithely the Americans seemed to take what, for them, was the disgrace of failure. Local investors also complained, castigating those who set up firms only to milk them. One economist wrote in 1820 that "every monied corporation is *prima facia* injurious to the national wealth, and ought to be looked upon by those who have no money with jealousy and suspicion." The Governor of Massachusetts thought that "these societies are one of the vices of our times."[21] Nothing could be done in those days before the Securities and Exchange Commission to prevent the eager speculator from parting with his money for all sorts of questionable issues. The fantasies of wealth operating during the tulip mania and just before the South Seas Bubble burst were duplicated in America during the late 1820s. Since the other idiot principle is one of the few laws governing bull markets, speculators often succeeded in realizing large profits. Those who bought United Mexican Mining at 35 in December, 1834, could have sold at 155 a month later. This was a spectacular performer, but there were many other large jumps during this bull market of the canal era.

Although activity on Wall Street increased, the Stock and Exchange Board was comparatively quiet. In those days more trading was done on the streets than in the auctions. In addition, the new issues, which appealed strongly to English investors, were traded at the Board only after the initial distribution had been made. Their activities, therefore, had to be followed in an underwriter's office, not at the market.

Still, the brokers benefited from the new business, and although they didn't spend more time at the auctions, their securities business increased to the point where some could abandon groceries and lotteries and concentrate on stocks and bonds. With the success of the Erie Canal flotation, Wall Street began to pull ahead of Philadelphia. One of the first to realize this was Alexander Brown & Sons, who set up a New York branch (later to become the parent of Brown Brothers, Harriman & Co.) in 1818. The Browns corresponded with their partners in Liverpool and tried to compete with the Prime, Ward & King —Barings combination for the English market. Fitch Brothers & Company, another new firm, worked with French houses in the same fashion. All three companies continued to rely upon factoring and importing, but their securities business was the fastest growing part of their operations.[22]

The Barings, who showed little concern with the threat posed by the Browns, corresponded with Prime, Ward & King until the Civil War era. The American firm enjoyed the confidence of the Barings, and was able to induce them to take up several issues that otherwise might have gone unsold. "There is no House here except them to draw largely," wrote Thomas W. Ward in 1831.[23] The Barings continued to use the Codmans of Boston, Willing & Francis in Philadelphia, and Robert Gilmore & Co. in Baltimore, but the New Yorkers' share of their business remained the largest in the next three decades.

The Browns never constituted a serious threat to the Barings, but the powerful firm of N. M. Rothschild & Sons did. In 1833 the Rothschilds took their first timid steps toward the American market, although selected stocks and bonds had appeared in their portfolios in earlier years. The firm soon became an important dealer in American bonds. By 1835 Rothschild agents or correspondents were situated in New York, Philadelphia, and Baltimore. The partners invested some $5 million in stocks and bonds, for the most part in conservative issues. In the same year the family was named English agent for the United States government.[24]

Others followed the Barings and the Rothschilds. Speyer & Co. of Frankfort entered the American markets after the short-lived panic of 1834. George Peabody of Baltimore, the great precursor and lineal ancestor of J. P. Morgan & Co., organized his firm in England in 1835. Peabody was the first important London broker other than the Barings to specialize in American securities. Although Peabody was to become prominent only after the 1837 panic—and then more as a result of international banking activities than stock and bond operations—his house was always concerned with the markets. Peabody and other European bankers controlled America's securities for a greater part of the century. When London sneezed, New York caught cold. As one member of Congress put it, "the barometer of the American money market hangs up at the stock exchange in London."[25]

The canal boom continued throughout the decade, and interest in the ditches remained for the rest of the century. But the peak of the early canal era came during the administration of John Quincy Adams (1825–1829), when the President supported federal public works, reversing the policy of Monroe and Madison. In addition, the government acquired stock in private canal companies. Of the $486,000 raised for the Dismal Swamp Canal Company, $200,000 came from Washington, $190,000 from the state of Virginia, and the rest from private individuals. Similar stories could be told of the Louisville and Portland Canal Company, the Chesapeake and Ohio Canal Company, and the Chesapeake and Delaware Canal Company: these firms received almost $1.3 million between 1826 and 1831.[26]

At the height of their popularity the canals were challenged by a new form of transportation: railroads. Although the English had been tinkering with schemes for power-driven railroads for over a century, it was not until 1829 that George Stephenson's *Rocket* pulled a thirteen-ton train from Liverpool to Manchester at fifteen miles per hour. On Independence Day of the previous year, Charles Carroll of Carrollton had dug the first spadeful of earth for the proposed Baltimore & Ohio Railroad. Thirteen miles of the new road were opened in 1830.

The decision to build the B. & O. was not made because of farsighted business statesmanship: it was primarily a result of the failure of the Chesapeake and Ohio Canal to be constructed at a reasonable figure. By 1827, when estimated costs reached $22 million, Baltimore businessmen looked for alternate routes and methods of tying their city to the markets of the coast and interior. A railroad seemed the best way of doing this. The B. & O. was to be capitalized at $3 million, represented by 30,000 shares of $100 each. Ten thousand were taken by the state of Maryland and an additional 5,000 by the city of Baltimore. The rest were bought by private individuals—and the Barings.[27]

A few months before the B. & O. received its charter, New York made a preliminary grant to the Mohawk and Hudson Railroad Company, which was later to become part of the famous New York Central. By the time the B. & O. was completed, a dozen or so smaller roads had been put into operation.

The coming of the rails intensified the competition for securities. Although public agencies provided a good deal of the capital for these early lines, a substantial part had to be raised from foreign and domestic investors. At first it was thought that most of the money could be gotten from local merchants and farmers who would prosper with the coming of a railroad; such schemes had worked with turnpikes and some canals. A few railroads, including the Auburn and Rochester, were financed in this way. This method was especially popular in the South, where Europeans were still wary regarding investments.[28]

There were two difficulties in such financings, however. Many were skeptical about the future of railroads, and unwilling to purchase stock in the new companies. Thus, outside capital in large amounts was needed. In addition, those holders of some early issues found ready markets for them at the exchanges, where they could be sold for sizable capital gains. In a short time the organizers realized they could get higher prices in the cities than by selling stock to local people, and they went to Wall, Chestnut, and Broad Streets first. One of the early experiences which taught New Yorkers this lesson involved the Hudson and Mohawk, a seventeen-mile road from Albany to Schenectady. Shortly after some rural merchants had taken up the issue, it was sold at the Stock and Exchange Board at a much higher price. In 1830 the stock was traded regularly, along with the debts, banks, insurance companies, and canals.[29]

The rise in volume turned the small auction into a bedlam. By 1835, the height of the rail mania, trading reached an average of about 6,000 shares a day; on June 26, 7,875 shares were sold at the auction, a new high.[30] Fortunately, the Board had made structural changes in its organization during the canal era, and was able to accommodate the increased business. The small auction room at 40 Wall Street soon became inadequate, and the brokers made the first of a series of moves that would spread over the next nine years. They tried to stay within the confines of Wall Street, although they went as far north as Broadway and Reade Street during a yellow fever epidemic that swept through the lower city in 1819.

Meanwhile they amended their original agreement to cover new situations. For example, the brokers would often tell nonmembers of their customers' activities, thus pinpointing the market leaders and predicting movements from their actions. In 1819, the governors resolved that "members of this Board do not communicate to members outdoors what members of this Board are purchasers or sellers of stocks at this Board, or what members offer to purchase or sell."[31] More amendments were added, and by the beginning of the following year it was decided to scrap the first constitution and write a new one. In part, the "Bye-Laws of the New York Stock and Exchange Board," adopted in 1820, read:

1st

Stock and Specie shall not be offered at this Board in less than Five Hundred Dollars, and Doubloons in less number than Forty, and no offer be permitted under one-quarter per cent. unless for sums of One Thousand Dollars and Upwards.

3rd

Any Member leaving the Room during the calling of the stocks, without permission of the President, shall be fined Twenty-five cents.

5th

Any Member requesting the President to revert to Stock already called shall pay Twenty-five cents for the same, and shall have the privilege of making the first offer either for buying or selling.

7th

Any member of this Board who shall be guilty of indecorous language or conduct toward another Member while in session, shall, by a vote of two-thirds of the Members present, be suspended from his seat at the Board for not less than one week nor more than one month; and a repetition of the offense shall subject the party so offending to expulsion....

10th

Any Member being duly elected an officer and refusing to act, or neglecting his duty as such, shall be fined a sum not less than Three nor more than Five dollars, at the discretion of a majority of the Board.[32]

In 1821 the brokers began meeting in Samuel Beebe's office at 21 Broad Street. In January, 1827, R. H. Nevins, a member of the Exchange, offered H. I. Wycoff $500 a year rent for a room at 43 Garden Street, "on condition that the doors of the adjourning room No. 41 may be thrown open for the benefit of a circulation of air during the sittings of the Board from eleven to twelve o'clock each day during the extreme hot weather between the months of June and October."[33] The Board met in this room for only four months, and in May, took up comparatively lavish quarters in the Merchants' Exchange, a new marble building erected on the block enclosed by Wall, William, and Hanover Streets and Exchange Place. Some brokers rented cubicles in the basement so as to be closer to both the auction and the mercantile dealings in the Exchange.[34]

Trading was regular but sometimes slow, on several occasions dipping to below 100 shares a day.[35] Still, the list of securities that were registered with the Board, and therefore qualified to be traded at the auctions, increased rapidly. By the end of the year there were twelve banks, nineteen insurance firms, and a few assorted gas companies, canals, and construction companies on the Board, as well as the many debt issues. Most canal stocks were traded outside the auction. Nonmembers would meet at the corner of Broad and Hanover Streets, on the same block as the Merchants' Exchange, and trade in the streets, in what was the beginning of the curb market.[36] The Board members tried to limit such dealings, pointing out that the securities traded on the curb were often less seasoned and sometimes outright frauds, but the curb grew even faster than the Board, and its volume was usually larger.

After 1830, with the influx of new rail issues, activity picked up, and the brokers were obliged to spend more time at the auctions. With this additional interest came greater chances for speculation. A group of younger men now entered Wall Street. Despised by their seniors as gamblers, they were to stage a series of market raids during the next two decades which would attract attention throughout the American financial community.

By this time Philadelphia had begun its decline. In 1834 the Boston brokers organized an exchange. But both cities took their cues from Wall Street during the railroad era.

The older members of the Board participated in some speculations with the newer brokers. Samuel Beebe, in whose office the Exchange had been formed, was a major operator in railroad securities. Jacob Barker began a new career as a money lender through the New York Exchange Bank, and he pulled off several coups in United States Bank shares. But the most flamboyant of the speculators was a new arrival, Jacob Little, who made the others seem unimaginative.

When the Board took up new quarters after the Civil War, one of the first portraits to be hung in the President's office was that of Little, the "Great Bear of Wall Street." Little deserved this honor, but not for the reason it was given. By the 1860s, he was a semilegendary figure, famed for daring coups and coolness in times of crisis. Today,

Little is recognized as the first original mind spawned by Wall Street, the first great, full-time stock "operator," and the first leader of the stock brokerage community. Duer was a carbon copy of European plungers, and Prime and Pintard were part-time Wall Streeters with other, more important interests. Little was completely identified with the securities market, a sign that the auctions had attained new maturity.

At first, Little found it impossible to enter the Wall Street community. He was blackballed several times before admitted as a member of the Board, and afterwards his speculations excluded him from the company of gentlemen. He favored the "manipulated short sale"— he would sell shares he didn't have for delivery in sixty days. He would then sell more shares in different brokerages, plant rumors as to the insolvency of the company, and thus force its shares down. Just before the time limit had expired, he would buy shares at depressed prices for delivery. These tactics were not always successful, and Little knew bankruptcy several times. He carried off enough raids, however, to be considered the uncrowned King of Wall Street, a title he held for a generation—until he lost a fortune and died poor.[37]

Wall Street and the other financial centers favored Adams in the 1828 election. Jackson was elected, and on taking office the following year, indicated his distrust of banks in general and the Bank of the United States in particular. Strongly anti-British, Jackson castigated those who worked with London in attempting to order American economic life. Both of these stands were feared by Wall Street: the brokers relied upon the Bank for financial leadership and most were either direct or indirect correspondents of English firms.

Despite these verbal attacks, Jackson was unable or unwilling to clash with the Bank during his first Administration, and although opposed to the spread of finance capitalism, he did little to hinder the growth of railroads and canals. His veto of the Maysville Road Bill, which would have allowed the federal government to subscribe to $150,000 worth of turnpike securities, was the only important gesture in this direction.

Though wary of the President, the brokers seemed to think he would not cut off the sources of their prosperity, and the markets continued the advances made during the Adams Administration. Demand for seats on the New York Board was such that their prices were raised from $100 to $150 in 1833.[38] The canal and rail booms also continued, and with them came more corners, speculative frenzies, and wash sales. The last practice, illegal on the Board, was often resorted to at the height of a bull or bear market. In the spring of 1832 an attempt was made to corner the Catskill Railroad, and several wash sales were made. The two brokers involved were called before a committee of the Board and asked to reveal the man behind the corner and the sales. Both named Alexander Hamilton, the son of the former Secretary of the Treasury, and all three were suspended. The ousting of Hamilton and the presence of men like Jackson in Washington made the older brokers uneasy. A new order seemed to be taking over, and they wondered what their places would be in it.[39]

Jackson based his re-election campaign on the issue of the Bank of the United States. He regarded that institution as the tool of British and American moneyed interests who operated it to the disadvantage of the middle and lower classes.[40] The Whig candidate in 1832, Henry Clay, had the support of the Bank's president, Nicholas Biddle, but to no avail; Jackson won a resounding victory. In an effort to shock the nation into support of the Bank's recharter, Biddle ordered a contraction of loans in 1833. Perhaps he thought that a financial panic would cause Jackson to change his mind as to the Bank's future, but the President refused to reconsider. Biddle's efforts only served to convince some conservative bankers that Jackson had been right; Biddle was irresponsible and should be disarmed. In addition, the private bankers came to realize that after the Bank was dissolved, its deposits would find homes in their vaults.

Wall Street had thought that the failure to recharter would presage a bear market. Instead, it marked the beginning of a three-year upward movement. Although the Bank remained in existence as a national institution until 1836, and as a state bank thereafter, its powers were gone with the defeat of Clay. A proliferation of state and local banks took up the slack left by Biddle's withdrawal. Many of these were unsound; they loaned money to questionable individuals for still more questionable enterprises. This gave the economy an aura of boom which was undeserved. In addition, Jackson distributed the Treasury surplus of about $28 million to the states, and much of this money went into internal improvements, which further stimulated the markets. Aided by easy money, the nation witnessed a speculative orgy of the first rank. The biggest bull market thus far in American history began in 1834. By the end of the year, thousand-share days were common at the auctions. During the following year, trading increased fivefold.

Little was in his element, and he engineered several corners in canal and rail issues.[41] He participated in the largest *coup* of the period, in the Morris Canal and Banking Company in late 1834. By gaining control of almost the entire floating supply of stock, Little was able to force short sellers to pay his price for shares they had contracted to deliver and could not buy on the open market. Little sold Morris Canal stock that he had bought in December at $10 a share for an average price of $185, a month later.

The Morris Canal *coup* was followed by several more in 1835. As a result of a corner in Harlem Railroad, James Bartow of the Albany Commercial Bank defaulted to the extent of $130,000, Buffalo speculator Banjamin Rathbun went bankrupt, leaving liabilities of $3 million, a London speculator fled Wall Street with $45,000 worth of Harlem stock, some members of the New York Legislature were found to have been involved in the corner, and one state senator was expelled from the Senate.[42]

The heat of speculation was not the only fire felt on Wall Street. On December 17, 1835, the Merchants' Exchange burned, as one part of the worst conflagration in New York's history. Almost 650 buildings valued at over $18 million were destroyed. But on the very next day the brokers demanded an auction, and space for one had to be found. The Board changed quarters frequently until 1842, when the brokers relocated to the new Merchants' Exchange Building, where they remained for five years. It is interesting and sad to note that almost all the records were destroyed during each move. The brokers were not trying to maintain secrecy; they simply could not understand how the records could be of interest to future historians.[43]

Although the 1835 fire stopped the auctions for brief periods, it did not interfere with trading, which continued illegally either on the streets or in local hotels. When the Exchange reopened new volume records were set and stock ran in short supply. Brokers sent agents to other cities—as far as New Orleans and Charleston—to buy shares to be offered in New York. They speculated heavily for their own accounts, sometimes to the disadvantage of their customers. At the height of the boom, John Thomson of 12 Wall Street advertised that "he will do nothing on his own account—his time and ability in all cases shall be devoted for the benefit of those who favor him with their orders."[44]

The brokers always found the curb sales profitable, and now they entered that market importantly, at times ignoring the auctions. In

1836 the Exchange forbade its members from dealing at the curb, on pain of suspension at "the pleasure of the Board." But since volume was still not high enough to warrant their full attention, the brokers continued their street activities. As the term "pleasure of the Board" was interpreted loosely, they were in no real danger of losing their seats.[45]

The stepped up volume led to a widening of the market. During the first months of 1836 there were thirty-eight banks, thirty-two insurance firms, twenty-one rails, four canals, and three gas companies on the list. Not all of these securities were traded regularly, however, but the length of the auction increased nevertheless.

In 1836, the boom began to level off. Although stocks still moved up, they did so at a slower pace than before. The effects of crop failures in 1835 were now being felt in the cities. Farmers could not fulfill their obligations to land speculators and merchants, who, in turn, were unable to meet their bills at the banks. As a result, some of the more insolvent banks were forced to close early in 1836. In addition, the loss of revenue due to the crop failures produced an import balance of trade. Gold began leaving America for Europe. At a time when expansion of currency was called for, Jackson added to the difficulties by issuing the "Specie Circular," directing that paper money could no longer be used to purchase government land. This weakened the already shaken banks, and more fell into bankruptcy. Toward the end of the year, England, America's prime customer, had a depression, and when southern cotton sales eased off subsequently, the economy and the nation were dealt a fourth blow. Philip Hone, the aristocratic anti-Jacksonian, saw signs of weakness as early as November 12, 1836, when he wrote:

> There has been for some time a severe pressure for money, which continues, and I feel the effects of it. Stocks have fallen very much. Delaware & Hudson, which was above par when I was abroad, has been as low as 60 and is now selling at 72. Boston & Providence Railroad, which was 120, is not worth now above par, and all others in proportion. The best mortgages cannot be converted into money without a sacrifice of 20 percent, and undoubted business paper is selling in Wall Street at a discount of three percent a month. . . .

Conditions got worse, and on April 21, 1837, Hone wrote:

> The immense fortunes which we heard so much about in the days of speculation, have melted like the snows before an April sun. No man

can calculate to escape ruin but he who owes no money; happy is he who has a little and is free from debt.[46]

By the end of May, every bank in the nation had suspended gold payments. Bank note circulation was slashed in half. Wall Street. was in deep gloom. After the greatest bull market up to that time, the brokers would have to suffer through a long bear period.

Notes

1. Studenski and Krooss, *Financial History*, p. 84.
2. In 1825 the "Suffolk System" was initiated by Suffolk Bank of Boston. Rural banks were required to keep deposits in the Suffolk Bank, which acted as a correspondent for the smaller institutions. Suffolk agreed to accept note issues from the country banks. This created the dangerous situation of pyramiding, which gave the banks an aura of strength, but later proved a source of weakness.
3. James K. Medbery, *Men and Mysteries of Wall Street* (New York, 1870), p. 288.
4. *Ibid.*, pp. 288–89; Myers, *New York Money Market*, p. 17.
5. Neill, *Inside Story of the Stock Exchange*, p. 33; Schultz, *The Security Market*, pp. 3–4; Meeker, *Work of the Stock Exchange*, p. 31.
6. Meeker, *Work of Wall Street*, p. 30.
7. Henry Lanier, *A Century of Banking in New York, 1822–1922* (New York, 1922), pp. 18–125.
8. *Ibid.*, pp. 14–15.
9. Myers, *New York Money Market*, p. 19.
10. Walker, *American Industry*, p. 79.
11. *Ibid.*, p. 80.
12. Myers, *New York Money Market*, p. 23.
13. *Ibid.*, pp. 25–26.
14. Nathan Miller, *Enterprise of a Free People* (Ithaca, 1962), p. 107.
15. Ralph W. Hidy, *The House of Baring in American Trade and Finance 1763–1861* (Cambridge, 1949), pp. 3–4.
16. Lewis Corey, *The House of Morgan* (New York, 1930), p. 45.
17. Nathan Miller, *Enterprise of a Free People*, pp. 105–106.
18. George Francis Train, *Young America in Wall Street* (New York, 1857). An improbable figure, Train was the model for Phineus Fogg in Jules Verne's, *Around the World in Eighty Days*. His book is interesting, but must be read with caution.
19. Neill, *Inside Story of the Stock Exchange*, p. 48.
20. Joseph Sands died in 1826, and the firm of Prime, Ward & Sands was dissolved and reconstituted as Prime, Ward & King. The new partner, James G. King, was a former English merchant with important London connections. Lanier, *Century of Banking*, p. 116.
21. William Z. Ripley, *Main Street and Wall Street* (New York, 1927), p.
22. The American's attitude toward bankruptcy was indicated by George F. Train in this way: "Germans hold a debt over a man for forty years. . . . In

England a man who fails seldom ever rises above the low-water mark. In America, where ninety-five out of a hundred come down, everybody floats in on the flood. An American stops once in five years and pays fifty cents on the dollar. . . ." Beard, *History of the Businessman*, pp. 626–67.

22. Myers, *New York Money Market*, pp. 69–70.

23. Hidy, *House of Baring*, pp. 109–10, 151–52.

24. *Ibid.*, p. 195.

25. George W. Edwards, *The Evolution of Finance Capitalism* (New York, 1938), p. 144.

26. Taylor, *Transportation Revolution*, p. 50.

27. Walker, *American Industry*, pp. 92–97.

28. Taylor, *Transportation Revolution*, p. 97.

29. Neill, *Inside Story of the Stock Exchange*, pp. 37–46.

30. Hedges, *Stock Market Before 1863*, p. 39.

31. Eames, *New York Stock Exchange*, p. 18.

32. *Ibid.*, pp. 23–24.

33. *Ibid.*, pp. 28–29.

34. Lanier, *Century of Banking*, p. 195.

35. On January 25, 1830, 31 shares were traded at a total cost of $3,470.25. E. C. Stedman, *The New York Stock Exchange* (New York, 1905), p. 85.

36. Noble F. Hoggson, *Epochs in American Banking* (New York, 1929), pp. 20–23.

37. Rufus Wilson, *Old New York and New* (Philadelphia, 1909), pp. 91–94; Henry Clews, *Fifty Years in Wall Street* (New York, 1908), p. 729; Smith, *Sunshine and Shadow in New York*, p. 219.

38. Eames, *New York Stock Exchange*, p. 85.

39. Neill, *Inside Story of the Stock Exchange*, pp. 46–47.

40. While estimates of the amount of British capital invested in American securities vary (Jackson thought it was $200 million in 1829), it was probably less than $50 million on the eve of the election. Instead of discouraging British investors, the election apparently acted as a spur to the purchase of new securities. Within three years an additional $108 million or so was sent to America. Jenks, *Migration of British Capital*, p. 85. Some Wall Streeters, hoping to use the Bank issue as a means of destroying Philadelphia's financial power, supported Jackson. See Bray Hammond, *Banks and Politics in America: From the Revolution to the Civil War* (Princeton, 1957).

41. A corner exists when a broker or group of brokers have control over a substantial amount of a company's floating supply of stock, thus being able to dictate trading in the issue.

42. Medbery, *Men and Mysteries of Wall Street*, pp. 13, 91–92.

43. Neill, *Inside Story of the Stock Exchange*, pp. 50–51; Eames, *New York Stock Exchange*, p. 29.

44. Eames, *New York Stock Exchange*, p. 30.

45. Neill, *Inside Story of the Stock Exchange*, p. 49.

46. Philip Hone, *Diary of Philip Hone, 1828–1851*, Allan Nevins, ed. (New York, 1949), pp. 1181, 1241.

4

The First Age of Rails: 1837-1857

> Within the last week many descriptions of what are called "fancy stocks" were inflated, by the progress of bubble-blowing, to prices double and quadruple those of the previous week. . . . This inflated state of things lasted three days, and then came the reverse which always follows these high-pressure operations. All of a sudden stocks fell back nearly to the place where the speculation found them; the sellers became buyers, pocketed their gains, and laughed at their dupes.
>
> Philip Hone

WALL STREET WAS QUIET AND PEACEFUL during the early spring of 1837. The trading areas belonged to the pigs and dogs until 9:00 A.M., when the first brokers arrived by horse and buggy from their homes uptown in Greenwich Village. The suburbanites of the day came in from New Jersey and Brooklyn a little later in the morning. For an hour or so the brokers would arrange commodity transactions or visit the curb to discover the state of that market. Then, perhaps after a quick coffee, they would head for the auction, where calls began at 10:30. The pace was unhurried; even during the more busy days, Wall Street gave the appearance of a narrow alley in some middle-sized upstate town. The roads were still unpaved, and clouds of dust were raised by the chaises which were later parked in stables that lined the street near the trading areas. The large number of horses gave the section the atmosphere and aroma of a country fair, especially during the hot days of early summer. The financial center of the city and the most important exchange in the nation was not a very impressive place in the last years of the Age of Jackson.

Within the shops, brokerages, and auctions, the tempo was much faster. In late March came news of a decline in cotton prices in New

Orleans, and speculators in cotton futures were hard hit. Then came word that southern merchants had been forced to constrict their businesses. Dozens of old Charleston, New Orleans, and Baltimore firms were obliged to declare bankruptcy, in some cases paying only five cents on the dollar. During the second week of April, Wall Streeters learned that southern accounts were in jeopardy. Those who had counted on cotton states' receipts to pay for market speculations were unable to cover their debts. A flurry of selling took place at the Board, as brokers tried to maintain liquidity in order to stay in business.

On May 4, John Fleming, president of the Merchants' Bank, fell dead at his desk—rumors had it that he was killed by overwork and fears as to the financial condition of his institution. A run set in at the bank, and it soon spread up and down the Street. On the next day a group of merchants who had overextended themselves announced their failures. The New York *American* stated that "it is vain to disguise that the whole frame of society is out of joint." More failures were reported on May 6. The exchanges were heavy, and stocks fell rapidly. For the first time since its inception in 1816, United States Bank stock went below par. By the end of the evening auction, every issue on the list had followed it down.

The next day was Sunday, and the markets were shut, but brokers went from church to downtown hotel rooms, where they traded for several hours. On Monday the decline accelerated. By Wednesday all banks had closed their doors, suspending specie payments, and three hundred New York businesses promptly announced their failures. During the last week of August scrip based on commodities had taken the place of banknotes, which were no longer trusted. By early September the entire nation was engulfed in a depression which would continue for seven years—almost 650 banks failed in 1837 alone. Bank note circulation, which had reached $149 million before the crash, dropped to $58 million by 1843. Van Buren, taking office in March, 1837, did little to alleviate the situation; although programs were initiated to reform the currency, land policy, and banks, government intervention during a depression was a century off. Van Buren did support a measure that enabled 39,000 people to cancel $441 million of debts, but this Bankruptcy Act did nothing to restore confidence or spur investment.

Some brokers hoped that Europeans would enter the markets and pick up cheap stocks and bonds, thus injecting new money into circulation and lifting the economy to its feet. But England had its own depression at that time, and instead of an influx of foreign capital, there came a general liquidation of American accounts. This served to deepen the depression, and also helped cause the collapse of several American correspondents of European houses: S. & M. Allen fell in the early summer; Joseph & Brothers, one of Wall Street's leading brokerages, was forced to declare bankruptcy in the fall.[1]

Trading at the Board was active during these months, but declined sharply soon after, as investors lost interest in securities. Companies whose stocks were prized in 1836 could not find bidders a year later. The brokers no longer trusted each other, not due to fears of breach of contract, but rather to thoughts of possible bankruptcy. Why extend a sixty-day payment period when your buyer could be in the poorhouse before then? At the height of the bear market almost all sales at the Board were made for cash. This not only discouraged speculation, but was an indirect form of currency contraction, and gave the economy another blow.[2] The Wall Street broker, hero of seven good years, was now castigated by the newspapers as the villain of the seven bad ones.

Wall Street was in a decline from 1838 to 1842. Americans who had lost fortunes in the crash were uninterested in speculation, and English investors likewise steered clear of foreign securities. In 1838, some $200 million of American stocks and bonds were held in Great Britain; almost $120 million of this investment were in shaky securities. By 1842, nine states had defaulted on their bonds. New York, one of the better governed states, managed to keep up payments, but Pennsylvania slipped deeper into bankruptcy, and the Chestnut Street brokers suffered another blow to their prestige. In the same year the American minister to Great Britain reported that the Rothschilds were no longer interested in federal bonds. The London *Times,* now more anti-American than ever before, wrote: "The people of the United States may be fully persuaded that there is a certain class of securities to which no abundance of money, however great, can give value, and that in this class their own securities stand pre-eminent." By 1844, South American state and municipal bonds, never considered anything other than rank speculations, were selling slightly above American federal bonds on the London Exchange.[3] The Barings, astute in international finance, cut back their commitments and did not participate in new flotations. Although the firm offered some American securities during the early 1840s, the volume of business dropped precipitously.[4] American credit on the continent reached rock bottom. The Paris Rothschilds, echoing their London cousins, told Duff Green, "You may tell your government that you have seen the man who is at the head of the finances of Europe, and that he has told you that they cannot borrow a dollar, not a dollar."[5] After Green reported this conversation, there was talk in Washington that the federal government might assume state debts to restore credit overseas, but nothing came of this rumor.

Whenever the securities market showed some signs of recovery, an untoward event would cause skittish speculators to dump their shares. A minor bull market in 1839 was cut short when Samuel Ward died and his firm of Prime, Ward & King was dissolved. Two new brokerages, J. G. King & Sons, and Prime, Ward & Co., appeared but neither was able to exert the leadership of the old concern. The latter failed within a year, and King & Sons lasted only a little longer.

Always ready to seize opportunities, Jacob Little reorganized his firm and tried to exercise leadership during one of the bull phases. Although Little was eager and able to lead, few brokers were left who were willing to follow.[6] Recovery still might have taken place, for the economy had begun to move up with the new decade, had not bad news prevented this. In February, 1841, Nicholas Biddle's Bank of the United States in Philadelphia, went into receivership. A new wave of repudiation began, and the securities markets were set back to where they had been during the worst days of 1837.[7] The New York *American,* attempting to show how severe the short panic of 1841 had

Table 4.1—New York American List

Stock	1837 High	Nov. 25, 1841 Price
United States Bank	122	4
Vicksburg Bank	89	5
Kentucky Bank	92	56
North American Trust	95	3
Farmers' Trust	113	30
American Trust	120	0
Illinois State Bank	80	35
Morris Canal Bank	75	0
Patterson Railroad	75	53
Long Island Railroad	60	52

been, published a list of prices late in the year; similar tabulations could be made for other stocks and other exchanges.[8]

Many Board members were able to ride out the panic. Because most brokers had interests other than the auctions, they were able to live on ordinary commodity trading and factoring while securities were stagnant. Only those who had conducted most of their business at the auctions suffered heavy losses, and a few of them went under in 1837.

The bear market had a more serious effect on the curb. Since the securities traded there were of a highly speculative nature, they collapsed with the first strong downward movement. Some of the curb brokers had formed a rival organization in 1836, after failing in an attempt to cooperate with the Board. During the pre-panic months, the "New Board" grew at a more rapid rate than the old, and hot rivalry developed between the two. On one occasion a member of the New Board dug out several bricks from the wall separating the auctions, to gain information on prices, purchasers, and so on.[9] But by 1839, three-quarters of the New Board's members were in bankruptcy. Six years later it was once more smaller than the Old Board, and in 1848 it was discontinued.

The brief history of the New Board, and of several other auctions which appeared during the bear market,[10] presaged future periods of high volume. At such times brokers who dealt outside the central market would experience sudden prosperity, as interest in unlisted shares and new issues mounted. Then, they would try to form rival exchanges. But after the market was broken, and volume returned to normal, the new institutions would usually close their doors. The major reason for the failures was often the unsound condition of most of the non-Board brokerages, but the generally hostile attitude of the older brokers toward interlopers was also important. In 1843, the Board passed the following resolution, which illustrates this sentiment:

Resolved—That upon the election of any person as a member of the Board, who may belong to any other Association for the transaction of Stock and Exchange business, that the person so elected be required to resign such membership before he signs the Constitution or takes his seat.[11]

The 1837 panic affected other financial districts as well as Wall Street. Baltimore, Charleston, and St. Louis were particularly hard hit; their hopes of becoming major trading areas were now ended. The Boston Exchange went into decline, although the city itself became the nation's first industrial center. The "Boston Associates," fifteen of the city's leading families, were able to buy defunct businesses at a fraction of their worth and consolidate them into a large economic empire. The Associates' first venture had been the Boston Manufacturing Company, organized in 1813. By 1850, the group controlled 20 per cent of the nation's cotton spindles, 30 per cent of the railroad mileage in Massachusetts, and 39 per cent of the state's insurance capital. In addition, 40 per cent of Boston's banking resources were in the hands of the Associates.[12] For a while the Boston brokers, working in conjunction with this early industrial giant, appeared to threaten the New York Board, but New York remained secure as the financial center of the nation.

Two major factors caused this centralization of power on Wall Street. First, there was a rapid decline of the Philadelphia brokers after the panic. Plagued by a weak and vacillating state government, a port that was declining in relation to New York, and an underwriting group that was losing ground to New York even before the crash, the Chestnut Street traders came out of the depression much weakened. As early as the 1840s, they began to follow the New York prices.

More important, however, were the technological changes affecting Manhattan Island. In 1832 Samuel F. B. Morse developed the first practical telegraph. With his associates, Ezra Cornell and O. S. Wood, he opened a small office near Wall Street where he demonstrated his device for an admission fee of twenty-five cents. He hoped to interest businessmen in his scheme of linking large cities by telegraph, but for ten years he attracted little attention. Then, in 1842, Morse scraped up enough capital to construct a line between Governor's Island in New York Harbor and the Battery. In 1844 he built the first land telegraph, a line which ran between Baltimore and Washington. Business finally awoke to the potential of such devices, and the Magnetic Telegraph Company was formed in 1844, to operate a line from New York to Philadelphia. The company was capitalized at $15,000, one-half of which was taken up by Morse and his associates, the other half by outside interests. For a while the line met with only a limited success, but within two years Magnetic Telegraph showed a profit, and began paying regular dividends. Significantly, the first customers—the men whose interest made success possible—were lottery dealers and stock brokers. Now Wall Street prices could be quoted the same day on Chestnut Street. The telegraph did away with the need for two major auctions, and Philadelphia slipped to second place. Other cities fell in line as soon as the telegraph was extended to their exchanges. By the mid-1850s there were over fifty telegraph companies in operation; in 1856 Western Union was formed, and began absorbing smaller firms. By the end of the decade Wall Street was connected to every important American city, and set prices for them all. Although local companies had their markets made on regional exchanges, their securities were often floated in New York.[13]

Now that Wall Street had become the market for the nation, the problem of transfer presented itself sharply. In the early days, buyer and seller were usually in the same location, and the delivery of certificates was a simple matter—during bull markets some brokers sent agents to other cities to pick up securities, but this was highly irregular. The need for intercity express service was evident after the telegraph appeared. If New York was to make a market for other cities, the Wall Street brokers would have to stand ready to deliver shares to other cities.

A beginning was made on May Day of 1840, when Alvin Adams went from Boston to New York, carrying money and notes for delivery on Wall Street. The trip was profitable, and Adams continued to make regular journeys between the two cities, eventually taking securities as well as money. A few years later he was joined by William Dinsmore, who became the New York agent for the express service, and shortly thereafter a branch was established in Philadelphia. By 1854 the express companies had offices in every important financial community, and most were directed from Wall Street.

The telegraph and express services made possible the nationwide purchase and delivery of shares traded at the New York market. Newspapers in all parts of the country began quoting Wall Street prices for their readers, and business news now became a feature of many journals. Charles Dana's New York *Transcript* and James Gordon Bennett's *New York Morning Herald* had financial columnists in 1840. Other papers throughout the nation added staff reporters to comment on the markets. In 1846 the *Banker's Magazine* carried Board prices, including those of "foreign shares," as securities traded at other than New York auctions were then called, and Freeman Hunt's *Merchants' Magazine* was established soon after.

Information and communication helped make New York the pivot of the continent during the 1840s and 1850s. Board membership became a prized possession. Even during the doldrums in trading the demand for seats grew, and dozens of would-be members were blackballed. Despite the depression, the price of admission was raised by the governors—it was the one important bull item of the bear market.[14]

Although the panic was felt on Wall Street until 1844, and full recovery did not come until the early 1850s, the economy moved ahead. By the end of the forties the Midwest was almost completely settled, and railroad terminals could be found in every town of respectable size. Similarly, the East was criss-crossed with new railroads. The new roads were usually backed by large capitalists who held the stock closely, although some were owned by small investors. Gone were the pre-1837 days, when a road could obtain all the money it wanted by going to Wall Street or London with its securities. Americans were wary of new ventures now, and London investors were more interested in selling than buying foreign shares.

This situation continued until the gold rush of 1849 ushered in a new prosperity and interest in shares picked up again. The urban investors seemed to have left the market. Promoters of new railroads preferred to have many stockholders rather than a few large interests in control of the line, because they could easily manipulate a firm in which no one held more than a small fraction of the shares. The Western Railroad in Massachusetts reported that 2,331 individuals owned shares in 1838; the New York Central's list ran to 2,445 in 1853; and the Pennsylvania had over 2,600 owners. Since the shareholder of the countryside usually lacked interest in trading on exchanges, shares in these companies were offered only irregularly at the Board. Because of this, the expansion which took place in the economy during the decade after the 1837 panic was not accurately reflected on Wall Street. In 1835 there were three rails listed at the auctions. On the eve of the panic the number had reached seven, and by 1840, it had gone to ten. A decade later, after total railroad mileage had increased from 3,300 to 9,000, there were only thirty-eight rails traded at the Board.[15]

The early years of recovery were filled with indecision on Wall Street. The brokers and their customers were unsure as to which way the market would go, and they tended to shy away from securities. Little, who participated in several corners in 1840, complained that he couldn't find any "action" at the auctions or at the curb. The period of the Mexican War (1846–1848) brought further prosperity to the nation, but the exchanges remained quiet, despite a small bull market in Texas bonds in 1846. Sales in other eastern cities were also sluggish, with the exception of Boston, which was having its short day in the sun.

Activity picked up in 1849, and volume rose sharply with the news of the California gold rush. The Wall Street brokers and speculators were fascinated by tales from the West. Fantasy, the prime ingredient of every bull period, was being manufactured for export to the exchanges, and it found a ready market. Europeans, long sour on American securities, were once again beguiled by dreams of huge profits. Visions of wealth flitted through the minds of investors, as they did during the canal and early rail eras. Europeans came to America, searching for the gold fields which had eluded the explorers of the sixteenth century, and many who stayed home once again sent their money to America.

It was not long before mining shares reached the curb markets, where they were traded by the thousands each day. At the Board the conservative brokers, realizing that railroads would be needed to carry the miners to midwestern depots, began a second phase of the rail boom. Manufacturers expanded their plants and extended credit to customers with a free hand.

In several western towns crude stock exchanges, where securities in questionable mines were bought by unsophisticated speculators, were formed. The rise in western mines led eastern traders to bid up their prices on the older exchanges. Thus, a banker in New York would lend money to a local speculator, who might buy mine shares on the St. Louis Exchange. The rise in St. Louis would encourage a similar advance in New York, and the bankers and speculators would then plunge more heavily into the St. Louis market. One exchange seemed to confirm the high hopes of another, although each was building on clouds. Telegraph and express companies connected all the exchanges, and rapid communication made for exaggerated price shifts, which in turn led to a new speculative period. To meet the demands for credit, the banks expanded their facilities almost to the breaking point. Notes, loans and deposits totaled $538 million in 1848. This figure reached $950 million by 1854, and two years later it jumped to $1,042 million.

Most investors believed that the bull market was founded on a storehouse of California gold, when it actually rested on promissory notes, commercial paper, and questionable railroad securities. But the gold shares did provide glamour for the market. Bullion shipments from California reached New York monthly, and the brokers and their customers would often meet the ships and wait for the unloading. They would rush back to Wall Street in time for the evening auction, and bid prices up to new highs.[16]

The rail stocks rose steadily, reaching their zenith during the summer of 1853. Then a decline set in, and by 1855 they had slumped below their 1844 levels. The usual picture of a booming market riding the crest of the gold and rail mania must be tempered by the fact that most common stocks did not share fully in the general prosperity after 1853, although activity in them continued to increase sharply.

The stagnation of prices was not due to lack of interest in the rails, however. It was the result of the flood of new issues which took up much of the investment capital available from Americans and Europeans. Almost as many corporations were chartered during the 1850s as had been in the previous half-century, and the majority of these went to the markets for financing.[17]

Enterprises seemed to spring up overnight during this decade. In 1851 a new bank was started during every month in New York City. Fifteen more were added during the next two years, at a total capitalization of $16 million, much of which was raised by Wall Street brokers. It is little wonder that stock prices remained stable when such huge outlays of money were required. The new companies had a glamour that the established ones could not match. During every bull market the new issue sector seems to attract the more venturesome of investors, and it is here we often see the greatest activity and price changes. The fact that many of the new concerns are shaky and are run by inexperienced managers doesn't seem to worry the investor —this is as true of the bull market of the 1850s as it is of the bull market of the 1950s. In writing of the new capitalists of the gold rush era, a banker of the old school said:

> One had acquired wealth by selling dry goods, and therefore he was fit to be a bank president; another had been equally successful in making shoes; another had been a ship chandler, and fortunate in the schooner coasting trade; another had been a stage driver; not a few were men of the narrowest minds, wholly lacking in mercantile education, and without the ability to conduct the simplest commercial correspondence.[18]

Yet, other bankers were of genuine ability. Jay Cooke, a partner in the firm of E. W. Clark & Co., received much of his training during the bull market. Cornelius Vanderbilt and his arch-enemy, Daniel

Drew, prepared for their future encounters during this period. And in 1853, Junius Spencer Morgan became a partner in the firm of Peabody & Co., beginning what would become the greatest house in the history of American finance: J. P. Morgan & Co.[19]

English and continental investors, who suspected the American market after the 1837 panic, were slow in coming back to Wall Street. As late as May, 1850, the Barings stated that they would refuse to invest in any American railroad with the exception of the Baltimore and Ohio.[20] But the gold fever hit London later in the year, and the Barings initiated a study of the American market which led to new investments by them in 1852. News of the California strikes captivated the British; the further one was from the fields, the more fantastic were the stories. British merchants realized that they could not hope to exploit the mines themselves, but when they heard of the high prices paid for clothes, meat, and equipment in California, they enlarged their factories. They also speculated in American securities. The rails were the prime glamour issue in London; by 1853, 26 per cent of all American rail bonds were in the hands of overseas investors, most of them English. The Philadelphia and Reading Railroad and the Illinois Central were directly controlled by groups of English investors. The Erie, which began operations in 1851 and within a year became the longest railroad in the world, was then substantially held by London interests. By 1856, there was some $1.5 billion worth of American securities outstanding, distributed as shown in Table 4.2.

Foreign investors held over $200 million of this amount, and were particularly attracted by the more speculative issues. Even the young American industrial issues attracted foreign interest; the Norris Locomotive Works of Philadelphia, which had delivered engines to England, Poland, and Russia, was a favorite on the London market in 1842.[21]

During the market decline following the 1853 highs, volume remained strong; most brokers seemed to think that an upturn was just around the corner. With the passage of the Kansas-Nebraska Act of 1854, the two new territories witnessed a heavy stream of immigrants from both North and South. The Graduation Act of the same year provided for low land prices, and thousands took advantage of it to buy homesteads. The year 1854 thus marked a change in Wall Street's relationship to the federal government. For the past half-century, the brokers had paid little heed to happenings in Washington, and except for Jackson's war on the Bank of the United States, politics was not a

Table 4.2—Outstanding Securities in 1856

	Number of Issues	Amount (dollars)
Railroad Stocks	360	433,286,000
Railroad Bonds	360	363,137,000
Bank Stocks	985	266,137,000
State Bonds	31	190,718,000
City and Town Bonds	113	79,352,000
United States Bonds	1	30,737,000
Canal Stocks	16	25,888,000
Canal Bonds	16	22,130,000
County Bonds	347	13,928,000
Insurance Stocks	75	12,829,000
Misc. Stocks and Bonds	30	18,783,000

Information in Hedges, Commercial Banking and the Stock Market Before 1863, p. 37.

primary factor in determining investment policy. The business cycle, the changes in transportation and industry, and the ties with Europe were considered more important than actions of presidents and congresses. Now, resurgent nationalism, the challenge of the trans-Mississippi West, and sectional rivalries focused attention on Washington's attitudes and programs. Jay Cooke and his brother, Pitt, turned their interests to politics at this time.[22] The "Young America Movement," begun in the 1840s, called for the more venturesome to forget sectional differences and concentrate on taming the frontier and twisting the British lion's tail. George Francis Train, one of its ardent popularizers, was convinced that the movement would prevent a sectional struggle, and he counted on a new bull market to finance western expansion. In 1851, Horace Greeley uttered, "Go West, young man, go West," and investors expected the young men would go by rail.

Although the New York Board churned about on heavy volume during the early 1850s—some days saw as many as 7,000 shares change hands—prices remained static or slipped further. The failure of the market to move upward cannot be blamed on a lack of optimism or ballyhoo; rather, it reflected the fact that lines of credit had been drawn to their utmost. In order to have further expansion, some of the rainbows would have to give forth their pots of gold.

Early in 1853, the Board moved from the Merchants' Exchange to temporary quarters in the Commercial Bank Building. No sooner had the brokers settled in the new location than the market broke downward. In July there were a series of bank contractions in the West which caused sharp declines at the auctions. The New York Legislature enacted a law requiring all banks to publish statements of condition, but this move, which was an attempt to demonstrate the soundness of New York banks, backfired. The institutions feared disclosures of questionable practices and began calling in large parts of their loan portfolios. The resultant contraction almost wrecked the state's financial credit. A short, painful panic followed, during which hundreds of speculators were wiped out.[23]

The brief recovery of early 1854 was halted by disclosures of fraud during the summer. Robert Schuyler, president of the New York and New Haven Railroad, had issued some $2 million in common stock, sold it for his own account, and pocketed the proceeds. About the same time Alexander Kyle, Secretary of the Harlem Railroad, defrauded his firm of $470,000. Other wrongdoings were uncovered at the Parker Vein and Vermont Central Railroads. In October came news of fraud at the Ocean, American Exchange, and National Banks. Each disclosure was accompanied by a selling wave at the Board.[24]

The Barings, along with other English banking houses, started to liquidate part of their American holdings in 1853 and 1854, and an important source of capital with which to finance new companies began to dry up. There was still enough American money to keep the market busy, however, and for a while the loss of foreign funds was not deemed of great significance. But it was still one more cause for uneasiness.

As the rails, canals, governments, and banks declined at the auctions from 1854 to 1856, a bull market developed among the mining issues. By the middle of the decade some of the mines had begun paying large dividends. A rush to get in on the gold boom took place at the curb markets, and soon the midwestern rails picked up, since they were tied to western transportation. Some of the issues were fraudulently bulled and beared; wash sales were the order of the day. But the mania was strong enough to attract even the more sober. Thus, North American Mines advanced from 17 to 75 in a period of two years, and at the same time, Rockland went from less than 1 to 12, and National from 3 to 32.[25]

The mines dominated trading, but few were offered at the auction, since the Board refused to admit the unseasoned issues. Brokers who specialized in mines retaliated by opening an *al fresco* auction opposite the old Merchants' Exchange. A busy day at the 1856 Board might see 6,000 shares change hands; volume on the curb went as high as 70,000, and over one million shares a month were traded during the fall of that year.[26]

Early in 1857 some curb brokers decided to establish a more formal organization. A constitution for the Mining Exchange was hastily drawn up, a room was secured at 29 William Street, and trading began in February. Little is known of the activities there. Some of the companies accepted for listing included gold and copper mines in North Carolina, New York and Pennsylvania lead mines, as well as the more familiar California golds. The leaders of the new organization, which included such old houses as Talmadge & Mawley and Fulton, Cutting, & Co., appear to have been honest; the same could not be said of the securities they traded. The Mining Exchange lasted only a few months, just long enough for some to make a killing and others to lose their shirts before the 1857 panic.[27]

The new auction was only one sign of the apparent disintegration of centralized trading in New York; smaller organizations were also started. Ezra Ludlow announced that he would "hold a sale of securities at 12 o'clock tomorrow at the Merchants' Exchange. In order to supply a ready mode of selling stocks this house will, on and after today, have a daily sale at noon at the Exchange." In January, 1856, Leonard Jerome, the grandfather of Winston Churchill, opened his office at 22 William Street, where he promised to "devote his undivided attention to the purchase and sale of all classes of stock securities," and he too, ran a private auction. The Board members, although forbidden by their constitution from engaging in outside trading, could often be found at these sales.[28]

The Board conducted two auctions a day in 1857, the first between 10:30 and noon, and the second at 2:45. During heavy markets more time was needed, and some members petitioned to have a third call; this was rejected by the governors. Nevertheless, the brokers meant to continue trading after the calls. Hotel rooms were taken by Board members, who bought and sold stock there after dinner. Jacob Little was usually to be found in one or another of these rooms, working around the clock and on Sundays to carry off his coups. A contemporary wrote of Little at the beginning of the bear market of 1857: "The only thing remarkable about this gentleman is his extraordinary appetite for securities . . . for he had been known to gorge and digest more stock in one day than the weight of the bulk of his whole body in certificates."[29] Little had gone bankrupt three times by then, but he was always able to pick up the pieces and start again, eventually redeeming pledges that were thought worthless. After he died it was said that "Jacob Little's suspended papers were better than the checks of most men."[30]

During the early months of 1857 the market declined in orderly fashion. The gold shares, though still prominent, had begun to lose their glamour, and they too slipped with the rails, banks, and other issues. By July the rails were down 50 per cent from their 1853 levels. Then in early August, the Ohio Life Insurance Company, which held many rail stocks, announced its failure, and a major panic gripped Wall Street. Thousands of shares were dumped; brokers rushed back to the financial district from their vacation places along the New Jersey shore and on Long Island. The telegraph clicked out sell orders to other exchanges, as the panic swept in from the West and returned there, reenforced by the New York brokers. There were some 200,000 stockholders in America at the time, and many of them sold out their portfolios in the months that followed.[31]

The panic was quickly felt in London, although the European depression had causes other than the American decline. "Despite my financial distress, I have not felt so cozy since 1849," wrote Karl Marx to Friedrich Engels, as he predicted the doom of capitalism. Engels, the son of a capitalist, answered that "The general aspect of the Exchange here was most delicious in the past week. The fellows grow black in the face with rage at my suddenly rising good spirits."[32] By November the American panic, added to an already tenuous situation, caused consternation on Lombard Street. The Bank Act of 1844 had to be suspended, and the financial structure of Great Britain seemed in danger of collapse. One London broker complained that "the chief blame should be laid to the wild go-ahead spirit of the Yankee." The plungers in American stocks had been burned in 1837, and now, burned once more, many vowed never to return to overseas markets. But this promise was not to be kept, for they would return to Wall Street again and again for the rest of the century.[33]

The 1857 panic was not as severe as that of twenty years before.[34] Its causes were the usual ones: overextention of credit, failure of gold and rail speculations to mature, a foreign war (the Crimean) which drained European capital from America when it was needed, and a European slump.

But the Wall Street financial community was badly damaged; rare was the broker who hadn't suffered heavy losses. Almost half of them were forced into dissolution. "The Western Blizzard" caused 985 merchants in New York to fail, representing a total loss of about $120 million. Violence erupted on more than one occasion, and troops were called in to keep the peace and prevent looting.[35]

Contrary to his essentially bearish nature, Jacob Little had speculated on a rise, and now he was wiped out for the fourth and last time. At the height of the boom he had been worth over $2 million; he lost half of this on a corner in Norwich & Worcester Railroad. Little was engaged in many such speculations, all of which failed, and his firm declared bankruptcy late in the year, with negligible assets and liabilities of $10 million.[36]

The Mining Exchange closed its doors; most of the brokers there were ruined. The curb traders almost disappeared. Their usual haunt on William Street was impassable in 1856; now it was quiet, and would remain so for several years.

The paper losses inflicted by the panic were severe, although not as bad as they had been in 1837. But the brokers had not been as heavily committed to securities at the earlier date. By 1857 many of them had abandoned their factoring and mercantile businesses to concentrate on stocks and bonds. Thus, while a broker could survive a 50 per cent loss in securities in 1837, a 20 per cent decline in 1857 could, and did, put him out of business. Because of this specialization, many of the older men were broken, and they left Wall Street for good.[37] The brash men of the Young America Movement, having overextended themselves, also suffered failures and withdrew, but not before they stoned Greeley's offices at the *Tribune*.

A third generation now took over Wall Street. They were not idealistic dreamers, like the corner brokers of Young America, nor were they basically London correspondents, like many of the older financiers. For the most part they were sober individuals: men like Henry Clews were as conservative as most of the older men, but were more likely to seize the main chance; men like Daniel Drew were larger versions of Jacob Little. Drew once remarked that the only mistake Little had ever made was in being born twenty years too early; he took up the master's mantle, and wore it for the next quarter of a century.

The new men had tried to gain admission to the Board prior to the crash, but they had been denied membership. Qualified in every respect but unable to join the club, they were forced to trade at the curb, and some had paid as much as $100 a week to listen to the calls at the keyhole of the auction room.[38] Now, with the withdrawal of the older men, they were able to pass the membership committee, pay their $400 fee, and participate directly.

Therefore, the 1857 panic was more than just another severe fluctuation in the business cycle. It marked the advent of a new, less polite period of American finance. Before 1857, a broker had to be a gentleman to be admitted to Board trading. He was genteel, well-bred, well-read, and well-connected; for him proprieties often came before profits. The new breed was made up of brokers to whom the amenities of the coffee-house would have appeared quaint and not very important. Where the older men had dealt in thousands of dollars, they gambled for millions. The "rules of the game," often broached but never disavowed by the former generation, were now completely disregarded. The panic of 1857 proved to be the watershed for the most exciting, lawless, and unscrupulous period in American finance.

Thus, on the eve of the Civil War, the business picture had changed markedly. The West still prospered, but the many bubbles in rails, mines, and internal improvements meant that it would have to rely upon other parts of the nation for its development. The North seemed wrecked by the panic. Under the debris, however, was solid strength, and recovery was on its way by 1861. The South, which suffered least of all, was led to believe that she alone had real economic power; soon, southern leaders would test that power in war. In the struggle that followed, the North defeated the South, and took financial control of the nation. By then Wall Street was the money center of the North, and the Board, its heart.

Notes

1. Otto C. Lightner, *The History of Business Depressions* (New York, 1922), pp. 135–50. The Josephs, worth over $500,000 in 1836, had to sell their furniture at auction in 1838. Other brokers took advantage of the panic to enter Wall Street and establish themselves. August Belmont, then the Havana agent of the Rothschilds, quit his job when news of the panic reached Cuba. He opened Wall Street offices and soon became a leading European correspondent.

2. One writer estimated that between 1837 and 1841, state securities depreciated $100 million and corporate issues another $80 million. Several states, including Pennsylvania and Mississippi, were obliged to default on their debts. Governor McNutt of Mississippi hit upon the international Jew as a scapegoat. He told the legislature that "The Bank of the United States has hypothecated these bonds, and borrowed money upon them of the Baron Rothschild. The blood of Judas and Shylock runs in his veins, and he united the qualities of both his countrymen. . . . It is for the people to say whether he shall have

a mortgage on our cotton fields, and make serfs of our children." Edwards, *Evolution of Finance Capitalism*, p. 149. Anti-Semitic outbursts took place after most panics, but Wall Street was usually much less bigoted than Main Street.

3. *Ibid.*, p. 150.

4. Hidy, *House of Baring*, pp. 368–70, 399.

5. Jenks, *Migration of British Capital*, p. 106.

6. Hidy, *House of Baring*, p. 351.

7. Jenks, *Migration of British Capital*, pp. 101–102.

8. Pratt, *Work of Wall Street*, p. 13.

9. Clews, *Fifty Years in Wall Street*, p. 89.

10. The newspapers of 1843–1844 mention a "Public Stock Exchange" and a "Commercial Stock Exchange," but nothing more of their existence is known. Neill, *Inside Story of the Stock Exchange*, p. 57.

11. *Ibid.*, pp. 57–58.

12. Cochran and Miller, *Age of Enterprise*, p. 70 ff.

13. Taylor, *Transportation Revolution*, p. 152; Pratt, *Work of Wall Street*, p. 15; Emerson, D. Fite, *Social and Economic Conditions in the North During the Civil War* (New York, 1910), pp. 155–56.

14. Edward C. Kirkland, *Dream and Thought in the Business Community 1860–1900* (Ithaca, 1956), p. 233; Hoggson, *Epochs in American Banking*, p. 205.

15. Hedges, *Commercial Banking and the Stock Market before 1863*, p. 36.

16. Cochran and Miller, *Age of Enterprise*, pp. 82–85.

17. *Ibid.*, p. 70.

18. Lanier, *Century of Banking in New York*, p. 213.

19. Corey, *House of Morgan*, p. 42.

20. Hidy, *House of Baring*, p. 411.

21. Hedges, *Commercial Banking and the Stock Market before 1863*, p. 37.

22. Henrietta Larson, *Jay Cooke, Private Banker* (Cambridge, 1936), pp. 75–76.

23. Clews, *Fifty Years on Wall Street*, pp. 504–505.

24. Pratt, *Work of Wall Street*, p. 16.

25. Medbery, *Men and Mysteries of Wall Street*, p. 274.

26. Hedges, *Commercial Banking and the Stock Market Before 1863*, p. 40.

27. Medbery, *Men and Mysteries of Wall Street*, pp. 275–77. The Mining Exchange fell in 1857, but reappeared two years later.

28. Neill, *Inside Story of the Stock Exchange*, pp. 58–59.

29. E. C. Stedman, *The New York Stock Exchange* (New York, 1905), p. 101.

30. Wilson, *New York Old and New*, pp. 91–92.

31. Medbery, *Men and Mysteries of Wall Street*, p. 201.

32. Beard, *History of the Business Man*, pp. 600–601.

33. Lightner, *History of Business Depressions*, pp. 142–43.

34. Prices continued upward for the rest of the year, and many stocks were back to their August 7, 1857 levels by March of 1858. Eames, *New York Stock Exchange*, p. 38.

35. Levinson, *Wall Street*, p. 126.

36. Edward Dies, *Behind the Wall Street Curtain* (Washington, 1952), pp. 38–39.

37. Little remained on the Street, a pathetic figure buying and selling five shares at a time. He died soon after, his last words being, "I am going up. Who will go with me?" Smith, *Sunshine and Shadow in New York*, pp. 219–22.

38. Clews, *Fifty Years in Wall Street*, p. 8.

5

The Fortunes of War: 1857-1865

Resolved, That we, the members of the New York Stock Exchange, impressed with a deep sense of the duty, which should animate every heart, of sustaining the Government of the United States in the support of the Constitution and laws, desire, in this period of public exigency, to give encouragement to the Government by pledging our fidelity to the Union, and our resolute determination to stand by it under all circumstances.

Resolution of April 7, 1861

THE PANIC OF 1857 began a depression that lasted for four and one-half years. The prices of securities traded at the Board declined sharply, leveled off, and then drifted down once more in the period from 1858 to 1861.[1] Volume was low at the auctions, as investors husbanded their resources, not trusting the mechanism which few of them really understood. The market for new issues was even duller; firms seeking backing were obliged to rely upon private financing or the support of local citizens.

At times a rise seemed imminent, and a flurry of buying would send the prices of selected stocks upward. But these minor bull periods never continued more than a few weeks, and afterwards the securities would settle back to their old patterns. Several of the upswings took place in telegraph stocks, the glamour issues of an otherwise unglamorous market. However, even here the spark of imagination found soggy tinder; investors had simply lost their daring, as they do during all depressions. For example, late in 1857, Cyrus Field appeared on the verge of success in his attempt to lay a transatlantic cable. Visions of simultaneous selling on both London and New York exchanges caused many brokers, especially those identified with Young America, to foresee more and better opportunities for trading profits.

After four disappointments, a 1,950-mile-long copper wire was strung between Trinity Bay, Newfoundland, and Valentia, Ireland, and on August 5, 1858, Queen Victoria sent the first message to President Buchanan. The auction responded with a mild upturn in prices, but the success and the rise were both brief. After a few more messages had been transmitted, the cable went dead. Field's failure seemed a symbol of the depression.[2]

Even during bear markets there were those who were willing to use the exchanges as gambling halls. As the bids for securities fell, fresh money began to trickle into the auction, hoping for bargains. Since prices steadied by mid-1858, it seemed that an upturn would occur. So even though there was no good news on the economic front, and despite threats of war, the volume of trading rose from the 1857 lows.

In addition, new brokers appeared to take the place of those who had been wiped out. Confronted with applicants and embarrassed by a small deficit, the governors felt justified in raising the price of seats to $1,000. In addition, brokers could buy permission for their clerks to attend auctions for $500. Many members grumbled about the clerks' fee, which was $100 more than full membership had cost in 1844, but most paid. Brokerage had become a complicated business, and the traders needed aid in carrying out transactions. As the lists grew longer, brokers got into the habit of bidding for those shares they wanted, and leaving the room while others were called. The free time was usually spent at the curb market, the volume of which was larger than that of the auction. In 1859 more clerks were added, for most brokers would absent themselves from the Board sometime during the day to listen to the calls at the new Mining Exchange.[3]

Trading in mine shares began in the spring of 1859 at 25 William Street, just two fronts down from the old Mining Exchange. The room was jammed during the first month, and the auction soon moved across the street to 24, where accommodations were larger. The element of risk was high at the Mining Exchange. Wash sales, corners, and fraud were everyday occurrences. Speculators from all parts of the country could be found there, the most prominent of whom were a group of Baltimore gamblers who acted together in bulling and bearing often worthless stocks.[4] The speculators concentrated on the market alone; political developments did not interest them, except insofar as they could affect prices.

The members of the Board were more prudent. Reading speeches of southern fire-eaters and northern abolitionists, they feared that what Senator William Seward of New York had termed "the irrepressible conflict" would further wreck the economy and bring down stocks. Hope never left the Board from 1858 to 1861, but caution predominated. Such news as there was of economic recovery was discounted; inventions and technological innovations stirred no interest. Two months before the 1857 panic William Kelley received a patent for conversion of iron to steel. In 1858 the first mail delivery was made to the West Coast by cross-country stage. The Pullman sleeping car, introduced the following year, made transcontinental rail trips more feasible. Shortly thereafter the Fifth Avenue Hotel bought its first passenger elevator (most patrons preferred to use the stairs, not trusting the new invention). In 1849 Moses Farmer installed the first electric lights in his Salem, Massachusetts home. The possibilities for wealth were great, and even more startling things were in store. But the brokers were either unaware of all this or indifferent to it. Their thoughts were on the coming war; they were no longer dazzled by dreams, as they had been in the early 1850s.

South Carolina announced her secession from the Union on December 20, 1860. On January 9, 1861, the federal supply ship *Star of the West* was fired on by the Charleston militia; on February 4, the Confederate States of America was proclaimed at Montgomery, Alabama. On March 9, five days after Lincoln's inauguration, the Confederate Congress authorized the issuance of treasury notes and currency. Now the Wall Street brokers, who had watched the events of the past three months with growing apprehension, began to panic. Southern speculators were leaving Wall Street, taking large amounts of gold, and some bankers refused to accept the American notes and bonds that started to flow north. The financial community showed concern over the large increase of paper obligations and the gold loss. Fear of fiscal and monetary difficulties drove the stock market down and the price of gold up. When Fort Sumter was shelled on April 12, marking what historians consider the beginning of the Civil War, news of the fighting came to a Wall Street that had operated under a war mentality for months.

Stocks drifted downward during the rest of the year. Southern merchants owed their northern counterparts almost $300 million; nearly all of this was a total loss. Approximately 6,000 northern firms with liabilities of over $5,000 each went into bankruptcy, and even more fell for less than that amount. The banking structure collapsed like a house of cards, with eighty-nine of Illinois' 110 financial institutions in the hands of receivers by the end of 1861. In all, the panic was more severe than the 1857 decline.[5]

Despite the market break, the first reaction of the Board and the unaffiliated curb brokers was of intense patriotism. Southern traders who remained in New York went about in fear of attack. This probably prevented many from selling out, thus retarding the decline; those who were bearish in April and May were considered Confederate sympathizers for many years thereafter.

On April 18, the Board voted to appropriate $1,000 to aid New York's Seventh Regiment, then preparing to leave for the fighting. On the next day, brokers B. M. Nevers and Peyton and Frank Jauden joined the unit. Shortly after, the Board passed this resolution:

> *Resolved,* That we, the members of the New York Stock and Exchange Board, hereby express to our associates our earnest appreciation of their gallantry and patriotism, and we assure them of our sincere sympathy and interest in the cause which it is their good fortune to vindicate and sustain.[6]

But almost all the members remained at their posts, raking in huge profits in the years that followed. Those who were drafted usually bought substitutes. Some developed pacifistic tendencies and converted to Quakerism.

On May 11, the Board published another of its many resolutions of this period:

> *Resolved,* That the members of the New York Stock and Exchange Board hereby pledge themselves not to deal in, or negotiate the bonds, stocks, or other securities of any state or states which may have been issued subsequent to the date of any act or declaration of secession by the authorities of such states, and any member of the Exchange violating this rule shall be expelled.[7]

But this admonition did not include shares that were floated prior to April, and they were traded during the war. The Mining Exchange suffered in the early period, primarily because many of its members were southerners and a large portion of its new issues had been southern mines, but activity there picked up in late 1861 and the Exchange prospered during the war.

Stock prices did not fluctuate strongly after the initial impact of the 1861 depression.[8] Such exotic securities as Panama Railroad and Pacific Mail Steamship Company, which had been placed on the list in 1860, went through several wild movements, but the rails, utilities, and debts held steady.

Indecision changed to optimism in 1862. In February, Union troops captured Roanoke Island, North Carolina. On March 6, a Confederate attack on Pea Ridge, Arkansas, was thrown back, and two southern generals were killed. A month later the Confederate Army of Mississippi was repulsed at Shiloh, Tennessee, after the bloodiest battle of the war, and in late May the southerners were bested at the Battle of Seven Pines. Every month brought news of fresh Union victories, and the prices at the Board, reflecting the national mood, started upward.

Interest in securities picked up during the summer of 1862, although the depression was just then reaching its bottom. The withdrawal of southern brokers, customers, and money did not have the anticipated bearish effect, and expected attacks on northern factories and railroads never materialized. Instead, the ties between the North and the West grew stronger, and industrial output increased sharply. The railroads, especially those running east-west, had to expand in the face of the economic upturn, and did record business. Government spending was up, and although many thought Lincoln's program was fiscally unsound and of dubious constitutionality, the brokers realized that together with his currency policies, it would bring both inflation and prosperity to the nation. The high tariff of 1861, Washington's interest in transcontinental railroads, and the open-handed issuance of military contracts, were to them clear signs of a business-minded Administration. Some feared government supervision of the exchanges, but this did not take place. In 1864 a tax of $\frac{1}{20}$ of 1 per cent was levied on stock, bond, and gold sales, and brokers were charged licensing fees—this was the extent of intervention.[9]

A good deal of the credit for this harmony must be accorded Jay Cooke, whose skill and imagination made him the most important American investment banker until the days of J. P. Morgan. Cooke became the mainspring of Union finance. Before the war he had developed techniques of selling securities which presaged the days of "people's capitalism." His agents would canvass the countryside, advertising securities in out-of-the-way places as well as at the exchanges. In 1861, Cooke underwrote a Pennsylvania state issue of $3 million, and distributed shares in almost every state in the Union. Without such distribution methods, large underwritings would have been close to impossible.

In mid-1861 Cooke transferred his talents to Union finances. Secretary of the Treasury Salmon Chase was unable to market government bonds successfully, and Cooke attempted to interest Chase in using him as an investment banker for the government. Chase showed little interest at first, but by October was obliged to accept the offer.

Cooke's greatest effort was the flotation of $500 million worth of government bonds in one issue. These securities were callable in five years, matured in twenty, and paid a 6 per cent rate. Cooke realized that it would be impossible to float so large an issue at the exchanges, even in those days of loose money and wild speculation. He also knew that his brokerage could not handle the distribution by itself, so he organized a syndicate of the ablest investment houses of the day. Livermore, Clews, & Co. in New York, Spencer, Vila & Co. in Boston, and John Wills in Baltimore were its leaders. None had participated in such ventures before; all would learn the lessons of syndication well, and become leaders in the field of underwriting and distribution. The group hired over 2,500 subagents, who took the "five-twenties" into almost every town and village in the Union. The syndicate appealed to patriotism: the bonds would win the war for the Union. But Cooke also pointed out that the bonds really returned more than 6 per cent, and since the interest would be paid in gold, which was then selling at a premium, the rate was closer to 8 per cent.[10]

This was something new for the American middle class. In the past, the banker had been viewed as a passive agent, always ready to serve, but rarely soliciting additional business. Securities he underwrote were usually kept by the bank or sold to friends and old customers. Now Cooke revolutionized the system. Just as Lincoln brought the power of the federal government to all parts of the nation, so Cooke spread the influence of Wall Street to parts of America that had never considered stock or bond ownership. In addition, the fact that the syndicate's first venture was in government bonds was symbolic of the growing influence of Washington on the securities markets in particular and the economy in general. Although government could be ignored on Wall Street during much of the pre-Mexican War period, it had to be considered during the 1850s. By the end of the Civil War, its programs and philosophy were of basic concern to the Wall Street community.

Cooke and his kind had yet another impact on the financial community: they marked the passing from power of the speculative broker and his replacement by the investment banker. Even the merchant-capitalist, who ran his factory, marketed his products, and always maintained control over the enterprise was to bow to this type of financier in the years that followed.

While Jay Cooke's men hawked bonds throughout the North and Midwest, Wall Street hummed with activity. The financial district had never been more alive, as speculation in securities became popular among the general public. Women invaded the Street, looking upon the market as a giant roulette wheel. Clergymen, generally from Brooklyn, would inveigh against speculators on Sundays, but on Mondays could be found on the Street, betting their salaries on a rise in Erie or a Union victory.

Many of the customers bought their stocks on margin, a device used prior to 1861 but now coming into its own. When a buyer purchased on margin, he would put up a small part of the price of the security (during the war, usually 10 per cent, but at times as low as 3 per cent). The rest would be borrowed by the broker from a bank, which charged as high as 10 per cent per month for this "call money." The effect of margin selling was to increase the amount of capital available for speculation, and at the same time draw money to Wall Street, making it scarce elsewhere in the nation. It brought prosperity to the banks, to the brokers—who by 1863 were averaging $3,000 a week in commissions alone—and to those who had guessed right about the direction of the market. Customers who believed a stock would fall might go short, selling stock they didn't own in the expectation of a decline. This would enable them to buy shares for delivery at lower prices than stipulated in the first contract. Those who thought the prices would rise bought long, or bought securities with the hope that when the payment was called for, the quote would be higher, giving them profits without their having put up the price. Like the margin sale, both of these devices relied upon credit for their operation. The short seller was borrowing stock, in effect, while those who bought long were borrowing money. Each was counting on a sharp shift in prices, and had the market remained steady for about three months, many Wall Street speculators would have been forced into bankruptcy. Fortunately for them the fluctuations did come, for never before had the prices of securities and gold changed so often and so rapidly as they did in the years between 1862 and 1865.[11]

The brokers, of course, were delighted with this kind of market.

Formerly they were sober during rises and falls (with the exception of the panics) and bored in periods of dullness. Now they screamed, ranted, and shouted themselves hoarse during bull and bear raids. Fist-fights were common at the auctions and outside the Merchants' Exchange, where the Board relocated on December 9, 1865. During lulls in the trading brokers worked off their energy in a variety of ways which would have shocked the men of the Tontine. "Crack-loo," a game similar to penny-pitching, but using half-dollars, was a favorite during the winter of 1863. Brokers also enjoyed shooting paper darts at the clergymen who attended the auctions. Whenever a broker pulled off an especially skillful coup, his friends would hoist him to their shoulders and march around singing, "For He's A Jolly Good Fellow." On news of a Union victory they sang "John Brown's Body," while "Dixie" was sung after Confederate breakthroughs. A broker of the period, trying to understand these shenanigans, wrote: "In an insane asylum, dancing and theatrical exhibitions are sanitary measures. And the tense brain fibres of these soldiers of finance would paralyse under the incessant strain of business, were it not for these occasional outbursts."[12]

Still, the Board was calm compared to the apparent chaos at other exchanges. There were literally dozens of separate trading groups in operation by 1865, which reflected two developments that had taken place during the war. First, the Board was found wanting in terms of speed, facilities, and daring. Since brokers there dealt in one stock at a time, and since demands were made for continuous trading —which the governors did not heed—speculators would go elsewhere to buy and sell after their stocks had been called. In addition, the Board members were unwilling to deal in many of the newer issues, arguing that these stocks were of doubtful value. Other brokers were not so scrupulous, and they traded in the new issues at different exchanges.

A second development was the changing nature of the markets and those who dealt in stocks and bonds. Prior to the war, the Wall Streeter was a generalist, which is to say he would speculate in many different securities in the hope of making profits. The merchant-grocer-broker of the Tontine was gone by the 1840s, but his successor still had varied interests. For example, Jacob Little preferred to deal in rail stocks, but he also bought and sold commodities, lotteries, and practically every other type of security. The war changed this. Now no single broker could expect to be informed as to the condition of shares in petroleum, rails, canals, bonds, gold, foreign issues, and the like, especially when high-speed transmission of information and the fluid conditions at the front lines made quick decisions necessary. In addition, competition demanded greater skill than ever to survive on Wall Street; the speculators of the war era were far more cunning than those of the preceding period. Specialization became the order of the day, and since the Board reflected prewar America, dealing as it did primarily in rails, canals, and debts, new exchanges were required for the newer types of securities.

The most famous of the early wartime organizations was Gilpin's News Room, where gold was bought and sold. The need for such a place became evident soon after the fighting had begun, for no one could be sure about the outcome of the conflict or the ability of the Union, even if victorious, to redeem its paper. The failure of Chase's first attempts to sell bonds was one obvious example of this lack of confidence; the hoarding of gold was another. When the North proved unable to quell the rebellion within a few months, hoarding intensified; the price of government bonds went down, while that of gold increased. The end of this first stage in gold speculation came in December, 1861, when northern banks stopped specie payments, followed shortly after by federal suspension.

In February the initial issue of greenbacks was released. This currency, backed by nothing but the credit of the government and not convertible into gold, immediately sold at a discount in relation to gold. "American gold" traded at the auction, would rise in price on bad news from the front, and fall on good. That is to say, when Union victories made it seem that the North would win the war, and thus be able to redeem the greenbacks in gold, the price of gold in relation to the paper would decline. Confederate victories, which might mean a dissolution of the Union and a repudiation of obligations by the North, caused the price to rise. Gold quotations were volatile, and speculators could make fortunes in hours by dealing in the metal.

Although the Board allowed gold to be traded, the brokers felt it was wrong to wager against Union victories, and in 1862 several resolutions were passed outlawing its sale at the auctions.[13] To serve brokers who were not so patriotic, Gilpin's News Room was organized in the spring, with membership open to anyone who could pay the $25 annual fee. For the next two years, despite charges of lack of loyalty and regulations and legislation aimed at curbing gold speculation, the Room prospered.

In April, 1862, the price at Gilpin's was 120, which meant that it took $120 in greenbacks to purchase $100 of gold certificates. After the Union defeat at Fredericksburg in December it rose to 134, and a month later, to 150. Not until Grant's victory at Vicksburg on July 4, 1863, did a decline take place. But Grant's failure to capture Richmond the following year sent the price to 185 on July 11. Soon thereafter the trend changed, and another downward spiral developed.[14]

In order to be better informed about the fortunes of war, which in turn would enable them to anticipate bull and bear periods in gold, the speculators used the wire services. Anyone who could learn of a victory or defeat an hour before his fellows would be able to make enough on the Gold Exchange to retire. Thus, in 1862 some brokers had agents traveling with the armies, sending back information as soon as it was available. A year later several private wires brought news to the financial district prior to its reaching Washington. By 1864, Wall Streeters had spies in the Confederate camp, and they knew of southern plans before the colonels of the Army of Virginia had been told of them. The ups and downs of the gold prices were the best barometer of the war; a shrewd observer could often predict the next step in the fighting by watching the bids closely. Lincoln, who was otherwise friendly to business, thought the gold speculators were no better than leeches. In 1864 he asked Governor Curtin, "What do you think of those fellows in Wall Street who are gambling in gold at such a time as this? For my part, I wish every one of them had his devilish head shot off."[15]

On June 20, 1864, Congress passed a bill declaring transactions in gold to be penal offenses unless they took place in the office of the buyer or seller. Insiders who knew of the proposed law before it was introduced reasoned that it would be interpreted in Wall Street as a sign of government weakness, and would thus increase the price of gold. They bought up all the gold they could, and sold on the news, making fortunes.

The legislation was a failure in that it did not stop trading. Instead of meeting in Gilpin's Room, which was now closed, the brokers would arrange to see each other on the street, where a conversation like the following might take place.

If I were in your office I would sell you twenty thousand gold at a hundred and seventy-five.

> If I were at my office, I would bid you a hundred and seventy for the lot.

> If I were at your office I would let you have it for seventy-three and that is the best I would do.

> Then I would take it.[16]

Memos passed hands, and the deal would be consummated the following day. All the congressional bill really did was to close Gilpin's and raise the price of gold to a new high of 250. Within a short period it was repealed, and the brokers formed the New York Gold Exchange in October, 1864.

The Gold Room, as it was called, was the most informal and certainly the wildest market in American history. We have the following description from a member of the Exchange.

> The gold room was like a cavern, full of dank and noisome vapors, and the deadly carbonic acid was blended with the fumes of stale smoke and vinous breaths. But the stifling gases engendered in that low-browed cave of evil enchanters, never seemed to depress the energies of the gold-dealers; from "morn to dewey eve" the drooping ceiling and the bistre-colored walls re-echoed with the sounds of all kinds of voices, from the shrill, piping treble of the call boys, to the deep bass of R. H————, J. R————, L. J————, etc., etc., while an upreared forest of arms was swayed furiously by the storms of a swiftly rising and falling market.[17]

All eyes were riveted on a large clocklike apparatus on the far wall, which indicated the current bid price for gold. With each tick up, hundreds of thousands of dollars could change hands—it was not unusual for a man to complete a week's trading with a profit exceeding 100 per cent. Similarly, bankruptcies were more common on the Gold Exchange than elsewhere.[18]

One of the biggest problems of the gold traders was how to transfer the merchandise from the seller to the buyer. Most of the buyers would contract for delivery and payment at a future date, intending to sell before settlement was necessary, so it would be possible for the identical gold to be sold several times without being moved from the vaults. But, where delivery was desired, the metal would be measured into canvas sacks, weighed, and sent by messenger from one Wall Street bank to another. Since the gold traders lacked the code of honor and obligation that existed at the Board, short-changing, adulteration, and late delivery were common. In addition, there was the danger of the streets. Specie-clerks carrying the canvas bags would be attacked by robbers who threw red pepper in their eyes and knocked them down, rushing the gold off in conveyances resembling modern supermarket carts. All this could be done in a matter of minutes, and the thieves would be gone before the police arrived.

After a half-dozen or so of these raids, the gold brokers decided to arrange for the issuance of private certificates, drawable upon deposits at the Bank of New York, which became a central depository and the largest non-federal holder of gold in the nation. Since the receivers of paper would usually demand payment from the Bank within one day, and the Bank insisted upon large balances in each broker's account, fraud seemed to be out of the question. Still, E. B. Ketchum, head of the house of Ketchum, Son & Co., was able to forge several millions of dollars worth of certificates in 1865 and to slip away before being found out. In order to prevent future incidents of this nature, a Gold Exchange Bank was set up, with new safeguards including daily statements on the reserves of every account. Despite all of these precautions, frauds still occurred, and the Gold Room was no place for the amateur at any time.[19]

Two other specialized exchanges came into being during the war. The Mining Exchange, which had existed prior to Fort Sumter, was reorganized in December, 1863, as a market for new issues. Such companies as the Woolah-Woolah Gulch Gold Mining and Stamping Company, the Federal Republic Gold Dust and Silver Dirt Mining Company, the Dry Digging and Gold Washing Company, and Gulliver Cañon Gold and Silver-Lead Mining and Water Sluice Company—all of them swindles—were floated at high prices and taken up by speculators to resell to the unwary.

A Petroleum Board was formed in February, 1865, to serve the "Coal Oil Johnnies" and their followers. For a while the price of petroleum fluctuated even more than that of gold, but since oil was then far less glamorous, trading was not nearly as heavy. Some saw a great future for kerosene, lubricating products, and illuminating oil, but most knew only its medicinal properties. One oilman said, "It was death to vermin, a capital disinfectant, and a gorgeous colorizer. As boot grease and as hair oil it was unequalled. The most delicious perfumes might be manufactured from it. It was a panacea for most of the ills that flesh is heir to. It was a liniment for rheumatism, a lotion for wounds, and a sovereign remedy for an inward bruise."[20]

The potential of petroleum was not guessed at; gasoline was considered a useless by-product.

Far more important than the Petroleum Board and the Mining Exchange were those rooms formed because of the inability of the Board to serve the financial community satisfactorily during the war. Some were started to expand the trading hours, others by those who desired to broaden the auction. And there were a few begun by men who simply wanted to wrest power from the older leaders of the Board.

The first of these exchanges to open after Fort Sumter was Godwin's Room, located in a hall adjacent to the Board.[21] In some ways it could be considered an adjunct to the regular auction. Attended by nonmembers, its habitués were permitted to station one of their number at the door leading to the Board to report transactions to his fellows, who would then continue trading the called stock. As might be expected, a good deal of arbitrage took place between the two rooms.[22] Godwin's was not really a new exchange, but rather represented an attempt to enlarge the old.[23]

In 1863 a group of venturesome brokers, unwilling to merely follow the auctions at the Board, withdrew to the cellar of 23 William Street to conduct their own exchange. The dimly lit room, which was called the "Coal Hole," made markets in Board stocks and gold. For a while it was able to compete with Gilpin's for the gold business, but the Hole eventually declined and had disappeared by the end of the war.[24]

The most important of the new exchanges in terms of its effect on the Board was the "Open Board of Stock Brokers." This organization had its origins during the hectic days of 1863, when the older brokers hired younger men to take care of the more vigorous side of their activities, such as waiting for calls, delivering stocks, and arranging arbitrage transactions. Some of these runners and clerks eventually found places in established firms; others united with former members of the Coal Hole to form the Open Board in 1864. The "Long Room" was rented on Broad Street, and the entrance fee was set at $50. The Open Board met between 8:30 A.M. and 5:00 P.M. Unlike the old Board, its transactions were continuous. Each security was traded at a specified place on the floor, and brokers interested in buying or selling stock would go to that area and deal with others who were there for the same reason. Thus, the auction market was rejected in favor of the less orderly but more responsive continuous market, which

characterizes the New York Stock Exchange of today. Since hundreds
of transactions were taking place simultaneously the volume was
much larger there than at other markets. By mid-1865 the new Exchange was doing ten times the volume of the old Board. In the very
same year, it was estimated that $6 billion worth of securities and
gold had been sold on Wall Street, or $20 million for each working
day. The two leading brokerages in terms of sales were Hallgarten
& Hartzefelt, which bought and sold $169,232,939 worth of securities,
and Gentil & Phipps, with $160,901,851. Both were members of the
Open Board.[25]

During the daylight hours Wall Street hummed with action, and
the activity was centered at the New Street entrance to the Long
Room. The old Board, or as it was renamed on January 29, 1863, the
New York Stock Exchange, was quieter, but considered more fashionable. "Guttersnipes," as the curb brokers were then called, con-
gregated at the south end of Broad Street. They were sneered at by
members of both boards, but then, as now, more shares and a larger
dollar volume were traded outside the established exchanges than in
them.[26]

After 5:00 P.M. Wall Street would begin to empty, although some
guttersnipes would remain as long as the sunlight lasted. With the
closing of offices on the Street, the members would move uptown to
hotel rooms and keep trading until their stamina gave out. At first,
the brokers met in the Fifth Avenue Hotel, near Washington Square,
where they would conduct their business in the reading rooms. The
management, deluged with protests from guests, soon posted notices
outside the impromptu exchanges, reading: "Gentlemen are requested not to buy or sell stocks or gold in these rooms."

In March, 1864, an enterprising businessman named R. H. Gallagher rented part of the Republican headquarters, at the corner of
Twenty-third Street and Broadway, and converted the rooms into an
evening exchange. This market was so successful that Gallagher
built a hotel on Twenty-fourth Street and Fifth Avenue and opened
the ground floor as an exchange, charging a yearly fee of $250. The
Evening Exchange closed soon after Appomatox, but while it lasted,
New York was the only city in the world that traded securities for
twenty-four hours a day.[27]

Speculation attracted many new men to Wall Street. Some knew
little of the economy, or for that matter, of the markets, but were
gamblers pure and simple, descendents of William Duer. Even more

than the investment bankers and brokers, they came to symbolize the wartime bull market. Some, like Anthony Wellman Morse, whose specialty was the bull corner in rails, made fortunes and quick reputations, and then lost all on a single roll of the dice. Morse was "The King of Wall Street" in 1863, and a year later he died in a shabby rooming house. The landlady refused to surrender his body to his family until his back rent was paid, but a few old friends finally redeemed it.[28] Others escaped Morse's fate. John Tobin, a bear, bluffed his way to a fortune which he never lost, and Addison G. Jerome, "The Napoleon of the Open Board," and his brother Leonard, made millions in a few months in 1863. Leonard left Wall Street while ahead of the game and went to Paris, where he lived a long and affluent life. Addison was not so fortunate. He lost everything in an attempt to manipulate Pacific Mail and Old Southern, and died of a heart attack in 1864. This colorful grand-uncle of Winston Churchill would have been destitute were it not for a birthday present of several hundred thousand dollars he had given his wife in lusher days.[29]

Men of this stripe were powers in their own right during the war. They entered Wall Street with the air of leading men in a play and, like actors, they were aware that every eye in the audience was on them. When they clashed, others stood by like hyenas waiting to scavenge around the dead loser. Pools, raids, wash sales, and corners were common between 1862 and 1865, and the men who ran them were viewed as gallant highwaymen. But as important as men like Jerome, Morse, and Tobin were in the popular literature of their time and ours, the fortunes of war were those of Cooke and his syndicates, whose innovations would outlast the flash and fire of the speculators.

Notes

1. Smith and Cole, *Fluctuations in American Business*, pp. 181–82.
2. Will Bowden, *The Industrial History of the United States* (New York, 1930), p. 274; Lanier, *A Century of Banking in New York*, p. 231; Walker, *Epic of American Industry*, pp. 172–73.
3. Eames, *New York Stock Exchange*, p. 85.
4. Wash sales on the Mining Exchange produced amazing results. North State Gold & Copper, with total assets of about $1,200, had 200,000 shares which were pushed to $4, giving the stock a valuation of $800,000. Similarly, Gardner Hill Gold and Copper, with assets of $30,000, was valued at $1,600,-000. Stedman, *New York Stock Exchange*, pp. 124–25; Medbery, *Men and Mysteries of Wall Street*, pp. 275–77.

5. Fite, *Conditions in the North During the Civil War*, pp. 105–106.

6. Eames, *New York Stock Exchange*, p. 41.

7. *Ibid.*, p. 42.

8. Smith and Cole, *Fluctuations in American Business*, pp. 181–82.

9. In 1862 a tax of 3 per cent was levied on railroad bonds. This affected securities holders, but not the exchanges themselves. Arthur Bining, *The Rise of American Economic Life* (New York, 1955), pp. 344–45.

10. Larson, *Jay Cooke*, pp. 123–24.

11. Medbery, *Men and Mysteries of Wall Street*, pp. 196–97, 205.

12. *Ibid.*, p. 146.

13. Neill, *Inside Story of the Stock Exchange*, pp. 65–66.

14. Fite, *Conditions in the North During the Civil War*, pp. 119–20; Stedman, *New York Stock Exchange*, pp. 187–88.

15. Pratt, *Work of Wall Street*, pp. 85–86.

16. A. W. Dimock, *Wall Street and the Wilds* (New York, 1915), pp. 129–31; Stedman, *New York Stock Exchange*, pp. 165–66.

17. William Fowler, *Twenty Years of Inside Life in Wall Street* (New York, 1880), pp. 411–16.

18. The young J. P. Morgan made $160,000 on one transaction, and was reported to have sung "Dixie" while taking profits. Corey, *House of Morgan*, p. 66.

19. Medbery, *Men and Mysteries of Wall Street*, pp. 234–35; Fowler, *Twenty Years in Wall Street*, pp. 419–20.

20. Fowler, *Ten Years in Wall Street*, pp. 188–89.

21. Some sources call the room "Goodwin's."

22. Arbitrage may be defined as the simultaneous purchase and sale of the same security in different markets in order to profit from unequal prices. If ABC were selling for 75 at the Board and 74 at Godwin's, the arbitrager would buy in the latter and at the same time sell in the former, thus making a one point profit.

23. Schultz, *The Securities Market*, p. 7.

24. Neill, *Inside Story of the Stock Exchange*, p. 68.

25. Stedman, *New York Stock Exchange*, p. 163.

26. Eames, *New York Stock Exchange*, pp. 70–71.

27. Medbery, *Men and Mysteries of Wall Street*, p. 42–44.

28. Fowler, *Ten Years in Wall Street*, pp. 314–22.

29. *Ibid.*, p. 162.

6

Consolidation, Expansion, and Panic: 1865-1873

When I came to New York and bought stock by the
hundred shares, they called me Stockwell. Then I began
buying in larger amounts, and they called me Mr. Stockwell. By the time I was trading in thousand-share lots,
I was known as Captain Stockwell. They promoted me to
Commodore Stockwell when word got around that I had
gained control of Pacific Mail. But when Jay Gould got
after me and booted me out of the concern all they called
me was "that red-headed son-of-a-bitch from the West."

Alden B. Stockwell

THE TUMULT AND SHOUTING of war died after Appomattox, and Wall
Street began to return to normal. Within a year the evening exchanges were closed, and some of the bucket shops at the far end of
Broad Street disappeared due to the lack of business. Still, the financial
district was far more active than it had been prior to the war. Most of
the stables and many taverns had been replaced by brokerages, insurance offices, and banks. The Wall Street area had jelled, taking on the
essential form of a banking-insurance-brokerage complex that characterizes it today.

This was the Wall Street that Sir Morton Peto and a group of fellow capitalists from England saw when, late in 1865, they visited
America to study investment opportunities. Sir Morton spoke of routes
to Chicago and St. Louis, of building a line to challenge Erie in her
own territory, and of financing new transcontinentals. The English
were impressed with what they were told by Wall Street bankers, who
enhanced their already optimistic outlooks.[1] Sir Morton's reports con-
firmed what they already felt; British investors had begun buying
heavily in American securities.

Foreigners poured tens of millions of dollars a year into the American economy, most of it for government bonds and railroad securities. The scope of this foreign investment can best be realized when one considers that approximately $52 million worth of railroad stocks and bonds were held outside the country in 1853, and by 1869, the figure had jumped to more than $243 million. In that year foreigners held over $1.46 billion of American securities.[2] More than half the stock of such important rails as Central Pacific, Louisville & Nashville, and Norfolk & Western were overseas. Two-fifths of the Pennsylvania was owned by foreigners, mostly English, as was one-third of the Union Pacific.[3] In all, almost 20 per cent of American rail stocks and bonds were foreign owned.

Most of these investments came through Wall Street. German bankers took up mortgage bonds of Ohio railroads through their New York correspondents, and British brokers contracted to purchase the bulk of Philadelphia & Reading convertible bonds in the same fashion. Jay Cooke was particularly prominent in this aspect of brokerage. He had come out of the war with the reputation of America's greatest financier. "The nation owes a debt of gratitude to Jay Cooke that it cannot discharge. . . ." wrote the *Philadelphia Press*. "No one who appreciates the genius and patriotism that led us through the fiery ordeal will hesitate to place the financier of the war alongside its great generals."[4] Cooke had not previously sold government bonds in Europe, but now he turned his attention to exporting railroad securities. He planned a London branch that would market stocks in England in much the same way as the five-twenties were sold in America. The Atlantic cable, finally completed in 1866, encouraged such foreign transactions by making instantaneous communication possible. Interestingly enough, the company that controlled the line, Anglo-American Telegraph Co., was underwritten and sold on both the New York and London markets by J. S. Morgan & Co., then a leading international house.[5] The cable was a fitting symbol of the increasing ties between England and America, and an important means through which orders could be placed on the New York Stock Exchange.

Fed by postwar prosperity, a probusiness Congress, foreign capital, and the rapid growth of railroads into the far West, the stock markets expanded, and by 1867 the level of activity on Wall Street was where it had been during the war. In the following year over $3 billion worth of securities were sold at the Exchange, while a larger volume was handled at the Open Board, and still more at the curb. Two other markets, the Gold Exchange and the Produce Exchange, also did record business, helping to make New York a larger capital market than all of its American competitors combined.[6]

Despite the intensified pace of business, the Exchange methods remained essentially the same as those of a half-century before. Membership was still limited; the Exchange attracted the more conservative of the Wall Street crowd. There were two auctions, one at 10:30 A.M. and the other at 1 P.M. Prior to and immediately after the calls, brokers would meet to bid on government securities, which were not sold at the auctions. In 1867 a Government Bond Department was organized by several members as a separate organization, and two years later it was incorporated into the Exchange.[7]

On a typical day the stock brokers—almost 200 members of the Exchange—would meet at 10:30 A.M. to buy and sell. The vice-president would call the meeting to order, and ask for bids on the list of securities registered with the organization. He would then auction the unlisted stocks. In the late 1860s there were over 250 in the first group, and a varying amount in the second, and on a fast day the calls could be concluded in little more than an hour. James Medbery, a member of the Exchange and one of the earliest historians of the organization, has left us the following transcription of a typical auction.

V.P.: Delaware and Hudson Canal. Any bids?
(*As no broker makes an offer, the mallet rings down upon the desk and the call proceeds.*)
Pennsylvania Coal, Central Coal, Cumberland Coal, American Coal, Spring Mountain Coal, Canton Company, Western Union Telegraph . . .
VOICE: I'll give '5 for a hundred,—'5 for a hundred,—'5 for a hundred.
OTHER VOICES: A hundred at ⅜. Five hundred at ½. Any part of five hundred at ¼.
FIRST VOICE: I'll take a hundred.
V.P.: At 5¼. A hundred at 5¼. Any bids? (*Rap. Rap.*) That will do for that stock.—Quicksilver.
ROBUST BIDDER: 12 for a hundred,—12,—12½,—13—14—
VOICE: Sold.
SIMULTANEOUS SECOND VOICE: I take that stock.
V.P.: One hundred to Snow at 14.
SECOND VOICE: I claim that lot, Mr. President.
V.P.: The Chair decides that Snow made the purchase.
SECOND VOICE: I appeal.
V.P.: Is the appeal seconded?

Fresh Voices: Second the motion.—Second the appeal.

(The vice-president brings the question before the Board, and Broker No. 2 has but three votes to show for it.)

V.P.: The Chair is sustained. Go on with the stock. Mariposa, Any bids?—Pacific Mail.

This would continue at a rapid pace until all the stocks on both lists were called, at which time the auction ended and the brokers retired to the Bond Room, the curb, the Open Board, or their offices. Every transaction was recorded by three secretaries, who sat near the vice-president.

There were several ways by which delivery and payment for shares could be made, for the most part depending upon agreements between buyers and sellers. In August, 1868, The Bankers' and Brokers' Association was formed as a clearing house for deliveries and payments. The organization lasted less than a month, as some brokers resented the publicity it gave to their dealings and others found it impossible to make deliveries on schedule.[8] As a result, each hired a small army of "pad shovers," who carried out orders, made deliveries, and did odd jobs while the auction was in session. By the time the calls had ended, the floor of the Exchange would be full of boys walking rapidly from broker to broker (running on the floor of the Exchange was forbidden, as it is today). Overseeing all was the large portrait of Jacob Little, which was hung above the vice-president's seat.[9]

The other exchanges did more business than the auction but seemed quieter, primarily because they used continuous selling rather than calls. The Open Board moved from the Long Room to its own building and handled the largest portion of organized sales in New York. On January 1, 1866, the Mining and Petroleum auctions were combined to form the Petroleum and Mining Board, which also used continuous sales, and soon became the hangout for the wildest speculators on the Street. In 1867 scandals regarding the sales and deliveries of shares were uncovered, and half its members left the Board. Quotations fell rapidly, along with prices for seats at the trades, which went from $1,000 to $100 in little more than a week. Some typical prices are shown in Table 6.1.

The Open Board, the Petroleum and Mining Board, and the Gold Exchange were the major competitors of the New York Stock Exchange in this period. At the same time, dissention broke out within the Exchange. Commodore Cornelius Vanderbilt, Jim Fisk, Jay Gould, and Daniel Drew, four of the wildest speculators on Wall Street dur-

Table 6.1—1866 Highs and 1870 Lows (Dollars)[10]

Stock	1866	1870
Consolidated Gregory	21.00	1.70
Smith & Parmelee	15.00	1.80
Quartz Hill	6.00	0.75
Grinnell	3.00	0.40
Benton	2.50	0.12

ing the war period, were busy manipulating the shares of the Erie Railroad and others.[11] Particularly objectionable was Drew's practice of printing new shares whenever he needed them to cover his short sales. After a series of wild coups in 1867 and 1868, both the Exchange and the Open Board decided to curb the speculators. On January 30, 1868, the two exchanges jointly declared that all shares traded at their auctions would have to be registered. A committee of members of both organizations was named to secure information from those companies already registered for trading.[12] This was not the first time such an attempt had been made; in 1866 the Exchange had asked the Delaware, Lackawanna, & Western Railroad for facts and figures regarding its capitalization. The president of the road responded that his firm "made no reports, and publishes no statements, and . . . (has) not done anything of the kind for the last five years." This time, however, the exchanges would not accept such answers. When Erie refused to comply, it was stricken from both lists.[13]

Drew and the Commodore planned reprisal. In late February they formed the National Stock Exchange, which was more generally known as the Erie Board. The new organization had a $500 entrance fee, but had no listing requirements, a fact which encouraged those firms which resented the other exchanges' actions to list their securities there. Eventually 300 brokers held membership in the Erie Board, but it was short lived. In September, after Vanderbilt had left Erie and Fisk and Gould had turned their attention to gold, Erie registered its shares at the New York Exchange and the Open Board and was readmitted to trading.[14]

The joint action against Erie led to closer relations between the Exchange and the Open Board. The Board was growing at the more rapid rate, but its members desired the prestige that came with Exchange membership. Early in 1868 a move toward reconciliation was made when the two forbade their members from dealings in the old Long Room, which had become a gathering place for shady curb brokers. In October, the Exchange made membership transferable for the first time. Open Board members, who viewed the Exchange as a gentlemen's club as well as a place of business, bid heavily for seats, and the price immediately jumped to $8,000, a figure that would not be topped until 1878. As a result of these sales, joint membership in both organizations was made possible.[15]

Merger talks were begun at this time. They were successfully concluded in late April, 1869, and on May 8 the two organizations joined to form a single securities market, with a membership of 1,060. A constitution was ratified, which provided for listing requirements, a "rigid scrutiny of all securities, . . . a proper surveillance over members in respect to their fidelity to contracts, . . . (and) a systematization of the whole business of brokerage." The Exchange was to be governed through a group of committees, and headed by a president. The auction was to continue, but the new methods employed by the Open Board would be practiced in the Long Room, reclaimed for this purpose. By 1870 all dealings were carried on there, as the auction became relatively unimportant. In the same year the organization purchased the Exchange Building, and concentrated all transactions on the first floor, reserving the second for offices. In 1882 the calls in stocks were ended, and twenty years later those in bonds also came to an end.[16]

Technological changes also transformed the market. The effects of the Atlantic cable have already been discussed; the centralization of the exchanges after 1869 made its use all the more effective, and further encouraged the sale of securities abroad. Just as important, if not more so, was the "ticker," patented by E. A. Calahan in 1867. An operator for the American Telegraph Company, Calahan was backed by William Muir, Elisha Andrews and others in the Gold & Stock Telegraph Company, which was formed in the summer of that year with a total capital of less than $200,000. The tickers, manufactured and leased by the company, sent out prices from the floors of both the Exchange and the Open Board to brokerages for a fee of $6.00 a week. The machine caught on immediately. Many brokers and customers had a vital need for price information, but had no desire to mix with others on the Exchange floors. Some wanted to follow the dealings, but wished to keep their interest secret. Previously, the broker had to remain on the floor to keep up with trends; now he sat in his office directing dozens of transactions simultaneously. William Heath, known as "The American Deer" for his swiftness in running from the floor to his office to register sales, now became sedentary. The small army of pad-shovers, whose primary job had been to relay quotations from the Exchange to the brokerages, was replaced by runners who carried buy-and-sell orders

The first ticker on Wall Street was installed in David Groesbeck's office, where Drew used it to carry out raids in 1868. Soon every major house had its crude battery-powered machine, which speculators consulted as one might the Delphic Oracle. A rival firm, the Manhattan Quotation Service, tried to develop a similar device, but Gold & Stock formed an alliance with Western Union to crush it. Stephen Field was more successful when his Commercial Telegraph Company competed with the older firm, lowering rates from $25 a month to $10. A price war resulted, which ended when both companies agreed to stop competing and raise the fees together. This collusion led the Exchange to take action. In 1885 reporters were hired by the organization to dispense prices to the tickers, thus obviating any manipulations of reports that might be attempted. Five years later the Exchange took control of Commercial Telegraph and reorganized it as the New York Quotation Company, and in 1892 the governors established their right to select telegraph companies to distribute quotations.[17]

Telephones appeared on Wall Street in 1878, making it possible for customers to buy and sell while away from the Street. Like the ticker, the telephone tended to decentralize buying and selling, and made Wall Street a less hectic place than it had been.

With the changes of this period, the Exchange began to resemble today's market. Important as they were, however, the changes were scarcely noticed by the bulls of 1868–1873, who were busy taking their gains. With the exception of Black Friday, a golden glow of prosperity seemed to have settled on lower Manhattan.

The postwar boom, which far surpassed the predictions of even the most optimistic bulls, had many causes. One was the influx of foreign capital, already mentioned; another was the continuance of government support for business, which had begun during the war. This was the age of the transcontinentals, which required heavy capital outlays. Funds came from private investors, who were encouraged by their brokers to sell conservative government bonds and buy riskier and more glamorous railroad securities. But most of the financing was by federal, state, and local governments. By 1871 approximately 131 million acres of land had been granted by Washington, while the states gave an additional 55 million acres. In addition, the federal government made loans of almost $65 million to the six transcontinentals.

Almost 40 per cent of the cost of all construction prior to 1870 was borne by one government or another.[18] The benefits of this largess went to the roads and those who controlled their stock. With full knowledge that governments were paying most of the bill, investors flocked to buy rail securities. Because of manipulation by insiders, the small stockholders did not share in the successes of most roads, but their money helped the managers to overexpand operations, construct unneeded roads, and practice corruption on a gigantic scale. The small investors did not question the operations of their roads, nor did they complain loudly when expected dividends did not materialize. The value of their holdings went up quickly in those days before capital gains taxes, and they were content. In addition, some roads did show remarkable progress, and this encouraged those who held shares in other new enterprises. The Union Pacific and the Central Pacific, completed in 1869, showed net earnings that year of over $2 million. This figure doubled within less than two years, with no end in sight.[19] Little wonder that the prices skyrocketed, dragging in their wake securities of questionable value. Even companies that had never shown profits, and had little hope of recovery, were sought after by the investors. The magic word was *rails,* and the Street's heroes were congressmen who voted new appropriations, presidents of favored lines, and foreign investors. The beneficiary was the small shareholder, who saw the bids rise almost daily. The price for this apparently limitless prosperity was to be a crash and the worst depression up to that time.

Perhaps the clearest sign of the market's strength in the late 1860s was its refusal to react downward on bad news. In 1866 the great English firm of Overend, Gurney & Co. failed, the London market sank sharply, and English investors were forced to sell American securities in order to meet their notes. Both the London and New York markets saw a general dumping of American shares followed by heavy demands for gold. The price at the Gold Exchange rose to 131 in the days that followed, a level not seen since 1864. Rumors flew that the Treasury had been sold dry, and would be unable to meet federal obligations, but the bulls discounted them and rushed in to buy depressed securities. Their confidence served to buoy the market during the summer and fall. When economic recovery came later in the year, investors were convinced that market conditions were sound; if Wall Street could survive the selling by foreign houses, it could survive anything.[20]

By this time, problems revolving around the currency had come to the fore. At the end of the war, $400 million in greenbacks were outstanding. Hard money forces favored their gradual elimination and redemption in gold, while inflationists demanded still more paper money. The first victory went to the former group, as in 1866 Congress passed a bill providing for the redemption of greenbacks at the rate of $10 million a year. During the campaign of 1868, Republican U. S. Grant came out for hard money, while the Democratic platform supported greenbacks. Grant won, but before he could take office, Congress voted to halt the further redemption of paper, leaving $356 million in circulation.

The problem was then transferred to the courts. In 1869 the Supreme Court, in *Hepburn vs. Griswold,* decided that greenbacks were not legal tender. The case involved a debt contracted before 1862, however, and therefore did not affect those greenbacks in circulation at the time of the decision. In 1871 the Court, in *Knox vs. Lee,* reversed the earlier decision, stating that Congress had the right to determine how debts should be met. But from 1869 to 1871 it appeared that the hard money forces had won the battle and the war.

To most investors, the victory seemed to mean stability and support for the economy as a whole. As the price of greenbacks fell, that of gold rose at the exchanges. Some unsophisticated speculators reasoned that the rise would soon be transferred to the stock lists, and they poured new money into the market. Wiser heads realized that much of the funds used to push gold higher had come from liquidations on the stock exchanges, which had left the securities markets considerably weaker than they had been in 1867. In addition, most of the speculation in securities was based on high margin accounts. The new buyers were a skittish lot, who panicked at the intimation of bad news and sold quickly when their stocks went up. These people were wiped out on many sharp rises and falls in this period.

The most shattering of the collapses involved machinations on the gold markets. In March, 1869, President U. S. Grant was inaugurated and for the next eight years more dishonest plans were hatched than in any other period of American history. Fisk and Gould were involved in the first of these scandals. In May, Gould arranged to meet the President's brother-in-law, Abel Corbin, an aged former speculator who was still on the make. Gould casually mentioned that a good deal of money could be made on the gold market, and that if the gold supply of the nation were constricted, prices would go up, assuring benefits to farmers, workers, capitalists—in short, to the entire nation. On the other hand, if gold expanded, it would lead to lower prices, followed perhaps by revolution. Corbin was impressed by this weird economics lesson, and promised to tell Grant about the dangers that lay in gold sales.

Shortly thereafter the President was introduced to Gould and Fisk. Within a few days Gould told Grant of his ideas, but the President seemed unconvinced. Fisk withdrew from the scheme, but Gould, who had been speculating in gold prior to the meeting, did not give up the possibility of a gold corner.

Realizing that Grant would not assist in the attempt to manipulate gold, Gould tested Corbin to see how much influence he had with the President. The Assistant Treasurer in New York had just resigned, and Gould told Corbin that his stepson-in-law, Robert Catherwood, would be an admirable choice for the post. When Catherwood refused to cooperate in the gold manipulation his name was withdrawn and that of General Daniel Butterfield, a more willing tool, was substituted. Corbin did have Butterfield named Assistant Treasurer: now Gould had his man placed in a vital office, and was also assured of Corbin's power over the President.

At this point Gould began buying heavily in gold, knowing that it would go up should the government stop public sales. He organized a pool with brokers Arthur Kimber and W. S. Woodward. Fisk refused to join, but offered his services, should they be needed. This offer was taken up, and although Jubilee Jim's try at manipulating Grant failed, his subsequent dinner party for Secretary of the Treasury George Boutwell was the signal for the beginning of a bull market in gold. Wall Street had sensed Gould's scheme; the dinner seemed to indicate that he had carried it off. The price of gold quickly went to 133, a postwar high.

On September 1, Grant ordered Boutwell to stop selling gold. Gould was overcome with joy, believing that Corbin had been responsible for the development. Actually, the President had come to the decision on his own, but the action fitted perfectly into Gould's scheme. To reward Corbin, he purchased $1.5 million in gold at 133, telling the brother-in-law that he needn't pay for it until the lot was sold. General Horace Porter, Grant's military secretary, had $500,000 bought for him under the same arrangement.

In mid-September the bears began to push gold down with concentrated selling, and Gould was panic-stricken. He called in his old friend, Fisk, and asked his aid in bulling the price up once more.

Telling him that almost the entire Administration, including the President, was in on the corner, Gould begged Fisk to do what he could to force the price higher. The next day Jubilee Jim appeared on Wall Street, and talked loudly of his purchases in gold; from time to time he would enter the Gold Room and buy for his account. The Street was impressed, and gold went up once more. Gould thought the situation was saved, and General Butterfield, agreeing with him, took up a previous offer of $1.5 million in gold with payment on its sale. Boss Tweed was in the ring, allowing Tammany-controlled banks to use their funds for speculation. By September 20, the pool members had amassed contracts for over $100 million in gold. There was a little more than $25 million in the city at the time, and the Government held less than $100 million. Three days later the gold price reached 144; the conspirators figured their total profit at that point in excess of $40 million.[21]

Then the corner began to crumble. Grant had learned of Corbin's speculation, and told him indirectly that he wanted it stopped. It was evident that Grant would soon tell Butterfield to sell federal gold once more, thus bringing down the price. Corbin avoided Gould at first, but later went to him and asked to be bought out. Gould promised to do so later if Corbin would keep quiet about the planned government gold sales. The shaken Corbin agreed, and Gould left, planning ways of selling his contracts before the price broke.

Gould began dumping gold on Thursday morning, September 23, but Fisk, unaware of what had happened, continued to bull its price. Acting through brokers William Beldon and Albert Speyer, he contracted for large amounts in their names. Since gold speculators saw what was happening, and didn't know of Gould's conversation with Corbin, they assumed that all was well, and the price would go higher. The opening bid on Thursday was 141; by noon, it had gone to 145, with no takers. Word that Gould had cornered the market was whispered from speculator to speculator. The bears, holding large contracts and believing them incapable of being filled, were frightened. Telegrams were sent to Washington requesting federal intervention, and Fisk was approached by brokers begging for mercy. Jubilee Jim refused to relent. This was his hour of triumph.

On Friday, September 24, the price continued to rise, and Speyer and Beldon continued to buy for Fisk's account. It is believed that Fisk had been told, finally, of Gould's plan, and allowed his brokers to keep on buying, with no intention of paying for the purchases. In any case, no one else knew of the pending government sales, and the price soon reached 150. Panic erupted at the Gold Exchange. The securities market also felt the pinch, as speculators liquidated stocks in order to buy gold. New York Central began to plunge downward, and Commodore Vanderbilt, mumbling invectives against Fisk and Gould, was obliged to pour over one million dollars into the market to bolster Central's price. As the price approached 160, with few takers, brokers began fainting on the Exchange floor. One of them, Solomon Mahler, committed suicide. Others were carted off to hospitals. The pandemonium was not to be matched until 1929.

The turning point was signaled by a telegram from Boutwell to Butterfield, telling the Assistant Treasurer to "sell four million gold tomorrow, and buy four million bonds." Butterfield promptly carried out the order, and at the same time sold his own holdings. Then he sent future President James A. Garfield to Wall Street to announce federal gold sales. Garfield mounted the steps of the Subtreasury, and screaming at the top of his lungs, declared: "Fellow citizens, God reigns and the Government at Washington still lives! I am instructed to inform you that the Secretary of the Treasury has placed ten millions in gold upon the market!" The price plunged twenty points at once, and continued to go down. So fast was the break that Albert Speyer, Fisk's broker, was still bidding 160 for gold at one end of the room while at the other it was selling for 135.[22] E. C. Stedman, a poet as well as a broker, wrote a lengthy poem about the corner, which read, in part:

> One Hundred and Sixty! Can't be true!
> What will the bears-at-forty do?
> How will the merchants pay their dues?
> How will the country stand the news?
> What'll the banks—but listen! hold!
> In screwing upward the price of gold
> To that dangerous, last, particular peg,
> They had killed their Goose with the Golden Egg!
> Just there the metal came pouring out,
> All ways at once, like a water spout,
> Or a rushing, gushing, yellow flood,
> That drenched the bulls wherever they stood!
> Small need to open the Washington main,
> Their coffer-dams were burst with the strain!
> It came by runners, it came by wire,
> To answer the bid of Israel Freyer,

It poured in millions from every side,
And almost strangled him as he cried—
"I'll give One Hundred and Sixty!"[23]

When the smoke cleared, the wreckage of "Black Friday" littered Wall Street. Dozens of brokers were ruined; hundreds of speculators were bankrupt. Beldon and Speyer, Fisk's two brokers, as well as Jubilee Jim himself, were penniless. But Gould shared a profit of over $11 million, with his partner. In addition, Fisk repudiated his buy contracts, contrary to the code of Wall Street but in keeping with his character. When a lynch mob came for them, Gould and Fisk slipped out a back door, leaving a parting message that blamed everything on Corbin. The two got off scot-free, and all attempts to make them pay back part of the money they had swindled were met with an injunction issued by Judge Barnard. Gould solemnly proclaimed, "I regret very much this depression in financial circles, but I predicted it long ago. I was in no way instrumental in producing the panic." And Fisk, in good form, added, "A fellow can't have a little innocent fun without everybody raising a halloo and going wild."[24]

By early 1870 the gold debacle had ended and the markets once more began to rise. But confidence had been severely shaken, although most investors did not realize it at the time. An awareness of the weaknesses underlying the apparent prosperity was evident for the first time, and the markets were far more susceptible to declines on bad news than they had previously been. We can see now that if the flow of foreign capital were to decline, if confidence in shaky rails were undermined, and if bad news came from Washington, the market would be sure to plunge downward.

The rail mania reached a climax in 1871. Not only was construction proceeding at a record pace in the United States, but many European nations were either planning or expanding their systems. In 1869 English investors held over $200 million of South American railroad construction bonds alone, and demands for capital from there as well as from Europe and the United States were straining the resources of the London money market. Funds for expansion became harder to get than ever before in the century, and credit facilities throughout the world were near their breaking point. By October 2, 1871, some New York banks were forced to call in several large loans in order to remain liquid. At the same time England raised its money rate from 3 to 5 per cent. News of the Chicago fire arrived in New York a week later. Millions of dollars were lost, and the demand for funds to rebuild the city, added to the loss of property by listed companies, caused a stock market break of major proportions.[25]

The October decline lasted only two weeks. Reports of great progress in the rebuilding of Chicago, rumors that the government would buy bonds at the market, thus supporting their prices, and optimistic announcements from the banks led to an upswing late in the month. The market had been oversold, said the speculators, and they rushed in to pick up rail stocks at bargain prices. By November the markets seemed back at the point where they had been during the summer. The appearance was deceiving, however, for the bull move had been further weakened by the October crash.[26] Few businesses had gone bankrupt, but dozens of brokerages failed early in the month, and by the end of the year, sixty-five of them had closed their doors. This figure, a postwar high, should have warned speculators of the flimsy condition of the market, but 1872 opened with a slight upturn in prices, a sign that confidence had been restored.[27]

During the first half of 1872 the railroad boom was reinforced by a new mining craze. For two months the San Francisco Stock Exchange was more active than its New York counterpart, as a gold mania based on reports and rumors of new strikes ran its course. New Yorkers soon learned of the speculative orgy and took the cue; a general rise began and carried through the summer. In early fall, Boss Tweed tried to precipitate a panic in order to help the Democratic candidate for President, Horace Greeley. Despite his not inconsiderable power, he could not halt the bulls. Confidence had apparently been restored, but it was built on clouds, for the fundamental economic and financial situation had not changed from the tense times of 1871.

Jim Fisk was murdered in January by his mistress' jealous suitor. Strangely enough, after Fisk died a legend of him as a modern Robin Hood began. Within a year a song appeared which related how Jubilee Jim reacted to news of the Chicago fire.

> When the telegram came,
> that the homeless that night,
> Were starving to death slow but sure,
> the lightning express,
> manned by noble Jim Fisk,
> flew to feed all the hungry and poor.[28]

The death of his old friend did not worry Gould, who was busy attempting another coup with Erie. Foreign investors, especially Germans, had begun accumulating Erie shares, apparently expecting that good news from Fisk and Gould would send them up. Feeling that the buying would continue, Gould bought heavily on the market himself. At the same time, Drew, the perennial bear, sold short. He was joined in this by Henry N. Smith, the senior partner in Gould's own firm of Smith, Gould, Martin & Co., who had made a killing by selling short on news of the Chicago fire. Now a millionaire in his own right, he prepared to take on his junior partner.[29]

Drew and Smith believed that Erie would go lower, and in March, they tried to oust Gould from his position at the road. The play failed, but when it was pointed out that his departure would cause a bull move in Erie from which he could benefit, Gould agreed to leave. When the news broke the stock advanced twenty points, and Gould made approximately one million dollars in profits. The new board of directors then charged that Gould had looted Erie, and must return the money. Smith and Drew thought that the protracted battles between the directors and Gould would cause the stock to decline, enabling them to make large profits.

All this did not happen, for Gould supported the price of Erie in order to make his bull contracts good. At the same time he moved to outflank Smith and Drew. While the two were speculating in Erie, they also sold short on Chicago & Northwestern, and the stock went from 85 to 75. But then Gould stepped in and began to buy heavily. Within two weeks the price had risen to 250 bid, with no takers. Gould had cornered the market, causing Drew to lose $2 million and Smith, still more.[30]

Now Smith moved to gain revenge. He released the books of Smith, Gould, Martin & Co., and showed the Erie Board how Gould had defrauded the road. General Barlow, a member of the Board, issued a complaint against Gould, and the former Erie president was arrested on charges of embezzlement. Bail was set at one million dollars, but this amount was raised with ease. Once freed, Gould told reporters, "The matter is very simple. Drew, Smith, and the rest of them were short of stock, and as a desperate resort they watched their time and arranged matters so as to have me arrested just at the moment they expected to create a panic in the Street."[31]

Gould never came to trial. Both sides wanted to avoid a protracted court fight, and they met to effect a compromise. The directors would drop all charges against Gould and pay him nothing for several parcels of land and securities which Gould told them was worth $6 million.

In addition, he would leave Erie for good.[32] This agreement was concluded on December 18. When the news reached the Street, a pre-Christmas rally began which went into full swing just before New Year's Day. And among other rises, Erie went from 52 to 60.[33] As had been the case a year before, the financial markets had a bull movement in early January.

If stocks appeared bullish while business and financial reports were bearish, the situation was no different from those in previous years. Rail construction was at a new high, although the utility of the new additions was questionable. The Republicans, led by Grant, were in power; manufacturers and farmers expected 1873 to be a record year. At the same time, however, weaknesses that had developed during the previous seven years were coming to the surface.

The United States was an integral part of the European financial community by 1873. The great American economic expansion had, in large part, been financed in foreign capitals, so that any move to limit credit or liquidate assets in London, Paris, Berlin, or Vienna could seriously damage the American markets. As has already been mentioned, the great rail boom was straining financial resources in all nations. In addition, London had to raise funds to pay for construction of the Suez Canal, which was completed in 1869. Italian states, involved in their wars of unification, were also borrowing heavily, as was Austria, which blocked the movement. The Franco-Prussian War cost approximately $2.7 billion in cash, and the Treaty that ended the war called upon France to raise an indemnity of one billion dollars. Much of this money was raised in France, but a good deal came from loans floated in London, which further weakened that city's reserve position.[34]

This was the situation in May of 1873, when Vienna was struck with a financial panic. Austrian bankers sought relief abroad, but funds were too tight, and the sharp decline continued throughout the summer and lasted several years. During the summer another sign of tight money appeared, this time in London. Purchases of American securities, which had increased sharply during the past few years, now declined. Even the well-advertised American Investment Trust, backed by the respected house of Glyn & Co., had to be withdrawn from the market due to a lack of investor interest. By early September, Europeans had begun selling securities on balance, and some forced dumping had started on Wall Street.[35]

Had the American financial structure been as strong as it was in

1866, when it survived the Overend, Gurney panic, the nation might have withstood the liquidations. But this was not the case. The railroads had been greatly overexpanded and financed by shady means, and were in shaky condition. The banks were also in sorry shape, having used their underwriting affiliates to finance the expansion and basing a good deal of their reserves on inflated rail stocks and bonds. Withdrawals in August seriously strained their capacities. When correspondent institutions in the Midwest began to call in their reserves in preparation for the fall crop movement, their position was further weakened. During August over $27 million in reserves was withdrawn for this reason alone. The national banks could not help, for their reserves were at a low point at the time.[36]

Adding to the fiscal problems was a monetary crisis. The demonetization of silver took place in February. Although silver hadn't been coined for several years, this action caused a fluctuation in the value of gold and greenbacks. Not only would it now be impossible to expand the currency through the issuance of silver certificates and coins should such a move become necessary, but confidence in the dollar was also being questioned. Gold began leaving the economy for hiding places in mattresses and back yards. In all, there were few bright spots in the picture. In May a commentator remarked that "Every financial man can see how with these safeguards a general panic is almost impossible and will continue impossible so long as our banks are kept strong in reserve."[37] By late August the banks were no longer strong, and panic was imminent.

The first crack in the wall of confidence came on September 8, when the New York Warehouse and Security Company, which was actually an underwriting house that had floated the securities of the Missouri, Kansas, and Texas Railroad, suspended payments. Five days later the brokerage of Kenyon, Cox, & Co., in which Daniel Drew was a partner, closed its doors. On the same day a small rubber importing company failed. Still the *Commercial and Financial Chronicle* noted that government bonds had fallen only 3 per cent: "In this, as in other points we have noted, the thoughtful man will see many gratifying indications of firmness and strength in the financial situation."[38]

Then came several days during which the markets held steady. The panic began on September 18, when Jay Cooke & Co., the most respected house on Wall Street, announced its failure. Cooke had invested in many railroads, and when they did not prosper as expected, he found himself in a financial hole. The actual event which precipitated his decline was the failure of his house to market Northern Pacific bonds. Cooke had gambled all on this venture, and when the public refused to respond to his advertisements, he found himself insolvent and bankrupt. Cooke did not cause the panic, but he was its symbol, and the spark which fired the conflagration.[39] The Philadelphia newspapers sadly noted that the firm was "The most enterprising and renowned of American monetary institutions, its name was everywhere the synonym for strength and solidity. An hour before its doors were closed, the Bank of England was not more trusted. The disaster was as unexpected as an earthquake is today."[40]

Cooke & Co. announced its failure simultaneously on the floors of the New York, Washington, and Philadelphia exchanges. Rail issues fell sharply on the news, as did Western Union, whose fate was tied to the transcontinentals. On the next day Fisk & Hatch suspended payments, along with nineteen other New York brokerages and a dozen or so more in Philadelphia. Lockwood & Co., which had rebounded from the panic of 1869, now went under for good. The senior member, who had celebrated the firm's salvaging operations with the purchase of a one million dollar home in Connecticut, announced his personal bankruptcy as well.[41] Runs began on the Fourth National Bank and the Union Trust, and both were forced to close their doors. The Bank of Commonwealth went into receivership. By the late afternoon of September 19, it was evident on Wall Street that the nation and the world were in the grip of the greatest international panic yet known.

The Board of Governors took emergency action. The Exchange was closed at 11:00 A.M. on September 20, and was not reopened for ten days. This was the first suspension of trading for more than twenty-four hours in the history of the money market. Although sales of listed shares continued at the curb, the Exchange's closing and its implications led to further panic, and shares dropped faster than before.

The Gold Exchange Bank was flooded with orders from people who wanted to convert their paper into gold, which they could hoard. The dealers were unable to fill the orders, and shortly thereafter the president obtained an injunction forbidding further clearances. This action heightened the panic. The Bank of New York, the most respected financial establishment in the city, undertook gold clearances in an attempt to steady the market. It failed to meet demands, and had to suspend such activities. Then a committee made up of twenty leading bankers and brokers tried to stabilize the gold market by pooling their resources. But when Smith, Gould, Martin & Co. refused to cooperate, this plan, too, collapsed. With each failure came a new frenzy of selling at the Exchange.[42]

The situation led President Grant and Secretary of the Treasury William Richardson to come to New York on September 20 and try to instill confidence in the market leaders. At Grant's right hand through most of this period was the old Commodore, who had not been seriously hurt by the panic. Vanderbilt, an expert on watering stock and manipulation, repeatedly told the President that "building railroads from nowhere to nowhere at public expense" was bad business. He offered to deposit $10 million with the Subtreasury if the Government would make deposits of from $20 to $40 million in various New York banks as a sign of its trust and a guarantee of payments: Wall Street was bargaining with Washington on equal terms. Grant rejected this proposal, and instead directed Richardson to begin buying government bonds on the open market. Within the next four days $13 million worth were purchased. This action served to support bond prices and inject new money into the market, but it did not stop the panic, and the Treasury was soon forced to stop purchases due to a lack of funds. Grant's action replaced some of the money that had been hoarded and helped the banks remain solvent for a while longer. As a means of supporting and injecting confidence into the money market, however, it was a failure.[43]

It remained for the bankers themselves to stem the decline. The New York Clearing House named a committee of five bankers to direct salvage operations. A central office was established which accepted deposits of securities and bills receivable, against which were issued clearing house certificates, which could be used to settle accounts between banks. During the next few months approximately $27 million of these certificates were issued, inflating the money supply. Reserves were encouraged to flow from stronger banks to weaker ones, thus preventing new failures. When the panic ended the holders of clearing house certificates were to receive their security plus 7 per cent interest. This plan worked within New York, but could not prevent withdrawals by noncity banks from their Manhattan correspondents. Such withdrawals were discouraged by requiring all country banks to send their individual depositors to the city for withdrawals when and if desired. Since few Pennsylvania farmers would make the trip to New York to draw against their accounts in a local bank, the net effect was a partial suspension of inter-bank transfers.

All of these measures, plus the fact that the panic had just about run its course when the clearing house plan was instituted, helped end the crisis. The selling eased off by late November, and the committee closed up shop, having redeemed the certificates and saved the New York financial complex.[44]

The 1873 panic ushered in a depression that lasted for six years.[45] During this period almost all the incompleted railroads were reorganized after foreclosure, and many of the others were also thrown into the hands of receivers. Although expansive Treasury policies aided the monetary situation, the equilibrium reached in 1874 was at a low level. There were three million jobless in that year, and this figure remained static until the upturn of 1878. Even then, full prosperity was not restored. Well over 23,000 commercial and industrial failures were recorded, and assets of more than one billion dollars were lost. The securities markets reflected the depression, as business slacked off and a generally low level of activity and prices set in.

Notes

1. Jenks, *Migration of British Capital to 1875,* pp. 259–60.
2. Myers, *New York Money Market,* p. 289.
3. Edward C. Kirkland, *Industry Comes of Age: Business, Labor, and Public Policy, 1860–1897* (New York, 1961), p. 289.
4. Fite, *The North During the Civil War,* p. 133.
5. Lanier, *Century of Banking in New York,* p. 231; Walker, *Epic of American Industry,* pp. 172–73.
6. Lanier, *Century of Banking in New York,* p. 233.
7. Schultz, *The Securities Market,* pp. 11–12.
8. Myers, *New York Money Market,* pp. 299–300.
9. Medbery, *Men and Mysteries of Wall Street,* pp. 20–29.
10. Fowler, *Ten Years in Wall Street,* pp. 463–64.
11. The fascinating stories of these four adventurers falls outside the scope of this work. See Bouk White, *The Book of Daniel Drew* (New York, 1937); W. A. Swanberg, *Jim Fisk: The Career of an Improbable Rascal* (New York, 1959); Wheaton Lane, *Commodore Vanderbilt* (New York, 1942); Jules Grodinsky, *Jay Gould: His Business Career, 1867–1892* (Philadelphia, 1957); Frederick Hicks, ed., *High Finance in the Sixties: Chapters from the Early History of the Erie Railroad* (New Haven, 1929).
12. Schultz, *The Securities Market,* p. 11.
13. J. A. Livingston, *The American Stockholder* (New York, 1958), pp. 179–82.

14. Neill, *Inside Story of the Stock Exchange,* p. 95; Eames, *New York Stock Exchange,* p. 52.

15. *Ibid.,* p. 51; Medberry, *Men and Mysteries of Wall Street,* pp. 16–17.

16. *Ibid.,* pp. 15–20; Schultz, *The Securities Market,* pp. 12–13.

17. Neill, *Inside Story of the Stock Exchange,* pp. 93–94; Stedman, *New York Stock Exchange,* pp. 436–40.

18. Harry J. Carman and Harold C. Syrett, *A History of the American People* (New York, 1952), Vol. II, p. 92.

19. Walker, *Epic of American Industry,* pp. 179–80.

20. Lanier, *A Century of Banking in New York,* p. 234.

21. *Ibid.,* pp. 234–35.

22. Swanberg, *Jim Fisk,* p. 153; Harris, *Memories of Manhattan,* p. 49.

23. Note that Albert Speyer's name is given as Israel Freyer. As had been the case in previous panics, and would occur in the future, anti-semitism played a role on Wall Street, although a smaller one than in the nation as a whole. It is interesting to note that Stedman, a young man in 1869, later discovered Emma Lazarus, the famed Jewish poetess. Eames, *New York Stock Exchange,* pp. 117–18.

24. Swanberg, *Jim Fisk,* p. 155.

25. Fowler, *Ten Years in Wall Street,* p. 531.

26. Walker, *Epic of American Industry,* pp. 196–97.

27. *Ibid.,* pp. 197–98; Clews, *Fifty Years in Wall Street,* pp. 329, 511.

28. Holbrook, *Age of the Moguls,* p. 48.

29. Fowler, *Ten Years on Wall Street,* p. 531.

30. Grodinsky, *Jay Gould,* pp. 108–109.

31. Richard O'Connor, *Gould's Millions* (Garden City, 1962), pp. 124–25.

32. The land and securities were later found to have been worth around $200,000. But Gould was never called to account for this shortage. *Ibid.,* pp. 125–26.

33. Clews, *Fifty Years in Wall Street,* p. 513; Eames, *New York Stock Exchange,* p. 58; Fowler, *Ten Years in Wall Street,* p. 529.

34. Lanier, *A Century of Banking in New York,* p. 235.

35. Walker, *Epic of American Industry,* p. 217.

36. Myers, *New York Money Market,* pp. 236, 278; Neill, *Inside Story of the Stock Exchange,* pp. 97–98.

37. Walker, *Epic of American Industry,* pp. 216–17.

38. *Ibid.,* p. 217.

39. Sparkes and Moore, *The Witch of Wall Street,* pp. 135–36; Larson, *Jay Cooke,* pp. 410–11.

40. Edwards, *Evolution of Finance Capitalism,* pp. 157–58.

41. Fowler, *Ten Years on Wall Street,* pp. 528–29.

42. Clews, *Fifty Years in Wall Street,* pp. 513–14.

43. Lane, *Commodore Vanderbilt,* pp. 276–77.

44. Myers, *New York Money Market,* pp. 236, 289, 357, 408.

45. Maurice W. Lee, *Economic Fluctuations: Growth and Stability* (Homewood, Illinois, 1959), p. 127.

7

The Rise of Investment Banking: 1873-1884

> The men I see before me are owners and managers of colossal capital. You are, doubtless in some degree, clinging to the illusion that you are working for yourselves, but it is my pleasure to claim that you are working for the public. (Applause.) While you are scheming for your own selfish ends, there is an over-ruling and wise Providence directing that the most of all you do should inure to the benefit of the people. Men of colossal fortunes are in effect, if not in fact, trustees for the public.
>
> Samuel Tilden

FROM 1873 TO 1878 the financial district and the nation suffered through a bear market and depression, the most drawn out in American history. But although the period was long, the decline was not severe. Volume dried up at the Exchange, money went into hiding, and the district took on an almost placid appearance. The price of a seat, which had risen to $7,700 before the crash, drifted down to $4,000 in 1876.[1] During this period, 287 brokerages declared bankruptcy, while only eighty-five closed their doors in the seven years following the depression.[2] Many of these liquidations were not caused by excessive speculation or reckless leadership, but by lack of business at the Exchange. The differences in volume between depression and boom can be seen in Table 7.1.

The averages told the same story. In 1878 the Exchange list was comprised of thirty-six rails, five coal companies, four each of telegraph and transport firms, three mines, one steamship, and one land company. Average prices of rails, by far the best indicator of market conditions, are shown in Table 7.2.

Table 7.1—Sales Volume 1875–1882[3]

	Shares Sold	Value of Shares Sold (dollars)
1875	53,813,937	2,862,903,683
1876	39,926,990	2,132,050,483
1877	49,832,960	2,601,280,512
1878	29,875,593	2,157,269,581
1879	72,765,762	4,136,633,570
1880	97,919,099	6,819,086,054
1881	114,511,248	8,197,506,403
1882	116,307,271	7,689,453,436

By both the volume and price levels, it can be seen that the market drifted lower from 1873 to 1878, while recovery came in mid-1879. The rail lows of 1877 were never again to be reached, while the highs of 1881 were not surpassed until 1901.[4]

A sharp decline in 1877–1878 was attributed to disclosures of ir-

Table 7.2—Average Rail Prices, 1873–1882[5]

	High	Low
1873	69.61	40.88
1874	58.79	41.79
1875	53.50	36.14
1876	47.28	27.58
1877	36.33	20.58
1878	37.77	25.51
1879	67.86	33.35
1880	87.04	51.74
1881	101.54	69.93
1882	94.85	63.77

regularities in New York savings banks and fears regarding the future of the nation's monetary system. In addition, a struggle for control of the Pennsylvania anthracite region ended in the failure of several rail and coal companies to form an effective combination. This led to a decline in their shares which spread throughout the list. The seriousness of the decline can be seen in the prices of those coal companies listed on the Exchange (see Table 7.3).

Table 7.3—Selected Coal Stock Prices, 1876–1877[6]

	1876 High	1877 Low
Delaware, Lackawanna, & Western	120⅜	30⅞
Delaware & Hudson	125	25½
New Jersey Central	109⅞	6

Despite the dark aspect of the bear period and the general despair of 1877, there were some signs of strength in both the economy and the market. One was the changing nature of the balance of trade. Prior to 1874, the United States imported substantially more than it exported, and the difference in payments was made up by foreign investments in American securities, gold shipments, and loans. The decline in American commodity prices in and after 1873 changed this. By 1874, foreigners were once more importing heavily from America, while the United States could no longer afford to purchase many European goods. This favorable balance was not a temporary phenomenon, for since then, with few exceptions, the nation has had an export balance.

Foreigners took a vacation from investment in American securities, with good reason: between 1873 and 1879 their holdings dropped approximately $600 million in value. By the end of the depression it was estimated that foreigners had lost $251 million on rail bonds alone.[7] *The Bankers' Magazine* complained that "this despoiling of European investors has been going on for more than a generation." A German banker stated that American railroad bonds could not be marketed "even if signed by an angel." An English publication remarked that "the consequences of rate wars on American railways are proving so disastrous to the holders of securities, and the prospects are so gloomy, that some heroic remedy must be resorted to, else the whole investment be lost."[8]

No remedy was forthcoming, and English investors began selling their American securities at heavy losses, importing their shrunken capital back to Europe. This served to further depress prices, and encouraged American exports still more, while discouraging imports.

Since the securities were sold to Americans at greatly reduced prices, the liquidations benefited the buyers. In effect, Europe had paid for railroads in the United States without having reaped their profits. For example, a group of English investors might have bought shares and bonds of a new railroad constructed in the postwar period. When completed, the United States had the road, and foreigners owned its securities. The stocks and bonds were then sold during 1873–1879 at a small fraction of their cost. Thus, when recovery came in the early 1880s, Americans had both the road and its securities. Without design, Americans were buying low and selling high, while the English were doing just the opposite. These periodic liquidations have always aided the United States, for when the new bull markets began, the Europeans would come back, investing more millions in foreign securities. Some Americans sensed this tendency, and went so far as to formulate rules as to how liquidations should be carried out.

The proper course for a merchant to pursue when he fails, is to go deliberately to work. When he finds he is to fail and cannot help it, if he owes a half a million dollars, he should immediately buy to the extent of a million—then turn it into cash, say $800,000. Then report that his failure is an immensely bad one, and that the unfortunate merchant will never pay two cents on the dollar. In this way he will be able to purchase all his debts for ten cents on the dollar or $100,000. This leaves him clear in bank or United States stock $700,000. All will join in saying: "What an honest man!" Let him give up every dollar and not have enough to buy a morsel of victuals, and every one will say: "What a damned scoundrel!"[9]

So it went during the depression. It might be said that the development of American commerce and industry was made possible by natural resources, the unwise investments of Europeans, and the dumb good luck of domestic investors. The period in question was perhaps the most striking example of this. Indeed, so much did Americans benefit from European liquidations that when the depression ended, many New York banking houses were in better shape than their London, Paris, and Hamburg counterparts, and Wall Street made it possible for the United States to begin its career as a capital-exporting nation. In 1879, for the first time, Wall Street began marketing foreign bonds in sizable amounts. An issue of $3 million in Province of Quebec bonds was floated successfully that year, and others followed.[10] Thus, the depression saw the end of the United States as a primarily capital-importing nation and the small beginnings of its capital-exporting phase. In the years that followed European funds would again pour into America, at times in greater volume than before, but they would never occupy the vital position they had before 1873.

Although the underwriting passed almost unnoticed, it was a harbinger of better times. During the spring of 1879 it appeared that the depression would be endless, and gloom settled like a shroud on Wall Street. Meanwhile, snow was falling in France, and England suffered through a frost of major proportions. People were gathered around their fireplaces in Paris and were wearing overcoats in London during July. In both countries crops were destroyed by cold and floods, and the meager harvests took on the importance of national disasters. On July 6 the Archbishop of Canterbury led England in prayers for fair weather, but this was to no avail; practically every crop in the British Isles was ruined. A similar story could be told of France, Germany, Austria, and Russia. Europe had to import grain or starve.

Meanwhile, American wheat production in 1879 exceeded the previous harvest by 29 million bushels; the oversupply led the wheat price to break downward and threatened the solvency of many farmers. Then came news of the European difficulties, followed by large overseas orders. The wheat price rose even more sharply than it had fallen, reaching new highs in August. In 1878 shipments of grain to Europe had averaged 2 million bushels weekly; by September, 1879, the United States was exporting a million bushels a day. The prosperity, the greatest the farmers had known in more than a generation, spilled over into other sectors of the economy, ending the depression and ushering in a boom period.[11]

The monetary situation also took a turn for the better. The seventies saw a bitter struggle between farmers, debtors, and many congressional Democrats who were inflationist, against those who favored the "sound dollar," including creditors, solvent businessmen, and the Republican party in Congress and the White House. In *Knox vs. Lee,* the Supreme Court had decided that greenbacks were legal tender, a gain for the paper money faction. The inflationists viewed the 1873 panic as an opportunity to make further gains, and in April of that year adopted a bill to authorize greenback expansion from $382 million to $400 million. To their chagrin, Grant vetoed the measure in 1874, and his congressional supporters were able to pass the Resumption Act the following year. Under its terms, greenbacks would be limited to $300 million, which meant that $82 million would be withdrawn from circulation. In addition, fractional paper money would be replaced by coins. Finally, and most important, on and after January 1, 1879, greenbacks would be fully convertible to gold.

The inflationists believed that this measure would result in the virtual disappearance of all greenbacks and a drastic reduction of the amount of currency in circulation. They counterattacked, demanding the repeal of the Resumption Act, and the isssuance of more paper money. In addition, they attacked the earlier demonetization of silver, demanding silver coinage as a further measure to inflate the currency. The debtors were able to gain some limited victories. In 1878 the compromise Bland-Allison Act was passed, which provided for monthly purchases and the subsequent coinage of from $2 million to $4 million in silver, and the greenback limit was raised through other legislation from $300 million to $347 million. But all attempts to repeal the Resumption Act failed.

As January 1, 1879 approached, the price of greenbacks—which were to become fully convertible after that date—rose in relation to gold. On December 7, 1878, for the first time in a generation, the price of gold dropped to par in terms of paper.[12] It was feared that the Treasury would be rushed on January 1 by greenback holders who wanted to turn their paper into specie. However, the full convertibility of the two currencies and the actions at the gold exchanges showed that the flood of paper into the Treasury would not take place. As it turned out only $135,000 in paper was redeemed for coin on that day, and $400,000 in gold was exchanged for notes.[13] This was a dramatic display of the soundness of the dollar. Wall Street greeted resumption with cheers, and optimism began to return to the district. Still, a leading financial weekly complained: "Wheat is no higher. Corn is no higher. There is no money in any of the earth's products. Where is the promised prosperity?" By June the London *Statist* could claim that "the effect of resumption has passed off, and we may expect to find gold steadily drifting from that side to this."[14] Then came the crop failures, and the American agricultural boom, backed by a hard dollar, led the nation out of the depression.

The advance agents of the new bull market were investment bankers, whose function it was to sell large issues of stocks or bonds to the public. Investment bankers were not new figures on the American scene; they dated back to the early period when firms like Prime, Ward & Sands would underwrite small issues, market government bonds, and act as private bankers for corporations. But before the war this side of their business was unimportant compared to factoring, brokerage, and lotteries.

Jay Cooke & Co. was a transitional organization in that it was the greatest of the old-style houses and the first of the new. Cooke was primarily interested in underwriting, as seen by his sales of government bonds during the Civil War, but after the war he gained control of the Northern Pacific, and for the first time a banking and brokerage house controlled a large-scale business enterprise. One writer stated: "the shift of power from the industrial to the finance capitalist came when the expansion of industry reached a size beyond the resources of individual entrepreneurs or banks, and when the movement for consolidation reached a stage where the services of a central investment house became necessary to handle the finance involved."[15] This period came immediately after the Civil War, when railroads requiring large amounts of money found it convenient to place a good deal of power in the hands of their bankers. During the depression, when almost all railroads were in trouble, in the process of liquidation, or undergoing reorganization, the investment bankers gained more power. The age of the industrial baron was just beginning, and Rockefeller, Carnegie, Harriman, Swift, and others occupied the center of the economic stage. As time passed, however, even they found it difficult to function without the aid of investment bankers, and throughout the rest of the century, power flowed from the hands of industrialists to those of financiers. To put it another way, it might be said that the builders, innovators, and organizers were giving way to individuals whose major functions were those of reorganization, consolidation of previously constructed enterprises, and financing. This transformation could be seen in the changing functions of Wall Street in this period.

In 1879 the House of Morgan was essentially an old-style financial institution, placing American securities in Europe, gathering together the scattered capital of innumerable investors by selling stocks and bonds, and participating in government financing. By 1889 the House of Morgan still did all these things, but in addition it participated directly in corporate affairs, combining, consolidating, centralizing, imposing the mastery of finance over industry by the institutionalized control of investment resources and of corporate industry itself.[16]

Typically, J. P. Morgan's first major venture in corporate investment banking came in 1879, when he was approached by William Vanderbilt, the Commodore's son, and asked to save control of the New York Central for the family by marketing stock overseas. The sale had to be conducted in such a way as to keep the New York price from falling. The underwriting was a success; Morgan sold 350,000 shares in Great Britain without causing the price to fall a single point. His reward for this feat was representation on New York Central's Board of Directors. From then on he was the road's banker; in short order it was apparent that Morgan controlled all of the Vanderbilt interests in this fashion.[17]

Morgan was forty-two years old at the time of the Central flotation. As head of Drexel, Morgan & Co., he was even then one of the most powerful men on the Street. Morgan was no parvenu; his father, Junius Spencer Morgan, was one of the great international bankers of the pre-Civil War era. John Pierpont, his maternal grandfather, was a Jacksonian reformer who enlisted in the Union Army at the age of seventy-six. The grandson did not take after this side of the family; he remained on Wall Street during the war, his major contribution to the Union being the sale of old faulty Hall carbines to the Army at an inflated price. When the rifles exploded in soldiers' faces, killing and maiming a few of them, Morgan apologized—but he didn't return the purchase price.

J. Pierpont Morgan & Co. became Dabney, Morgan & Co. in 1863, through a merger. Dabney, who had been Morgan's supervisor when both worked at Duncan, Sherman & Co. in 1857, probably was more interested in establishing contact with J. S. Morgan & Co., the London brokerage which had succeeded Peabody & Co. after 1864, than in working with his former clerk. The Dabney-Morgan partnership lasted seven years, during which time it was a great success, showing a profit of $1 million and scars from battles with Gould and Fisk. Shortly after its dissolution Morgan joined with Francis A. and Anthony J. Drexel of Philadelphia to form Drexel, Morgan & Co. *The Commercial and Financial Chronicle* observed that "the combination of these two conspicuous banking firms with the branch houses and connections named must place the new firm among the few leading banking houses of the world."[18] Connections were made with Drexel & Co., the leading Philadelphia brokerage, and Drexel, Harjes & Co. of Paris. In addition, J. S. Morgan & Co. of London was closely tied to the new house.

Drexel, Morgan & Co. was a powerful, well-financed and excellently connected organization, and posed a serious challenge to Jay Cooke's leadership of American finance. Its first clash with Cooke came when both firms bid for a federal bond issue in 1871, and Cooke triumphed. But in 1873, Drexel, Morgan, in combination with the Barings, was able to gain a half share of an important government underwriting while Cooke and the Rothschilds won the other half. Six years later Morgan received a good deal of the Rothschilds' American business. During the depression, the firm became recognized as the financial leader of the district, and Morgan, not the Drexels, was its driving force.[19] Within a decade the tall, solidly built Morgan, whose fierce expression and large red nose cowed many a banker and politician, was to become the most powerful man in the nation.

Although never as influential as Drexel, Morgan & Co., the second most important underwriting establishment was Kuhn, Loeb & Co. The partnership was originally a mercantile business, owned and run by two German-Jewish merchants, Abraham Kuhn and Solomon Loeb. The firm ventured into private banking and underwriting, but met with little success; the inherent anti-Semitism of the Street was hard to overcome. Things took a turn for the better when Jacob Schiff joined the organization in 1875 after marrying Teresa Loeb, Solomon's oldest daughter. Schiff was a warm person, less impressive but every bit as crafty as Morgan. Before joining Kuhn, Loeb, he had organized and led the small but respected house of Budge, Schiff & Co. Most of this firm's business came from Germany, and by the time it was merged with Kuhn, Loeb, it had become a major medium through which central European funds were invested in American securities. With this background, Schiff was able to transform his father-in-law's concern into a powerful Wall Street house. The senior partners were talked into expanding operations, and by the end of the decade they had a large and select clientele among those railroads which were dodging Morgan's attempts to merge them into larger systems. In addition, Kuhn, Loeb & Co. entered the field of industrial underwriting before Morgan, and had financial control of several manufacturing concerns and steel companies by the mid-eighties.

The Kuhn, Loeb dynasty has been called the American Rothschilds because of its power and great amount of intermarriage. Otto Kahn, Schiff's eventual successor, entered the firm by marrying Addie Wolf, the daughter of an early partner; Paul M. Warburg, a German-Jewish broker, married Nina J. Loeb. His brother, Felix M., made the Atlantic crossing, and he married Frieda Schiff. In addition, marriage tied the family to Thomas Fortune Ryan, the colorful tycoon and enemy of J. P. Morgan, and George F. Baker, president of the First National Bank and Morgan's right-hand man.[20]

By the early 1880s, there were approximately two dozen underwriting concerns on Wall Street. Their origins were diverse. Some, like Drexel, Morgan and Kuhn, Loeb, began as mercantile establishments. J. & W. Seligman, which had offices in New York, San Francisco, New Orleans, London, Paris, and Frankfort, each presided over by one of the eight Seligman brothers, originated as a commercial house. James Stillman, who, as head of the National City Bank, was involved in many important investment decisions, began his business career as a cotton merchandiser. Levi Morton, who later became Vice-President in the Harrison Administration, was also an investment banker. Kidder, Peabody & Co., a leading house which was the first to underwrite issues of American Telephone & Telegraph, had mercantile origins, as did many other investment concerns.[21]

Other underwriters began as private banks and factoring companies, and only later went into the sale of securities. Lehman Brothers began as "cotton bankers" before the Civil War, and afterwards became a leading investment house. Marcus Goldman and Samuel Sachs formed a partnership in 1882. Sachs had banking connections while Goldman was in the commercial paper business. The new firm continued in paper, and only later did Goldman, Sachs & Co. turn to underwriting. During the 1880s the firm specialized in buying short term notes from small local businesses, thus building up capital and experience which would be used during the twentieth century.[22]

Another group was made up of brokerages which turned to investment banking after the Civil War. In this category were Fahnestock & Co., Charles D. Barney & Co., Fisk & Hatch, and Marquand & Dimock.[23] Some went into investment banking as a logical extension of their brokerage businesses. Others abandoned brokerage or considered it secondary to the more dangerous business of buying and selling large blocks of securities. Together with former banking and mercantile establishments, they formed an aggressive group which viewed its major functions to be the rationalization of the economy, the control of individual enterprises and, for some, the bilking of the public through the flotations of inflated securities. An example of the last was Henry S. Ives & Co., who would take control of a railroad only to loot its treasury. Some of the illegally obtained funds would be transferred to Ives' own account, while the rest would be used to enable him to take control of another, larger road. Ives carried off several of these actions, but he fell in his attempt to raid the Baltimore & Ohio.[24] Firms, like Drexel, Morgan and Kuhn, Loeb, although often unscrupulous, were honest and sincerely believed that they were serving the nation and the public as well as themselves.

The large investment concerns employed small armies of clerks, runners, recorders, bookkeepers, and salesmen, a marked contrast to the days when brokerages operated with a half-dozen clerks and the partners. By 1870, the employment in financial institutions stood at 0.3 per cent of the nation's total work force, and it was increasing rapidly due to the expansion of the financial district's activities.[25] Despite the doldrums of the mid-seventies the working population of the Street expanded, a change from previous depressions.

The would-be investment banker was advised to start as a runner and work his way up—advised by banking leaders and brokers who more often than not had been born to their positions. The semi-official philosophy of American business was social Darwinism, as it still is today, to a great degree. A combination of old style Calvinism and the new biology of Charles Darwin and his followers, social Darwinism held that in the struggle for existence on all levels, the fittest would survive. A corollary to this was the belief that education, background, and connections were unimportant in comparison to inner strength. This aspect of social Darwinism also fit in with the tenets of democracy as viewed by many post-Civil War intellectuals. The notion that the United States was a land of opportunity, where even a rail-splitter could become President, was part of the national creed. This sentiment was evinced by the great popularity that Horatio Alger books had in this period and after. Everything seemed to combine to lead bankers and brokers to prefer bright, eager young men, fresh off the farms, to trained intellectuals who came to Wall Street from the colleges. As one writer put it, "from the business point of view the indictment against the American college was that it delayed the start in business life, taught what was useless, and gave students bad habits and bad attitudes, the worse of which was a desire to live by wit rather than work and a disbelief in the dignity of labor."[26] This anti-intellectual bias was not to fade until after World War I, and even today it can be found in parts of the district.[27] This, despite the assertion by several businessmen that they were "all in favor of education and mental culture; should anyone doubt this in this age?"[28]

Although by no means typical, the career of E. H. Harriman, the rail tycoon who proved the equal of the great Morgan, offers an example of the myth. Harriman was a poor, scrawny boy who was raised in Hempstead, Long Island. At the age of fourteen he took a job as a five-dollar-a-week runner in the offices of broker D. C. Hayes. After a while he was promoted to the rank of pad-shover, and began to learn the ins and outs of Wall Street. Harriman was smart enough to see Black Friday coming, and he sold short, clearing a small fortune. He used this money to buy a seat on the Exchange and finance his early career as a Wall Street plunger. At this time, in 1871, Harriman was only twenty-one years old. He helped one brother to get a job in the offices of Lawrence Jerome, and another to begin in real estate. Harriman always preferred boys without education in his offices, and seldom trusted anyone with college training.[29] One businessman expressed relief when his son failed his college entrance examinations. "Whenever I find a rich man dying and leaving a large amount of money to found a college," he said, "I say to myself, 'It is a pity he had not died while he was poor.' "[30] In actuality, the poor boy usually could hope for a dispatcher's job if he did his work well; the theory was rags to riches, but the practice was riches to greater riches.[31]

The bright young men from poor families apparently never bothered to check the backgrounds of corporate directors. They believed in this dream, and made Wall Street their Mecca. A flood of talent came to the district during the 1870s and 1880s, the most able group it was to have. Like electronics and other glamour industries of today, finance provided a fascination for that generation which attracted to the banks and brokerages many ambitious young men, who otherwise might have sought different positions. In part, this explains why politics was so barren of good men from the end of the Civil War to the turn of the century.

During the 1880s the Wall Streeter—which meant the successful banker, broker, or speculator—was lionized by polite society. At long last, the spiritual descendants of the Fuggers were accepted by the aristocracy. One contemporary wrote:

The leaders of New York were, a few years ago, porters, stable-boys, coal heavers, pickers of rags, scrubbers of floors, and laundry women. Coarse, rude, uncivil, and immoral many of them are still. Lovers of pleasure and men of fashion, bow and cringe to such, and approach hat in hand. One of our new-fledged millionaires gave a ball in his stable. The invited came with tokens of delight. The host a few years ago, was a ticket taker at one of our ferries, and would have thankfully blacked the boots or done any menial service for the people who clamor for the honor of his hand.[32]

This is, of course, poetic exaggeration, but it does show how one of the genteel viewed the influx of the Wall Streeters into his world. This was the period of Ward McAllister, who claimed that Mrs. Astor's ballroom could contain four hundred people, or just the amount which made up "society"—thus, the term "the four hundred." In 1890 a popular magazine remarked that the four hundred had risen to the fifteen hundred because Wall Street had taken control and watered the stock.[33]

The Street was a gay place during the post-depression years. At its heart was the New York Stock Exchange, never again to be seriously challenged by a rival organization. The Mining Exchange, begun in 1875, and other smaller markets still existed, but their position was definitely minor. A new "Open Board of Brokers" appeared in 1879, but when denied the use of Stock Exchange instruments, it declined and in 1881, dissolved.

Then, as now, almost all companies regarded listing at the Exchange as a sign of their having "arrived." The Exchange underwent no major changes in this period, but rather was content to bask in its success. A clearinghouse was proposed and tried, but an experiment in clearances failed in February, 1880, as would a third attempt in 1883. Wall Street settled down to a static period as far as organization and institutions were concerned.[34]

In this period, as usual in prosperous times, the Street had its share of colorful characters. One of the weirdest was Hetty Green, the "Witch of Wall Street," an eccentric, a miser, and a religious fanatic. She was also the richest woman in America, having turned a small fortune inherited from her father into a larger one through speculation and investment. One of her most bitter moments came when Russell Sage died and left a fortune to his wife. The legacy made Mrs. Sage richer than the Witch, but not for long. The wealthy widow placed the bulk of the inheritance in the hands of the Russell Sage Foundation—an act which must have set Russell revolving in his grave, for he was even more miserly than Hetty Green.

A Connecticut grocer turned banker, Sage came to Wall Street shortly after the war. His greatest contribution to the Street was the innovation for which he is rarely given credit: "puts and calls." These are options to sell a certain amount of stock for a specified price within a specified time, and options to buy shares at a set price on or before the date specified in the contract. This device enabled speculators to operate on limited capital. Sage would sell the contracts, operating what amounted to a stock bank. Should a great demand for calls in certain stocks develop, he would raise their price, and then buy more stock on the open market. In the case of puts, he would sell short, thus making money any way the price went.[35]

One of Sage's earliest customers was James R. Keene, the slender, bearded "Silver Fox of Wall Street," who sometimes rented his considerable talents at speculation to more famous figures. One of those was Henry Villard, one of the earliest and most important plungers in western rails. Charles Woerishoffer, who had inherited Drew's title of the "Great Bear of Wall Street," called Villard the most talented speculator of them all. "Villard had probably no superior in that important department of railway management," he stated.[36]

These were the men who dominated the scene during the bull market. Even then, however, none could match Jay Gould for skill, power, and cunning. By the late 1870s Gould had graduated from the gutter he had shared with Fisk and Drew during the Erie period, to become the most influential and respected Wall Streeter of his day. The leading financial historian of the period described Gould's power:

> That Gould had a genius for making combinations is unquestionable; but in almost every instance—the Wabash Railway, the Union Pacific, the Missouri Pacific, and the elevated railways of New York are notable examples—he obtained his power by tempting other men to join in a speculation for personal profit. . . .[37]

In addition to using others, Gould was one of the first to understand the importance of public opinion for financial operations. "The public be damned," attributed to Vanderbilt, pretty well summed up the attitude of many capitalists, Wall Streeters, and bankers during the 1880s. Gould realized that the public voted, bought stock, and influenced their representatives in government. If the public were truly to be damned, he reasoned, it might as well be damned for rather than against him. As a boy he had bought favorable notices in his home-town newspapers, when good publicity served his ends. Now he loaned Whitelaw Reid, publisher of the *New York Tribune,* enough money to remain solvent, and got in return a controlling interest in the paper. Shortly thereafter, he bought majority interest in the *New York World,* a paper which had previously been critical of his operations. Now he had his own voice in the city, and he used the *World* to discredit the managements of companies he wished to take over. When he gained control of a firm, the Gould newspapers would praise him as the stockholders' friend, a man who saved the public from the avarice of the former owners.[38]

Gould's major interest during the bull market was rails, which had begun to move upward once again. Approximately 28,000 miles of new roads were constructed from 1879 to 1882, and thereafter the pace accelerated. Foreigners returned to the American markets, picking up at high prices securities that they had dumped a few years before. By 1883, Europeans held more than $1.5 billion in railroad stocks and bonds alone, and the total foreign holdings exceeded $2 billion. They were more circumspect, however; from 1882 to 1885 they also returned $25 million worth to America, but this was small in comparison to the net holdings. In any case, American corporations no longer needed foreign funds as much as they had in the past, for domestic savings were at a level where they could support a good deal of new construction. At the height of the 1873 boom, for example, the total assets of American financial institutions stood at little more than $3 billion. In 1879, after a long depression, the figure had risen to $3.6 billion, and at the peak of the bull market in 1884 it had gone to $4.7 billion.[39] The rise continued for the next decade, making the American investor a prime target for new issues. Because of this the major impact of the new bull market was felt in New York; London was considered peripheral for most underwriters. The salesmen did their jobs well, and the average annual volume at the Exchange went from 51,244,048 shares in 1875–1879 to 104,388,480 in 1880–1884.[40]

Although trading was heavy, prices at new highs, and optimism in the saddle, the bull market had understones of fear and doubt. The long depression could not be forgotten so quickly and the slightest hint of bad news could cause a sharp dip in stock prices—followed by an equally sharp recovery. It was this raggedness that made Woerishoffer's bear raids possible. Speculators were not convinced that upswings would last for long, and they were quick to take profits, thus causing new declines. For example, the Gould-inspired merger of Western Union, American Union, and Atlantic & Pacific Consolidated in January, 1881, led to a sharp rise along the entire list. But two months later John R. Duff's unsuccessful corner in Hannibal and St. Joseph led to a spring decline. In June the market hit a new high, one which would not be surpassed for twenty years.[41] But President Garfield was shot on July 2, and died on September 19, and the market plunged downward. In 1882, the volume increased, but the prices of stocks declined.[42]

Rumors that Gould was on the verge of bankruptcy caused a sharp flurry in March. Actually, he was never stronger; he held more large systems than any man or combination in the nation. Nevertheless, the market collapsed on the rumors, perhaps remembering what had happened eight years before when Jay Cooke had folded. Gould met the situation head on. He invited several brokers to his office, and then took a "little tin box" from his drawer. Gould opened it, and showed his visitors $23 million worth of Western Union, $12 million of Missouri, Pacific, $6 million of Manhattan Elevated and $10 million in bonds of Metropolitan and New York Elevated and Wabash preferred. He offered to show the brokers an additional $30 million in other securities if they so desired, but they had seen enough, and left, amazed. The market must have learned of this show of power, for it began to rise. Even the price of an Exchange seat went up to a new high, $32,000.[43] But there were signs of weaknesses. In March, 1882, gold exports to Europe picked up; by June $32.5 million had been shipped—the largest amount since 1876.[44]

Throughout this period Presidents Garfield and Arthur were paying off the national debt, thus contracting the amount of notes in circulation. During 1883 more than $105 million of the debt was redeemed. At the same time gold shipments continued to rise, and some Americans began hoarding gold as well. In addition, the silver coined as a result of the Bland-Allison Act began to drive gold from circulation. By 1883, it had superseded gold in the payments of government obligations, a sign that the reserves had reached a dangerously low level. Although the markets held steady, an erosion of confidence had begun.[45] Then came news of poor crops and a slackening of trade. Political uncertainties regarding the 1884 election also damaged confidence on Wall Street. Good corporate and railroad news still appeared almost daily; indeed, during the summer of 1883 record earnings and construction figures were released. The newer speculators continued to buy in expectation of a rise, but the older men began to liquidate their holdings, perhaps remembering that the market is often at its most optimistic just before a crash.

In August, 1883, a rumor circulated that several brokers had manipulated the statements of the Wall Street National Bank. An examination showed that bank officials had overcertified checks to the amount of $200,000. In order to avoid receivership, the institution went into liquidation, and this led to the failures of several medium and large mercantile houses. Although Wall Street did not know it as yet, the panic of 1884 had begun.[46]

Early in 1884 a receiver was appointed for the New York and New England Railroad, and failures of other lines soon followed. At the same time European liquidations of American securities reached a new seven-year high—over $33 million in gold left America during March and April alone, as a result of the sales. In January Henry Villard announced that his scheme to take over the Northern Pacific had run aground. His subsequent bankruptcy caused a sharp decline at the Exchange, and the volume of sales rose as well. Then came the most devastating blow of all: the failure of Grant & Ward.[47]

U. S. Grant had left the White House in 1877 an honored and respected man; despite the corruption of his Administration, he himself had avoided taint. Offers of lucrative business connections poured in. Grant's slow-witted son, Ulysses Jr., who was also known as "Buck," urged his father to go into brokerage as a partner of young Ferdinand Ward, a rising Wall Street figure. Buck had met Ward through his father-in-law, who also supported the scheme. The President agreed to meet Ward, and was impressed with him after being flattered with attention. The partnership of Grant & Ward was formed shortly thereafter. For helping in this, Buck received a gift of $100,000 from his father-in-law and a monthly drawing account of $3,000.

Ward proved to be one of the slickest crooks of his day. Using the General's name, he was able to convince several wealthy people to invest in his financial schemes, promising them large dividends and safety. Most of his ventures failed, but Ward made a pretense of success, paying dividends illegally out of capital rather than earnings. This could not last, for in time the entire capital structure was erected on credit. When the banks began to fail in April, Ward realized that he was in serious trouble. Most of his business had been contracted through the Marine National Bank. Its president, James D. Fish, who was in on the schemes, notified Ward that unless the institution received $300,000 from the partnership it would collapse, and with it would go Grant & Ward.

Ward told the former President of his manipulations, simplifying and coloring them for the gullible Grant, who agreed to ask the Wall Street brokers for aid.[48] Ward made the rounds of other banks in an attempt to cover his losses.[49] He placed the funds received by Grant in his private account, as a prelude to leaving the country. Ward was imprisoned before he could leave, however, and Grant might have been prosecuted were it not for his glorious past. Lonely, broken, and suffering from cancer, Grant spent the last days of his life writing his memoirs with the aid of Mark Twain.[50]

The Grant & Ward failure set off a series of collapses on the Street. John Eno, the spectacular young president of the Second National Bank, absconded to Canada with almost $4 million of the depositors' funds. George I. Seney's Metropolitan Bank went under, and with it the Seney fortune. Within a few weeks, New York Central fell 28 points at the Exchange, Western Union went down 26, and Delaware, Lackawanna & Western fell 34. Fisk & Hatch, whose senior partner was the president of the Exchange, went into bankruptcy for the third time in a generation, and many others followed suit.

The panic led Wall Street to once again question Jay Gould's solvency. Despite his impressive showing in 1882, Gould had been in serious trouble, characteristically escaping through the use of guile and bluff. Now the bears descended upon him *en masse,* hoping to wreck him in return for the damages done them in previous years. Henry Smith had never forgotten how his former junior partner had ruined him in 1873; now he predicted that Gould would end his days as an organ-grinder. Keene, who had lost his first fortune to Gould, joined with Smith, as did Woerishoffer and Addison Cammack. Once again, however, Gould proved the master of Wall Street. He transferred his holdings to others and then threatened to go bankrupt, and cause a crash that would dwarf the previous decline. Since his enemies had all taken bull positions, such a move would have wiped them out, but Gould would have emerged from the debris still a multimillionaire. So instead of destroying him, the group was forced to enter into an agreement to buy 50,000 shares of Western Union from Gould for $2.5 million, enough to tide him over until the panic passed.[51]

During the months that followed, prices continued to fall. In December a wave of selling forced many houses to close the week before Christmas; there was no caroling in the streets that year. On January 15, Hetty Green withdrew $25 million in securities and $475,000 in cash from J. J. Cisco & Co., demanding the stocks and money at once and refusing to leave until she got them. Unable to respond to such a heavy call, the firm went into bankruptcy, and a new wave of failures was initiated.[52]

Most of these insolvencies were suffered by brokerages, however, rather than manufacturers and commercial houses. Twenty-eight failures were recorded on Wall Street, as against eight in the pre-panic year of 1883, seven in 1882, and five in 1881. But although business fell off in mid-1884, it began to swing upward early the following year, while the markets were still declining. The exchanges leveled off in 1885, and by the end of the year a new bull market was in the making.

The panic did prove several points, and marked the end of an era on Wall Street. Clearing House certificates, which had been so useful during the 1873 panic, once again enabled weak houses to gain support from stronger ones. Before the panic had ended, $24,915,000 of them had been issued against commercial paper, which at the time was not marketable. The bankers and brokers proved that joint action could buoy up the financial apparatus of Wall Street, and were to use this method of self-help in several important crises in the years that followed. In addition, the panic demonstrated that the economy could weather financial difficulties, an indication of the growing maturity of the American business structure. Finally, it marked the end of Jay Gould's career as a plunger. "In what had almost happened to him . . . he discerned the eventual fate of all speculators, even the smartest. The lesson could be summed up in a two-word resolution: never again."[53] Gould would live for another eight years, but his days of daring ended with the 1884 panic.

At first, no one seemed capable of filling Gould's place. He so dominated Wall Street during the 1870s and early 1880s that he seemed to require several joint successors. This was not to be, for J. P. Morgan had already shown signs of greatness, and soon after the panic he began to take over. In the summer of 1884, Morgan declined re-election to the Board of Northern Pacific, claiming that the Villard clique—which had regain control in 1882—was not acting in accord with his wishes. The stock immediately dropped, and in time the directors invited Morgan to return on his own terms. Shortly thereafter he gained control of the road. Villard was obliged to leave the Board, but he rebounded once more, going on to a career as an electric utilities magnate. Meanwhile, Morgan stepped into a dispute between Vanderbilt's New York Central and the Pennsylvania Railroad, inviting both sides to his yacht and forcing them to accept his mediation. It was agreed that Vanderbilt would stay out of Pennsylvania territory, while the Pennsylvania allowed Morgan to reorganize one of its lines and attach it to the Central. Morgan emerged from the meetings with enhanced status.[54]

In the midst of the panic, Cyrus Field, who had collaborated with Sage and Gould in several deals, sent a cable to Junius Morgan, urging that he take action.

Many of our businessmen seem to have lost their heads. What we want is some coolheaded strong man to lead. If you should form a syndicate in London to buy through Drexel, Morgan & Co. good securities in this market, I believe you would make a great deal of money and at the same time entirely change the feeling here.[55]

J. S. Morgan entered the market and helped restore confidence, but the key man in this operation was his son, John Pierpont.

The election campaign of 1884 was conducted during the panic. The G.O.P. nominated James G. Blaine, whose dishonesty was suspected by most and known to many, and the Democrats put up Grover Cleveland, then Governor of New York. Although dull and unimaginative, Cleveland was honest, a refreshing change from most post-bellum political figures. For the first time since the Civil War, Wall Street backed a Democrat. According to his son-in-law, Morgan cast his ballot for the Governor, admiring his "rugged honesty, directness of thought, and frankness of speech."[56] Although the two men had never met, their paths were soon to cross, and nine years later they would collaborate to save the nation from financial collapse, causing Cleveland political embarrassment and making Morgan the most powerful American of his time.

In 1885, shortly after William Vanderbilt died, Drexel, Morgan & Co. was called in for consultation by the Vanderbilt heirs. Financial circles felt that his death would cause a widespread panic on the Exchange, which had still not recovered from the bad days of 1884. Representatives of Drexel, Morgan met with Russell Sage and Cyrus Field, with Gould joining the group later. It was agreed that they would form a syndicate to buy 250,000 shares of railroad stock the following day should such a course of action become necessary to support the market. As it turned out, the fears were groundless; the market held fast with a few spotty declines and some advances. But it did mark the first time a group undertook to support the entire market rather than single issues, a clear demonstration of the growing power of the men involved. Symbolically, on this occasion Gould, the old master, followed the leadership of young Morgan.[57] In such ways did the baton of leadership pass hands.

Notes

1. Eames, *New York Stock Exchange*, p. 85.
2. *Ibid.*, p. 96.
3. *Ibid.*, p. 95.
4. John Hinkling & Co., *Men and Idioms of Wall Street* (New York, 1875), p. 53. Seventy per cent of nongovernment issues were rails, approximately the same percentage as was traded at the London Stock Exchange. Edwards, *Evolution of Finance Capitalism*, p. 34.
5. Pratt, *Work of Wall Street*, p. 254.
6. Eames, *New York Stock Exchange*, p. 61.
7. Edwards, *Evolution of Finance Capitalism*, p. 173.
8. *Ibid.*, pp. 173–74; Corey, *House of Morgan*, pp. 145–46.
9. *Ibid.*, p. 26.
10. Edwards, *Evolution of Finance Capitalism*, p. 182.
11. Alexander Noyes, *Forty Years of American Finance* (New York, 1898), pp. 54–57.
12. Lanier, *A Century of Banking in New York*, p. 239.
13. Bining, *Rise of American Economic Life*, p. 446; Noyes, *Forty Years of American Finance*, pp. 39–47.
14. *Ibid.*, pp. 51–53.
15. Harold U. Faulkner, *The Decline of Laissez Faire, 1897–1917* (New York, 1951), p. 37.
16. Corey, *House of Morgan*, p. 132.
17. Faulkner, *Decline of Laissez Faire*, pp. 37–38.
18. Corey, *House of Morgan*, pp. 56, 74–76, 116–17; Larson, *Jay Cooke*, p. 313.
19. United States, *Corrected Opinion of Harold R. Medina, dated February 4, 1954, in The United States of America vs. H. S. Morgan et al.* (Washington, 1955), pp. 58–59 (hereafter referred to as *Medina*).
20. *Ibid.*, pp. 64–65; B. C. Forbes, *Men Who Are Making America* (New York, 1916), pp. 218–20, 331; Ferdinand Lundburg, *America's 60 Families* (New York, 1937), pp. 12–13; Larson, *Jay Cooke*, p. 218.
21. Smith, *Sunshine and Shadow in New York*, pp. 269–70; Corey, *House of Morgan*, p. 43; *Medina*, p. 76.
22. *Medina*, pp. 17–18, 71–72, 79–80.
23. *Ibid.*, pp. 18, 65–66; Dimock, *Wall Street and the Wilds*, p. 74; Smith, *Sunshine and Shadow in New York*, p. 270.
24. Stedman, *New York Stock Exchange*, pp. 331–33.
25. Sidney M. Robbins and Nestor E. Terleckyj, *Money Metropolis: A Locational Study of Financial Activities in the New York Region* (Cambridge, 1960), pp. 3–4.
26. Kirkland, *Dream and Thought in the Business Community*, p. 87.
27. Paradoxically, bankers thought that gifts to universities and membership on their boards of trustees were not only correct practices, but admirable ones. So it is that today's Wall Streeter should be a graduate of one of the "right" colleges, but should not show too great an interest in matters intellectual.
28. *Ibid.*, p. 62.
29. H. W. Eckenrode and Pocahontas W. Edmunds, *E. H. Harriman: The Little Giant of Wall Street* (New York, 1932), pp. 11–15, 63.

30. Kirkland, *Dream and Thought in the Business Community*, p. 101.

31. B. C. Forbes, *Men Who Are Making America* (New York, 1916), pp. 174–240. This book, a compilation of interviews with business leaders, shows that almost all thought formal education was a waste of time.

32. Smith, *Sunshine and Shadow in New York*, pp. 35–36.

33. Holbrook, *Age of the Moguls*, p. 328.

34. Alexander Noyes, *The Market Place* (Boston, 1938), pp. 52–53.

35. Robert Warshow, *The Story of Wall Street* (New York, 1929), pp. 196–97.

36. Collins, *Money Town*, p. 263.

37. Noyes, *Forty Years of American Finance*, pp. 63–64.

38. O'Connor, *Gould's Millions*, pp. 158–60.

39. Myers, *New York Money Market*, pp. 290–91; Edwards, *Evolution of Finance Capitalism*, p. 184.

40. H. Parker Williams and Jules I. Bogen, *Investment Banking* (New York, 1936), p. 228.

41. Clews, *Fifty Years in Wall Street*, p. 517; Pratt, *Work of Wall Street*, pp. 378–79.

42. Eames, *New York Stock Exchange*, p. 95.

43. Clews, *Fifty Years in Wall Street*, p. 518; Eames, *New York Stock Exchange*, p. 85.

44. Noyes, *Forty Years of American Finance*, p. 85.

45. *Ibid.*, p. 95.

46. Lightner, *History of Business Depressions*, p. 175.

47. Warshow, *Story of Wall Street*, p. 205.

48. Noyes, *The Market Place*, p. 45.

49. Warshow, *Story of Wall Street*, p. 211.

50. *Ibid.*, pp. 205–12; Noyes, *The Market Place*, p. 46; Dies, *Behind the Wall Street Curtain*, p. 41.

51. O'Connor, *Gould's Millions*, pp. 233–35.

52. Warshow, *Story of Wall Street*, p. 214.

53. O'Connor, *Gould's Millions*, p. 235; Noyes, *Forty Years of American Finance*, p. 100.

54. Herbert L. Satterlee, *J. Pierpont Morgan: An Intimate Portrait* (New York, 1939), pp. 225–28.

55. Corey, *House of Morgan*, p. 131.

56. Satterlee, *J. P. Morgan*, p. 218.

57. O'Connor, *Gould's Millions*, p. 243.

8

All Roads Lead to Wall Street: 1884-1896

> Pierpont Morgan calls in wan iv his office boys, th prisi-
> dint iv a naytional bank, an' says he, "James," he says,
> "take some change out iv th damper an' run out an' buy
> Europe f'r me," he says. "I intend to re-organize it an'
> put it on a payin' basis."
>
> Mr. Dooley (Finley Peter Dunne)

GROVER CLEVELAND narrowly defeated James Blaine in 1884, and for the first time since the Civil War, a Democrat occupied the White House. Cleveland had a reputation of honesty, ability, and courage which seemed to foreshadow great changes in Washington. But this was only an illusion, for he was content to keep the old system, only making sure that it ran more efficiently than it had before.

Abram Hewitt, the Democratic Chairman of the House Ways and Means Committee, was considered by his contemporaries to be a sound and sober man. Nevertheless, a month before the inauguration he wrote the President-elect in great distress:

I am satisfied that we are in the presence of a great peril. When in New York yesterday I ascertained that the receipts of the Custom House are now mainly in silver certificates. The stock of gold in the Treasury is being exhausted, and cannot be replenished, except through practical purchases, which will soon put gold at a premium—already the banks and trust companies are hoarding gold, or investing in sterling exchange. The Secretary of the Treasury is striving to maintain gold payments until the 4th of March, so that the inevitable suspension shall take place under a Democratic Administration. He has had a conference with the Republican presidents of the United States banks who are being appealed to and have agreed to take silver certificates at the New York Clearing House, so far as may be necessary to keep up the balance of gold at the Treasury to the point to avoid suspension.[1]

As Hewitt indicated, the currency question was the greatest problem facing the nation at the time, and it would remain the prime political and economic issue for the next eleven years. At first centered around greenbacks, by 1885 the controversy had been distilled into agitation for and against unlimited coinage of silver. The silverites, who included every inflationist element in the nation, argued that rising prices would bring prosperity, and that the volume of money in circulation—which had actually decreased during the past decade due to payments on the national debt—was inadequate to an expanding economy. When told that no other major power coined silver, which was unacceptable in international settlements, the silverites responded that it was time the Europeans began following us.

Those who followed the gold banner included businessmen, creditors, those with significant European connections, and almost all the investment bankers and Wall Street leaders. They believed that inflation was little more than legal robbery of savings; those who worked hard for their money had a right to see its purchasing power remain constant. In addition, silver would soon drive gold out of circulation, and when that happened, foreign trade and investment would cease, and the nation would suffer the greatest economic decline in its history. Traders and speculators might favor silver coinage, as did some bulls, thinking that inflation would lead to an expanded market and an upswing, but power was in the hands of the bankers, and they called the tune. Led by Morgan, they trusted Cleveland to back the "sound dollar," but they feared the inflationists—the legislators who had pushed through the Bland-Allison Act and who were said to represent "at least three-fourths of the Democratic Party."[2] The bankers asked whether Cleveland would be willing to do battle with such a broad and powerful group; the answer was not long in coming. Cleveland told the new Congress that when he took office on March 4, he would not only oppose further expansion of the Bland-Allison Act but would favor the suspension of all silver purchases. The message was so strong that it frightened some of his banker friends, who thought that Cleveland was too blunt and direct in their support.

During the next four years business was better represented in the White House than at any time since the Civil War. This was not so because Cleveland was pro-business, but, rather because he had a laissez-faire policy. Business no longer needed the great benefits given it by previous administrations; it wanted neutral government that would view all interference in the economy as wrong, unnatural, and futile, if not wicked. Cleveland, the leader of the conservative Bourbon Democracy, was the embodiment of these ideals. The President "narrowed his role to that of a bold protector of the *status-quo*,"[3] and "turned his back on distress more acute than any other president would have had the *sang-froid* to ignore."[4]

Had the economy and society been static, perhaps such a point of view could have been successful. But the period from the end of the 1884 panic to the election of 1896 saw greater social and economic concentrations develop than at any other time in the nation's history. Tensions built up in a pressure-cooker atmosphere, and when freed, they erupted with violence.

The laissez-faire presidents of the time considered economic and social discontent to be outside the purview of government. Thus, the relative decline of the farmers, the problems of workers in an industrial society, the growth of big business, and the whole complex of difficulties involved in the transformation from an agrarian-commercial to an industrial society were ignored or glossed over by both major parties. The United States was far less class and status conscious than European nations in the late nineteenth century; America had not known feudalism and its very foundation was the Enlightenment belief in the equality of man. But the pressures of the period were such that special interest alignments gained power and clashed as never before in the country's history. The farmers had their granges, agricultural wheels, and in 1891, the People's, or "Populist" Party. Workers organized in local unions, the Knights of Labor, and the American Federation of Labor, in part a response to the organization of business into more powerful groups.

The combinations entered into by businessmen took many forms. Some, like the pools, were agreements to share profits and risks, on the theory that such practices would discourage competition and rate-cutting and maximize profits. The Kentucky Distilleries' Association regulated output; the Gunpowder Manufacturers' Association set prices. Albert H. Veeder, a lawyer for Swift & Co., organized a highly successful pool of meat packers which effectively set the rules, established rate structures, and divided territories for the industry. Such organizations depended upon the integrity of the participants for their success—as a result, they were generally unsatisfactory. The president of the Whiskey pool said that he was "well convinced there is cutting going on secretly now, and unless provision is made at once to arrest it, it will be done openly, until there is nothing left of the market." In addition, the Interstate Commerce Act of 1887 declared railroad pools illegal, causing a decline in the instrument.[5]

By then pools had been largely replaced by trusts, led by John D. Rockefeller and the giant Standard Oil complex. In a trust, the individual corporations deposited controlling portions of their stock with a set of trustees, receiving trust certificates in return. The trust would then act as a separate entity, usually with control over an industry. Rockefeller's Standard Oil Company was formed in 1879, and in the next few years was followed by the Distillers' and Cattle Feeders' Trust, the Sugar Refineries Company, the Windowglass Trust, and others. There were eventually combinations in rubber, coal, threshing machines, iron nuts and bolts, stoves, and lead. Even the school slate manufacturers formed a trust. After 1890 other forms of organization appeared, but the trust, though circumscribed by law, dominated large-scale enterprise for the rest of the century.[6]

The trust operated within the corporate form and was usually made up of operating companies. In the period after the 1884 panic the corporation came into its own, as America entered a new phase of the industrial revolution. By 1900, 21 per cent of the labor force was engaged in manufacturing, and only one worker in three could be classified as a farmer.[7] Till then the business scene had been dominated by the railroads and agricultural processing businesses, which were closely dependent upon each other for prosperity. Now heavy industry began to develop rapidly. The percentage of the national income invested in capital formation during the period from 1899 to 1908, when the manufacturing industries were in their heyday, stood at 12.6; even during the halcyon years of the 1920s, this figure was only 10.2.[8] From 1887 to 1897, eighty-six industrial corporations capitalized at more than one million dollars each were formed, including Diamond Match, Electric Storage Battery, General Electric, United States Rubber, and Westinghouse Air Brake. Approximately one-third of these new combinations could be classified as trusts.[9] Most of them were financed and organized on Wall Street; some appeared on the Stock Exchange, while others were traded over the counter. They did not replace rails as investment favorites until after the turn of the century, but their growth was by far the more rapid.[10]

Pools needed management, and often found it among their lawyers and executives; the same was true for trusts. Oftentimes the combines lacked the managerial genius needed for vast operations, however, and it was a rare trust indeed in which the participants trusted one another. So it was that investment bankers were often named to the directorships of these organizations.

The leader in railroad, and later industrial organization, was Drexel, Morgan, which in 1895 became J. P. Morgan & Co. At one time the head of the house controlled 341 directorships in 112 corporations. Morgan always made sure that a corporation would be solvent; he would then refinance the debts at lower rates, maintain dividends to insure investor confidence, replace loose cooperation with controlled coordination, and take charge of the boards of directors. In addition, he refused to deal with anyone whose character he suspected. The benefits for those who would submit to and work with Morgan were great. In January, 1889, he told a group of railroad men who were interested in a "morganization" of their roads that he would undertake the job under certain conditions.

> I am authorized to say, I think, on behalf of the banking houses represented here that if an organization can be formed practically upon the basis submitted by the committee, and with an executive committee able to enforce its provisions, upon which the bankers shall be represented, they are prepared to say that they will not negotiate, and will do everything in their power to prevent the negotiations of, any securities for the construction of parallel lines, or the extension of lines not approved by that executive committee. I wish that distinctly understood.[11]

Morgan's organization was indeed formidable; in Wall Street it was referred to as "Jesus Christ and his Twelve Apostles." Charles H. Coster, the "financial chemist," was then Morgan's right hand man. A master of detail and a genius at organization, Coster was probably responsible for most of the work until his death in 1900, at which time he was a director in fifty-nine corporations. Egisto P. Fabbri became a Morgan partner in 1876 and continued until 1885. An economist and mathematician, he kept Morgan informed as to new technological developments, and among other things, interested the House in the Edison Electric Illuminating Company, formed by Morgan interests. Others of the group were George S. Bowdoin, who was a partner from 1884 to 1900; J. Hood Wright, who cooperated with Fabbri in the Edison transaction; Charles H. Godfrey, a railroad specialist; and Walter Burns, Morgan's voice in London. They were ruthless men, hard working and well rewarded. By 1900 they had either burned themselves out or had retired, having helped make Morgan the most powerful economic force in the nation.[12]

When Morgan took over a group of railroads or industrial firms, he would merge them, conduct extensive refinancing, and float new securities at the New York money market. This was the method used by Kuhn, Loeb, the Seligmans, and other investment houses as well. In 1887 alone approximately $180 million in bonds and $98 million in stock issues were listed on the Exchange after being floated by the bankers, and these figures do not include sales in other cities or those off the Exchange. In that year 84,914,616 shares were traded at the market, with a total value of $4,508,778,899.[13]

The 1887 flotations represented new highs for both stocks and bonds, but the volume and values of that year were both below that of the previous year. Throughout the 1884–1892 period, activity at the Exchange eased off; while the average volume from 1880 to 1884 was 104,388,480 shares, the 1885–1893 figure was 84,943,820.[14] Stagnation of sorts, had set in at the Exchange, as can also be seen in the average prices of sixty active rail issues (Table 8.1) and in the cost of an Exchange seat (Table 8.2).

Table 8.1—Average Prices of Sixty Rail Issues[15]

	High	Low
1884	66.28	38.58
1885	63.47	43.45
1886	71.99	55.28
1887	72.35	59.03
1888	65.09	55.71
1889	66.29	59.55
1890	69.93	53.61
1891	66.78	55.29
1892	68.49	62.32
1893	66.31	41.71

Table 8.2—Cost of an Exchange Seat

	High (dollars)	Low (dollars)
1884	27,000	20,000
1885	34,000	20,000
1886	33,000	23,000
1887	30,000	19,000
1888	24,000	17,000
1889	23,000	19,000
1890	22,500	17,000
1891	24,000	16,000
1892	22,000	17,000

There were several reasons for this stagnation. First, rivalry from other markets as well as a temporary growth in private auctions took some business from the major market. Then too, there were no major bull and bear raids or major corners; the Drew-Gould period had passed, and the giant raids of the Morgan period were yet to come. Finally, there was the nature of morganization, which created giant complexes and offered securities to the public. Although many of these paid good dividends, the public tended to shy away from the trust certificates, knowing the chicanery and stock-watering often indulged in by the managers. During the 1890s and the first decade of the twentieth century, railroad stocks and bonds dominated the list, although few new issues in rails were floated in comparison to the previous two decades. So, with the rails in balance, and the industrials yet to be accepted, the Exchange quieted down to a period of steady but unexpanded trading.[16]

From 1885 to 1889 the economy prospered. Despite a short financial panic in 1886 and a drought in 1887, most economic indices set new records almost every year. National wealth rose from $43.6 billion in 1880 to $65 billion in 1890. In 1880 the total assets of financial institutions stood at $3,817,000,000, while ten years later the figure was $7,096,000,000.[17]

Much financing for new industries came from domestic investors, but foreigners, having recovered from the 1884 panic, also bought heavily. Germans were interested in rails, while the English took mining shares. By 1890 there was approximately $3 billion of foreign capital in American firms, a 50 per cent increase over the pre-panic year of 1883. Since most of these shares went overseas, where they were tightly held or traded on European markets, their sales were not reflected in New York Stock Exchange volume figures.[18]

A financial journal estimated that there were some 1,250,000 shareholders in America in 1893. While this figure may be exaggerated, and some economic historians question whether shareholder growth actually took place in this period, most are of the opinion that ownership did expand toward the end of the nineteenth century.[19] During the colonial era local citizens took shares in canals and turnpikes, and as we have seen, the first railroads relied in part on such purchases. By the 1890s these investors were willing to buy shares in companies farther from home. This was part of the trend which began with Jay Cooke, and would end with people's capitalism.

The buyer of small lots was not welcomed at the Exchange, however. It was felt that the commissions were not worth the broker's trouble. In addition, many Exchange members were loath to sell stock in quantities below a "round lot," or one hundred shares. The refusal to service the "odd lot" buyers was one major reason for the formation of the Consolidated Stock Exchange in 1886, through a merger of four smaller exchanges. It was attended by some 400 former members of the New York Stock Exchange, who broke relations with the older organization over the odd lot and other issues. A charter member of the Consolidated, who lived to see the New York Stock Exchange adopt odd lot instruments, later wrote:

> In raising the standard of what may be described as the retail odd lot trade, as distinguished from the jobbing trade in odd lots in the primary market, we have performed a public service. We have made it legitimate trade and brought it to two markets, where it naturally and logically influences prices. There always must be an outlet for this trade, and for its decent development we are responsible.[20]

The existence of the Consolidated did not disturb the financial district, but it did lead to a significant change in the New York Exchange's methods. The Consolidated had employed clearing-house techniques from its founding, and these worked efficiently, preventing frauds and the reneging of contracts. The older exchange had tried three times without success to initiate such a method of delivering securities. Because the Consolidated was successful with a clearing-house and because such institutions also existed in every major European exchange, several bankers urged the New York to try once more. In April, 1892, a fourth attempt at centralized clearings was made, and by the end of the year, twelve securities were using clearing-house facilities. The system was gradually extended to other shares, until the entire list used centralized clearing methods. Although techniques changed, no broker seriously thought of doing away with the institution thereafter.[21]

By the early 1890s, communication was almost instantaneous at the Exchange; every brokerage had its batteries of telephones and its ticker. The Exchange installed an electric annunciator to page members from the floor, and trading became more orderly and quieter.[22] Raiders still operated on Wall Street, but they found it difficult to run pools and corners since the information facilities made secrecy difficult. In addition, such services as Poor's, Moody's, and Dun's, which published data on corporations and offered analysis of their situations, made outright fraud rare. The Exchange did not require listed companies to file annual reports until 1895, but many of them offered financial information before then. Not until 1900 did the Exchange feel that its position was so secure that it could require earnings statements and balance sheets as a prerequisite for listing.[23] Although the days of full disclosure were still a half-century away, a beginning was made during the 1890s.

The outstanding external development from 1884 to 1893 was the Baring failure of 1890. The large English house had sent a good deal of capital to the Argentine from 1885 to 1890, viewing that region as a new United States and the future investment area of the world. Other English houses followed the Barings, and an Argentine craze developed on Lombard Street, temporarily diverting more English funds from investments in American securities. In 1889 several large mining ventures in South Africa failed, and late in the year the Argentine wheat crop was all but completely lost. A revolution began in that nation, further endangering foreign investments, and a selling wave sent the London markets down sharply. Realizing that a failure at Barings would affect the entire nation, the Bank of England undertook to help the firm, borrowing money from other nations to support the markets.[24] Late in the year the Barings fell, with liabilities of $75 million. The English financial community was thrown into a gloom reminiscent of the dark days of the Napoleonic era.

At first the failure of the Argentine was thought to be good news for Americans, since Europe would have to import more American grain. Since harvests were at record levels in the Midwest, the price of stocks advanced in late 1888 and early 1890. Foreign investments continued to pour into Wall Street for the time being; from February to August of 1890, £100 million of new American securities were marketed in London. The Baring failure, which came in November, ended these sales, and at the same time caused a sharp decrease in English imports from America and other nations.[25] This inevitably caused a slowing of economic activity in the United States.

Despite the apparent good times of early 1890, some Americans realized that the nation was in financial trouble. The gold reserves were dropping, partly as a result of the Bland-Allison purchases of silver. The retirement of the national debt and the increasing surplus at the Treasury, strange as it may seem to the American of today, were serious problems, since they took money out of circulation and thus hindered economic activity. Free silver agitation grew; the monetary problems seemed to augur well for the inflationists. The bankers feared that should gold payments be suspended, the silverites would win free and unlimited coinage, which would wreck America's standing in international financial circles. In January, 1890, Harriman wrote the directors of the Northern Pacific that "It would be unwise at this time to pass any resolution adopting a policy for a large expenditure of money." Railroad baron James J. Hill told an interviewer in May that "We are going to have a panic next September. It will take five years to get over it." The depression would be particularly severe, he said, because the nation was "built up," and the frontier had disappeared. Hill sold his securities, turning everything he had into gold, and put the $50 million in a safe place.[26]

The panic came in late summer. It was short and sharp, but did not cause extreme hardship on Wall Street. Twenty-nine brokerages failed, compared to seven in 1889 and twelve in 1888. This figure was one more than had gone under during the 1884 panic, but was far below the seventy-nine failures of 1873.[27] Clearing house certificates, which had proved so important during the two previous panics, were again issued, this time to the extent of $16,645,000. Security prices declined, but not as far as they had in 1884 or 1873. The Atcheson, Topeka, and Santa Fe, which was widely held by Baring accounts, went from a high of 50⅜ to a low of 23½ during the panic, and other representative issues showed similar declines, as can be seen in Table 8.3.

Table 8.3—Declines in Representative Stocks, 1890[28]

	High	Low
Missouri Pacific	79¼	53
Union Pacific	68⅞	40
Louisville & Nashville	92½	65½
New York Central	111	95¼
Erie	29½	16
Tennessee Coal	89	28
Western Union	87	71¾
Edison General	119	65

The decline began in August, reached its nadir during the first week in November, and was over by the middle of the month. Writing to London banker Ernest Cassel on November 25, Jacob Schiff said:

Things look brighter today, but it seems that the public has already forgotten the lesson of recent weeks. I myself am still pondering so intently the abyss which the financial world faced, and which has fortunately been bridged by the courageous intervention of London's *haute finance,* that I am unable to entertain the idea of another bull movement for the present.[29]

Nevertheless, a bull movement developed in December and carried into 1891. The panic was mild, despite the dire predictions of men like Harriman, Hill, and Schiff. This can best be realized by noting that the high-low range of Dun's rail index was 16.32 points in 1890. The spread of the previous year was only 6.74, but in 1887 it had been 13.32.[30]

The most important result of the panic could be seen in Congress. Already faced with demands from organized business, labor, and agriculture, who asked for legislation favorable to their interests, and pressured by unorganized middle class voters who wanted to curb the powers of each of these groups, Congress was prodded into action and passed three significant pieces of legislation. Business received greater protection through the adoption of new rates in the McKinley Tariff, which raised duties to a new high. In addition, the subsequent decline of imports attendant upon higher duties was expected to lead to a gold inflow as well as stimulate domestic industry.

In order to get their tariff demands, businessmen were obliged to accept the Sherman Anti-Trust Act, which stated: "Every contract, combination in form of trust or otherwise, or conspiracy, in restraint of trade or commerce among the several states or with foreign nations, is hereby declared to be illegal." President Harrison, who defeated Cleveland in the 1888 election, showed no desire to enforce this act and neither did the next two occupants of the White House.

The third piece of legislation, and for the short run the most significant, was the Sherman Silver Purchase Act, which was supported by farmers, miners, and inflationists in general. Under its provisions, the Treasury would buy 4.5 million ounces of silver a month, issuing notes in exchange which would be legal tender, and could be redeemed in gold. The legislation stated that in the future the federal government would "maintain the two metals on parity with each other." The amount of silver to be purchased was practically the entire American production, doubling the intake under the Bland-Allison Act. During the next three years, purchases would average $51,977,000 a year, which meant that that much new money in the form of government notes was injected into the economy annually.[31] From 1880 to 1890 outstanding bank notes had declined from $344 million to $185 million. Now this deflationary influence was ended, and the debtors cheered the increase of currency. In the last half of 1890 some $100 million was added to circulation through silver purchases, gold coinage, and the issuance of new Treasury notes.[32] The effects on gold reserves, however, were equally startling. In 1890, the government had received 95 per cent of its customs receipts in gold. This figure began to drop immediately and, by 1893, had declined to 5 per cent, the rest being paid in silver and greenbacks. This was a sure sign that the public no longer trusted its currency.[33] During the same period foreigners, still shaky after the Baring failure, liquidated some of their American holdings and began to withdraw gold from the United States. In the first six months of 1892, $41.5 million left the country. At the end of May, the Treasury announced that reserves had dropped to $114 million, and were declining at the rate of between $5 million and $6 million a month. Hoping to stem the tide, the sound-money men in Congress were able to pass a bill declaring that the minimum gold reserves should be set at $100 million,[34] but within a year, reserves fell below this figure, as the President was obliged to disobey the Reserve Act.

The election of 1892 was a replay of the 1888 campaign, pitting as it did President Harrison against Cleveland. Leaders of both parties demanded the demonetization of silver as a first step in restoring confidence. Vocal elements in each party were equally insistent that "the free and unlimited coinage of silver and gold at the ratio of sixteen to one" be adopted. In addition, the Populist Party, which nominated James B. Weaver for the presidency, adopted the slogan and a platform which was anti-business and anti-urban.

Cleveland won the election with a plurality of the popular vote. The silver faction in Congress was enlarged, however, and Weaver received over a million popular votes—more than one-fifth of either major candidate's popular vote—and the electoral votes of Kansas, Colorado, Idaho, and Nevada, for a total of twenty-two. The silverites rejoiced, and prepared to do battle when Congress began its sessions in January, 1893.

Wall Street was uneasy about the rise of Populist power and the decline in gold reserves, but had cause for optimism in that cotton and wool manufacturers reported good earnings. In addition, more iron was produced during the first half of the year than at any comparable period in American history. Despite the higher duties of the McKinley Tariff, imports increased, and a favorable balance of payments position was established. During the election campaign industrial conditions improved, and toward the end of the year, manufacturers, railroaders, and financiers voiced the hope of continued prosperity despite the Sherman Silver Purchase Act and inflationist successes in congressional elections.[35] On December 31, R. G. Dun & Company, in its *Weekly Review of Trade,* reported: "The most prosperous year ever known in business closes today with strongly favorable indications for the future."[36]

Cleveland re-entered the White House in 1893 an even more conservative man than he had been during his first Administration. He had spent most of the interim years as counsel to Bangs, Stetson, Tracy and MacVeigh, a law firm which handled a good deal of J. P. Morgan's business. Early in his career Cleveland had formed a friendship with William C. Whitney, who was Secretary of the Navy during his first Administration. Now the two men became still more intimate; Cleveland thus formed a connection with other Wall Street influences. Whitney was allied by marriage to Oliver H. Payne, an original founder of Standard Oil, and the former Navy chief was a major stockholder in the gigantic trust. Whitney later managed Cleveland's 1892 campaign, and Morgan contributed to the war chest. The two giants of the day—Morgan and Rockefeller—were suspicious of each other, but they could agree that Cleveland was their kind of politician.

In December of 1892 and January of 1893, over $25 million in gold was withdrawn from the Treasury. By the end of January, the reserves stood at $108 million, only $8 million more than the legal minimum.[37] Several New York banks aided the Treasury by exchanging part of their reserves for notes, but the outflow continued. By the time Cleveland took office on March 4, the reserves had fallen to a bare $982,410 over the legal limit. Rumor circulated that the new Administration would soon announce the suspension of gold payments. Purchases of Treasury bullion continued, and one newspaper, observing that annual payments of interest and dividends to Europe amounted to over $350 million alone, doubted whether the nation could avoid bankruptcy if this amount were taken in gold.[38] In addition, the crop outlook was poor, business was stagnant after the 1892 boom year, and the foreign trade picture was grim.

While Cleveland organized his cabinet, news of business failures began to shake Wall Street's confidence further. Henry Villard warned his German friends to keep their accounts liquid. Woerishoffer and Cammack staged several bear raids which met with great success.[39] Railroads were eyed with apprehension; insiders realized that most were overbuilt and shoddily financed, and could fall on bad economic or financial news. James Hill's Great Northern was completed in January, and began taking business away from the Northern Pacific and the Union Pacific, his transcontinental competitors. Reports of decreased loadings came in from almost all the major lines. Then, on February 20, less than two weeks before Cleveland would take office, the Philadelphia & Reading Railroad, capitalized at $40 million, went into bankruptcy. This caused widespread alarm, and stocks declined on heavy volume throughout the nation.[40]

Cleveland, following tradition, attacked the problem indirectly. Correctly concluding that one of the major sources of the trouble lay in a failure of confidence in the currency, he called upon banks to buy government bonds in order to bolster federal gold holdings. By March 25, this policy had succeeded in raising reserves to $107 million, but by April 22, outflows caused this figure to dip below the $100 million limit. Still, the market showed little sign of panic, although prices drifted downward in slow trading.[41]

The crisis came on May 4, when the Cordage Trust (National Cordage Company) went into bankruptcy. The firm's common stock fell 14⅛ points on the announcement, and set off a series of declines in other issues. But there was no real panic, for prices rose sharply the following day. "The nearest approach to a panic which the Stock Exchange has witnessed since 1884 occurred today," wrote the *New York Times* correspondent. "The excitement, however, was confined to the industrial group."[42] Still, the brokerages of Henry Allen & Co., H. L. Smyth & Co., and Schuyler, Walker & Co. declared bankruptcy. All reorganized and settled their debts within two years, but their failures eroded confidence on the Street. Some were calm about the decline. S. V. White, a noted speculator, stated:

> I am not badly off at all. If a man is struck by a runaway team he may have an arm broken or his back broken. In my case, it is not my judgement going to be worse than a bad bruise. Any man connected with business will appreciate that borrowing as I was millions of dollars with a drop of $23 a share in 23 minutes on some of the securities I was carrying, it was perfectly evident that calls would be made for margin greater than I could respond to on the instant and it was my duty under the laws of the Exchange to promptly notify them of the fact. I did it and did not then know how bad the storm was going to be. As it appears this morning things are looking not at all serious for permanent results.[43]

For the rest of the spring and summer, declines on heavy volume —which then was approximately 300,000 shares a day—were followed by short rallies on light volume of under 100,000 shares daily. Bullish rumors were common. A week after the National Cordage failure it was announced that "Russell Sage has been the biggest buyer in Wall Street. He has told his friends that he now has twice as many stocks as he had held at any time during the last eighteen months." A later rumor had it that "the Rockefellers (will) take a more active interest in Wall Street," while another was that "George Gould's friends insist that he has twice as many stocks now as he had a year ago, having bought through all the recent declines."[44] Keene was said to be forming a bull pool in Chicago Gas, the Sugar Trust, and Western Union, and "Friends of the Northern Pacific Company are much elated. over the improved financial outlook for their property."[45] But the stocks kept declining.

Foreign liquidations picked up during the summer, and shipments of gold from New York to interior banks also hurt the situation on Wall Street. Railroad bankruptcies became common, and construction slowed down. During the 1880–1890 period the annual additions to railroad mileage had been 7,000 miles, but from 1894 to 1898 the average was less than 2,000 miles a year. Financial news was black. In June, twenty-five national banks closed, the largest one-month total ever recorded. Before the financial community could digest this fact, seventy-eight more suspended in July, and thirty-eight in August. Gold exports picked up sharply, as the Treasury began to run dry. Within a year reserves would reach the lowest point since the early national period (see Table 8.4).

Table 8.4—Gold Reserves, 1890–1894 (Dollars)[46]

June 30, 1890	190,232,405
June 30, 1891	117,667,723
June 30, 1892	114,342,367
June 30, 1893	95,485,413
June 30, 1894	64,873,025

In 1893 alone 642 banks and 15,242 businesses declared bankruptcy. Out of a total of 177,823 miles of railroads, 32,379 belonged to lines which were bankrupt in that year. Business losses in terms of liabilities reached $2.2 billion in 1893,[47] and conditions were getting worse. The corn crop of Iowa, Kansas, and Nebraska was 548 million bushels in 1893; production the following year fell to 137 million bushels. In 1893 the Erie, Philadelphia & Reading, Northern Pacific, Atcheson, Topeka and Santa Fe, Union Pacific and many others were in the hands of receivers. By 1895 there were 169 railroads in the process of reorganization, representing 37,855 miles of track.[48] In the 119 largest industrial centers alone, 800,000 were thrown out of work. This figure does not include the additional hundreds of thousands of jobless in smaller towns and on the farms.[49]

The Columbian Exposition opened in Chicago in 1893, its theme being the great progress made in America since its discovery. Antonín Dvořák premiered the New World Symphony in New York, ushering in what many critics hoped would be a "classical period of American music."[50] The seventeen-story Manhattan Life Insurance Building rose in New York, the first structure in the city taller than Wall Street's Trinity Church. With the aid of Jacob Schiff, Lillian Wald founded the Livingston Street Settlement, which later grew into the Henry Street Settlement. On February 1, Edison Laboratories opened the first film studio in West Orange, New Jersey, and two months later Henry Ford completed the construction of his first gasoline engine. The nation was in the midst of the bicycle craze in 1893, their number rising from 20,000 in 1882 to over one million eleven years later.[51]

While these things mirrored an optimistic America—the period of the gay nineties—many feared drastic changes in the national fabric, if not revolution itself. Homeless and jobless workers roamed the streets; cases of starvation were reported in several large cities. Farmers saw wheat fall to forty-nine cents a bushel, an all time low, while workers could not afford to buy bread. In 1894 Charles Lawler wrote "The Sidewalks of New York," when the city had breadlines and soup kitchens along its streets. Coxey's Army, a small group of less than 1,000 jobless men which frightened those who feared revolution, marched toward Washington in the summer. Other forces, including the Commonwealers, Fry's Army and Kelly's Army (with Jack London in its ranks) committed acts of violence as they roamed the countryside. Strikes hit the coal mines, factories, and railroads. The Pullman strike, one of the bloodiest in American history, threw Chicago into panic and required intervention of federal troops. In New York tailors went on strike, protesting against sweatshop conditions. Wall Streeters, saddened by liquidations, dividend cuts and omissions, fearful of revolution, now found that they could not get delivery on their winter suits. One writer, finding some humor in the situation, wrote that "the social fabric is on the point of disintegration."[52] But humor was rare; the nation was facing its gravest peril since the Civil War.[53]

The Exchange mirrored the discontent in a steady bear market. On July 26, 1893, "Black Wednesday," industrial stocks fell steadily as support melted. During the next two weeks new lows were made daily by the high flying issues of the 1880s[54] (Table 8.5), and the yearly highs and lows told the same story (Table 8.6).

Table 8.5—New Lows, 1893

	Price on Jan. 1	Year's Low	Date of Low
American Sugar	111	61⅛	July 26
American Tobacco	121½	43	July 31
Baltimore & Ohio	94	54⅜	July 27
Chesapeake & Ohio	22	12	July 26
Chicago, Mil. & St. Paul	77	46⅜	July 26
New York Central	109¼	92	July 26
Pacific Mail	27	8⅛	July 27
Western Union	96¼	67	July 26

Table 8.6—Yearly Highs and Lows, 1893

	High	Low
Atcheson, Topeka & Santa Fe	36½	9½
Missouri Pacific	60	16½
Northern Pacific	50⅜	15½
New York Central	111½	92
Erie	26⅝	7¾
Chicago, Milwaukee & St. Paul	83½	46⅜
Richmond & West Point	12	⅛
General Electric	114¼	30

The brokers and speculators were frantic in the face of such a collapse. Even the bears, who made fortunes on the decline, were worried. In August a delegation of brokers and traders marched on the Board of Governors, demanding that the Exchange close, as it had under similar circumstances in 1873, but the directors refused to act. Hopelessness descended on the district, as the brokerages filled with customers who stood around the tickers watching their fortunes melt away. Even the short rallies, which had marked trading during the early months of the decline, were lackluster affairs by the end of 1893. The district was deserted and still, as though resigned to its fate. Although the market declined, the bears were not in evidence, for making money at such a time was like robbing a corpse. They watched the agricultural and industrial news get progressively worse, saw the gold reserves dip weekly, and acted as though they expected the world to come to an end.[55]

On June 30, 1893, Cleveland issued a call for a special session of Congress, which was to meet on August 7 to consider repeal of the Sherman Silver Purchase Act. By the time the congressmen assembled, gold drafts were selling for a premium in New York; by paying higher prices Americans were able to import gold from England, most of which was buried in backyards or in mattresses. A serious "flight from the dollar" was in progress. Employees' paychecks, drawn on suspended banks, were being sold at large discounts, providing a strange type of currency. Clearing-house certificates entirely replaced gold in inter-bank dealings. Six days before the special session met, the National Bimetallic League, made up of 810 delegates from forty-two states, announced that it was willing to repeal the Sherman Act—and in its place accept the free and unlimited coinage of silver at the ratio of 15½ or 16 to 1. Unless this was accepted, the League intimated, violence might take place.[56]

Haggard and drawn after a secret operation for cancer of the jaw, Cleveland sent a message to Congress outlining the seriousness of the reserve situation, and asking for an end to silver purchases. A bitter debate followed, but when the vote was taken, the sound money forces won. The victory over the silverites was hailed by conservative politicians and businessmen; Cleveland was the man of the hour in industrial circles. But business activity continued to fall, agriculture showed no improvement, and bankruptcies were daily affairs. The Exchange greeted the news of repeal with a two-day rally, but then prices leveled off, showing no sign of further recovery.[57]

Gold reserves continued to fall through most of 1894, despite the end of silver purchases. Hoarding, gold exports, and Gresham's Law, together with the low level of economic activity prevented the Treasury from attaining the $100 million gold reserve desired by the President and the business community, and required by law.[58] Early in the year, the Treasury sold a 5 per cent bond issue which brought in $58 million, but half of this amount came from gold withdrawn from the Treasury to make purchases, and the issue was considered a failure.[59] During the first eighteen days of the year reserves fell from $80 million to $69 million. Secretary of the Treasury John G. Carlyle, who had gone to New York in February to float the loan, returned in November to borrow another $50 million. The issue was taken, but again gold was withdrawn from the Treasury to pay for most of the bonds. At the same time, silver certificates were being redeemed in gold, put back in circulation, and again returned for more gold. In his annual message of December 4, Cleveland complained that "we have an endless chain in operation, depleting the Treasury's gold and never near a final rest."[60]

By February 8, 1895, the gold reserve stood at little more than $41 million. Forced to take drastic action, Cleveland sent a special message to Congress requesting power to withhold notes brought to the Treasury for redemption, thus contracting the currency as well as stopping the "endless chain." He also asked for legislation requiring the payment of certain debts owed the government in gold. These proposals were rejected.[61] Reserves kept falling, and the President, realizing the credit of the nation was at stake, decided to act in a dramatic fashion. He would, in effect, bring Morgan into the government, thus demonstrating to the country and European bankers that the most powerful American of the time had confidence in the nation's future. Cleveland could not save the country with his prestige, but he thought that Morgan could with his.

Morgan met with the President in early February, informing him that the New York Sub-Treasury had only $9 million in its vaults and that he knew of one check then outstanding for $10 million.[62] Morgan suggested that by using an act passed in 1862, Cleveland could sell him a private bond issue to be paid in gold, which would save the reserves. At first the President was adamant; what would prevent the "endless chain" from once more going into action, as in the two previous flotations? Intimating that his credit was better than that of the government, Morgan guaranteed that this would not happen. Cleveland was satisfied; with Morgan he drew up plans for a bond issue that would bring 3.5 million ounces of gold—worth approximately $62 million—to the Treasury. Half of this amount was to come from overseas. The President was denounced by the silverites for his "sell-out" to Wall Street, but the nation's credit was saved. The French banking house of Lazard Fréres had a ship loaded with $18 million in gold ready to leave New York for France. When news of Morgan's bond issue came through, the gold was redeposited in New York. Far more important than the $62 million in gold that Morgan brought to the Treasury was the restored confidence of foreigners and American bankers in the dollar. Morgan was castigated for making large profits in time of emergency, Cleveland lost whatever control he had over the silverites in his own party, and both men were condemned by the inflationist press. The *New York World* charged that a conspiracy had been formed to wreck the nation, and saw "the iron band of contraction wielded at the dictation of England."[63] Nevertheless, on July 8, 1895, the gold reserve stood at $107.6 million; the nation's credit had been secured through the power of J. P. Morgan & Co. American issues were once again favorites on European exchanges.[64] Morgan emerged from this crisis as the most powerful, feared, respected, and hated man in the nation.

Morgan's operations in saving the currency were only part of his activities during the panic and depression. He became the greatest single factor in railroad reorganization, as well. As has been seen, the 1893 panic wreaked havoc among the nation's railroads. The House of Morgan reorganized many of them through refinancing and the introduction of new managements, earning for itself the title of "Doctor of Wall Street."[65] In 1893 Morgan took over the operation of the Richmond & West Point Terminal Company. The holding company owned 9,000 miles of track, most of it in bad condition, and had defaulted on its debts, which were represented by more than 100 stock and bond issues. Aided by Coster and others, Morgan recapitalized the combine, absorbing it into the Southern Railway Company, which had $370 million in capital, and within a year showed a profit of $3 million. During the next five years the same salvaging operations had been carried out for the Northern Pacific, Erie, Lehigh Valley, and others.

Morgan's motives in these reorganizations were many. First, he always considered himself to be a patriot who would help his country in time of need. To a less innocent age this appears naïve, but Morgan was always a flag-waver. In addition, Morgan had important European connections, who had invested heavily in railroads, and he wanted to protect their positions as well as his own.[66] Then, too, Morgan was power-hungry. He was never one of the richest men in America, although he could easily have been, but he was the most powerful for several years, and this gave him much satisfaction. Finally, Morgan had a passion for order; it is significant that his favorite card game was solitaire, in which the player makes neat piles of cards out of a jumbled deck.

During his first period of greatness, Morgan saved both the currency and the nation's railroads. It should be noted, however, that other banking houses, especially Kuhn, Loeb, were also important. Jacob Schiff was active in Erie and Chicago & Atlantic reorganizations as early as 1886. In February, 1893, he took an interest in the Chesapeake & Ohio and the Louisville & Nashville. The Norfolk and Western had Kuhn, Loeb help during the late 1880s and the early 1890s, as did the Denver & Rio Grande. In 1881 the firm became banker for the Pennsylvania, which was then trying to resist Morgan's blandishments. By 1895, Schiff was second only to Morgan as a reorganizer.[67]

By 1900 most of the rails were controlled by six large systems or groupings; shown in Table 8.7.

Table 8.7—Railroad Groupings, 1900

	Miles
Harriman	20,245
Vanderbilt	19,517
Morgan	19,073
Pennsylvania	18,220
Gould	16,074
Hill	10,373

Since Morgan was in indirect control of the Vanderbilt system, he was considered the leader in railroads, which then were still the most important segment of the investment market.[68] At the same time, however, Schiff could have claimed even greater power. His house was banker for the Pennsylvania, and had cordial relations with Gould and Hill. A great plum fell into his lap in 1885, when the Union Pacific reorganization was turned down by Morgan, and the road's directors turned to him. For almost a year Schiff worked on a refinancing scheme, but found himself blocked at every turn by some unknown opponent. He went to see Morgan, asking whether he was behind the opposition. J.P. said that he had nothing to do with Union Pacific, but promised to find out who was thwarting the reorganization. In short order the mystery man was uncovered; it was E. H. Harriman, a man who Morgan despised as a person and as an industrialist. Schiff and Harriman were able to come to terms, and Kuhn, Loeb became the banker for many of Harriman's ventures. Together they would challenge Morgan's domination of the railroads, and would administer to the great man one of his few Wall Street defeats.

Notes

1. Allan Nevins, *Grover Cleveland: A Study in Courage* (New York, 1938), pp. 201–202.

2. *Ibid.*, p. 203.

3. Horace S. Merrill, *Bourbon Leader: Grover Cleveland and the Democratic Party* (Boston, 1957), p. 168 ff.

4. Richard Hofstadter, *The American Political Tradition and the Men Who Made It* (New York, 1954), p. 184.

5. Victor S. Clark, *History of Manufactures in the United States* (New York, 1929), Vol. II, pp. 175–76.

6. Hoggson, *Epochs in American Banking*, p. 207; *Medina*, pp. 18–19.

7. Thomas C. Cochran, *The American Business System: A Historical Perspective, 1900–1955* (New York, 1962), pp. 24–25.

8. *Ibid.*, p. 25.

9. Harold U. Faulkner, *Politics, Reform and Expansion, 1890–1900* (New York, 1959), p. 75.

10. *New York Times,* December 21, 1896.

11. Edwards, *Evolution of Finance Capitalism*, pp. 173–74.

12. John Moody, *The Masters of Capital* (New Haven, 1921), pp. 32–34; Satterlee, *J. Pierpont Morgan*, p. 208.

13. Eames, *New York Stock Exchange,* p. 95.

14. Willis and Bogen, *Investment Banking,* p. 228.

15. Pratt, *Work of Wall Street,* p. 254.

16. Clark, *History of Manufactures,* Vol. II, pp. 162–63; *Medina,* pp. 18–19.

17. Edwards, *Evolution of Finance Capitalism,* p. 184.

18. Myers, *New York Money Market,* pp. 290–91, 303–304.

19. Kirkland, *Industry Comes of Age,* p. 70.

20. Pratt, *Work of Wall Street,* p. 203.

21. Myers, *New York Money Market,* pp. 303–304; Neill, *Inside Story of the Stock Exchange,* p. 113. Bernard Baruch, making his start on Wall Street as a runner for E. A. Houseman, wrote that his major function at the time was to deliver shares from his firm to those who acted for purchasers. "Up and down those stairs we boys would clatter, making our deliveries. I would shove a bundle of securities through the cashier's window, crying out, 'Hold the check for Houseman,' and rush off to make the next delivery." *Baruch: My Own Story* (New York, 1957), p. 86.

22. Neill, *Inside Story of the Stock Exchange,* p. 112.

23. Livingston, The *American Stockholder,* pp. 180–82.

23. Livingston, *The American Stockholder,* pp. 180–82.

that loans of £3 million from France and £1.5 million from Russia were floated by the Bank of England. Since France was then recovering from the collapse of the Panama Company and Russia was hardly in condition to export capital, this seems questionable. In addition, the three nations were rivals in Africa and Asia, and this too would make such a loan or loans questionable. In any case, the author has found no other record of these transactions.

25. Noyes, *Fifty Years of American Finance,* pp. 155–56.

26. Josephson, *Robber Barons,* pp. 379–80.

27. Eames, *New York Stock Exchange,* p. 96.

28. *Ibid.*, p. 66.

29. Cyrus Adler, *Jacob H. Schiff: His Life and Letters* (New York, 1929), Vol. I, p. 30.

30. Pratt, *Work of Wall Street*, p. 26.

31. Harold U. Faulkner, *American Economic History* (New York, 1958), p. 519.

32. Walker, *Epic of American Industry*, pp. 204, 219–20.

33. This phenomenon is known as Gresham's Law, which states that bad money forces good money out of circulation. It operates when doubt exists as to the value of currency in a nation.

34. Noyes, *Forty Years of American Finance*, p. 167.

35. Lanier, *A Century of Banking in New York*, p. 188; Clark, *History of Manufactures*, p. 165.

36. Lightner, *History of Business Depressions*, p. 188.

37. Noyes, *Forty Years of American Finance*, p. 183.

38. Faulkner, *Politics, Reform and Expansion*, p. 152.

39. Nevins, *Grover Cleveland*, p. 510; Noyes, *The Market Place*, pp. 103–104.

40. Noyes, *Forty Years of American Finance*, p. 188.

41. *New York Times*, March 22, 1893.

42. *New York Times*, May 5, 6, 1893.

43. *Wall Street Journal*, May 6, 1893.

44. *New York Times*, May 9, June 11, 1893.

45. *New York Times*, May 22, July 7, 1893.

46. Lightner, *History of Business Depressions*, p. 193.

47. Eames, *New York Stock Exchange*, p. 67.

48. Lightner, *History of Business Depressions*, p. 354; Noyes, *Forty Years of American Finance*, p. 221.

49. Clark, *History of Manufactures*, p. 166.

50. *New York Times*, December 1, 1893.

51. Gorton Carruth, *The Encyclopedia of American Facts and Dates* (New York, 1956), pp. 366–70.

52. *Wall Street Journal*, December 20, 1894.

53. Lightner, *History of Business Depressions*, pp. 196, 355.

54. Eames, *New York Stock Exchange*, pp. 67–68.

55. Noyes, *Market Place*, pp. 106–107.

56. Faulkner, *Politics, Reform and Expansion*, p. 151; Noyes, *Forty Years of American Finance*, p. 196.

57. Nevins, *Grover Cleveland*, pp. 546–47.

58. *New York Times*, May 22, 1894.

59. Nevins, *Grover Cleveland*, pp. 598–99.

60. John K. Winkler, *Morgan, the Magnificent* (New York, 1931), p. 139.

61. *New York Times*, February 9, 1895; Faulkner, *Politics, Reform and Expansion*, pp. 154–55.

62. Nevins, *Grover Cleveland*, p. 290.

63. Edwards, *Evolution of Finance Capitalism*, p. 172.

64. Noyes, *Forty Years of American Finance*, pp. 243–44.

65. Winkler, *Morgan the Magnificent*, p. 129.

66. Moody, *Masters of Capital*, pp. 28–29.

67. Adler, *Jacob H. Schiff*, pp. 53–81.

68. Corey, *House of Morgan*, pp. 208–209.

9

The Morganization of America: 1896-1903

> Finally, Mudd decided that the chances were about fifty-fifty that the sulfur content of Bryan Mound was rich enough to be mined profitably. Back in New York, I reported this to Mr. Morgan, explaining that we could buy the whole property outright, including royalties, for $500,000. I added that I was willing to "gamble" half of this sum from my own funds.
>
> "Gamble" was a poor choice of language. I should have said "invest." "I never gamble," replied Mr. Morgan with a gesture that signified that the interview was over and the venture closed as far as he was concerned.
>
> Bernard Baruch

EARLY IN JANUARY, 1896, the Appellate Division of the New York Supreme Court rejected a proposal for a subway in the city, basing its decision, in part, on Luke 14:28, in which Jesus asked: "Which of you, intending to build a tower, sitteth not down and counteth the cost, whether he have sufficient to finish it?" In April the first motion picture program was put on at Koster and Bial's Music Hall, after a "concert" which included "There'll be a Hot Time in the Old Town Tonight," the most popular song of the year. The *New York Times* called the show "all wonderfully real and singularly exhilarating," and predicted a great future for motion pictures. Toward the end of the year, Guglielmo Marconi perfected wireless telegraphy, and the Duryea brothers announced that their plant had turned out ten automobiles during the previous twelve months.[1]

The overshadowing event of the year was the presidential contest between William Jennings Bryan and William McKinley. Populists and silver Democrats, angered at Cleveland's economic conservatism, all but threw him out of the party and named Bryan, a young but well-known former congressman, as their candidate. McKinley, the political protégé of traction and iron magnate Mark Hanna, was counted on to protect business's interests. For the first time since the Civil War vital issues were discussed during a long and bitter campaign marked by threats, violence, and indications of growing class hostilities. The key issue was silver, Bryan standing for its coinage at a ratio of sixteen to one and McKinley supporting the gold standard. The Republicans won, carrying every eastern state and the entire Midwest east of North Dakota and Minnesota, as well as Oregon and California. Bryan took the South, the mining states of the Rockies, and the western tier of states in the Midwest. The electoral vote was 271 to 176, but so close was the election in some states that a switch of 500,000 votes, properly placed, would have put Bryan in the White House.

The vote was considered a victory for business and the last great stand of the farmers. The investment bankers, who had all but suspended business from the time of Bryan's nomination to Election Day, were particularly pleased. The election of McKinley has been called the coming of age of industrial America, a symbol of the end of the agrarian era. A standard interpretation of the result was offered by William Allen White, a pro-McKinley Republican:

> I do not believe, as the academicians have said, that McKinley won because Hanna spent so much money. Few votes were actually purchased in that campaign. McKinley won because the Republicans had persuaded the middle class, almost to a man, that a threat to the gold standard was a threat to their prosperity. Incidentally, labor as a class was persuaded to the point of coercion that if McKinley was defeated industry would shut down, and that if McKinley won prosperity would return because capital had confidence in the Republican party, and because the gold standard and the protective tariff as national policies would be established. The coercion was bold, unashamed, and effective. Hanna had more money than probably was ever spent in a campaign before. But Bryan had enough to present his case fairly to the people.[2]

Paradoxically, Bryan's major theme—that only inflation of the currency could bring full recovery and prosperity—was soon vindicated. This was done not through silver coinage, but rather through a great influx of gold into circulation. The amount of gold *per capita* in 1891 had been $10.10; during the election the figure stood at $8.40.³ It had been this growing scarcity that led to the farmers' support of free coinage at sixteen to one. For the silver miners, this would mean an assured market; the farmers wanted silver coinage primarily as a means of inflating the currency. They backed silver in 1896 for the same reason they had supported greenbacks during the 1870s: the desire to pay off debts in depreciated dollars. Starting in 1897 gold production began to rise, giving the farmers their increased supply of money. With this, many of them began to leave the Populist Movement.

The increase in gold production was due primarily to two developments: the discovery of new mines and the perfection of the cyanamide process for ore reduction. News of gold strikes in South Africa and Australia came in 1896, and on August 12 gold was discovered in Klondike Creek in the Yukon. News of the new deposits did not reach America until after McKinley's victory, but when it did the gloom of the depression lifted. The Bryan defeat and the gold strikes led the *Review of Reviews* to claim that "For the present and for some years to come the cause of free silver in the United States is thoroughly and hopelessly defeated." The *Nation* added its amen. "For the first time in twenty years the silver menace is cleared away from the financial horizon. . . . The silver lining no longer adorns the Western sky."⁴ The overwhelming popularity enjoyed by McKinley during his presidency paralleled the gold expansion. The production figures from the mines tell the story most graphically (see Table 9.1).

Table 9.1—Gold Production, 1893–1898⁵

	Value of Gold Mined (dollars)	Increase over Previous Year (dollars)
1893	157,494,800	10,843,300
1894	181,175,600	23,680,800
1895	198,763,600	17,588,000
1896	202,251,000	3,487,400
1897	236,073,700	33,824,700
1898	286,879,700	50,806,000

By 1908, when Bryan made his third try for the presidency, gold production stood at $442,837,000, while silver mining stagnated. Thus, within a few years after the bitterly contested election, the causes of discontent had almost disappeared, with each side able to claim victory. The businessmen had the gold standard, while the farmers received an expanded currency.

The election year of 1896 offered a further benefit to American farmers in the form of a wheat famine in India, which caused the grain prices throughout the world to rise sharply. Continued high prices and a record harvest in 1897 added to the agrarian prosperity, which carried over into the urban centers during the year. The Dingly Tariff, passed during the summer, raised duties to new highs, thus discouraging imports while exports were expanding rapidly. This would create difficulties in the long run, but for the time being it helped fortify the agricultural and industrial boom. Although Europe was undergoing a similar upturn in the business cycle during the late 1890s, American goods were successfully competing with domestic manufactures in every west European nation. In 1897, exports passed the one billion dollar mark for the first time, and the excess of exports over imports—$286 million—was the largest in American history up to that year. And the trend continued; in 1901 the export figure reached $1.5 billion and the trade balance $615 million.[6]

Despite the rising export balance, very little gold was shipped from European vaults to America. Instead, European importers would buy American securities on foreign stock exchanges and then send them to New York, where they were sold to obtain the needed funds to pay for American goods. This liquidation reached its height just before the most powerful stage of the bull market. Once more, the Europeans had bought high and sold low.

It was during this period that Wall Street made its real start as a capital market for the world. The Province of Quebec issue of 1879 has already been mentioned. At the time the $3 million flotation was considered to be very large. During McKinley's first Administration, Americans exported over $100 million to Canada. In 1889, $2.2 million in Chinese bonds were sold on the Street. The Swedish government floated a $10 million issue through the National Park Bank in 1900, and in the same year Germany borrowed twice that amount through Kuhn, Loeb. National City Bank underwrote a $25 million Russian rail issue. Even the British, dominant capital exporters for over a century, were obliged to borrow some $227 million, mostly from Morgan, during the Boer War. After peace returned to South Africa the bonds were repurchased, and London again had no peer as the world capital center. But from 1900 to 1909, American foreign investments increased every year, reaching $2.5 billion by the spring of 1910. Jacob Schiff, angered at the Russian treatment of Jews, was able to avenge himself by lending the Japanese government over a quarter of a billion dollars during the first decade of the twentieth century.

Europe's private investors returned to the American exchanges in full force in 1904, seeking a share in the phenomenal bull market. From that year to 1909 foreign investments increased steadily, reaching a total of $6.4 billion by early 1910. Thus, what was a small beginning for Wall Street as a capital exporter was reinforced by European investments. In effect, private citizens in western Europe were buying American stocks with their gold, which was then returned to Europe in the form of loans to governments. This gave the foreign loans an appearance of solid strength. But had overseas purchases of American stocks and bonds been cut to any great extent, the loans would have also declined. For the time being, however, Wall Street seemed not to notice this. New York had replaced Philadelphia as the nation's capital market during the early nineteenth century, and now it would supersede Lombard Street and take the title of Banker for the World.[7]

In 1896 such an idea did not exist in even the wildest dreams of Wall Street men. The economy and the market were both stagnant, each waiting for the voters' mandate in November. The *Financial Chronicle* was probably correct when it wrote:

> There has been no lack of investment funds any more than there has been a lack of capital to engage in reproductive enterprises. The real trouble has been that in view of the pending uncertainty—and uncertainty at once menacing the standard of values and threatening to derange all values—neither the investor nor the capitalist was willing to tie up his money or to let it go far out of his reach.[8]

The McKinley victory, the agricultural and industrial revivals which followed, and other signs of vitality in the economy, added to news of gold strikes, led timid investors back to the markets. Having returned to Wall Street, they sought investment opportunities in the group which had led the market down in 1893: the rails. Even a cursory look at the industry was enough to convince them that the carriers were getting back on their feet. In 1895, there were 169 insolvent railroads with 37,856 miles of track and $2.5 billion in liabilities. Economic revival and reorganizations brought many of them back to life. By the middle of 1898, only ninety-four were still in the hands of receivers, representing 12,745 miles of track and $661.5 million in liabilities. Two years later railroad earnings were 50 per cent over 1895, and the industry was in the midst of a construction and modernization boom that eclipsed that of the immediate post-Civil War period. The roads floated new issues (see Table 9.2), which were eagerly taken up by domestic and foreign investors, who could not know that this was to be the last great era of the rails.[9]

Table 9.2—Value of New Rail Issues, 1898–1902 (Dollars)

1898	67,000,000
1899	107,000,000
1900	199,000,000
1901	434,000,000
1902	527,000,000

There was some liquidation in foreign accounts during 1898 and 1899, as European issues were more attractive than American. But as substantial as European expansion was at the close of the century, American industrial and rail growth out-stripped it, and, as we have seen, capital flowed across the Atlantic to New York when the new century began. So great was the American threat to the European capital markets that Count Goluchowski, the Austrian Foreign Minister, warned that "European nations must close their ranks and fight, shoulder to shoulder, in order successfully to defend their existence."[10]

The first test of the nation's financial strength after the recovery came in April, 1898, when the United States declared war on Spain. Three months later the Treasury offered $200 million worth of 3 per cent bonds. The issue was quickly oversubscribed as $1.5 billion in tenders were received; within a few months the bonds were being quoted at a 6 per cent premium.[11] In April, 1899, when the government paid Spain $20 million for the Philippines, the Treasury reserve increased despite the large gold exports. Indeed, so sound was the government's financial position that the nation was able to underwrite most of Great Britain's loans during the Boer War, increase the rail network, sustain an industrial and agricultural boom which made heavy demands upon the capital markets, increase the standard of living, and maintain prices without inflation, all at the same time. And there was still a large surplus in the public purse after all this was paid for. From 1897 to 1906, total assets of financial institutions increased at a more rapid rate than ever before in the nation's history (see Table 9.3).

Table 9.3—Assets of Financial Institutions, 1897–1906 (Millions of Dollars)[12]

	Bank Assets	Life Insurance Assets	Total Assets
1897	7,822	1,334	9,156
1898	8,869	1,463	9,531
1899	9,905	1,595	11,500
1900	10,786	1,742	12,528
1901	12,358	1,911	14,269
1902	13,364	2,092	15,456
1903	14,303	2,265	16,568
1904	15,199	2,499	17,698
1905	16,918	2,706	19,624
1906	18,148	2,924	21,072

These were optimistic years, during which scarcely a problem arose which seemed incapable of being solved. Even when panic appeared, it was short and not as fearful as those of the past. When danger threatened, J. P. Morgan and his colleagues, the leaders of high finance and the bulwarks of the nation, would step in and set things aright. Late in 1899, a break developed at the Exchange. Several brokerages declared bankruptcy and others suspended operations. Some talked of an end to the two-year bull market, but Morgan announced that he would lend one million dollars to those in trouble at below the going rate, and added that he would get together an additional $9 million if necessary. The decline was halted, and the bull market resumed.[13]

A ten-year advance began in 1897 and ended with a dramatic crash in 1907. To those who profited by the advances, Morgan was both a symbol and a guide. Only Kuhn, Loeb, was considered in the same class as the House of Morgan, and even then, Jacob Schiff's influence never approached that of the Great Man. Although other banking houses did underwriting and acted as financial associates of large firms, Morgan and Schiff were Wall Street's leaders. This was not to change for another two generations, but the growing importance of investment banking led to increased business for the other houses as well as for the Big Two. Goldman, Sachs & Co. and Lehman Brothers cooperated on many joint ventures, finding that together they could challenge the leaders. Speyer & Co. did well, primarily due to the trust the Street felt for James Speyer. Kidder,

Peabody & Co. made its niche in utilities, an area neglected by Morgan and Schiff. Other leading specialist houses were Harris, Forbes & Co., Charles D. Birney & Co., and N. W. Harris & Co.[14] Although merged and re-formed during the past half century, these firms still exist today. All date back to the Civil War era, but their real starts as investment houses came during the 1898–1907 period, when under-writing was in its first great wave of prosperity.

As had been the case during every previous bull market, a group of traders appeared during the late 1890s whose antics livened the scene. These were not merely raiders and petty dealers who, through shrewd manipulations, could pull off *coups* worth millions. They could and did put together great industrial empires, float large issues of securities, and, as was the case with Bernard Baruch, become important figures in fields other than finance.

Baruch appeared on the Street before the 1893 panic and from the first showed signs of becoming an important dealer. His most noted features were his calm demeanor and his ability to learn from mistakes. "Both my failure in whiskey and my success in copper emphasized one thing," he later wrote, "the importance of getting the facts of a situation free from tips, inside dope, or wishful think-ing. In the search for facts I learned that one had to be as unim-passioned as a surgeon. And if one had the facts right, one could stand with confidence against the will or whims of those who were supposed to know."[15]

Baruch was a charter member of what came to be known as "The Waldorf Crowd." During afternoons of trading days he would lunch with such luminaries as Richard Harding Davis, Mark Twain, Jim Corbett, Mark Hanna, Diamond Jim Brady, and James Keene. The most flamboyant of them all, a man who Vanderbilt might have thought a reincarnation of Jim Fisk, was John W. "Bet-A-Million" Gates. A born salesman and promoter, Gates began his business life as a "drummer" in the Midwest. In 1890 he combined two small barbed-wire companies into a larger unit, the first of his many financial deals. Two years later, with a capital of $4 million, he formed the Consolidated Steel and Wire Company. From there he went on to become important in the petroleum industry and in iron and steel. There were few operators shrewder than Gates; even Morgan, who had contempt for the man, respected him as a financier.[16]

Thomas Fortune Ryan, a good friend of Baruch and later a colleague of his as financier of the Democratic Party, was another great trader and industrialist. Baruch called him "lightning in action and the most resourceful man I ever knew." Jacob Field, also of the Waldorf Crowd, was something of a character. When asked by a lady at a dinner party what he thought of Balzac, Field replied, "I never deal in dem outside stocks."[17] Harry Content, "the prince of brokers," and another regular, had been on the Street during the 1873 crash, and would live through the 1929 collapse. During this period he helped Baruch gain control of National Lead, worked for James Keene and the Guggenheims, and was one of the most trusted figures in the district. He liked to tell friends of the advice his mother gave him before he left for New York. "Son," she said, "never cheat for money."[18]

Wall Street's stormy petrel near the end of the bull market was Thomas W. Lawson. While still in his teens, Lawson made $50,000 by speculating in rail stocks on the Boston Exchange, and then lost it in his very next venture. Lawson vowed to become the leading financier in America, and although he never succeeded, he gave it a good try. By the time he was twenty-one, he was Boston's best known plunger. Lawson then went to New York, where he earned his first million before he had reached the age of thirty. It was during this period that he wrote a history of the Republican party, some copies of which were printed on satin and given to special friends.

Lawson usually operated as a bull, particularly in rails and mining shares, but when the occasion called for it, he would turn to the bear side. Feeling flush at the turn of the century, Lawson commissioned a sculptor to do a statue for him of a bull and bear in mortal combat. He instructed the artist that neither animal was to be shown as having an advantage over the other. The bull was to have his horns braced against the bear's side, while the bear was to stand in such a position as to be able to kick the bull's belly. The statue won a gold medal at the Paris Exposition and was later enshrined at the Stock Exchange Luncheon Club.[19]

It paid to be a bull during the 1897–1906 period, and most of the speculators and operators acted as such, making and spending fortunes. With the perspective of a half-century we now know that this was one of the two biggest bull markets in the nation's history, and that 1901 was an even better year for optimists at the exchanges than 1929. In addition, not even the wild years of the 1920s could compare with the late 1890s and early 1900s in terms of consolidation, expansion, rationalization, and production.[20]

From 1895 to 1904, over 3,000 firms disappeared as a result of mergers. This movement began slowly, picking up momentum as it went. The peak year for mergers came in 1899, when 1,208 companies capitalized at $2.27 billion, went into consolidations.[21] The most striking effect of the merger movement was the rise of the large industrial complexes that characterize the twentieth century. In 1897 there were but eight industrial firms capitalized at over $50 million; six years later the number of these giants reached forty. Small entrepreneurs still controlled the bulk of industrial production, but during this period they began to give way to much larger organizations.[22]

Many of the nation's most famous companies had their beginnings in the six hectic years of 1898–1903. International Silver, National Biscuit, and the forerunner of Union Carbide made their appearances in 1898. The peak year of 1899 saw the formations of American Car and Foundry, American Chicle, Borden's Condensed Milk, Diamond Match, Electric Boat (the forerunner of General Dynamics), National Carbon, National Distillers, United Fruit, and Standard Oil of New Jersey. The steel industry also was swept by a series of mergers; Federal Steel, American Steel and Wire, American Tin Plate, Colorado Fuel and Iron, Carnegie Steel, and Tennessee Coal and Iron were either formed or underwent important mergers during the six peak years. A leading commentator on the period wrote that the merger movement reached fantastic heights:

> When one of the smaller "trusts" was being formed, a party of steel men were on their way to Chicago one night after a buying tour. The men had been drinking and were in a convivial mood. Said one, "There's a steel mill at the next station: let's get out and buy it." "Agreed!"
>
> It was past midnight when they reached the station, but they pulled the plant owner out of bed and demanded that he sell his plant.
>
> "My plant is worth two hundred thousand dollars, but it is not for sale," was the reply.
>
> "Never mind about the price," answered the hilarious purchasers, "we will give you three hundred thousand—five hundred thousand."[23]

The next four years saw the modern formations of Allis-Chalmers, American Locomotive, Corn Products, DuPont, Eastman Kodak, Elliot Fisher (forerunner of Underwood) and United States Gypsum. The greatest merger of the era, however, was that of United States Steel in 1901, which took in eleven major firms and contained what were once 170 independent companies. This giant billion-dollar complex alone accounted for 26 per cent of all the mergers in the 1895–1904 period.[24]

The movement continued into 1902 and 1903. In the latter year the American Tobacco Trust, formed from seven firms representing 162 mergers, made its appearance.[25] Scarcely a month went by from 1898 to 1903 in which a major merger was not announced by one or another of the investment houses, which presided over the operations, carried out the refinancing, and marketed the securities. And more often than not, when the excitement subsided, the investment bankers could be found controlling the boards of directors of the giant combinations. Charles H. Dow, editor of the *Wall Street Journal* and the most famous analyst in the history of the Street, prophesied on March 3, 1900:

> It is as certain as anything in the future that industrial securities will form the principal medium for speculation in this country. The field for the formation of industrial corporations is vast and varying degrees of skill in management, coupled with the succession of good times and bad times, will make constant changes in values which will be discounted by movements in the prices of stocks.

A year later, Dow noted the rise of the steel combine, and said that "the industrial market is destined to be the great speculative market of the United States."[26]

The reasons for these mergers were many, and it is not within the scope of this work to analyze them. It should be noted, however, that the desire to end or curb competition so as to achieve marketing and productive advantages was important, as was the expectation that the end of cutthroat tactics would bring greater profits. Some writers believe that the lack of rationality in the nation's railroads was a prime cause for mergers in that industry, but this view does not take into account the fact that companies with low costs and great growth potentials merged along with the others. At one time it was fashionable to view the mergers as a first attempt at introducing economic fascism to the nation, which was stopped by the Progressives from 1903 to 1914. Some believe that Morgan and other investment bankers wanted to create efficient plants and railroads only to end the chaos that existed in the economy after the 1893 crash. But, by so doing, they were greatly responsible for the economic successes enjoyed by the nation in the twentieth century. In addition, they performed a valuable service by acting as central bankers at a time when the federal government was unwilling or unable to take up that task. As Charles H. Dow noted in 1899, the bankers had, in effect, underwritten not only corporations, but the very future of the economy.

> This is preeminently the period of industrial speculation, yet the creation of industrial stocks has become pronounced only within a year. It is impossible that any large portion of the industrial stocks created in the last six months should have been marketed. As it is the intention of the promoters of industrial combinations to sell a portion, at least, of the stocks which they have made, it follows that there must be a very strong body of capitalists prepared at present to resist anything like collapse in the industrial market and to promote by every means in their power firm or advancing prices for the market as a whole.[27]

Were these men robber barons or captains of industry? This question has not as yet been tackled dispassionately by economic historians, and it remains, as it has been for the past half century, the battlefield for propagandists.

The interrelationships between the merger movement and the stock exchanges are evident to those who study the nation's capital markets.[28] Without an organized market place, the flotations of large issues of securities would have been difficult, if not impossible. The only alternative would have been a return to Jay Cooke's Civil War practice of selling securities directly to customers through a large army of salesmen. The capital offerings at the turn of the century were far too large for such a device, and the exchanges were invaluable to the investment bankers. In the first quarter of 1899, new industrial companies capitalized at $1.59 billion were incorporated, and the total for the entire year ran to $3.59 billion. Common stock issues accounted for $2.35 billion of this figure, while bonds and preferred stock made up the rest. In the first four months of the year automobile companies alone floated $338 million in stock.[29] Not all of these issues reached the markets, to be sure, but many did, and they were taken up by eager investors. Most buyers realized that common shares in the new corporations were often backed by nothing but hope, but since the economic outlook was rosy, they were willing to "take a flyer." Why not buy Colorado Iron common, worth nothing in terms of its book value, when the price of iron advanced from $15.45 a ton in 1894 to $29.50 a ton toward the end of 1899?

Dreams of wealth exceeding those of any previous bull market dazzled investors who, looking at first for signs of economic weakness and not finding them, did not bother to look again until it was too late. All of the production figures seemed to be headed upward in 1900, especially those of gold and steel, the two key figures for the Wall Streeter of the time. The capital markets seemed in sounder shape than at any other period in history. This was no illusion, for the Morgan-directed banking fraternity was dedicated to maintaining order and liquidity, carrying out functions which in other countries were assigned to central banks.

The influx of foreign investment capital, the increase in the gold supply, industrial prosperity, and firm leadership in the formation of large combines would have assured a bull market. There was another element, however, which added to the excitement and helped make the rise of prices spectacular.

Although the merger movement created hundreds of thousands of new shares, it also retired securities of companies that disappeared in the reorganizations. On balance, the number of shares listed on the New York Stock Exchange declined from 1897 to 1903, while demand for securities, fed by the bull fever, increased, causing a shortage of shares. This factor served to reinforce the advance and heighten the optimism of the Street.[30] Never before or since did the turnover rate of listed shares reach the levels of the 1900–1907 period. During four of these years the rate was over 200 per cent; even 1928, the most active year of the twenties, saw a turnover of 132 per cent. The highest rate of the "turbulent fifties" was the 23 per cent of 1950. In 1900, the reported stock volume reached 102,386,252 shares, while 59,579,694 shares were listed, giving a turnover rate of 172 per cent. On the most active day of 1900, November 12, 1,627,031 shares changed hands, which in terms of today would be equivalent to a 105 million-share day.[31]

The churning markets of 1900 were far overshadowed by the outbursts of speculative fever that gripped the district the following year, when the turnover rate was 319 per cent. In writing to his friend Cassel about the market conditions in late March, Schiff said that "it is almost terrifying to contemplate the way in which the market has risen, by leaps and bounds," and he closed by prophesying that "the reaction must come; it is only a question of time."[32] Discussing the Street two months later, Stedman said:

> The business of commission houses swelled beyond all precedent, and weary clerks toiled to midnight adjusting the accounts of lawyers,

grocers, physicians, waiters, clergymen, and chorus singers who were learning to acquire wealth without labor. From every lip dropped stories of fortunes gained in a week by this or that lucky strike. Florists, jewellers, perfumers, restauranteurs, and modistes rejoiced in the collateral prosperity secured to them by the boom in stocks.[33]

Prices rose almost daily, and volume went up even faster. In January an average day saw some 500,000 shares traded. The figure reached one million by April, which was the heaviest month in Exchange history until the late 1920s.[34] On April 2, the Board of Governors announced its plans to construct a larger building to house the Exchange. Until then, trading was to shift to the Produce Exchange, where expanded facilities could take care of the increased activity. Despite the dislocations caused by moving, volume continued to rise, making the trading floor an unorganized, sweaty arena. The temporary quarters were ready by April 28, and on the day of the move, when the old building had been stripped of every facility, volume topped the million-share mark.

At the third session in the temporary quarters, the traders staged a fantastic display of buying power. On April 30, 3,250,000 shares were sold. Without first having had a 2 million-share day, the Exchange witnessed its first 3 million-share session.[35]

The bull market had picked up steam during the election campaign of 1900. McKinley's reelection in November was the spark that ignited the 1901 period of wildness, and Morgan's activities helped keep it alive. This was to be one of the most important years in J.P.'s career, and certainly the most eventful.

In 1898 John Gates drew together seven wire factories to form the Consolidated Steel & Wire Company. Since Consolidated bought most of its steel from the Illinois Steel Company, it was natural that the two should seek a merger. Working together with Elbert Gary, counsel for Illinois, Gates was able to bring the firms together to form the American Steel and Wire Company. Morgan was contacted for aid in proposed expansions, and together with Gary, formed Federal Steel, capitalized at $200 million, out of American Steel and Wire and five other companies. The new firm was headed by Gary, and Robert Bacon, a Morgan partner who had risen to take Coster's place in the organization, represented the Wall Street interests on the Board. Gates was excluded from membership. "I don't think property is safe in his hands," said Morgan, who controlled the new giant company.[36]

Andrew Carnegie had dominated the iron and steel industry during the 1890s. Together with his on-again, off-again partner, Henry Clay Frick, he undercut competition, bullied other ironmongers, and in general ruled his sector of the economy like a tzar while talking like a saint.

He had mixed feelings regarding the Federal Steel merger; he disliked the new competition which could be construed as a threat from Wall Street. Carnegie distrusted the Exchange crowd, viewing the bankers as parasites. At another time he might have relished the idea of destroying Federal through price competition, but by 1899 he was ready to retire to a life of philanthropy. In his *Gospel of Wealth* he later wrote that "the day is not far distant when the man who dies leaving behind him millions of available wealth . . . will pass 'unwept, unhonoured, and unsung.'" Carnegie believed that "the man who dies rich, dies disgraced."[37]

In 1899, Carnegie broke with Frick, reorganized his company, and made affable Charles M. Schwab its president. Frick had represented those in the firm who supported cooperation with the new iron and steel companies in pooling arrangements. Carnegie had tried this policy, indicating his willingness to join in a pool with Federal and other producers. But when it was suggested that each member be treated as an equal, Carnegie withdrew from the negotiations and abandoned support of the Frick policies. Schwab represented those who wanted to combine with the new companies to form a giant trust, which would control most of the iron and steel production in the nation. "A big business enterprise," he said, "is invariably built up around one man."[38] With Carnegie's support, he wanted to be that man.

Carnegie had granted William Moore an option to buy his company for $157,950,000 in 1899. When Moore was unable to meet the terms in the specified period, he forfeited one million dollars, which was held in escrow. Later in the year Carnegie offered to sell the company to Rockefeller for a quarter of a billion dollars. Although John D. was in the industry through control of Lake Superior Consolidated Iron Mining Company, he was not interested in taking over the firm at that price. Reluctantly, Carnegie was forced to admit to himself that if he was to sell his holdings, it would have to be through Morgan, the distrusted leader of the hated Wall Street Crowd.

In 1900, Carnegie announced a great expansion program, one

which would threaten the very existence of Federal and the other steel firms. The other companies were panic-stricken, and they asked Morgan to buy out Carnegie and set the steel industry aright as he had formerly rationalized the rails. At first Morgan refused, thinking the project unworthy on Carnegie's terms. But he did not dismiss the idea entirely; he hated Carnegie, as he did all disruptive forces in the economy, and he was still smarting from the Scot's withdrawal from the pooling plan. It would be a great triumph to rid the industry of him.

On December 12, 1900, Morgan heard Schwab give an optimistic speech concerning the future of steel. If only integration could be carried out, he said, the possibilities for the industry would be boundless. Morgan saw Schwab later that evening, and told the young man that he might be willing to do business with Carnegie if the price were right. A few days later he called Gates to his office, and asked whether Schwab was the best instrument through which to approach Carnegie. Bet-A-Million said that he was, and Schwab was called to the Morgan offices in New York. After some haggling, the two men agreed on a price of $400 million for the Carnegie properties, of which Carnegie's own share was $217,720,000. The Scot insisted that he be paid in first mortgage bonds. Some believe that he requested this settlement because he expected the new steel trust to fail, after which he would foreclose and take over once more.[39] This seems unlikely, however, for Carnegie spent the rest of his life in philanthropic work, and never gave any serious indication of wanting to return to the business world. He enjoyed this last great coup, however, since he received an amount far in excess of the firm's worth from Morgan. "Pierpont feels that he can do anything because he has always got the best of the Jews in Wall Street," he said. "It takes a Yankee to beat a Jew, and it takes a Scot to beat a Yankee!"

The new United States Steel Company was formed through the merger of Carnegie properties with Federal, Rockefeller's Lake Superior Iron, and other firms in February of 1901. As expected, Schwab was made president. The company was capitalized at $1,-404,000,000, with $304 million in bonds, and the rest divided equally between the preferred and common stock. Since the physical valuation of the properties was only $682 million, a good part of the preferred, and all of the common, was water.[40] This presented a serious problem to the Morgan interests: would the public, especially those who knew of the mergers and the nature of the capitalization, accept the stock?

A banker's syndicate was formed to guarantee successful flotation to the extent of $200 million, and Morgan put his entire organization behind the issues. James Keene was called in to act as field marshal at the Exchange during the flotation. The brokers were organized behind Harry Content to push the stock. Keene was asked why he bothered to take such work, since he was a millionaire in his own right. "Why does a dog chase his thousandth rabbit?" he replied. "All life is a speculation. The spirit of speculation is born with me."[41]

Keene carried out the task with his usual perfection. He would sell a thousand shares, and then buy back a hundred to support the stock, thus playing with the price while at the same time buoying it. The fluctuations made some rich, but others lost heavily. The winners stayed in the market to get richer, while the losers remained to recoup their losses. An air of unreality was introduced when the "Pittsburgh Crowd" entered the arena. These were men who had sold their properties to Morgan, and now had millions to burn. They contributed to the wild market conditions, and helped support the demand for the two Steel issues. The initial price of the common on the curb was 38, while the preferred sold for 82¾. Half a million shares of each were sold during the first two days of trading. In this period the common rose four points and the preferred, five. Within a month the prices had risen to 55 and 101⅞. The Steel flotation sparked an April rise, and the bull market went into high gear. In a state of exuberance, and not a bit tired after his great success, Morgan boarded the *Teutonic* in early April for his annual spring trip to England. For the moment, at least, there seemed not a cloud on the horizon.[42]

While Morgan was away, E. H. Harriman began to play, busying himself by organizing a rail empire in the West. In February he had wrested control of the Union Pacific from Speyer & Co., and by creating a mortgage of $100 million on the road, he was able to take the Southern Pacific as well. This gave him a system that rivaled the Hill-Morgan combine of the Great Northern and the Northern Pacific. Between the two systems lay the Chicago, Burlington & Quincy, which was controlled by Northern Pacific. Harriman had sought an interest in the Burlington, but had been tricked out of it by James Hill. He then decided to stage a raid on the Hill-Morgan citadel itself: the Northern Pacific.

Harriman understood the magnitude of the task he had set for himself. By 1901 the House of Morgan was the center of a gigantic financial empire which would later be characterized as "the money trust." George F. Baker, head of the First National Bank, was Morgan's ally, and had thrown his weight behind Hill and the Northern Pacific. The National City Bank, whose gold reserves were second only to those of the U.S. Treasury, could usually be counted upon for help, although its dour president "Sunny Jim" Stillman had significant connections with the Rockefellers as well as with Morgan. The Bankers and Guarantee Trust Companies, among the largest in the nation, were in the Morgan camp, along with several important insurance companies.[43] The Morgan community of interests was a juggernaut in 1901.

Despite this, Harriman had good reason to hope for success. After besting Schiff in the contest for Union Pacific, he employed the Kuhn, Loeb leader as his investment banker. Unlike Morgan, Schiff did not control banks directly, but he had close relations with several New York firms as well as a strong hold on many central European houses. In any fight with Morgan the Harriman-Schiff forces could call on Rockefeller and the "Standard Oil Crowd," which had clashed with Morgan on several occasions and could be counted upon to aid his enemies. No one knew exactly how much money John D. and his family and friends controlled, but it was easily the largest fortune in the nation.[44]

In late April, while the stock market boom was at its peak, James Hill was in Seattle on an inspection trip of the Northern Pacific and Great Northern. Although he had scant interest in the Exchange, always considering himself a builder and leaving his financial matters to Morgan, he noticed that concentrated buying was taking place in Northern Pacific. Ordinarily he would have contacted Morgan and allowed the banker to take care of whoever dared buy large amounts of the stock. But Morgan was in Europe, and Hill, not taking any chances, ordered a special train to take him to New York. Without bothering to stop at Morgan's offices, Hill headed straight for Jacob Schiff, who he knew was Harriman's banker. Ignoring the usual pleasantries, he got right down to business: was Harriman behind the purchases? Schiff was equally frank: not only was he buying shares for Harriman, but he boasted of having gained control of Northern Pacific for his customer. Then followed a strange scene in which both men claimed to have a majority of stock and each believed he was telling the truth. In this case, Schiff's knowledge was superior to that of Hill. That morning he had bought a block of

35,000 preferred shares from a Morgan associate who did not suspect a raid was on. This was done without notifying Bacon, who was in charge during Morgan's absence. With this sale, control of the total amount of preferred and common combined passed to the Harriman-Schiff group.[45] Hill-Morgan still had a good block of the common shares, but the preferred had voting rights. Hill stormed out of the Kuhn, Loeb offices and told Bacon of the developments. A few hours later, on the evening of May 3, Bacon cabled Morgan asking authority to buy 150,000 shares of Northern Pacific common. His plan was simple: Hill-Morgan would gain a majority of the common shares, and then vote to retire the preferred at the next Board meeting. This would leave Harriman with a sizable amount of cash and a large block of common stock, but without control of the road. Morgan wired back his approval at once, but Bacon did not receive the cable until Sunday, May 5. On Friday evening, therefore, Bacon awaited the reply, as Schiff retired for the night, convinced that he had Northern Pacific in his pocket. Bacon planned a council of war for the following morning, while Schiff, as usual, expected to go to his synagogue for Sabbath services.[46]

During that evening Harriman paced his bedroom floor. One of the shrewdest men in America, he never made the mistake of underestimating Morgan. In order to insure his control of the road, he decided to buy an additional 40,000 shares of common stock the following day, thus giving him a majorty of the common as well as the preferred. On Saturday morning he called Kuhn, Loeb, and put in the order for execution at the market. He then relaxed, feeling that he had outsmarted Morgan and had taken control of the railroad empire of the Far West. His order, however, was never carried out. Schiff was contacted by his partner at the synagogue, and asked for the go-ahead for the purchase. Refusing to do business on the Sabbath, Schiff told the partner not to execute the order; he would take full responsibility for whatever happened.[47] Harriman thought he was safe that Sunday, but Bacon, having received the Morgan cable, called in James Keene and planned a buying campaign to secure Northern Pacific for the Hill-Morgan group.

On Monday morning the Kuhn, Loeb forces led by Otto Kahn, entered the Exchange arena, while from another entrance came Keene and Harry Content, who had carried off the U.S. Steel flotation. Keene, who was not a member of the Exchange, retired to the offices of broker Talbot Taylor, and directed operations from there. Content stayed on the floor, receiving messages from the Silver Fox through broker Edward Norton. The transfer of orders was done with a secrecy that would have done credit to the F.B.I.[48] During the first hour, while no one realized what was happening, Keene started to buy his 150,000 shares. In the middle of the day, Schiff announced that Harriman had control of Northern Pacific. Keene knew better, and continued to buy. By evening Morgan had a clear majority of the common shares, in the process having run the price up from 110 to 149¾. Harriman apparently thought that he too had bought enough shares to give him a majority of the common. Meanwhile, some traders, thinking the price could not hold and ignorant of the Morgan-Harriman duel, had sold blocks of stock short, expecting to buy them back when the price fell. Morgan and Harriman were not trying to gain a corner, however; each man expected to hold on to the shares he had bought. On Tuesday more shares were sold short, and Keene fulfilled his quota of 150,000 shares. Wednesday saw more heavy trading in Northern Pacific. The rude awakening came on Thursday, May 9, when the shorts, trying to buy shares for delivery and finding that none were to be had, panicked and threw the Exchange into a turmoil.

The night before, rumors had circulated at Peacock Alley of the Waldorf that there were no shares of Northern Pacific to be had. The following morning several brokers called for delivery of shares, causing a flurry of buying at the Northern Pacific post. The stock opened at 170, went to 200, stabilized, and then shot upward, reaching 1000 before trading had ended. Baruch, who was present at the Exchange on Black Thursday, recalls the hectic trading most vividly.

> When one broker walked into the crowd, other traders, thinking he might have some Northern Pacific stock, charged him, banging him against the railing.
>
> "Let me go, will you?" he roared. "I haven't a share of the d——d stock. Do you think I carry it in my clothes?"
>
> Then, through the desperate crowd strode Al Stern, of Hertzfield & Stern, a young and vigorous broker. He had come as an emissary of Kuhn, Loeb & Company, which was handling Harriman's purchases of Northern Pacific. Stern blithely inquired: "Who wants to borrow Northern Pacific. I have a block to lend."
>
> The first response was a deafening shout. There was an infinitesimal pause and then the desperate brokers rushed at Stern. Struggling to get near enough to him to shout their bids, they kicked over stock tickers. Strong brokers thrust aside the weak ones. Hands were waving and trembling in the air.

Almost doubled over on a chair, his face close to a pad, Stern began to note his transactions. He would mumble to one man, "All right, you get it," and then complain to another, "For heaven's sake, don't stick your finger in my eye."

One broker leaned over and snatched Stern's hat, with which he beat a tattoo on Stern's head to gain attention.

"Put back my hat!" shrieked Stern. "Don't make such a confounded excitement and maybe I can do better by you."

But the traders continued to push and fight and nearly climbed over one another's backs to get to Stern. They were like thirst-crazed men battling for water, with the biggest, strongest, and loudest faring best.

Soon Stern had loaned the last of his stock. His face white, and his clothes disheveled, he managed to break away.[49]

In order to raise money for the Northern Pacific purchases, the shorts had to sell their other holdings. As a result, almost every stock except Northern Pacific fell during the day. Atchison, Topeka, and Santa Fe broke 47 points, Delaware and Hudson 74 points, and Union Pacific 57 points. Prices declined $30 on the average during the record 3,336,695 share session.[50] The apple of Morgan's eye, the six-week-old U.S. Steel was no exception to the collapse. The record of the trading is shown in Table 9.4.

Table 9.4—Transactions in U.S. Steel, May 9, 1901[51]

1000	shares at	40
600		39½
1500		39
2900		38½
500		38
300		37
500		36
200		34½
100		34
400		32
1000		34½
100		34
200		32
500		31
800		32
200		30⅞
100		29¾
1000		29
4000		28
500		27
100		26

Neither Harriman nor the Morgan forces had expected this collapse, and they both stepped in to bring order. Each agreed to settle their contracts at $150 a share, and four banks raised $19.5 million to lend cash for the purchases. The market calmed down, and within a week conditions were back to normal. The opposing forces held a series of meetings to decide what would be done regarding Northern Pacific. When Morgan returned from Europe in July, he presided over a reorganization of the railroad, which gave Harriman representation on the Board; he was also given a voice on the Burlington, his original aim. That road was pledged not to compete with the Union Pacific and Southern Pacific, and to remain neutral in any future clashes between Harriman-Schiff and Hill-Morgan.[52]

Morgan had been fought to a standstill for the first time since his dominance of the Street; Harriman gained a reputation as a financial power to match his fame as a railroad tycoon. Each had learned to respect, if not to like, the other. Shortly after they formed the Northern Securities Pacific Company, a trust that included the Great Northern, the Northern Pacific, and the Burlington. As for Schiff, he rested for several months before returning to full time duty. Bacon retired the following November and was replaced by George W. Perkins. Morgan's right-hand man had power and financial rewards, but the battle had been man-killing.[53]

Harriman went on a European tour after the Northern Securities deal was completed, and met many of the crowned heads of the continent, with whom he conferred as an equal. He had hoped to speak with Emperor Franz Joseph, but a meeting could not be arranged. Harriman realized that emperors had pressing schedules. "I am in a position to realize the magnitude of this monarch's task," he said.[54]

Back in New York, Bet-A-Million Gates, who had suffered heavy losses on Black Thursday, refused to be dismayed. When a friend remarked that "a lot of fellows going around here (are) saying you had your head kicked off," the philosophical Gates, twirling his cigar and rolling his eyes, replied:

Well, I will tell you. Once out in Youngstown, there was a yellow dog. He was a homely cur, and every one that came along gave him a kick in the rear. The dog became cock-eyed from watching for these kicks from behind, and also got in the habit of walking sideways. Well, they had me cock-eyed and walking sideways for a while, but I managed to straighten out in the stretch, and I was coming strong at the finish.[55]

Morgan turned his attention to plans for still bigger things after the crash. *Life,* the humor magazine of the day, published a cartoon about his activities during the summer:[56]

Question: Who made the world, Charles?
Answer: God made the world in 4004 B.C., but it was reorganized in 1901 by James J. Hill, J. Pierpont Morgan, and John D. Rockefeller.

The market continued its upward climb during most of 1902. Although volume was below that of 1901, the share turnover reached 207 per cent, making it second only to the previous year in activity. Over one billion dollars worth of new securities were listed on the Exchange, many coming from those companies which had merged the previous year. The consolidation and merger movement began to slow down, however, as the second quarter of the year was the only one in the past three years in which fewer than 100 firms disappeared.[57] The railroad average hit a new high, the peak of that stage of the bull market (see Table 9.5). In addition, business conditions remained good, and production would continue to rise through the first half of 1903 (Table 9.6).

Table 9.5—Railroad Average, 1897–1902[58]

	High	Low
1897	59.99	45.46
1898	67.04	52.55
1899	76.79	66.72
1900	84.87	68.49
1901	103.98	81.36
1902	116.27	101.03

But there were troubles. The money market was strained, as demands for capital exceeded even the increasing supplies of 1902. Some of the newer mergers seemed shaky, and it became difficult to float several issues. This situation was considered temporary by the Morgan group; J.P. called the unbought issues "undigested securities." Hill, who realized that the market was outrunning the economy, was more realistic; he called them "undigestible securities."[59]

Another cause of worry involved the new President, Theodore Roosevelt, who took office when McKinley was assassinated in September, 1901. Although T. R. was given to bombast, his actions during

Table 9.6—Industrial Production, 1897–1900[60]

Year and Quarter		Industrial Production, Adjusted (1947–1949 = 100)
1897	1	13.8
	2	14.4
	3	15.8
	4	16.5
1898	1	16.3
	2	16.3
	3	16.0
	4	16.6
1899	1	17.2
	2	17.7
	3	18.5
	4	18.6
1900	1	18.6
	2	18.7
	3	17.4
	4	17.4
1901	1	19.0
	2	20.0
	3	20.3
	4	20.2
1902	1	20.5
	2	20.3
	3	21.2
	4	22.4
1903	1	22.8
	2	23.1

his first few months in office were conservative, and business thought that he could be trusted to protect its interests. Then, in February, 1902, Attorney-General Philander Knox entered an antitrust action against Northern Securities, which he attacked as a "virtual consolidation of two competing transcontinental lines."[61] The news was noticed, but not considered important on Wall Street.[62] On April 10, 1903, a circuit court decided for the government, and a brief panic hit the Street; Morgan delayed his European vacation for a week so as to set things aright. The trust appealed to the Supreme Court, however, and the financial district, including the analysts of the *New York Times* and *Tribune,* expected the decision to be reversed.[63]

On April 22, several days after the circuit court decision, the Exchange announced that its new building was ready for occupancy. The day was sunny, and the brokers gathered outside the new building—the present Exchange—to cheer the officials and officers of the organization. Morgan, Exchange President Keppler, Mayor Seth Low and others spoke to the happy group. Henry Clews, by then a patriarch, described the quarters:

> The Stock Exchange building is a fine, solid structure, devoid of anything showy, pretentious or decorative. It was designed by James Renwick, the architect of Grace Church and of St. Patrick's Roman Catholic Cathedral, on Fifth Avenue and Fiftieth Street. The cost of the building was nearly $2,000,000. It costs nearly $200,000 a year to pay the salaries of the various officials and keep the building in proper repair. The apparatus for ventilating the building is one of the best. Its cost $30,000, and supplies an abundance of pure air and perfumes at the same time. The heating and cooling arrangements are the best of their kind, and the lighting is admirable. There are three chandeliers containing 200 electric lamps, which throw a flood of beautiful soft light around the whole interior. The building is well supplied with rooms for members, lavatories, and closets, which contain more than a thousand safes for the safe keeping of securities. About 400 of those safes are let to people who are not members. The vaults and safes are considered the strongest in the world.[64]

To Clews and his fellow brokers, the new Exchange symbolized the permanent triumph of finance capitalism, which was as secure as the vaults in the basement. The nation was prosperous, peaceful, and apparently pro-business. Within little more than a decade, however, the foundations of the Exchange would be shaken. Attacks from government, depression, war, and the only important suspension of the market place would test the institution as never before.

Notes

1. Carruth, *Encyclopedia*, pp. 375–77; Walker, *Epic of American Industry*, p. 334; Lloyd Morris, *Not So Long Ago* (New York, 1949), pp. 15–16.

2. William Allen White, *The Autobiography of William Allen White* (New York, 1946), p. 285, as quoted in Faulkner, *Politics, Reform and Expansion*, p. 209.

3. *Ibid.*, pp. 209–10.

4. *Ibid.*, p. 268.

5. Mark Sullivan, *Our Times: The Turn of the Century* (New York, 1927), pp. 298–99.

6. Faulkner, *Decline of Laissez Faire*, p. 24.

7. Clark, *History of Manufactures*, Vol. II, p. 10; Noyes, *Forty Years of American Finance*, pp. 272–73; Studenski and Krooss, *Financial History of the United States*, p. 249; Forbes, *Men Who Are Making America*, p. 331.

8. Edwards, *Evolution of Finance Capitalism*, p. 161.

9. Noyes, *Forty Years of American Finance,* pp. 278–79; Willis and Bogen, *Investment Banking,* p. 230.

10. Noyes, *Forty Years of American Finance,* p. 273.

11. *Ibid.,* p. 279.

12. Edwards, *Evolution of Finance Capitalism,* p. 184.

13. Corey, *House of Morgan,* p. 226.

14. Medina, pp. 19–20, 25–26, 79–80, 105–106; Victor Perlo, *The Empire of High Finance* (New York, 1957), pp. 182–83; Forbes, *Men Who Are Making America,* p. 365.

15. Baruch, *My Own Story,* pp. 131–32.

16. Robert Warshow, *Bet A Million Gates: The Story of a Plunger* (New York, 1932), pp. 62–63.

17. Baruch, *My Own Story,* pp. 109, 152.

18. Sparling, *Mystery Men of Wall Street,* p. 240.

19. Holbrook, *Age of the Moguls,* pp. 169–70; Neill, *Inside Story of the Stock Exchange,* pp. 159–60.

20. Ralph E. Nelson, *Merger Movements in American Industry, 1895–1956* (Princeton, 1959), p. 6.

21. *Ibid.,* p. 37.

22. Cochran, *American Business System,* pp. 58–59.

23. Moody, *Masters of Capital,* pp. 84–85.

24. Nelson, *Merger Movements,* p. 55.

25. *Ibid.,* pp. 161–63.

26. George W. Bishop, Jr., *Charles H. Dow and the Dow Theory* (New York, 1960), p. 137.

27. *Ibid.,* p. 135.

28. T. R. Navin and M. V. Sears, "The Rise of a Market for Industrial Securities, 1887–1902," *The Business History Review,* June, 1955, as quoted in *ibid.,* p. 89.

29. Holbrook, *Age of the Moguls,* p. 202.

30. Nelson, *Merger Movements,* p. 90.

31. New York Stock Exchange, *Fact Book, 1961* (New York, 1962), pp. 42–43.

32. Adler, *Schiff,* Vol. I, p. 34.

33. Stedman, *New York Stock Exchange,* p. 276.

34. Noyes, *Forty Years of American Finance,* pp. 300–301.

35. *New York Times,* May 1, 1901.

36. Winkler, *Morgan the Magnificent,* p. 202.

37. Forbes, *Men Who Are Making America,* p. 36.

38. Moody, *Masters of Capital,* p. 79.

39. Josephson, *Robber Barons,* p. 431.

40. Edwards, *Evolution of Finance Capitalism,* pp. 186–87.

41. Baruch, *My Own Story,* p. 157.

42. Noyes, *Market Place,* pp. 188–89; Satterlee, *J. Pierpont Morgan,* pp. 350–51.

43. Fritz Redlich, *The Molding of American Banking: Men and Ideas* (New York, 1951), Part II, pp. 392–93.

44. Corey, *House of Morgan,* pp. 260–61.

45. Satterlee, *J. Pierpont Morgan,* p. 354; Frederick Lewis Allen, *The Lords of Creation* (New York, 1935), p. 55.

46. Satterlee, *J. Pierpont Morgan,* pp. 354–55.

47. Winkler, *Morgan the Magnificent,* pp. 188–89.

48. Baruch, *My Own Story,* p. 145.

49. *Ibid.*, pp. 143–44. Baruch states that this happened on Tuesday. But from his description and the newspaper accounts, it would appear that the incident took place on Thursday.

50. *New York Stock Exchange Fact Book, 1961*, p. 43. Given the amount of shares listed at the time, the May 9 trading would be equivalent to a 38 million-share day, today. Not until 1925 was the volume figure of that date topped.

51. Allen, *Lords of Creation*, pp. 61–62.

52. Winkler, *Morgan the Magnificent*, pp. 196–97.

53. Moody, *Masters of Capital*, p. 104.

54. Eckenrode and Edmunds, *E. H. Harriman*, pp. 232–33.

55. Warshow, *Gates*, pp. 98–99.

56. Sullivan, *Our Times*, Vol. II, pp. 369–70; Winnkler, *Morgan the Magnificent*, p. 197.

57. Nelson, *Merger Movements*, p. 164.

58. Pratt, *Work of Wall Street*, p. 254.

59. Faulkner, *Decline of Laissez-Faire*, pp. 26–27.

60. Nelson, *Merger Movements*, p. 164.

61. Sullivan, *Our Times*, Vol. II, p. 412.

62. *New York Times*, April 2, 1902.

63. *Ibid.*, April 15, 1903; *New York Tribune*, April 18, 1903.

64. Clews, *Fifty Years in Wall Street*, p. 88.

10

The End of the Golden Age: 1903-1913

The Ten Commandments

1. Remember a bear market always begins when everything is brightest and the public most bullish, and when volumes of transactions are largest on the advances.
2. A bull market begins at the end of a bear campaign when everything is darkest and the public are selling stocks.
3. Again, watch for the large volume days when you may reasonably suppose the bottom has been reached.
4. Remember, by the time the news gossip has reached you it is very apt to be stale and is probably sent out for the very purpose of getting the public on the wrong side of the market.
5. New extreme movements when they pass old extreme movements nearly always come back to former extreme movements.
6. On the bear movement watch for days of large bear volumes, note the lowest figures recorded, and when the market starts upward immediately send in your order to buy on the second downward movement to the previous low figures. On an extreme bull movement reverse the operation.
7. Never trade in more than your capital will allow you to. Margin at least five points and preferably ten, because then when you have to take a small loss you will not feel it so seriously as would be the case were you to trade on narrow margin. Let small loads and big margins be your watchword.
8. Drop all sentiment, pay no attention to new gossip, points, or tips, but merely become a machine with sufficient power to execute your orders according to market movements as previously explained.

9. Always stop your trade at a small loss in case it should go beyond former extreme figures on the second movement, and in this way you are always in a position to make large profits with a probability of doing so largely in your favor, while your losses will always be limited to a small amount.

10. When the market starts in any direction, continue buying or selling as the case may be, using your profit for additional margin, always keeping plenty of margin in your favor. Your profit would then be something immense in proportion to the amount invested.

Golden Rule: When in Doubt, Do Nothing.

L. C. Van Riper, *The Ins and Outs of Wall Street*

IF THE CIVIL WAR ERA witnessed the emergence of the securities salesman, the postwar period saw the first significant beginnings of financial journalism. Fathered by the growing interest in securities, it led more investors and speculators to Wall Street. Financial journalism was not new, nor was it originally American. A weekly review of London commercial activities was published by a J. Haughton in 1692. The historian Macauley gleaned his information on the stock markets from Haughton's short discussions. As far as is known, this shadowy figure was the first of the market "tipsters."[1]

There were analysts in colonial America—writers who tried to find meaning in the commodities markets wrote in New York, Boston, and Philadelphia. During the early national period the New York press reported on the activities of William Duer and Jacob Little, and columnists attempted to foresee their next moves. *Prices Current, Niles' Weekly Register,* and the *United States Commercial and Shipping Register,* business publications all, wrote of the securities markets in the 1840s and 1850s. *Hunt's Merchant Magazine* was the *Fortune* of that day, while the *United States Economist* and the short-lived *Bankers' Magazine* resembled *Barron's* and *Forbes,* respectively.[2]

During the post-bellum period, Henry Varnum Poor's *American Railroad Journal* became the most important publication in its field. "A reformer, geographer, statistician, journalist, man of business, and an accepted expert on American railroad finance and operation," Poor was also the first of the modern market analysts.[3] He always considered himself a spokesman for industry and Wall Street, and worked for a better understanding of both by the literate public. In 1868 he began to collect information for his *Manual of the Railroads of the*

United States which, by the early 1880s, had over 5,000 subscribers. The *Manual* analyzed securities as well as offering information, and may be considered the first stock market service in this country. Poor's writings of this period sound familiar a century later. In 1851, for example, he wrote:

> We would advise our country friends to keep out of the market for the present. In a short time the immense amount of bonds which have been recently thrown upon the market will gradually find their way to the holders for investment, and thus create an opening for a new supply. A few weeks we believe will witness a favorable change, of which we will give our readers timely notice. The quickest and surest way to improve the market, is to guard against overstocking it.[4]

In the 1880s John Moody, an analyst for a Wall Street firm, got the idea of publishing information on market conditions in bound volumes, to be sold at stiff prices. His first *Manual of Industrial Statistics,* released in 1900, did for the growing industrials what Poor had done for the rails.[5] C. W. Barron, a Boston analyst, began striking off handbills with market information in 1887. In those days "the Barron Service consisted chiefly of C.W.B. legging nimbly around State Street, C.W.B.'s nimble fingers flying over copy sheets, the little hand-fed press banging away, and the two delivery boys running around with C.W.B.'s little hansards."[6] Charles H. Dow, who was later to eclipse all other financial journalists, came to New York in 1880, after a newspaper career which had taken him from Providence, Rhode Island to Leadville, Colorado. Following a short period during which he worked as a financial reporter for the Kiernan News Agency, he organized the Dow-Jones service in 1882. With Edward D. Jones, he published "flimsies" (short newsletters) at first and bought a seat on the Exchange three years later. (In January, 1899, the partnership dissolved, although Dow never took Jones' name from the door.) On July 8, 1899, Dow turned his flimsies into the *Wall Street Journal,* which soon became the most influential nonbanking voice in the district.[7]

Before financial journalism in general and stock market letters in particular could reach a degree of maturity and importance, the companies had to release sufficient data so as to make meaningful analysis possible, and there had to be a market for such information.

Poor found that only half the states in the nation had enough information for him to use in the *Manual,* and that others were publishing incompetent and incomplete records. The *Commercial and Financial Chronicle,* commenting on a report issued by the government on the Union Pacific, wrote: "The champions of government supervision and control of railroads may find somewhat of a damper thrown upon their enthusiasm when they reflect that it takes a government official nearly seven months after the close of any period to get up his report for that period."[8] Part of the reason for this inefficiency was government laxness, but mainly it reflected a desire on the part of management to keep financial and other information private.

Conditions began to change during the 1880s. The Interstate Commerce Act of 1887, the first in a series of regulatory measures, marked the start of a new era in government-industry relations. One of the provisions of the Act required the carriers to submit regular reports, and this information was released to the press, making more accurate analysis possible. As we have already seen, the Exchange had required listed companies to submit annual reports as early as 1895, and five years later such reports were made a prerequisite for listing. Despite this, there were no reports in 1895 and 1896. Then, in 1897, the Kansas City Gas Company announced that it would "from time to time, make publication of its new profits not less than twice each year." Most other Exchange firms followed suit, but full disclosure was still more than thirty years away.[9] In 1903 Henry H. Rogers, later a member of the Rockefeller inner circle but then a promoter of copper and other interests, told Thomas Lawson to "just tell those people (stockholders) that our way of doing business is to send out reports when we decide it is time for them to be seen."[10] Peter A. B. Widener, a director of U. S. Steel and chairman of the Metropolitan Street Railway of New York, was able to conduct a stockholders' meeting with an iron fist in 1902.

WIDENER: The teller will now take the vote.

STOCKHOLDER: We wish a discussion of this matter. Let us discuss it before we vote for it.

WIDENER: Well, you can vote for it and discuss it afterward.

STOCKHOLDER (*amazed, incredulously*): Do you mean to say that we must vote and then discuss?

ANOTHER STOCKHOLDER: You wish us to be executed first, then tried, is that it? We object to voting before discussion.

WIDENER (*bored, smiling*): Well, sir, you may withhold your vote until after the discussion. The Chair orders that the vote shall be taken.

Widener pushed his proposal—one which manipulated the lease of a line and granted it to another corporation—and got it accepted over the minority protests. It should be noted that the opposition was not made up of small stockholders, but of a group that was trying to seize control of the line in order to milk it even more.[11]

Bankers and businessmen resented government and Exchange attempts at extracting information from corporations, and they gave short shrift to the financial reporters. Once, after waiting for several hours, reporters were given the following communiqué by two of the most important businessmen of the day:[12]

The United States of America is a great and growing country.
Signed, James Stillman
Henry C. Frick
This is confidential and not for publication unless names are withheld.

Yet, several years later Otto Kahn could say that "Finance, instead of avoiding publicity in all its aspects, should welcome and seek it. Publicity won't hurt its dignity. A dignity which can be preserved only by seclusion, which cannot hold its own in the market place, is neither merited or worth having." The banker told his fellows that "We must more and more get out of the seclusion of our offices, out into the rough and tumble of democracy, out to get to know people and get known by them."[13]

Whatever Kahn's motivations might have been, the nature of the stock market during the bull period of 1897–1906 made such an attitude useful, if not mandatory. This was not so because of government and Exchange regulations, or an awakening of honor among the bankers. Rather, it came about due to the fulfillment of the second condition: the growth of a market for financial information.

During the bull market Main Street came to Wall Street where it would stay, much to its ultimate regret, until late 1929. The small investor, faced with the choice of buying hundreds of old securities, or perhaps becoming interested in the new flotations, was grist for the mill as far as financial writers and would-be experts were concerned. If corporations did not issue information (accurate or adulterated), if bankers were not careful of how they treated the press (if not the shareholders), their projects might not be bought by the small investors, whose funds became increasingly more important during the years preceding 1907.

During the early years of the nineteenth century financial news was printed in a dispassionate manner along with lists of stock, bond, and commodity prices. What advertisements there were on the financial pages consisted of notices of new incorporations, dividend reports, and commercial statements. By the end of the century this had changed. Financial news was colored, sometimes by writers in the pay of or under the influence of promoters. The future dean of American finance journalism, Alexander Noyes, a young reporter at this time, wrote:

> In 1902, outspoken criticism . . . was not the less necessary, because much financial writing of that day was based on the mistaken view that to praise a rising speculative market of whatever character, and to predict its indefinite continuance, was to help American prosperity. Perhaps because of this idea, a writer's judgement was sometimes unhappily perverted by engaging personally in speculation. In no instance known to me was money actually paid by interested speculators or promoters for newspaper articles approving unqualifiedly speculative undertakings. But in those days, "underwriting syndicates" formed to guarantee the successful floating of a Wall Street enterprise, frequently ended, after making little or no actual requisition on the guarantors, by distributing to such participants the large cash commission which had been agreed upon. . . . To a degree which today would be difficult to understand, principals in such undertakings, during 1902, endeavored to interest a financial writer for the press—usually through assuring him that responsibility incurred through the placing of his name on the underwriting list was purely nominal, that the subscriptions would never be called up, but that he would share the resultant profits. Comparatively few of the financial critics accepted such overtures. . . .[14]

Since a writer might have to raise funds should the issue fail, and could make a large amount of money should it succeed, he would often "help it along" with well-placed stories about the rosy future of the corporation. This type of reporting did not end with reporters and other small fry; even the publishers could be reached. Frank Munsey, owner of *Munsey's Magazine,* was one of the leading muckrakers. His publication attacked the evils of big business in almost every issue, and led crusades against corruption during the Progressive era. Munsey never attacked U. S. Steel however, and with good cause; from 1907 to 1911, he was its biggest stockholder.[15]

Toward the end of the century a new kind of advertisement appeared on the financial pages, and as "finance grew more frenzied" it increased in importance. This was the "tipster report," which today is an important constituent of most financial pages. Most reports bordered on the sensational. In December, 1904, for example, the following appeared in the *New York Times:*[16]

> Subscribe immediately to our *Daily Message* and secure this GUARANTEED SPECIAL #29. Trade upon it heavily. We know what we are talking about. Ask no further questions. Just get our message and trade. The more you carry the more money you will make. All of our previous promises have been fulfilled to the letter.
>
>   *Hunter's Daily Message—*$10 a month.

The claim of "all . . . previous promises have been fulfilled" was not hyperbole; such claims were often true. Sometimes this was done through manipulations and "matching orders." A manipulator would sell himself stock at increasingly higher prices. This would cost him nothing but broker's commissions, and on the following day, the newspapers would print stories of how XYZ stock had risen on heavy volume. Outsiders would then be attracted to the issue, and then they would send it up in the usual manner. Another reason for rises after these predictions was the self-fulfilling prophecy which has been described earlier: if one predicts that a stock will rise, and enough people believe in and act on the prediction, their purchases will cause the rise to occur. Another device used by the tipsters was double-talk; many had a facility with words which enabled them to ramble on for pages without actually having said anything. Then, no matter which way the selected stock would go, the writer would claim to have predicted the movement.[17] Finally, there was the "sucker list," which became important toward the end of the bull period.

> These lists are classified into ten dollar investors, twenty-five to one hundred dollar investors, one hundred to five hundred dollar investors; and investors having $1,000 or more available. The $10 investors are mostly made up of a class of people who are in the habit of taking a small flyer occasionally of not more than $10, investing this amount on the theory that it may turn out with a big profit, but that in any event the loss cannot exceed $10. . . . In number these $10 investor lists run into the hundred thousands, and are the main avenue for floating all schemes of the cheaper and more openly fraudulent variety. The $25 to $50 list is made up of country investors, Methodist and Baptist ministers, country doctors and all classes of teachers; also barbers, waiters, hospital nurses, and the general class of people who are able in one way or another to set aside for a rainy day from $25 to $100 a year. . . . The $100 to $500 investors consist of doctors of a

slightly higher grade than those referred to above; also college teachers and professors, small Wall Street lambs, Episcopal and Presbyterian ministers, mercantile clerks, some country merchants and other thrifty people who annually accumulate a few hundred dollars over and above their cost of living. . . . The higher grade lists, covering $1,000 to $100,000 investors, largely explain themselves.[18]

One writer, eschewing the sucker lists, merely sent his tips on post cards to a list taken at random from the telephone directory. He recommended a worthless stock that was then selling for one dollar, telling his "customers" that it would soon hit $30.50. The suckers bought heavily—from the promoter—and the price did rise to $30.50. Soon after, however, it was below one dollar.[19]

Such financial journalism and advertisements were an important part of the bull market. The movement of prices was based on solid economic advances and excellent business conditions, which justified the upward swing. However, it was greatly oversold, and when the public's dreams of wealth were punctured, the market collapsed with greater force than should have been the case. Morgan and his like still dominated the market, but the age of the giant was passing, and the public—made up of millions of usually uninformed or poorly informed individuals whose actions were often irrational—was becoming the most important influence on the Street.

For the time being, however, the small investor played second fiddle to the great soloists. On November 6, 1906, the *Times* could write that "the four most powerful figures . . . are E. H. Harriman, H. C. Frick, H. H. Rogers, and William Rockefeller," along with the ever-present Morgan.[20] Men like these were still kings, but the small investor was gaining an important veto power.

Although he appeared more like a court jester than a ruler, Bet-A-Million Gates was one of the leaders of the Street. He went on a European business trip and vacation in 1902, and returned just in time for the 1903 panic. "I am surprised at the condition of the stock market," he told reporters who met his ship. "It is not natural. The causes are purely artificial, and they rest on a false basis. I do not believe there was ever a better time to invest in reasonable securities. I have come back stripped for the fray and I am going down into Wall Street."[21] Gates immediately plunged into the market, forming a syndicate to buy up those shares he felt were underpriced. Nevertheless, the market collapsed in the spring and fell heavily through early summer. This so-called Rich Man's Panic was over by late August, and J. P.

Morgan's return from his annual European art-collecting expedition helped restore confidence. By October, prices were on the way up. The Rich Man's Panic was merely a brief interlude in the bull market, but it was of great significance. The upper class, the insiders, suffered in 1903, not the small investors. Early in the year the latter went on a "buyers' strike," having decided that prices were too high. They sold in the early spring—along with the astute managers of the Standard Oil Empire—while Gates and most professionals bought. It was the first example of the new power of the small investor, a power which would not be fully recognized by the usually sensitive Wall Streeters for another generation.[22]

After 1903 the investment bankers consolidated their positions, destroyed competition, and expanded into new fields. The titans were not power hungry; rather, their expansion was a necessary part of the investment picture of the period. The huge combines formed by Morgan, Schiff and others rested on the market's ability to absorb new securities. The 1903 panic demonstrated that the small investor could not be relied upon completely, so the bankers turned to new sources of funds, and found them in banks, trust companies, and insurance companies, which were growing rapidly during the early twentieth century. In 1900 total bank assets were $10.79 billion and assets of life insurance companies stood at $1.74 billion. By 1907 these figures had risen to $18.15 billion and $2.93 billion, respectively.[23] If an investment banker could gain control of a large bank or insurance company, he could sell it his undigested securities and maintain a market for other offerings as well. Thus, the investment bankers took control of the financial and insurance firms during the early years of the century.

Commercial banks had always invested in securities, but they did not become important investment agents until the turn of the century. At that time Baker's First National Bank acted as Morgan's ally, bringing with it the Chase National, the Bankers Trust Company, the National Bank of Commerce, and the Guarantee Trust, all of which were controlled through stock ownership. By 1904 Baker was buying heavily in Morgan's undigested securities. Four years later he organized the First Securities Company by declaring a 100 per cent stock dividend to holders of First National equities. This securities affiliate continued to absorb Morgan's issues until the New Deal era, when such practices were outlawed.[24]

James Stillman's National City Bank followed a similar path. Always in the securities business, it underwrote Amalgamated Copper for the Rockefellers in 1899, and later floated issues for Armour and Company and others. After the 1903 panic Stillman pushed further into the securities field, working sometimes with Morgan and sometimes with the Rockefellers. A power in his own right, Stillman alone, of all commercial bankers, could afford to act in this fashion. In 1911 he formed the National City Company by paying a 40 per cent stock dividend to holders of National City stock. Like the First Securities Company, the Stillman concern acted as a purchaser of undigested stocks, usually from Kuhn, Loeb, the Rockefellers, and Harriman's heirs.[25]

These investment affiliates often bought stock forbidden to the banks by law, thus acting as a speculative influence on the Street and playing with depositors' money. Although not illegal in the strict sense of the word, this practice circumvented the spirit of the law, and was called by one writer "a masterpiece of legal humor."[26] By 1912 the securities holdings of all national banks had risen to 9.45 per cent of their assets, as compared with the 0.59 per cent of 1863. Two years later C. W. Barron estimated that two-thirds of the assets of commercial banks were invested in securities, and only one-third was being used for commercial transactions, thus making them "important institutions of developed security capitalism."[27]

In 1905 James Hazen Hyde, the effete son of the founder of the Equitable Life Assurance Society, was eased from his chairmanship by a group of financiers and capitalists headed by Hill and Frick. Hyde sold his shares in Equitable—502 out of the 1,000 issued—to Thomas Fortune Ryan. Harriman approached Ryan and told him that his friends in Albany would investigate the transaction unless half the shares were sold to him, and Ryan capitulated.

The situation at Equitable interested the publishers of the *New York World,* which in the past had been controlled by the Ryan clique and was still sympathetic to the traction magnate. The editors demanded an investigation to determine whether the Harriman group had been guilty of wrongdoing. The hue and cry set up by the *World* was soon echoed by other newspapers, and late in the year the Armstrong Committee was formed to investigate the entire insurance industry in New York. Its young, able leader, Charles Evans Hughes, quickly disclosed that many companies were under the direct or indirect control of investment bankers. Morgan ruled the New York Life Insurance Company, and loaded it with nearly $150 million of his securities. Similar stories were told of the Mutual Life, which was a Rockefeller firm, and the Equitable, controlled by the Ryan-Harriman group. For example, Mutual's assets were $500 million in 1906, and 57 per cent of this was in securities, as opposed to 11.3 per cent in 1871. Of this total, 41.4 per cent was in Rockefeller railroads. The same situations existed in the other "captive companies," which had the poorest records of any in the industry, primarily due to their rape by the investment houses. The directors were held responsible for these sorry showings. Equitable's board included Hill, Frick, Schiff, and Harriman; Mutual's directors were led by Baker, Rogers, William Rockefeller, and Speyer. The New York Life board included Stillman and the National City crowd, and its president, John A. McCall, was ranked along with Baker, Hill and Morgan as one of the most influential men on Wall Street.[28]

Thus, a complex of investment-commercial banks together with life insurance-trust companies constituted a power with enough resources to control the market under almost any circumstances, and for a while was able to counter the moves of the capricious public.[29] This Money Trust was a cause for alarm in Progressive circles, and it became a target for reformers in the 1903-1914 period. Backed by well-to-do farmers, middle class intellectuals and businessmen, and aristocratic eastern families, the Progressives mounted an attack on Wall Street which rivaled in intensity that of the New Deal a generation later.

On May 14, 1904, the Supreme Court ordered the dissolution of Northern Securities, a decision that led to a quick decline on the Exchange, caused a chill wind to pass through the investment houses, and gave Roosevelt a reputation as a trust-buster. Morgan had been stopped for the first time; unlike the Northern Pacific episode of 1901, there was no compromising differences with the Court. But Morgan seemed to realize that Roosevelt was not as anti-business as was thought at the time. After all, former Secretary of State Elihu Root defended the Morgan interests before the Court and none of the defendants went to jail.[30] Roosevelt often spoke of his capitalist convictions, and his approval of "good trusts," but the public preferred to think of Roosevelt as an enemy of big business.

The antitrust crusade reached its height on August 3, 1907, when Judge Kenesaw Mountain Landis fined Standard Oil of Indiana $29,-240,000 following convictions on 1,462 counts for accepting rebates in violation of the Elkins Act of 1903. Although the company had assets of only $10 million, the fine stood; Landis ordered the parent company, Standard of New Jersey to pay it. The Rockefeller complex underwent attacks throughout the spring and early summer of 1907, as the Progressives applauded what appeared to them the beginning of the end of the Standard Oil empire. Characteristically, they hardly noticed the fact that the Landis fine and others were set aside by higher courts.

The Armstrong investigation of 1905 sparked a wave of anti-Wall Street sentiment, leading to legislation which the insurance companies, advised by their lawyers, promptly circumvented. During the following year a movement against adulterated foods and drugs got under way, and again the corporations were under fire. The Standard Oil decision of 1907 was an indication that the attack had gone into high gear; the hero of 1901 had become the villain of 1907, and some businessmen feared he would be the corpse of 1910.

Morgan was showing signs of weakness and age, and it appeared as though his world could collapse of its own weight, even without Roosevelt's intervention. In 1903 Charles Schwab resigned from U.S. Steel to take command of reinvigorated Bethlehem Steel. In the same year the giant firm failed to earn its dividend, and the common shares fell precipitously when its payment was skipped. Morgan's International Mercantile Marine Company, formed in 1902 to control the world's seaways, ran into tough competition from the English and German state-supported lines, and was never a success. His most serious reverse came when he tried to unite the railroads of New England into a viable combination, and ended with a $400 million loss. Evidence of stock-watering, extortion, bribery, and mismanagement were later produced, and the Morgan interests were shown to have secreted $12 million from the New Haven Railroad treasury. It was also demonstrated that in the ten years after 1903, the firm had raised the capitalization of the New Haven from $93 million to $417 million, and only $20 million of this was used to better conditions on the line. Never before had such evidence of waste and malfeasance been unearthed regarding a firm of the stature of J. P. Morgan and Company.

Even more significant than these business failures was Morgan's inability to see the future of new industries. He refused to put his house solidly behind automotive firms, and he ignored motion pictures completely. It appeared as though Morgan had lost his touch, and might go the way of Jay Cooke. There seemed little likelihood of this in 1907, but it must be remembered that Cooke had appeared invulnerable in 1872.

There was, of course, a brighter side to the picture. A few months after Northern Securities was overthrown, the American Tobacco

Trust was formed. In 1900 there were 149 trusts capitalized at $4 billion; after more than seven years of attacks, and after a concerted assault on the Money Trust, there were, in 1909, 10,020 trusts capitalized at $31 billion.[31] In addition, despite the rocky road the financiers were traveling, prices on the Exchange continued to rise. The rate of the upswing in 1904, 1905, and early 1906 was the most rapid in modern American history, as prices of listed stocks doubled (see Table 10.1).

Table 10.1—Stock Prices, 1904–1906[32]

Year and Quarter		Dow-Jones Average
1904	1	36.4
	2	36.8
	3	40.6
	4	50.0
1905	1	55.9
	2	57.9
	3	60.9
	4	65.7
1906	1	73.5

The strong bull market had many supports. Industrial and agricultural prosperity continued; the wheat crops of 1904 and 1905 surpassed all previous ones save that of 1901. World gold production reached new highs, pushing prices up and stimulating the economy. Wages also rose, so the worker had his share of the general prosperity and his purchases could keep the factories humming. The Russo-Japanese War of 1905 added to the already great demands for capital for expansion of established firms, for the initiation of new enterprises, and securities. This was the case not only in America, but in other Western nations as well; 1905 and 1906 marked a high point in world-wide speculation and expansion, which strained the financial resources of every country and caused money rates to rise steadily. By the autumn of 1905 stock market booms were taking place in such cities as Alexandria, Tokyo, and several South American capitals.[33] In the summer of 1906, Harriman suddenly raised the dividend of Union Pacific from six to ten dollars. The stock rose forty points in a week, taking with it practically the entire list. Within a week a stock craze gripped Wall Street, and formerly worthless shares were taken up at inflated prices. By early autumn, the boom had extended as far as Tokyo and Berlin, with no end in sight.

At the beginning of 1907, industrial production was at an all-time peak. From an index of 20.7 in the fourth quarter of 1903 it had gone to 29.1 by 1907's second quarter.[34] Traveling securities salesmen coming back from their spring trips reported that orders had never been heavier.[35] The majority of the nation entered the year with confidence, and they grew more sure of themselves with each succeeding month.

Under the veneer of optimism, however, were several important weaknesses that caused prescient observers many sleepless nights. A real estate boom, taking place at the same time, was draining money from industry into land speculation, and this added to an already stringent financial situation. Safe loans could be had at a 6 per cent rate, while stocks were so high that medium grade issues paid around 3.5 per cent. Under such conditions, many small investors began to withdraw from the equity market to invest in bonds. Thus, while industrial production shot up during the last quarter of 1906 and the first of 1907, the Dow-Jones average fell from 71.4 to 61.3. There was no panic selling in this period, but a withdrawal of funds was evident.[36] This situation was aggravated by the financial aftermath of the San Francisco earthquake and fire of April, 1906. Reconstruction costs of some $350 million were met largely through borrowing on Wall Street, causing money to leave the market and prices to fall. In addition, the Wall Street dominated insurance firms were hard hit; after paying claims little was left to buy the undigested securities. The combination of speculation, sudden demands for funds, and an inelastic currency contributed to the money squeeze of early 1907. "Speculation on the Stock Exchange was not the chief contribution to the collapse of 1907," said Horace White in 1908, "but speculation on a much wider scale, through the length and breadth of the land, was the . . . cause."[37]

The money problem led Jacob Schiff to predict disaster as early as January 4, 1906. On that date he told a group of bankers that "If the currency conditions of this country are not changed materially . . . you will have such a panic in this country as will make all previous panics look like child's play."[38] As late as the summer of that year Schiff's fears seemed groundless; European authorities assured Americans that if they wished, they could "borrow from Europe to a practically unlimited extent."[39] But the increase in American speculation during the summer led to large exports of gold from London to New York, and by autumn, the Bank of England's reserve had fallen to a thirteen-year low. By then Europe was in no condition to help America in case of trouble. This, at a time when Hill was telling the

Merchants' Club of Chicago that unless one billion dollars were raised for railroads and industry within the next five years, "commercial paralysis" would result.[40]

A tightening of credit was evident early in 1907. This was not consequent upon poor business conditions, but rather because there simply was not enough money to pay for the world-wide expansion. It could be seen as early as April in Alexandria, when a financial crisis which had begun in January culminated in a panic. At the same time the Tokyo boom collapsed. Hamburg began to feel the pinch soon after, as did Santiago.[41] By early October the world was in the grip of a money crisis.

This financial stringency has led two leading scholars to conclude that "the panic of 1907 was exclusively banking."[42] On the surface this would appear to have been the case,[43] but the psychological aspects of the crash were also very significant, and they made the panic deeper than it might have been had only monetary forces been at work.

A year after the panic, the *Commercial and Financial Chronicle* stated that "adverse legislation, national and state, directed against railroads primarily, but also against corporations generally; political attacks against men of wealth and men of capital; the serious advocacy of political and economic doctrines which would completely change the theory of our Government and revolutionize social relations—these and kindred matters had threatened the security and stability of investment values."[44] The railroad presidents blamed the Hepburn Act of 1906 for the panic, as well as for their other difficulties. Other Progressive legislation on the federal and state levels also hurt the roads, and when Bryan proposed government ownership of the rails, the executives feared a new revolution.[45] The Pure Food and Drug Act of 1906, the disclosures of the insurance company investigations and the subsequent election of Hughes as governor of New York led many businessmen to be cautious and the public to be wary of finance. The Standard Oil fine and the general anti-business attitude of the federal government and the courts also undermined confidence. The Metropolitan Street Railroad investigation in New York, which led to new railroad and utilities legislation, caused bankers to see the long arm of the Progressives in their own back yard. All of this was behind what today would be called an erosion of optimism on Wall Street, at a time when the economic picture seemed brightest.

In 1905 Thomas Lawson wrote about his experiences on Wall Street in *Everybody's Magazine*. The brash speculator, who had conducted a spectacularly successful campaign with Amalgamated Copper, had been brought down by the Standard Oil interests, and now, posing as a friend of the "little fellow," he told how "the System" controlled Wall Street, the financial district, and the nation. His articles were immensely popular, boosting the magazine's circulation to 500,000, and were later published in book form as *Frenzied Finance*. The book was important in the calling of investigations of American finance, and opened new doors for Lawson. In late 1905 he began publishing full-page advertisements in newspapers urging the public to take advantage of his inside information to buy those stocks which he was prepared to bull, and sell those he was going to bear. In one of his statements he said:

> The price of copper, the Metal, will break suddenly to a very low figure. This is not a prediction. It is not a surmise or manipulation. It is a statement of fact. . . . This is to give fair warning that I intend to make full use of the knowledge I have to profit by the break at the expense of the stock gamblers. . . .[46]

The public sold heavily—and Lawson bought. The price of copper did not fall, and Amalgamated, in which Lawson had an interest, went from 88½ on August 25 to 110 on December 29. Lawson made another million at the expense of his followers, and he enjoyed his new wealth for several years before losing it in a series of wild ventures. In 1906, however, his manipulations, disclosures, and general demeanor caused further uncertainty on the Exchange and angered the Standard Oil leaders.[47]

While Lawson was battling Standard in New York, Frederick Augustus Heinze, a Brooklyn-born son of a Yankee mother and German father, clashed with the giant corporation in the Far West. His search for copper proved so successful that Rockefeller paid him $10.5 million for his claims on condition that Heinze would leave Montana for good. Rather sure of himself after licking the largest industrial force of the day, Heinze went to New York to make a career as a stock manipulator. Together with his brothers he organized the firm of Otto Heinze and Company, which became the base for his operations.[48]

At this point Heinze met a kindred soul, Charles W. Morse, a dealer who had made a fortune through the manipulation of American

Ice Company. Morse was then planning an ambitious program for taking over all Atlantic seaboard shipping and consolidating several firms into a large trust. He had taken over the Bank of North America and ten other financial institutions, all of which were interconnected through stock ownership and were firmly in his hands. Now Morse joined forces with Heinze to form the United Copper Company, a firm with a few mines which was capitalized at $80 million. This shaky concern was financed through the Mercantile National Bank, one of Morse's pets.

The new company proved even more successful than the promoters had expected. By 1906 it was threatening the Rockefeller-controlled Amalgamated Copper by underselling it at the metal market. Standard Oil vowed revenge. "We are going to settle this," said a high official in the organization, "but we are going to settle it in our own way."[49]

In March, 1907, the stock market began to show signs of weakness. Loans became more difficult to obtain, as the tightened money situation began to make itself felt in the district. Rates rose, banks refused to lend money, and several stockbrokers, hit by a downward dip on heavy volume in March, declared bankruptcy. Casting an eye toward Washington, Harriman explained a twenty-five point decline in Union Pacific by saying, "I would hate to tell you to whom I think you ought to go for an explanation of all this."[50] Mining stocks— except United Copper—began to fall at the curb, wiping out hundreds of speculators. Over 32 million shares were traded in March, as the bottom seemed to fall out of the market.

There was a brief rally in April and May, but it lacked conviction. Then, in July, came news that U.S. Steel's backlog was down. Railroad earnings fell sharply, and several large trusts reported financial difficulties. Morse's shipping empire crashed, and his banks began to show the strain of his activities. A City of New York bond issue was unsold; $15 million worth of 4 per cent bonds brought bids of only $2,713,815. Kuhn, Loeb's $75 million issue of Union Pacific 4 per cent debentures, which were offered at 90, had to be bought by Schiff himself, as the market absorbed less than $2 million of the issue.[51] Hill had said that unless capital for industry could be raised in increasing amounts, the economy would be paralyzed. Some noted that there seemed to be a twenty-year cycle between panics, so that the next panic would be due in 1913, not 1907. They also believed that "the coordination of American industry" since 1899, the establishment of the gold standard, and the great power of the investment bankers, would act as brakes on any major decline. As a result of these conflicting hopes and fears, the market was skittish on low volume in September. Banking and industrial leaders organized conferences and began to issue highly optimistic reports. Even Frick and Stillman began to speak to reporters. This deliberate show of confidence led smart financial analysts to realize that both the economy and the market were in severe straits.[52]

On October 14, United Copper went from 37½ to 60, while all other important mining shares declined. The *Times* of the following day thought that this was due to increased earnings and "a degree of speculation." In fact, the company was in sound shape. The rise was not due to earnings, but rather to an attempted corner by the Morse-Heinze group. By evening they thought the corner had been gained, and in the time-honored tradition, Morse and Heinze prepared to squeeze the shorts the following day.[53]

It was at this point, although no one knew it at the time, that the panic of 1907 began. Morse and Heinze had guessed wrong; they didn't have their corner. Perhaps through the aid of Standard Oil or other enemies of the two men, the shorts were able to buy enough shares to deliver to the ring. Instead of rising, the price of United fell from 60 to 38, and Heinze and Company found itself with a large block of stock which diminished in value by the hour. On the morning of October 16 the price fell to 10. Heinze and Company closed its doors, ending the meteoric career of its founder and seriously crippling the Morse interests.[54]

Since United Copper was controlled by the Mercantile National Bank, of which Heinze was president and Morse a director, that institution was obviously in danger. It had provided the margin money for the pair's purchases, and now it was left holding a block of depreciated shares. Depositors staged a run on the institution, which was drained of its assets in a few hours. Heinze sent an appeal to the Clearing House for help, but the directors replied that they would do nothing until he and Morse had left the bank. Later, Heinze claimed that this was the price exacted by Standard Oil for his previous victory over the Rockefeller empire. In any case, he had no choice; on October 18, Heinze and Morse announced that they were leaving all of their banking positions.[55]

The brief panic seemed over. The Clearing House announced that it would examine the books of the Mercantile and all other Heinze-Morse banks, and would correct abuses and shore them up if necessary, but it was too late to repair the damage of October 18. The public, aware of the tight nature of the money market and frightened by the Mercantile run, began to withdraw deposits from other banks and trust companies. The run started on Monday, October 21, at the branch banks, and during the late morning it spread to the main offices. By early afternoon a selling wave hit the Stock Exchange, and a panic which had not been known since the wild days of 1901 was set into motion. Morse's American Ice fell from 16 to 9⅞, and his Knickerbocker Ice of Chicago went from 51½ to 20. Other afternoon declines are shown in Table 10.2.

Table 10.2—October 21 Declines[56]

	High	Low
American Telephone & Telegraph	100	98
Canadian Pacific	159½	155
Chicago, Milwaukee, & St. Paul	113¼	107¾
Delaware, Lackawanna & Western	435	425
Northern Pacific	118½	112
Union Pacific	116	112⅜
U.S. Steel	24¼	22⅜

Westinghouse Corporation also had many financial difficulties early in 1907. By a stroke of bad luck the firm announced its insolvency at the same time the Heinze-Morse empire toppled. Westinghouse's price fell from 103 to 79⅞ that day, and was suspended from trading. The stock opened at 35 over the counter on Tuesday, causing the failures of two brokerages and the ruin of hundreds of speculators.[57]

As the market collapsed, trouble was brewing at the Knickerbocker Trust, a company controlled by Charles T. Barney, one of Morse's closest collaborators. Barney was forced to resign by the Clearing House, and was strongly attacked for alleged incompetence and thievery. On the first day of the run the National Bank of Commerce, controlled by a Morgan-Ryan group, announced that it would not clear checks for Knickerbocker. At the time there was a Day and Night Bank on Fifth Avenue; the institution was packed that evening with depositors withdrawing from their Knickerbocker accounts. Wall Street was gaining its revenge on the Heinze-Morse clique, but at the same time was committing suicide. The Knickerbocker run continued on Tuesday, and its leaders warned Clearing House members that unless aid was forthcoming, they would have to close their doors. The members refused aid, and on Wednesday the Knickerbocker collapsed.

The failure of the Knickerbocker seemed to sober the vengeful Wall Streeters. Even before the company failed, attempts had been made to bolster confidence. Jacob Schiff said "the trouble is over and the general situation sound." On October 22, John D. Rockefeller added: "I think that the existing alarm among investors is not warranted, and I hope the good common sense of our American people will control the situation. Personally I have absolute faith in the future of the value of our securities and the soundness of underlying conditions."[58] Wall Street leaders spoke with unbounded optimism during the rest of the week, indicating their belief that recovery was imminent, and that it was a good time to buy stocks at depressed prices. With each statement, prices sank lower.

J. P. Morgan was in Richmond as a member of the General Convention of the Episcopal Church, when the trouble developed. By Sunday morning, October 20, he was back in his offices and preparing to take charge of the situation. He had silently acquiesced to the destruction of the Heinze-Morse group, but like the others, had not thought it would lead to a panic. Morgan was seventy years old at the time, and had lost some of his great vigor. The failures of the International Mercantile Marine and the difficulties with the New England railroads had taken some of the luster from his reputation, but he was still the kingpin of Wall Street and was expected to save the district from ruin. Reporters formed a ring around his house which remained for four weeks. A parade of Wall Street leaders—Harriman, Stillman, Baker, Keene, the Rockefeller men—came and went from the Morgan library during this period as if they were visiting the Pope at the Vatican.[59]

The failure of the Knickerbocker had set off a chain of other collapses. The National Bank of North America folded, and there were runs at the Trust Company of America and the Lincoln Trust, as well as dozens of smaller institutions. The long lines outside virtually every bank and trust company led to this exaggeration in *Life*.[60]

> Hello, Dinny, you look prosperous—got a job now?
> You bet, an' its a good one!
> What is it?
> Gettin' in early on de bank runs, an' sellin' me place in de line.

At first the government allowed the panic to run its course. Then Roosevelt, who was strangely ignorant of economic and monetary matters, was moved to act. As a first step, $36 million was deposited in needy banks, an ironic example of the President's true feelings about the "malefactors of great wealth." Secretary of the Treasury Cortelyou agreed to add additional funds should they be needed, and all but put himself at Morgan's disposal. The conditions of 1893 seemed to be repeating themselves, with Roosevelt taking Cleveland's role. Once more Morgan was supreme, and presidents bowed to his power.[61]

As Morgan and his colleagues were leaving Cortelyou's office, they were met by a mob of reporters. As usual, J. P. Morgan had nothing to say, but Baker intimated that if the Trust Company of America applied for aid, it would be given. Either by accident or design, the *New York Evening Sun* printed a garbled story of the interview, and the *Times* of the following morning indicated that the Trust Company was in sad shape.[62] A run developed at the institution that morning, and President Oakleigh Thorne rushed to Morgan's home and pleaded for aid. With little sleep and suffering with a severe cold, J.P. dragged himself from bed and met with Thorne. After assuring himself of the Trust Company's solvency, he announced his willingness to lend the institution one million dollars, and Thorne's firm was still functioning when the business day ended. The following afternoon Morgan decided that the Trust Company of America was the key to the panic. "Then, this is the place to stop the trouble." He called a meeting of trust company presidents and told them that since it was a trust company panic, they should help out with their reserves. He already had the First National and the National City banks in his corner, and now the other companies fell in line. At first they demurred, but the wrath of Morgan was a terrible thing to behold; they meekly signed the pledge and walked out of the Morgan mansion.[63]

On Thursday, October 24, Morgan met with the bankers. He arrived at his offices at ten A.M. and found the building surrounded by worried onlookers. Morgan was cheered; the depositors realized that only he could save their money.[64] Soon America's leading businessmen began to come and go, in a repetition of the Sunday evening visits, and the onlookers' mood took a turn for the better.

Several hours later R. H. Thomas, President of the Stock Exchange, was ushered into Morgan's library. Prices had fallen on Wall Street all day, and by one P.M. a selling wave threatened to wipe out a majority of the brokers. Unless something was done soon, the financial apparatus of the district would grind to a halt. Thomas suggested closing the Exchange until a more moderate tone appeared on the Street. Morgan refused to hear of this; such an action would only serve to further erode confidence. He undertook to raise enough money so as to keep the shaky brokers solvent. Morgan's operations in this moment of stress were thus described by his son-in-law:

> Mr. Morgan immediately had a telephone message sent to the presidents of all the banks in the neighborhood, asking them to come to his office. At two o'clock they were there. When they had gathered in his room he explained the situation, which was that the Stock Exchange houses needed in the aggregate at least $25,000,000, and unless that sum could be raised *within the next quarter of an hour* he feared that at least fifty firms would go under. Mr. Stillman was the first to speak up and said that the National City Bank would furnish $5,000,000 to loan on the Exchange before closing time. Mr. Morgan called on each of the other men present to state how much his bank would lend, and in turn they said, "$500,000," "$1,000,000," or "One-half million"; and Perkins took down the figures. Some of them kept quiet, and Mr. Morgan had to speak to them pretty plainly before they announced their contributions to the fund. However, in not more than five minutes $27,000,000 was at Mr. Morgan's command to loan to the Stock Exchange at 10 percent.[65]

News of the consortium was rushed to the Exchange, where there was still about a half-hour of trading left before closing. In this period $18 million was absorbed by the needy houses. A roar of approval for the Great Man's actions went up from the floor at the close, and Morgan heard it in his offices a block away.[66] "If the people will keep their money in the banks everything will be all right," he said, and he left for home. There were no callers at the Morgan mansion that evening of October 24; the first glimmerings of confidence appeared among the financial leaders, and the panic seemed licked.[67]

On the following day Morgan agreed to the issuance of clearing-house certificates as a means of easing the money squeeze. Eventually $100 million were issued in New York, and together with the Morgan funds they saved several large institutions. On Friday evening Morgan rallied the clergymen of the city the way he had previously organized the bankers; he arranged for the spiritual leaders of the major Catholic, Protestant, and Jewish houses of worship to deliver encouraging sermons over the weekend; like the bankers, they fell into line.[68]

During the second week of the panic Morgan commanded the banking forces with consummate skill, throwing his millions of reserves into each breech that appeared. On Sunday afternoon he agreed to deliver $30 million to the city fathers of New York, who told him that the municipal coffers were empty. One group of Morgan men reviewed municipal finances, another, led by Keene, kept the stock market at an even keel, and a third directed operations at the banks and trust companies.[69] Morgan sat in his library, directing and co-ordinating these efforts while playing endless games of solitaire.

It was at this point, when the crisis seemed over, that the medium-sized brokerage of Moore & Schley found itself in trouble. Grant B. Schley—who was George F. Baker's brother-in-law—had borrowed money on a large block of Tennessee Coal and Iron, which had been used as collateral for a previous loan. This practice of using the same securities for two notes was illegal, but not unusual at the time. Had the market risen, Schley would have made a fortune; as it was, he was on the brink of bankruptcy. His partner, John Moore, was a popular Wall Streeter, famous for his capacity for food and drink. Moore had many friends in Washington, and he tried in vain to en-list their aid for the partnership.[70] When this failed, he and Schley turned to Morgan.

The Great Man was ready to help Moore & Schley, taking its shares of Tennessee Coal and Iron for his trouble. At the same time, he had to shore up a run on several banks. Needing funds for these two enterprises, he called the bankers to his home on the evening of November 2. Morgan told them that he would require an additional $25 million to take care of "new problems." After a short period of hesitance during which several bankers protested that they lacked the money, they all fell into line. Morgan merely locked the door and told them they couldn't leave until he had his money. He laid the pledge on his massive desk, and waved at it. "There you are, gentle-men." One by one they approached and signed—Morgan even guided the shaky hand of one banker as he stood over the paper. Thus did the district's leaders pay homage to the seventy-year-old giant.[71]

Morgan could have easily loaned Moore & Schley enough money to save the firm; a short-term transfer of $5 million would have done it. But this would not have gained the Tennessee Coal and Iron shares for U.S. Steel. Against Frick's objections—he argued that such a pro-posal was immoral—Morgan called Judge Gary to his offices, and told him to rush to Washington and inquire of Roosevelt whether the government would block a merger of U.S. Steel and Tennessee Coal and Iron under the provisions of the Sherman Act. Gary caught a late train and was in the capital and at Roosevelt's office on Monday morning.

Roosevelt was then considered an implacable foe of big business, but we now realize that he was quite conservative in his economic views. Robert Bacon, who had acted for Morgan during the Northern Pacific contest of 1901, was an assistant secretary of state in 1907 and would soon head that department. Morgan's biographer and son-in-law, Herbert Satterlee, was an assistant secretary of the navy for a brief period. In the election of 1904, and again in 1912, most Wall Streeters were in Roosevelt's corner. There was good reason for this; T.R. might have talked tough, but he acted soft. He continued to make a distinction between "good" and "bad" trusts, and considered that most were good. "As a matter of fact," he later said, "I have let up in every case where I have had any possible excuse for so doing."[72]

Gary told Roosevelt that unless the merger were allowed to take place, further difficulties could be expected in New York. Frightened by the panic, the President agreed to the takeover. Morgan bought the Tennessee Coal and Iron shares at a fraction of their actual worth, Moore & Schley was saved, and the Street praised Morgan for his actions. A "sunshine movement" began in the district, led by the "Prosperity League." In time the lines disappeared from the banks and trust companies. By the end of November the financial community was back on its feet, and the casualties either left the Street or went away for a few months to lick their wounds. Heinze was through with Wall Street for good; Morse was indicted for malfeasance and served a term in the Atlanta Penitentiary. He appeared in New York during World War I, but not as a tycoon; by then he was a petty speculator. Gates retired to a small Texas town where he regaled one and all with stories of his former glory. Morgan went to Europe as usual the following year, and began grooming his son, J.P. Jr., to take over the firm. Roosevelt's antitrust days came to a quiet end; shaken by the panic, he withdrew suits against International Harvester and other trusts. Charles Barney, whose Knickerbocker Trust failure had been a key event in the panic, left Wall Street a fallen man. After trying to see Morgan, with no success, he went to a sanatorium for a while and, on November 14, committed suicide.[73]

The 1907 panic was one of the most severe in the nation's history. Still, fewer firms declared bankruptcy in that year than in 1903, and by 1908 the economy began a two-year upward swing. By the end of 1909 both the economy and stock market prices were back at their 1906 levels,[74] but the recovery was followed by a decline in 1910–1911.

Some expansion took place in 1913, but early 1914 saw bad business again. Not until war orders flooded the nation later in the year did business pick up important momentum.[75]

The Exchange quieted down after the panic, and was in the doldrums for the next seven and one-half years. The share turnover declined each year from 1909 to 1914, as did the average daily volume.[76] Rallies and declines were of short duration. The scars of 1907 were not healed until war prosperity ushered in a new bull market.

During the 1908–1914 period Wall Street was under constant scrutiny from one government agency or another. The Hughes Committee of New York investigated banks and insurance firms in 1909, and also looked into Stock Exchange operations. As far as the market place was concerned, the committee recommended:

> The Exchange should . . . adopt methods to compel the filing of frequent statements of the financial condition of the companies whose securities are listed, including balance sheets, income and expense accounts, etc., and should notify the public that these are open to examination under proper rules and regulations. The Exchange should also require that there be filed with future applications for listing, a statement of what the capital stock of the company has been issued for, showing how much has been issued for cash, how much for property, with a description of the property, etc., and also showing what commission, if any, has been paid to the promoters or vendors.[77]

The committee found, however, that speculation "is a necessary incident of productive operations" and "when carried on in connection with either commodities or securities it tends to steady their prices." Thus, an indirect approval of the market place was granted, and the Exchange itself was absolved of any major wrongdoing. As a result, the state did not pass new legislation to control trading. The Exchange did make some changes due to the investigation, however. In 1910 the Unlisted Department was abolished, members were prohibited from dealing with bucket shops, and the Law Committee was given a mandate to investigate member firms when wrongdoing was suspected. In addition, the Exchange acted to curb the more flagrant excesses of manipulation. In the past a broker could offer to buy a thousand or so shares, "all or none," simply to influence the market; he could then refuse to buy them. In a similar manner, he might offer to buy a huge block of stock—with no intention of taking it— only to give the appearance of an active market. Now the Exchange declared that if a broker bid for shares of any quantity, he would have to buy them in any multiple of 100 offered.[78]

As an indirect result of these Exchange actions, the New York Curb Agency, which had been founded by a group of street brokers in 1908, formed a Listing Department. This organization moved toward tighter control in 1911, when it opened a central office. Ten years later operations were transferred to 86 Trinity Place, and in 1952, the Curb became the American Stock Exchange, now the nation's second largest market.[79]

In 1911 the Taft Administration hit hard at the trusts, dissolving, among others, the Standard Oil and American Tobacco companies. DuPont was hit by antitrust actions, as was U.S. Steel. Then, in 1912, the House of Representatives authorized its Committee on Banking and Currency to discover whether there really was a Money Trust in the nation. One group, headed by Carter Glass, worked on legislation while another, under Arsené Pujo, conducted the investigations. Aided by counsel Samuel Untermyer, Pujo showed clearly that such a trust did indeed exist. Morgan defended his actions with vigor, and Untermyer got little from him except his belief that character was the best collateral for a loan. But Baker admitted that control of the nation's credit mechanism was too concentrated, and could do immeasurable harm to the country.[80]

Meanwhile, the Glass group prepared new legislation. The Aldrich-Vreeland Act, passed in 1908, had authorized national banks to issue circulating notes based on commercial paper. Under this act, the banks could borrow from the federal government up to 90 per cent of their pooled assets. In effect, this put the power of the Treasury behind any future consortium of bankers that would operate privately to stem a panic. The act, drawn up by Paul Warburg of Kuhn, Loeb, Morgan partner Henry Davison, and Benjamin Strong of the Morgan-dominated Bankers Trust, among others, was applauded by those Wall Streeters who bothered to read it. Glass and his colleagues drew up a proposal for the Federal Reserve System which was largely based on the Aldrich-Vreeland Act and became the Glass-Owen Act. As a concession to the Progressives, the Federal Reserve was not to be a central bank in the European sense of the term; it would not be a resurrection of the Second Bank of the United States. Instead, the members would be selected by the President, although once named, they would be free of his control. Since the System was to have twelve branches, it was hoped that New York's influence would be lessened. The Federal Reserve was, in effect, an attempt to institutionalize and impersonalize the work that Morgan had done for the past quarter-century. The Banks would control currency, discount paper, and act to stem crises. They did their jobs with moderate success, although the Progressives' plan for separation from Wall Street never materialized. The first Governor of the New York Bank, which soon was the recognized leader, was Benjamin Strong, who was solidly in the Morgan camp.[81] Not until the New Deal would the System gain real independence from Wall Street.

In the next five years Morgan lived in semi-retirement, devoted to art, the Episcopal Church, and his family. Harriman died in 1909, and Morgan took over the Guarantee Trust Company and the Mutual Life Insurance Company, the foundations of the Harriman empire. Soon after the Equitable Life passed from Ryan to Morgan, putting the Great Man in virtual control of the nation's insurance industry.[82] But there were failures as well. In 1908 Morgan refused to see the future of William Crapo Durant's proposed International Motors Company, and Durant was later obliged to take his renamed General Motors to Lee Higginson & Co. for financing.[83] Morgan wasn't alone in this shortsightedness; Chauncy Depew told his nephew, who wanted to invest $5,000 in the Ford Motor Company, that "Nothing has come along to beat the horse. Keep your money. Or, if you must spend, buy a horse and you'll have enough left over to furnish it with feed for the rest of its life."[84]

The New England railroads continued to give Morgan trouble, and he was never able to straighten out the mess. His son Jack resembled him, but he lacked the father's genius and lived in an age when such genius, even if it did exist, would be hampered from exercising its full range of powers. Jack failed to bring order to the New England rails, a fact which must have saddened the old man in his last years.[85]

In 1913 Morgan fell ill during his annual trip to Europe, and from February on, rumors regarding his condition circulated. On March 30 a communiqué from his Rome hotel suite announced that he was seriously ill, and on the following day he grew delirious, speaking of religion and his past triumphs. Then, just after midnight, he had a moment of lucidity. Morgan pointed to the ceiling and turned to Satterlee. "I've got to go up the hill," he said. Morgan fell into a coma and never recovered consciousness.[86]

"There will be no successor to Morgan," wrote the *Wall Street*

Journal the following day. "Now Wall Street is beyond the need or possibility of one-man leadership. There will be co-ordination of effort, union of resources, but Morgan will have no successor," wrote the *Times*. "He was the last of his line. Never again will there be another J. Pierpont Morgan" was the judgement of the *World*. Roosevelt said that he was fundamentally opposed to Morgan, but was "struck by his very great power and truthfulness. Any kind of meanness and smallness were alien to his nature." But another writer said:

> We verily believe that J. Pierpont Morgan has done more harm in the world than any man who ever lived in it. It was Morgan who started the idea that the trust is an economic necessity. . . . The enslavement of labor, the crushing of individual initiative, the blighting of womanhood, the premature aging of children, these are the awful sidelights thrown on the terrible journey of this modern juggernaut—crushing, crunching, and destroying all who tried to resist it. . . . It will be a weary fight for the American people to get from under the continuing burden which J. P. Morgan has left upon them. . . .[87]

Secretary of State William Jennings Bryan—whom Morgan had despised—arranged for the return of the body to America. On April 14, Morgan's hearse was drawn through the district; trading was suspended from 10 A.M. to noon in his honor, the only time this has ever been done for a private individual. Memorial meetings were held in Westminster Abbey and in Paris. Financial circles around the world felt his passing.

A few days later Morgan's will was read to his family. It contained no reference to his business activities, but rather was a semi-religious tract—one could almost hear Morgan dealing with St. Peter.

> I commit my soul into the hands of my Saviour, in full confidence that having redeemed it and washed it in His most precious blood He will present it faultless before my Heavenly Father; and I entreat my children to maintain and defend, at all hazard and at any cost of personal sacrifice, the blessed doctrine of the complete atonement for sin through the blood of Jesus Christ, once offered and through that alone.[88]

Morgan was dead, but his House remained, and the structure he had erected on Wall Street was undamaged. Even today, more than any other American, he symbolizes industrial and financial America.

The Balkan wars of 1913 helped stimulate the American economy, but the nation was still in the doldrums on June 28, 1914, when Archduke Franz Ferdinand was assassinated at Sarajevo. The nation, and for that matter, the entire world, took little notice of his death. A week after the event reporters of the London Stock Exchange saw no change in trading as a result of the act; Parisian reporters remarked as late as July on the "large numbers of members of the Stock Exchange who are absent in the country." On July 9 the London *Economist's* Berlin correspondent wrote that "the Norway visit of the Kaiser marks the beginning of the dead season in German politics." American financial reporters did not mention the possibility of a new European war until the last week in July.[89] Thus, when Germany sent its ultimatum to France and Russia on the last day of the month, most international financiers were caught unprepared. War soon followed, along with the most complete financial paralysis the world has ever known. Panic hit the Paris Bourse, Lombard Street, and the Berlin Exchange. Even the small St. Petersburg Exchange suffered a selling wave. On Wall Street, brokers stopped one another and asked what the war would mean. Many noted that Morgan could not have picked a worse time to die.[90]

As every exchange in the world announced suspension, the governors of the New York Stock Exchange tried to keep trading going on an even keel, but this proved impossible. Morgan had been able to keep the market open in 1907, but nothing could prevent the closing of July 31. The Exchange did not reopen for over five months; not even during the great panic of 1873 had it been closed for more than one week. When it managed to begin limited, formal trading on December 12, America was on its way to becoming the most important economic power in the world, and Wall Street had begun to replace Lombard Street.

Notes

1. Pratt, *Work of Wall Street,* p. 199.
2. Alfred D. Chandler, Jr., *Henry Varnum Poor: Business Editor, Analyst, and Reformer* (Cambridge, 1956), pp. 72–73.
3. *Ibid.,* p. 87.
4. *Ibid.,* p. 83.
5. Moody's autobiography, *The Long Road Home* (New York, 1933), is a curious work, in which the author's mixed commercial and religious drives often clash.
6. Clarence W. Barron, *They Told Barron* (New York, 1930), pp. xxi–xxii.

7. George W. Bishop, Jr., *Charles H. Dow and the Dow Theory* (New York, 1960), pp. 35–41.

8. Kirkland, *Industry Comes of Age,* pp. 234–35.

9. *New York Times,* February 12, 1929.

10. Thomas Lawson, *Frenzied Finance* (London, 1906), p. 266.

11. Corey, *House of Morgan,* pp. 283–84.

12. Levinson, *Wall Street,* pp. 161–62.

13. Forbes, *Men Who Are Making America,* p. 220.

14. Noyes, *Market Place,* pp. 220–21.

15. Lundberg, *America's 60 Families,* p. 107.

16. Neill, *Inside Story of the Stock Exchange,* p. 157.

17. Today's analyst may say, "The stock will turn out well for those who are willing to hold it for the long run." Translated, this means, "If it doesn't go up, don't blame me."

18. John Moody, *The Art of Wall Street Investing* (New York, 1909), pp. 118–20.

19. Noyes, *Market Place,* p. 218.

20. By 1906 Morgan was often left off lists of powerful Wall Streeters, his position by then was such that his leadership was taken for granted.

21. Warshow, *Bet-A-Million Gates,* pp. 125–26.

22. Noyes, *Forty Years of American Finance,* p. 311.

23. Edwards, *Evolution of Finance Capitalism,* p. 184.

24. Redlich, *Molding of American Banking,* Vol. III, p. 390.

25. Cochran and Miller, *Age of Enterprise,* pp. 194–95.

26. Faulkner, *Decline of Laissez-Faire,* p. 42.

27. Redlich, *Molding of Investment Banking,* Vol. III, p. 389; Edwards, *Evolution of Finance Capitalism,* p. 166.

28. Lundberg, *America's 60 Families,* pp. 79–81; Faulkner, *Decline of Laissez-Faire,* p. 39.

29. During the 1950s and early 1960s it was believed that the mutual funds would act in a similar way to balance the vagaries of the small investor. In the decline of 1962, however, their efforts could not keep prices up. They bought heavily, but the public sold faster. *New York Herald Tribune,* October 30, 1962.

30. Lundberg, *America's 60 Families,* p. 70.

31. *Ibid.,* p. 100.

32. Nelson, *Merger Movements,* pp. 164–65.

33. Noyes, *Forty Years of American Finance,* pp. 312–29.

34. Nelson, *Merger Movements,* pp. 164–65. These figures are seasonally adjusted with 1947 − 1949 = 100.

35. Lightner, *History of Business Depressions,* p. 208.

36. Nelson, *Merger Movements,* p. 165.

37. Clews, *Fifty Years in Wall Street,* p. 799; Lanier, *Century of Banking in New York,* pp. 256–57.

38. Noyes, *Forty Years of American Finance,* p. 329.

39. *Ibid.,* p. 355.

40. *Ibid.,* p. 359.

41. *Ibid.,* pp. 360–62.

42. Studenski and Krooss, *Financial History of the United States,* p. 252.

43. In addition to the banking problems were problems brought by margin accounts. In 1907 even "widows and orphans" commonly bought on margin. Edwin Lefevre, *Wall Street Stories* (New York, 1901), p. 12.

44. Faulkner, *Decline of Laissez-Faire,* pp. 28–29.

45. Noyes, *Forty Years of American Finance,* p. 352.

46. Neill, *Inside Story of the Stock Exchange,* pp. 158–59.

47. Lawson spent money as fast as he made it. Within three years he had built Dreamwald, a castle set in a thousand-acre estate in Massachusetts, had built a yacht to compete for the America's Cup, and had become a leader in New York society. Holbrook, *Age of the Moguls,* p. 173.

48. Moody, *Masters of Capital,* pp. 138–39.

49. Lundberg, *America's 60 Families,* pp. 91–92.

50. Allen, *Lords of Creation,* p. 124.

51. Kahn, *Jacob H. Schiff,* Vol. I, p. 113.

52. Moody, *Masters of Capital,* pp. 142–45; Noyes, *Forty Years of American Finance,* pp. 363–64.

53. Allen, *Lords of Creation,* p. 118.

54. *New York Times,* October 17, 1907.

55. *New York Times,* October 18–20, 1907.

56. *New York Times,* October 22, 1907.

57. *New York Times,* October 23, 1907.

58. *New York Times,* October 23–24, 1907; Corey, *House of Morgan,* p. 341.

59. Satterlee, *J. Pierpont Morgan,* p. 461.

60. Sullivan, *Our Times,* Vol. III, p. 504.

61. Eventually almost $80 million was deposited in banks in New York, Chicago, Pittsburgh, Cincinnati, and other cities, thus buoying the whole nation, not only Wall Street. Charles A. Conant, *A History of Modern Banks of Issue* (New York, 1915), p. 714.

62. The *Sun* was published at the time by William Laffin, a close friend of the Morgan clan, and Adolph Ochs of the *Times* owed money to George W. Perkins, a Morgan partner. Because of this, Lundberg (*America's 60 Families,* pp. 92–93) suggests that they may have been influenced to print pessimistic reports about the Trust Company of America. Lundberg believes that Morgan wanted to see the firm in trouble, so that it would be forced to sell to U.S. Steel its holdings of Tennessee Coal and Iron Company. All of this, however, is based on surmise.

63. Satterlee, *J. Pierpont Morgan,* pp. 468–72.

64. One enterprising real estate firm offered to redeem the suspended certificates of the Knickerbocker Trust on that morning. They could be used, at full face values, for deposits on lots in such places as Garden City and Floral Park. Other real estate companies offered similar deals for lots in Valley Stream and elsewhere on Long Island. Those who took advantage of these offers saw their investment increase in value at a far more rapid rate than the Dow-Jones averages. *New York Times,* October 24–26, 1907.

65. Satterlee, *J. Pierpont Morgan,* pp. 474–75.

66. John A. Garraty, *Right Hand Man* (New York, 1960), pp. 203–204.

67. Satterlee, *J. Pierpont Morgan,* p. 476.

68. *Ibid.,* pp. 480–81; Conant, *Modern Banks of Issue,* p. 714.

69. Garraty, *Right Hand Man,* pp. 207–8.

70. Holbrook, *Age of the Moguls,* p. 177; Lawson, *Frenzied Finance,* pp. 179–80.

71. Allen, *Lords of Creation,* pp. 137–38.

72. Lundberg, *America's 60 Families,* p. 88.

73. Satterlee, *J. Pierpont Morgan,* p. 490.

74. Nelson, *Merger Movements,* p. 164.

75. Lee, *Economic Fluctuations,* p. 132.

76. *New York Stock Exchange Fact Book,* pp. 42–43.

77. Myers, *New York Money Market,* p. 310.

78. Neill, *Inside Story of the Stock Exchange*, p. 178.

79. *Ibid.*, pp. 178–79; Schultz, *The Securities Market*, p. 15.

80. Moody, *Masters of Capital*, pp. 181–219. Moody has collected the most important sections of the testimony.

81. Lundberg, *America's 60 Families*, pp. 121–22; Cochran and Miller, *Age of Enterprise*, pp. 294–97.

82. Moody, *Masters of Capital*, pp. 149–50.

83. Faulkner, *Decline of Laissez-Faire*, pp. 230–31.

84. Walker, *Epic of American Industry*, pp. 289–90.

85. Corey, *House of Morgan*, p. 421.

86. Satterlee, *J. Pierpont Morgan*, pp. 581–83.

87. Sigmund Diamond, *The Reputation of the American Businessman* (Cambridge, 1955), pp. 92–93.

88. Corey, *House of Morgan*, p. 412.

89. Alexander Noyes, *The War Period of American Finance* (New York, 1926), pp. 54–55.

90. *New York Times*, August 3, 1914.

11

Genealogy of the Giant Bull: 1914-1924

Six New Basic Leaders.—Look at the list: First come the oils with a new fuel epoch ahead of them and no readjustment to face. Motor and tobacco stocks reflect the tremendous prosperity of the country and the tendency to spend money on luxuries. Food stocks with the group embracing companies in the packing industry, cereals and baking, refining of corn, production of vegetable oils, appeal to the buyer of securities because he has faith in the basic soundness of the enterprises. Leather issues have been featured as never before and no one who realizes the demand for shoes the world over will criticize this selection. Shipping shares have been firm because the average buyer of stocks believes the commerce of the world will have need for the equipment and the organization of our leading mercantile companies.

Market Letter, 1920

THE NEW YORK TIMES' FINANCIAL ANALYST, noting that stock prices had fallen during the week of July 18–25, 1914, told his Sunday readers that "the causes of the decline could be traced to the war scare in Europe. As for America, business was not at the 1913 level, but prospects seemed good and recovery was expected by year's end." He quickly discounted the war talk. "Everyone spoke of the possibility of conflict involving practically all Europe," he noted, "but no one here really believed that such a thing was likely to come about."

The lead article in that Sunday's magazine section was entitled "We Face the Most Acute Crisis of History." Its author, Dr. Rudolph

Euken, a German winner of the Nobel Prize for Literature, was not referring to the impending world conflict; rather, he feared the effects of the falling off of church attendance throughout Europe. Further on in the section was an essay by a now obscure economist, who told his readers that war could not last, if indeed it ever came, because business was against it. "No modern war has been conducted to which the business world as a whole was unalterably opposed, for war must draw its sinews from the money chests of business."

Toward the end of the main section was a short statement by Professor Irving Fisher of Yale University—the same man who, just before the 1929 crash, predicted continued prosperity on a "permanently high plateau." Professor Fisher stated that a European war of long duration would wreck the American economy. As soon as the conflict began, the Europeans would sell their American holdings and start to import gold, which would be used to build up national defenses. There would be autarchy; imports from America would cease. In short order the Europeans would offer attractive interest rates to American investors so as to get additional financing for the war efforts. This would drive the domestic rate to a new high. American industrialists would be unable to compete for capital, and would be prevented from expanding. This would usher in a panic and depression that would last throughout the war.[1]

Many Americans seemed to share Professor Fisher's beliefs. Toward the end of the month stock prices fell in heavy trading. The headline of July 28 read, "War Scare Draws American Gold to Europe." Although stocks showed some resistance to foreign selling on July 27, a sharp dip took place the following day, when the Treasury announced that Europeans had imported $13 million in gold from the United States. Practically every stock on the list fell on this news, the rails leading the way with Canadian Pacific down fifteen and Delaware, Lackawanna and Western off seven. Industrials followed, as U.S. Steel fell three and one-half and American Smelting and Refining closed with a four-point loss. There was an "abrupt recovery on light volume" the following session, but the list suffered its sharpest selloff since 1907 on July 30. Some of the leaders are shown in Table 11.1.

Two days before the crash the Montreal, Toronto, and Madrid Exchanges closed down. On the following day those in Vienna, Budapest, Brussels, Antwerp, Berlin, and Rome were suspended. The St. Petersburg and all the South American Exchanges announced their

Table 11.1—Closing Prices on July 30, 1914[2]

	Closing Price	Loss
Baldwin Locomotive	41	− 7½
Bethlehem Steel	36	− 5⅞
General Electric	139	− 4
General Motors	58⅞	−19⅞
International Harvester	83	−13
U.S. Steel	51⅞	− 4⅞

closing during the July 30 decline. On Friday morning, July 31, the London Stock Exchange was officially closed for the first time in its history. Not even during the Napoleonic period was such an action deemed necessary. When the news reached New York, the Governing Committee of the Exchange called a hurried meeting. But by the time it had begun, a line of customers had formed outside the trading area, and people were queuing around the brokerages as well. It was evident that they were there to sell. The New York Stock Exchange was, at the time, the only major market which had not suspended. If it had opened, all the bears of the world might have descended on Wall Street, causing the greatest collapse in all history. The way was clear; within a few minutes the governors decided to close trading indefinitely. When calm was restored, they said, trading would be re-opened on a limited basis. The governors expected that at such time some liquidation would take place, but in a quieter atmosphere sufficient buyers would appear to pick up bargains and steady the market. Led by Ernest Groesbeck (David's son), the governors also decided that delivery of previously transacted securities be suspended until further notice, and that a committee of five be established to take care of the crisis and agree upon an opening day for trading.[3]

From early August through late November the Committee dealt with the many problems involved in running a closed Exchange. One of the greatest concerned the relationship between the institution and the "outside brokers," who had always bought and sold securities without a formal organization. At first the small group of traders which habitually gathered on New Street was quiet and orderly, but by the end of the first week in August, business picked up. The Exchange frowned upon its members trading on New Street. Such brokers were viewed as conscious underminers of the price structure, and they were warned that a continuation of such practices could lead to their expulsion. These admonitions were useless, however, and on August 12 the

Committee decided to recognize the outlaw market and regulate it in such a way so as to benefit the district and the nation. The following ruling was handed down that evening:

> Members of the Exchange desiring to buy securities for cash may send a list of same to the Committee on Clearing House, 55 New Street, giving the amounts of securities wanted and the prices they are willing to pay.
>
> No offer to buy at less than the closing prices of Thursday, July 30, 1914, will be considered.
>
> Members of the Exchange desiring to sell securities, but only in order to relieve the necessities of themselves or their customers, may send a list of same to the Committee on Clearing House, giving the amounts of securities for sale.
>
> No prices less than the closing prices of Thursday, July 30, will be considered.[4]

The attempt to form an exchange at the Clearing House, which would provide a degree of marketability for securities above the July 30 prices, was futile. During the dark days of late August, quotations for U.S. Steel and Amalgamated Copper were ten points below their last quotes at the Exchange, and with most other stocks were traded surreptitiously on the outlaw market. Realizing that the Clearing House scheme had failed, the Committee declared that "transactions with bargain-hunters should not be countenanced and your Committee will not approve the closing of transactions coming under this head." Nonetheless, it continued, and even broadened in the weeks that followed. Soon after, the Committee received protests from its counterparts in other American cities, who lodged complaints against Exchange members who were bootlegging bonds to banks and trust companies below July 30 quotations. Attempts to crack down on such practices were usually futile.[5]

Another major problem involved the question of whether quotations of stocks on the outlaw market should be permitted. Also, if such prices were to be published, how would they be obtained from the unrecognized outlaw market? The committee opposed the issuance of prices on the grounds that such publicity would encourage speculation, and it prevailed upon the financial writers to refrain from reporting over-the-counter activities. The press gave perfect cooperation to the committee, and even went one step further; in order to keep the public calm, the writers reported that the lists were not being printed because dealings "have not yet reached a scale that justifies the acceptance of prices made outside of the Stock Exchange as a basis for buying or selling."[6] This, at a time when activity was estimated to be at a higher level than that at the pre-panic Exchange.[7] Instead, the financial writers encouraged potential buyers to transact their business at the Clearing House market and keep away from "shady" New Street traders. This attempt failed, for the over-the-counter prices were published surreptitiously and handed on from trader to trader until the cheap paper on which they were printed fell apart. Only those stocks which had not declined—and there were precious few of these—were traded at the Clearing House. The success of the outlaw market was a compelling reason for considering an early opening of the Exchange.

The possibility was talked about at the first session of the committee after its formation. Not only was there pressure from shareholders, bankers, and speculators for a reopening, but the member firms told the committee that they could not stand the loss of commissions indefinitely. Although most of them kept their full staffs during the stagnation, some were obliged to cut salaries and a few dismissed their clerks. An employment bureau was formed at the Exchange to take care of the temporarily unemployed, but despite this, some clerks were out of work for over four months. The same held true for financial analysts and business writers; they were either shifted to new assignments or released. From those whose livelihoods depended upon a healthy market as well as the general public came the cry for an end to the suspension.

During the period of closing the public offered the committee many plans under which trading could recommence. Some were extreme, although most suggested that trading in limited shares under strict supervision during shortened hours would be the best solution. One western banker offered the slogan "Buy a Share of Stock," to be stated as a patriotic appeal. If you supported your country, he reasoned, you would purchase one share at the July 30 closing price to prove it. This would counter the foreign selling with a mass of small buy orders. Another suggestion was that all sales be made under sixty-day contracts, for cash. This would discourage the in-and-out speculators, and would attract only those investors who had long-term goals in the market. The sellers would be wary under such a program, for manipulation and hypothecation under time orders would be extremely difficult. The Committee rejected both plans as cumbersome and unworkable. A third suggestion was that sales of American securities by foreign shareholders be allowed, while domestic holders should be forbidden to enter the market except to buy. Since prices were artifi-cially depressed, it was reasoned, the plan would enable Americans to buy at low prices, which would rise as soon as the panic ended. A fourth plan, to restrict sales to odd lots, and a fifth, to have a brokers' consortium buy shares at a fixed price to bolster confidence, were rejected along with many others.[8]

Instead, the committee adopted a wait-and-see attitude. On Sep-tember 1, it questioned the brokers as to the situation regarding Euro-pean buy-and-sell orders. If those which had been entered on July 30 were completed, how would the money market be affected? The re-sponses showed that such completions would result in a transfer of over $18 million of gold to European sellers. Clearly this could not be allowed, and the committee decided to wait for buying pressures on the part of domestic investors before opening trading. The situation got worse before it got better, however. By late October the unofficial prices at the outlaw market were at their lows, and the Committee members began to wonder whether regular trading during wartime could ever be instituted.

With hindsight, we can see that this pessimism was unjustified, even allowing for the fact that the committee could not foresee the great economic boom of the war period. First, the banks were sound. It had been expected that the suspended trading would force the clos-ing of weaker institutions, but only six national banks suspended during the Exchange holiday, as against the 158 that closed as a result of the 1893 panic and the twenty-two failures of 1907. The reforms following the last panic and the aid given by the Federal Reserve were important factors for the maintenance of liquidity following the out-break of the war. Although $80 million was withdrawn from the New York banks in the last week of July and the first of August, the banks held fast. Some institutions were able to pay their depositors with little difficulty, while others refused to transact some aspects of their business until conditions settled down. Still others raised the loan rates to fantastic heights and, in the case of the savings banks, exer-cised their rights to receive prior notice before withdrawals were made. Reserves proved sufficient, and there was no banking panic in the summer of 1914.[9]

Another factor, one which aided the Exchange enormously, was the low level of prices at the market in the immediate pre-panic period. From a high of 71.4 in the third quarter of 1906, the Dow-Jones aver-age had fallen to 60.7 in 1914's second quarter. During this period, industrial production had risen from 26.3 to 30.4.[10] The meaning of these figures is evident; the investors of mid-1914 had not forgotten the 1907 panic, and refused to buy stocks at moderate prices even though there had been considerable economic recovery. Therefore, stock prices in July, 1914, were low, even by the conservative standards of that day, and shares remained fairly stable at the New Street market. Had the price earnings ratios of 1907 prevailed, a decline of disastrous proportions might have developed.

By early November the forces of panic appeared to have been spent, and the Committee decided to reopen trading on a limited basis. On November 12, the Clearing House was permitted to sell unlisted securities at prices below the July 30 closing. This indication of confidence was immediately reflected on New Street, where prices began to turn upward. Four days later a small bull market developed at the Curb, and the way to complete resumption seemed clear. On the 28th, bond trading was reopened, and instead of the expected decline, prices began to rise. Encouraged by this, common stocks of a noninternational nature were readmitted to trading on December 11. Once again prices rose, and three days later the entire list was reopened to trading on a cash basis. With this, the Committee of Five was dissolved. Although all restrictions were not removed until April 1, 1915, the Exchange was, for all intents and purposes, back in business by mid-December.[11]

When an assessment of the New Street market was made a few weeks later, it was seen that average prices had dipped on the war news and continued to fall until late October, but had recovered soon after and were back to their late-July levels by December 12. Some representative prices are shown in Table 11.2.

Table 11.2—Averages, July–December, 1914[12]

	Last Price, July 30	Low, October 23	Last Price, December 12
Amalgamated Copper	49	37½	52⅛
American Smelting	52½	46	56½
New York Central	80	72½	83
Southern Pacific	87⅞	76¾	91
U.S. Steel	51⅞	38½	50

In all, 1914 was a dull year so far as volume was concerned, which must be viewed as a sign of confidence. Average daily volume, excluding the period of closure, was 270,262 shares, the lowest of the century.

On December 30, as prices leveled off after the reopening, volume was 49,937 shares, also a twentieth-century low. The feared panic had not developed, but on New Year's Day, 1915, there seemed no reason to assume that prosperity and a great bull market were in the offing. The range of market leaders of 1914 is shown in Table 11.3.

Table 11.3—Range of Market Leaders, 1914[13]

	January 1	High	Low	December 31
American Smelting	63¾	71⅛	50¼	56¼
Baldwin Locomotive	39	52⅛	38½	40½
Bethlehem Steel	30	46⅝	29⅛	46⅛
General Electric	140⅝	150⅝	137½	139
General Motors	37⅜	99	37⅜	81½
U.S. Steel	59⅛	67¼	48	49⅜

A year later, after the first full year of American neutrality, the *New York Times* wrote: "The tremendous speculation of 1915 stands out as truly remarkable when the unpropitious setting of last New Year is considered."[14] A major bull market, which few expected and none predicted, began in early January and, with the exception of a sharp correction on May 7, continued through the rest of the year. Significant moves among market leaders are shown in Table 11.4.

Table 11.4—Ranges of Market Leaders, 1915[15]

	January 1	High	Low	December 31
American Smelting	56¼	108⅞	56	108⅛
Baldwin Locomotive	40½	154½	26⅝	117⅞
Bethlehem Steel	46⅛	600	46⅛	459½
General Chemical	165¼	360	165	328½
General Electric	139	185½	138	174
General Motors	81½	558	81½	500
U.S. Steel	49⅜	89½	38	88⅞

The reason for this bull movement, which saw the Dow-Jones average go from 55 in the last quarter of 1914 to 93.8 in the first quarter of 1916, is not difficult to find: it was the prosperity that came with neutrality.[16] Railroad earnings in 1915 were 203 per cent above 1914 figures; foreign trade boomed, aiding the rise of Bethlehem Steel (the nation's leading shipbuilder and a major war material supplier) and contrary to Professor Fisher's expectation. The excess of exports over imports in 1915 was over $1.7 billion, as against over $324 million the preceding year, for an advance of 438.8 per cent. Instead of leaving America to pay for Europe's industrial expansion, gold came to New

York to settle accounts for imports, for investment in safe industries, and for participation in the American bull market. Gold imports in 1915 were 661.9 per cent over those of 1914. All the other major indices also rose, as America became a major supplier of arms and food. During the first four months of 1915, American wheat exports were 98 million bushels, as against 18 million in the same period of 1914. Heavy industry did not feel the impact of war until later in the year, and during January, only 50 per cent of the nation's steel capacity was in use. U. S. Steel was in financial difficulty, not having earned enough to cover its bond interest for the first two months of the year. As late as May the New York Chamber of Commerce announced that "hopes earlier entertained by American steel manufacturers, that they would profit by the conflict through an expansion of exports, were ill-founded."[17] But orders picked up in the fall, and by the end of the year the furnaces were going full blast, as production showed a 28.4 per cent increase over 1914.[18]

The war prosperity began to level off in 1917. Production reached all-time highs, as did prices at the stock markets. America's entry into the war had been discounted by Wall Street and the manufacturers, and did not have an important impact on the growth rate in late 1917 and during the rest of the war. Industry was at its peak when Wilson delivered his war message on April 2, and agriculture had formed the broad base which would lead farm production upward during the rest of the conflict. It is clear that armed neutrality and trade with belligerents, not actual participation in the fighting, brought prosperity to America (see Table 11.5). This expansion was, for the most part, taken up in the nation's foreign trade, as seen in Table 11.6.

Table 11.5—Production Figures of the Neutrality Period[19]

	1914	1917
Bituminous Coal	422,703,000 short tons	551,790,000 short tons
Zinc	343,000 short tons	588,600 short tons
Copper	575,500 long tons	943,100 long tons
Iron Ore	41,493,000 long tons	75,288,000 long tons

Table 11.6—Foreign Trade, 1914–1917 (Dollars)

	1914	1917
Export Balance of Trade	435,800,000	3,567,800,000
Explosives Exports	6,272,000	802,789,000
Chemicals Exports	21,924,000	181,028,000
Iron and Steel Exports	251,486,000	1,133,746,000

It was said that the du Pont powder factories "saved the cause of the Allies in 1915." The company had produced 6,000 tons of explosives in 1914; by 1918, it was turning out explosives at the rate of 200,000 tons a year. Together with other chemical concerns, it profited from the loss of German dye and drug exports to the Allies. During the war period, American production of coal-tar chemicals increased from $13.5 million to $133.5 million, and the value of drugs, from $176.7 million to $418.2 million.[20]

In the neutrality period the nation set the pattern of financing for the war. In effect, America loaned Europe money to buy goods here, having first caused the belligerent powers to sell most of their securities. At first Wilson and Secretary of State Bryan opposed the granting of credits to either side, as part of their neutrality program. But the pro-Allied bias of the nation which was evinced from the first, the desire on the part of investment bankers to benefit from the war, and the rapid diminution of foreign treasuries which made it impossible to finance purchases without loans, led to Bryan's resignation and the reversal of his policy in 1915.[21] Early in that year the British and French asked permission to float a billion-dollar loan in America. After long negotiations with New York investment bankers, this plan was scrapped in favor of a $500 million offering of 5 per cent bonds, to be sold to the public at 98, and payable in gold. This was the largest flotation up to that time; the former high was the $200 million Spanish-American loan of 1898.[22] At first the issue went slowly; German-American influence, the natural wariness of the public, and uncertainty as to the outcome of the war led investors to shy away from the bonds. But after a sales campaign that would have done credit to Jay Cooke, the entire issue was taken. Other underwritings followed. The French placed a $100 million loan, the British had two offerings of $250 million each, and a Russian Imperial loan came late in the year. By December 1, 1916, the total foreign offerings—almost entirely Allied—had reached $1,794,000,000.[23]

This staggering figure brings us back to Professor Fisher's prediction: why didn't this massive borrowing raise the domestic interest rate and cause stagnation? The answer lies in the fact that during the first two years of the war, the Allied nations deposited their gold in New York for safekeeping. This caused inflation, not depression. Most of the gold used for coins was gathered in at the beginning of the war and sent to America. The more than $200 million per annum production of British mines in South and West Africa found its way to America, along with a good deal of the reserves of London and Paris. In 1915 and 1916 alone, over one billion dollars in gold came here. This enabled America to lend money to the Allies and to finance war material purchases, and at the same time allowed industry to expand. It also helped the Exchange absorb the $2 billion of American securities which were resold by European nations and private investors. At the same time it enabled prices to rise to new highs.[24] Thus, having taken most of Europe's gold, Americans loaned the old continent the funds needed to enable her to continue the war through purchases from American factories.

Wilson's declaration of war put the credit facilities of the government at the disposal of the Allies. This came at a propitious time; private offerings of foreign securities were meeting with resistance, and it was doubtful whether more English and French issues could have been absorbed. Now the methods of collecting the money for loans were changed, even though the results were similar. The American government would float Liberty Bond issues, and grant credits to the Allies based upon the money collected. Three days after the declaration of war the Allies began to sound out the Wilson Administration on the question of government loans. It was decided that an initial credit of $3 billion would be granted, and on April 17 a law enabling the transfer to be made passed both houses of Congress and was signed by the President. During the next nineteen months such loans reached the total of $8,171,976,000, or over six times the national debt in 1917. From 1917 to early 1919—a little more than the period from America's entry in the war to the Versailles meetings—the national debt rose from $1.3 billion to nearly $27 billion, mostly as a result of direct participation in the fighting, but also due to the granting of credits to the Allies. Had a banker of 1913 been presented with these figures, he would have declared that such a rapid expansion would destroy the credit and banking facilities of the nation as well as its currency. But the Federal Reserve, buttressed by the European gold exports, handled the situation skillfully. While taxes did rise, most of the financing came from reserves, European liquidations and, most important, from war loans.

There were four Liberty Loan drives and one Victory Loan from 1917 to 1919. The first, begun in May, 1917, had a goal of $2 billion. Although the facilities of the Federal Reserve were thrown behind the drive, it went slowly at first. But when the trust companies began to buy to the tune of $300 million, it picked up steam, and wound up with a total of $3 billion in sales. A second drive, which called for $3 billion, netted $4.6 billion from almost 10 million subscribers. The third appeal, made in May, 1918, was for an additional $3 billion, and brought subscriptions for $4.1 billion. In October the Treasury asked for $6 billion, and this too was oversubscribed, with almost $7 billion in bonds taken up by more than 22 million separate buyers. Thus, the public helped finance the war, in the bargain raising the national debt from about $12 per capita in 1917 to $250 per capita in 1919.[25] There was an unexpected dividend from the drives, which affected the securities markets of the next decade. The "hard sell" of 1917–1919 led the general public to participate in securities offerings, many for the first time. This experience led many to the Stock Exchange, where they bought war stocks in odd lots. In this way, the wartime financial and monetary necessities helped create the broad-based bull market of the 1920s.

The investment bankers were also affected by the loan drives. Most of the campaigns had been conducted solely by government agencies. The sales and purchases were made through banks and other financial institutions, and not through the investment bankers. This undermined the positions of the leading houses, and enabled newer firms to gain small footholds on Wall Street. "In the money market of the twenties, syndicates of relatively obscure or new houses could handle hundred-million dollar issues without recourse to the old financial leaders."[26] The significance of this development will be seen in the following chapter.

The unprecedented prosperity, financed through liens on the future, was not shared by most workers, whose economic positions during the war were the worst since the early 1890s. Although union membership increased from 2,772,700 in 1916 to 4,125,200 in 1919, the benefits of prosperity did not trickle down to the workers until 1920, while the increased cost of living brought by war shortages and inflation wreaked havoc with their paychecks (see Table 11.7).

Table 11.7—Cost of Living Increase, 1913–1920[27]

	Wages per Hour	Cost of Living	Real Wages
1913	100	100.0	100.0
1917	128	142.4	89.9
1918	162	174.4	92.9
1919	184	188.3	97.7
1920	234	208.5	112.2

The benefits of the economic boom went to business, and were heightened by the comparatively stable wage level, which helped keep costs down while profits were rising. Bethlehem Steel, for example, had a backlog of $24.9 million at the end of 1913, and $46.5 million at the end of the following year. Because of British orders for shells, by the end of 1915, the backlog had risen to $174.5 million.[28] The industry leader, U.S. Steel, increased its capacity by over 40 per cent during the war in order to keep up with Allied and American demands, spending over a billion dollars in the process. The gross receipts from sales in 1918 reached a peak of $1,744,312,000 as against $1,683,962,000 the previous year and $1,231,875,000 in 1916. Gross earnings rose in a similar fashion, but increased costs of raw materials and especially the payments of war taxes cut the 1918 profits to $512,839,000, which was $120,071,000 below those of 1916. General Motors had a similar experience, as did General Electric and other important war materials suppliers. The du Pont powder plant in Wilmington grossed $10,276,000 more in 1918 than in 1916, but net earnings after taxes were $34,792,000 less.[29] These figures are all for *reported* earnings, and do not include writeoffs for capital improvements, depreciation, special charges, and the like. If these are taken into consideration, the picture changes drastically. The du Pont assets, for example, rose from almost $75 million in 1913 to over $308 million by the end of 1918. In addition, although profits in 1918 were generally below those of 1916, they were much higher than those of prewar America. The pattern was the same for Standard Oil, U.S. Steel, Bethlehem Steel, U.S. Rubber, Baldwin Locomotive, and Amalgamated Copper. Together with the writeoffs, such profits enabled the corporations to build their facilities and pay off their debts. U.S. Steel's 1914 assets were $1,735,257,492; by 1918 they were $2,571,617,175. Figures such as these could be given for almost every producer of war materials, which meant most of American industry.[30] If 1918 brought a degree of stagnation to the economy in terms of profits, it was stagnation at an extremely high level.

A similar story could be told of the stock market, whose boom continued in 1916, braced by reports of business and agricultural prosperity. But the rapid rise could not be maintained indefinitely, and from November, 1916 to December, 1917, prices fell steadily (see Table 11.8). The market leaders showed the effects even more vividly (see Table 11.9).

America's entry into the war did not boost prices, as many market analysts had expected; instead, the fears of war taxes caused the early-

Table 11.8—Quarterly Dow-Jones Averages, 1916–1917[31]

	Quarter	Dow-Jones Average
1916	2	90.2
	3	92.3
	4	102.8
1917	1	94.2
	2	94.7
	3	88.4
	4	73.6

Table 11.9—Prices of Market Leaders, 1915–1917[32]

	1915 Low	1916 High	1917 Low
American Smelting	56	127⅞	67⅝
Baldwin Locomotive	26⅝	118⅝	43
Bethlehem Steel	46½	700	66¼
General Electric	138	187¼	118
General Motors	82	850	74½
U.S. Rubber	44	70¾	45
Western Union	57	105½	76

year decline to broaden. Rails and shipping issues rose slightly on the news, but the rest of the list fell. Within a week analysts were pointing out that direct participation in the war would mean government loans, which would divert money from the Exchange to the Liberty Bonds. Industry might boom, they said, but stock prices would level off as a result of this drainage. In addition, the anticipated war taxes led to the selling of many glamour issues.

Once again the analysts were proven wrong. The Dow-Jones industrials average rose from 73.6 in the last quarter of 1917 to 84.2 one year later.[33] But the Liberty Loan drives did have an effect on volume. Share turnover, which had reached 145 per cent in 1916, declined to 103 per cent in 1917 and 74 per cent in 1918. Average daily volume likewise declined from 1916 to 1918, going from 842,873 shares to 677,516 to 528,701.[34]

Activity began to pick up in July, 1918, as Marshal Foch's offensive pushed the Germans back. From September through early November each new rumor caused a tremor on the Street. By November 7, when the false peace news reached New York, the ending of the war had already been discounted, and prices fell moderately. The actual armistice, which came four days later, did not change prices much at the Exchange.[35]

The initial excitement of peace was soon replaced by uncertainty.

The war had brought prosperity, which had sent stock prices upward. In 1917 and 1918 the excesses of hope and fear had been corrected. Having mistaken the nature of war's effect on the economy in 1914, the brokers and their customers were unwilling to wager on the effects of peace in 1918 and 1919.

There were two contrary views as to what would happen when "peace broke out." The bears observed that war industries, which had reached top capacity in early 1918, would suffer a letdown when government buying stopped. This would cause layoffs harmful to both capital and labor, which would spread throughout the economy. In addition, the Europeans would soon repatriate their gold, causing further declines and more distress. Such had been the case after the Napoleonic Wars and the Civil War, said the bears, and since the World War was so much greater than either in the employment of capital, the depression following the peace would be one of the worst in history.

The bulls did not believe that the situations of 1815 and 1866 had much to teach their generation. Even those who believed in historic parallels could observe that the Franco-Prussian and Spanish-American Wars were each followed by booms, as industry and consumers concentrated their purchases in order to make up for the lost years. Thus, they said, the initial peacetime prosperity would equal, and perhaps surpass, that of the war. True, there would be a slackening off after the large initial purchases had been made, but this would be gradual, and industry, aided by the Federal Reserve, would have ample time to prepare for it.

During the war Wilson had, in effect, suspended the antitrust laws. Men like Bernard Baruch were brought into government, and were transformed from sharks of Wall Street to heroes of Pennsylvania Avenue. It was universally recognized that the same capitalists who had been castigated during the Progressive era had played a vital role in defeating the Central Powers. In some respects, the businessman stood higher in the public esteem in 1919 than ever before—and during the next decade he would rise still higher.

The war years had transformed the American economy into the world's greatest, and had enabled New York to replace London as the central market of the world. The London bankers realized that their positions would be crippled during the war, and that the burdens of the fighting would drain their gold, force sales of foreign securities, and hurt their prestige, but they could not foresee how complete the American takeover would be. The United States, a net debtor in 1914 to the extent of more than $3 billion, was a net creditor by $5 billion in 1917. The implications of this shift were realized at the time of Wilson's war message, when the *Manchester Guardian* editorialized:

> European financiers would be well advised to face the fact that the war has radically transformed the relations between the United States and Europe. . . . The United States . . . by the end of the war will have wiped out most of its debt to foreign investors. It will have a currency of unimpeachable magnitude. The American bankers will have acquired the experience they have hitherto lacked in the international money market and all this strengthened financial fabric will rest upon an economic fabric which the war will have much expanded. It can hardly be doubted that under these circumstances, New York will enter the lists for the financial leadership of the world.[36]

This prediction must have seemed rash at the time, but it was proved moderate. By the end of the war the period during which England financed American development had ended, and the era of American hegemony had begun. When one adds to these economic facts the crusading ardor of war, which extended through the peace negotiations at Versailles, and the Wilsonian dream of a Parliament of Nations that captured the imaginations of people throughout the world, the fact that the bulls outnumbered the bears can be easily understood.

The optimism of 1918 seemed false in January, 1919, however, as the steel mills reported operations at 65 per cent of capacity; advance orders at U.S. Steel had dropped 42 per cent since the November armistice. The huge war material exports of 1914–1918 shriveled in early 1919 and sank lower as the year wore on. The war industries suffered a dislocation which, had it spread throughout the economy, would have been of the greatest magnitude. This slack was more than taken up, however, by exports of cotton goods, boots and shoes, agricultural implements, hardware, and other peace goods. Orders for rails with which to reconstruct Europe's transportation network stood 40 per cent higher than the prewar figure. These factors caused the 1919 export surplus to rise to $7.9 billion as against 1918's $6.2 billion. In 1920 the figure reached $8.2 billion; the expected dislocation had been overcome.[37] And what was true for exports was also true for the domestic markets. Instead of the feared breadlines, there was a major labor scarcity in civilian industries in 1919.

All of this was transmitted to the Stock Exchange which, after an initial fall in the immediate postwar period, began a sharp rally which carried prices 21.1 per cent over their 1918 lows.[38] The 1919 advance continued into early 1920. It was as frenzied as that of 1915, the major difference seeming to be that clothing manufacturers, machinery companies, and food processors were given the aura of glamour which had previously fallen to the steel, chemical, and munitions manufacturers. The Dow-Jones average stood at 84.2 in 1918's last quarter, and rose to 110.4 a year later. More than 318 million shares were transacted in 1919, a new high, and the turnover rate of 153 per cent in that year has not been surpassed since.[39] There seemed to be solid economic reasons for these advances. Prosperity never appeared so real, unemployment was negligible, and prices, though rising, were still within the grasp of the consumers. Dividends were generous in 1919, with cash payments reaching a record.

A long list of companies issued stock dividends that year, along with the cash payouts. Stock dividends were unusual at the time, and the public needed some education as to their meaning. The boards of directors told their stockholders that the corporations had a good deal of money in their surplus accounts, which would be needed at some future date for expansions of plants. Instead of paying the surplus to the shareholder in cash, its equivalent in stock would be issued, and the cash would be stored for later use. Thus, American Woolen, with a $2 million surplus, paid roughly $2 million in new shares which, in theory, was backed by the reserve fund. In those days, when net asset value meant far more to the investor than it does today, this was an important consideration.[40]

The popularity of these payouts led the corporations to continue them, and today they are of great importance.[41] It also enabled the corporations to set a regular pattern for cash dividend payments. Before the war, the capital surplus had been divided among the stockholders as dividends. In good years, the payments would be high, while in bad ones, they could fall to zero. A few firms, such as American Telephone and Telegraph, paid regular dividends, but such cases were comparatively rare and almost entirely limited to utilities. After the war many firms went on a regular basis, their payouts usually set at below normal earnings expectations. For the investor, this meant a degree of assurance as to the return on capital which had formerly not existed for owners of common stock. In prewar days the small investor would usually buy bonds if he needed regular income, and stocks only for speculative purposes. After the war he became more willing to buy stocks, and a sharp shift from bonds began. If the war taught the small investor how to buy securities in the Liberty Loan drives, the regularization of dividends helped accustom him to stock purchases.

The initiation of regular dividends was both a symptom and cause of a new attitude on the part of the corporations toward their financing. In effect, it signaled the beginning of a shift from dependence upon Wall Street bankers. In the past, a typical corporation would pay out its surplus and, when funds were needed for expansion, float a new bond issue through an investment house. With the growth of capital surplus accounts, a good deal of the financing could be accomplished internally, making bankers less necessary than they had once been. Thus, the combination of the government's role in the Liberty Loans, the growth of small underwriting syndicates, and the new power of the Federal Reserve, added to the growing importance of surplus accounts, caused a diminution of the power of the Money Trust.

While these underlying currents were being set into motion, the public enjoyed itself in the rising bull market, recklessly pouring its wartime savings into the district. A minor land boom diverted some money from the Exchange, but on balance it probably added to the speculative fever, and in that way drew many more people to Wall Street. By early 1919 there seemed no reason to expect a downturn.[42] The Federal Reserve, influenced by the Treasury which wanted low interest rates to ease debt servicing, did nothing to curb speculation. By mid-year loan rates of 25 per cent and time loan rates of 9 per cent were not uncommon, and the daily turnover at the Exchange was usually in excess of one million shares.

It was at this time that the most fantastic figure of the bull market appeared. In the summer of 1919 Charles Ponzi, an ex-convict whose former jobs included day laborer, clerk, fruit peddler, and waiter decided to become a financier. Armed with brashness, a look of innocence, and $150 in cash, he announced his willingness to borrow money and pay 50 per cent interest in forty-five days, or 100 per cent in ninety days. His plan for accomplishing this seemed simple and foolproof. Taking advantage of differences between the official and actual rates of foreign exchange, he would buy international postal coupons in one country where the rate was low and sell them in another for a higher price. Ponzi meant well; at least there is no evidence that he was intentionally dishonest. However, the exchange fluctuations were extremely complex and Ponzi made all the wrong guesses.

He paid the promised interest promptly, and all seemed well, but the investors did not know that Ponzi was paying them off with the fresh capital brought in by new buyers of his notes. Thus, the more successful his program became, the more people who came to buy his notes, the deeper in debt he went. Within the first eight months of his operation, Ponzi took in $9,582,000, for which he issued notes for $14,374,000. The large commissions paid to his agents, the failure of his plan to mature, and the inefficiencies of the operation led to a shutdown and exposure in July, 1920, at which time Ponzi was taking in money at the rate of one million dollars a day.[43]

The Ponzi scheme, begun during the last stage of the postwar bull market, ended at the beginning of a bearish period. The high hopes of December turned to gloom by July, 1920, when the prices of listed securities dropped 33 per cent. Some of the glamour issues, which had done so well until the market broke in April and May, are shown in Table 11.10.

Table 11.10—Glamour Issues, 1920[44]

	April High	December Low	Close
American Car & Foundry	147	111	121
American Locomotive	109½	74	82
American Woolen	165	55	60½
Baldwin Locomotive	118½	78	86
Crucible Steel	278	70	75
General Motors (new)	42	12	14

From the 110.4 Dow-Jones average of the fourth quarter in 1919, prices fell to 68.3 in 1921's second quarter.[45] While the market declined steadily the nation suffered through a series of strikes, highlighted by a walkout at U.S. Steel that led to labor violence. In September, 1919, the city of Boston was hit by a police strike, and seven months later the shoe factory robbery that led to the Sacco-Vanzetti case took place. At noon on September 16, 1920, a bomb exploded near the offices of J. P. Morgan & Co. on Wall Street, killing thirty-eight people and severely wounding fifty-seven. Race riots erupted in all parts of the nation, the most important in Washington, D.C. and Chicago. And in the midst of all this came the election campaign of 1920, the final debate over the League of Nations, and the start of the crime wave that began with prohibition. In this way, the nation entered the Roaring Twenties, its supposed period of regained adolescence.[46]

There was fear of "red infiltrators" in the land in 1920 and 1921.

Woodrow Wilson, the carrier of America's liberal tradition, had begun a campaign against civil rights during the last stages of the war which led to the greatest abuses of the Constitution in American history. Under Attorney General A. Mitchell Palmer—whose house was later bombed—people suspected of thinking un-American thoughts were harassed.[47] Seen in this context, the stock market decline was all the more frightening.

In December, 1920, Charles Schwab of Bethlehem Steel gave an interview to selected members of the press. After the questioning was completed, Schwab spoke to the reporters about stock prices, and asked their opinions of what was happening on Wall Street.

> What is the matter with this market? Here is Pneumatic Tool at 60 paying its regular dividend and earning a great deal more. It has a $10,000,000 plant at cash values that is selling for nothing. In fact, Pneumatic Tool is selling for less than its treasury.
>
> Bethlehem Steel is near 50 and its real book value is near 300. It will earn $40 a share this year before charge-offs and between $25 and $30 according to what we can charge off.[48]

To Schwab, this simply made no sense, and he advised his audience to buy stocks. But this recommendation went unheard, for the economy was stagnating or even declining. Construction slowed to a crawl; crop prices fell sharply, as did those of manufactured goods. Consumers, tired of inflated prices and perhaps taking a cue from the workers, staged a buyers' strike. The 1920 election was won by the business-oriented Republicans under the pliable Warren Harding, but the overwhelming victory did not bring a revival of confidence. Between Election Day and the end of the year, stock prices fell almost 25 per cent.[49]

In 1921 steel production fell from 42 million tons to less than 20 million; there were almost 100,000 business failures, and mercantile bankruptcies alone accounted for a loss of $350 million. By mid-year there were approximately 5 million unemployed. Retail prices bowed to the buyers' strike, and fell over 30 per cent, but there were few takers at even those low prices. The railroads reported that freight loadings were down 25 per cent, and some failures were noted. President Harding called several conferences of business leaders, politicians, and financiers, but did little else to stop the decline.[50]

The recovery, which began slowly that summer, was aided by several factors, the most important of which, from a financial point of view, were the actions of the Federal Reserve. In 1920 the governors, freeing themselves from Treasury influence, began raising the discount rate in an attempt to stem the wild speculation. For this tightening of credit they were blamed by some for having precipitated the panic. In 1921 the System started lowering the rate, and by year's end it had fallen from seven to 4.5 per cent. This was done to aid member banks, which loaned money to shaky firms that otherwise might have fallen. By so acting the governors demonstrated that they could function in a manner similar to that of Morgan, who had aided banks in 1893 and 1907. By bolstering confidence and providing capital, the Federal Reserve began exercising a leadership missing in the financial community since 1908. In 1923 this leadership was augmented by the inauguration of "open market operations," designed "to accommodate commerce and business and with general reference to credit conditions." Now all twelve governors acted in unison to expand or contract the currency through the sale or purchase of government securities. Although the System had been in operation since 1914, the 1920 panic and recovery marked the beginning of its power.[51]

Equally important was the inventory situation in mid-1921. At that time it had reached a level where companies were forced to place new orders or go out of business. The first choice was usually made, and industry and employment were thus strengthened. The decline of prices and the end of the buyers' strike, while often overrated, were also factors contributing to the end of the depression.[52]

While quite severe, the business falloff was not as dramatic as the two previous panics, and did not scar the national imagination. Its shortness was undoubtedly a factor in this, as was the fact that the bears had made a good case for a decline as early as 1919, and when it came, it was considered a natural correction. Indeed, some believed that such "shake-out depressions" were beneficial to the economy; they rid the nation of poorly run companies and allowed the fit to take over a larger share of the market, speeding up an operation which would have been accomplished in any case. The end product was a healthier, stronger economy. This was the view of many economists of the early 1920s, and was applauded by those businessmen who had survived the panic.

The role played by the Federal Reserve was supported by followers of the English economist, R. G. Hawtrey, who claimed that the business cycle could be corrected through the use of monetary devices and regulation of credit. If this were so—and it was a popular belief at the time—prompt action by the System could iron out future downturns and assure prosperity. With this, business entered the 1920s with confidence, and looked upon the postwar crash as little more than a minor cold, which could have been corrected with the early use of monetary medication.[53] "With the assistance of the Federal Reserve System," wrote Paul M. Mazur of Lehman Brothers in 1928, "we may expect freedom from the unwarranted and annoying financial panics of the past."[54]

This analysis seemed justified in the light of the recovery that followed. Not a single important bank had failed in 1921, and by the end of the year some leading bankers had begun poking among the debris, picking up bankrupt corporations and putting them back on their feet through new financing. It was generally believed that the prosperity that seemed to permeate the economy (with several notable exceptions) was due to the strength and wisdom of the banks; the banker, who, as we have seen, had redeemed his reputation during and immediately after the war, was lionized in the decade that followed. He was the true "advance agent of prosperity" for millions of Americans. He would always be there, as he had been in the past, to bail the nation out of economic difficulties.

Few thought of such problems in the eight years that followed the recovery. This was a truly spectacular period, although not as great in some respects as that of 1896–1907. In the 1920s business added $100 billion in new capital equipment, advanced an additional $10 billion to foreign nations, and at the same time paid off $7 billion of the national debt,[55] all without inflation (see Tables 11.11, 11.12).

It can be readily seen that the gross national product and consumer expenditures rose at a slightly more rapid rate than gross capital formation from 1923 to 1929, indicating that the prosperity was, to an extent,

Table 11.11—Selected Economic Indicators, 1921–1928[56]

	Industrial Production	Wholesale Prices	National Income (billions of dollars)	Real Income Per Capita (dollars)
1921	58	97.6	59.4	522
1922	73	96.7	60.7	553
1923	88	100.6	71.6	634
1924	82	98.1	72.1	633
1925	90	103.5	76.0	644
1926	96	100.0	81.6	678
1927	95	95.4	80.1	674
1928	99	96.7	81.7	676

Table 11.12—Gross National Product, Gross Capital Formation and Consumer Expenditures 1904–1929 (Billions of Dollars)[57]

	Gross National Product	Gross Capital Formation	Consumer Expenditures
1904–13	29.7	6.0	23.7 (averages)
1914–23	62.7	13.3	49.4 (averages)
1922	67.8	11.6	56.2
1923	79.7	16.7	63.0
1924	80.1	13.9	66.2
1925	84.2	17.5	66.7
1926	90.4	18.0	72.4
1927	88.9	17.0	71.9
1928	90.8	16.5	74.3

based on the high levels of consumption. Although new industry and improved technology were significant contributors to the boom, it was the ability to absorb consumer goods that shaped the market. This point, which is of prime significance for any understanding of the 1920s, will be discussed later.

The stock market reflected the prosperity, and magnified it to an unreasonable extent. The Dow-Jones quarterly averages show how selected market leaders reacted to the bullish economic news. (see Table 11.13).

Table 11.13—Dow-Jones Quarterly Averages, 1921–1929[58]

	1	2	3	4
1921	75.2	74.3	68.3	75.6
1922	83.8	92.9	97.6	97.5
1923	101.0	96.2	90.2	91.0
1924	97.4	91.9	101.9	108.2
1925	120.8	124.7	138.4	153.0
1926	152.9	143.0	160.5	155.3
1927	157.6	167.2	184.8	192.6
1928	199.9	213.4	225.8	267.0
1929	308.4	312.0	354.3	

It should be noted that while industrial production doubled from 1921 to 1929 and the gross national product went up approximately 50 per cent, prices of stocks in the Dow-Jones average quadrupled. In the 1896–1907 boom, both stock prices and industrial production doubled; there was no runaway stock market. This was a major difference between the two prosperity periods, and a major reason why the decline following the 1907 break was less severe than that of 1929.

There were many factors that made the prosperity of the 1920s possible, and to isolate any one would distort the picture. Among the more important, however, was the ability of America to recover from the war and the adjustment that followed at a faster rate than Europe. American businessmen had captured many foreign markets during the neutrality years, and they maintained their hold after the war, in some areas strengthening it. A good deal of the nation's surplus capital was used to buy foreign bonds, especially in South America. Because of this, America's long term direct investments in foreign countries jumped from $1.74 billion in 1912 to $7.47 billion in 1929.[59] General Motors alone invested some $50 million overseas, most of it during the 1920s. Through aggressive salesmanship, Americans were able to increase their exports during every year but one of the prosperity decade while decreasing imports, in part through the passage of two high tariff bills in three of the years (see Table 11.14).

Table 11.14—Balance of Trade, 1923–1929 (Billions of Dollars)[60]

	Imports	Exports
1923	3.79	4.17
1924	3.61	4.59
1925	4.23	4.91
1926	4.43	4.81
1927	4.18	4.87
1928	4.09	5.13
1929	4.40	5.24
Per cent change	16	26

This favorable trade balance enabled American industry to expand through producing for the foreign markets, and at the same time the tariff program prevented competition. It was not recognized at the time that such a policy might lead to short-run prosperity but eventual ruin.

Another factor in the prosperity was the development of technology, especially that of power generation, and the reorganization of industry. Between 1920 and 1929 the amount of fuel used in power plants rose by about 25 per cent, and the production of kilowatt hours increased more than 100 per cent. The amount of factory machine equipment electrified in 1929 was double that of 1914.[61] The use of power increased worker productivity by more than 40 per cent in this period. This was the major factor in raising production while capital investment stagnated. At the same time a new wave of mergers, not so large as those at the turn of the century but still quite impressive, brought greater efficiencies and savings, causing profits to rise faster than employment. Like the situation in foreign trade, the technological developments and industry reorganizations brought prosperity, but also great problems.[62]

Government's benevolent role was a key element in the economic boom. Andrew Mellon, who resigned directorships in fifty-one corporations to become Secretary of the Treasury under Harding, and who served in three administrations, was convinced that high corporate taxes were not only unsound economically but also wrong morally. The head of a huge aluminum-petroleum-banking complex, Mellon spent a good deal of his time working on tax reductions and rebates for the large corporations and leading capitalists, most of whom were also important contributors to the Republican war chests. The Mellon program had several effects. It gave business a feeling of confidence that the antitrust era had passed forever; optimism prevailed throughout the decade, and this certainty of government sympathy helped business. On the other hand, the concentration of wealth in the hands of the few—by 1929 the 60,000 families at the top of the economic scale were worth the same as the 25 million at the bottom—resulted in a lack of broadly based purchasing power and an increase of savings by the wealthy. This also helps explain why capital formation did not expand greatly during the decade. Together with the growth of technological efficiency, the inability of the consumer to keep pace with productivity would eventually lead to a diminution of demand.[63]

A good deal of the "Mellon dividends" which were retained by the corporations and were not used for new capital formation, were distributed to shareholders. Dividends rose 65 per cent in the 1920s, even with the large surpluses set aside by the big companies in the form of reserve accounts. The higher dividends attracted the large investors—who had also been aided by Mellon—to the Exchange, where they helped make the utility and industrial stocks rise sharply in the bull market. Before Mellon, many of these people invested in tax-free bonds, keeping their stock commitments comparatively low in order to avoid taxes. But when Mellon cut taxes, and the market's rise seemed to assure large capital gains, this money flowed from the bond market to stocks and became the backbone of the bull market of the 1920s.[64]

Despite this capital leakage, the factories hummed and goods were sold in increasing amounts. As we have seen, it was the nation's ability to absorb consumer goods that propped the economy throughout the decade. The reason for this expansion of consumption while wages lagged behind can be expressed in two words: credit and advertising. Prior to the war, most expensive goods were bought for cash or, at most, on thirty- or sixty-day credit. American factories were able to produce desired goods, but the consumers had no way of buying them. In 1920 there were only thirteen bathtubs and six telephones for every hundred people in the nation's cities, and the figures were lower for the farms.[65] Had the unwashed and unwired the opportunity, they would have become prime targets for salesmen, and when long-term credit purchases were instituted, this became the case. By 1929, more than 15 per cent of all goods sold were on the installment plan. Over 85 per cent of furniture, 80 per cent of phonographs, 75 per cent of washing machines, and more than half the radios, sewing machines, and other large items, were owned jointly by the consumers and the finance companies.[66] Credit was made easy by the retailers, and glamorized by the advertising men. The magazines, newspapers, and radio were glutted with appeals to buy, to consume, to "enhance your status," with the statement, "easy credit arranged" appended. In 1927 the annual volume of advertising reached over $1.5 billion, and it rose to $1.8 billion two years later.[67]

An unwitting accomplice of the advertising man, the motion picture industry, did much to change the nation's standards in the 1920s. If the ideal of 1900 was the Horatio Alger hero who rose "from rags to riches" through "pluck and luck," the idol of the 1920s was the consumer: Douglas Fairbanks in a white convertible and Gloria Swanson in a black evening gown. If Rudolph Valentino lit a cigarette with a silver lighter, hundreds of thousands of nickel-plated imitations would be sold in the months that followed.

All of these purchases took massive amounts of credit, and involved the mortgaging of tomorrow for today. The American consumer was willing to make this deal, and he traded a decade of unemployment and hunger for a decade of tinsel, much like the man who sold his soul to the devil. When the credit structure collapsed, the unwise buying of the twenties would lead to a far worse depression than might otherwise have been the case.

At the center of the credit complex was the automobile. While output in that industry rose 255 per cent for the decade, the production of railroad cars dropped 41 per cent and that of locomotives, 69 per cent. The age of rails was passing—in 1930, for the first time, railroad mileage showed a decrease for the year—and that of automobiles had arrived. The impact of the automobile on the economy cannot be overstressed. It helped create a new kind of petroleum industry, and caused great expansion in the glass, fabric, plastic, road construction, servicing, and steel industries, among others. It helped change the moral fiber of the nation, and opened new vistas to a previously all but immobile population. As far as the stock market and credit were concerned, it meant an expansion and boom; a person did not own his railroad car, but he felt he had to own his car. This helped the industry increase production from 1.5 million units in 1921 to 3.6 million in 1925. In that year nearly $3 billion in new and used cars— approximately 60 per cent of the total—were sold on time, and the president of Studebaker Corporation estimated that almost $1.5 billion in unpaid installment notes were outstanding. He said that an awkward situation could develop "if there should be another 1893."[68] Two years later, at a General Motors show in New York, a company economist upheld installment buying. In his view, the car was a necessity, and not a luxury, and if time purchases were the only way for the average man to buy his automobile, then they were good. In addition, the general trade expansion caused by large scale installment buying would, in his opinion, "ensure a proportionate increase in the installment buyers' personal incomes." Thus, an upward spiral would be put into action which would make fears about payments cancellations needless and groundless.[69]

It was a decade of optimism, which some have called an unconscious attempt to return to the womb of prewar America. The age which produced F. Scott Fitzgerald, Henry Ford, Charles Lindbergh, Calvin Coolidge, Primo Carnera, Rudolph Valentino, and Amos 'n Andy was certainly not dull; even today, the adjective "roaring" usually precedes the noun "twenties." But there were cracks in the façade. Farmers never recovered from the 1921 depression, the textile industry operated at a low level, and the miners knew starvation even as the oil fields boomed. Hardly anyone would have known this from sentiment on Wall Street, where everything seemed to be going well and all stocks appeared headed for the stratosphere—where a broker was a king and his shoeshine boy could make a fortune, so it was said, if he would invest his tips in "sound common stocks." If the Age of Morgan was the golden era of Wall Street, the Age of the Great Bull Market was its silver period.

Notes

1. *New York Times,* July 26, 1914. Fisher had a longer article in the August 30 edition, in which he elaborated upon these ideas. One of the great American economists, Fisher nonetheless had a facility for saying the wrong thing at the wrong time.
2. *New York Times,* July 26–31, 1914.
3. H. G. S. Noble, *The New York Stock Exchange in the Crisis of 1914* (New York, 1915), pp. 8–9.
4. *Ibid.,* pp. 42–43.
5. *New York Times,* October 5, 1914.
6. *New York Times,* October 7, 1914.
7. *New York Times,* January 4, 1915.
8. Noble, *The Crisis of 1914,* pp. 67–71.
9. Noyes, *War Period of American Finance,* pp. 45–56, 73–74, 99–101.
10. Nelson, *Merger Movements,* p. 165.
11. Noble, *The Crisis of 1914,* pp. 82–83.
12. *New York Times,* January 3, 1915.
13. *Ibid.*
14. *New York Times,* January 3, 1916.
15. *New York Times,* January 4, 1916.
16. Nelson, *Merger Movements,* p. 165.
17. *New York Times,* January 3, 1916; Noyes, *War Period of American Finance,* pp. 93–98.
18. *New York Times,* January 2, 3, 1916.
19. Faulkner, *American Economic History,* pp. 584–85.
20. Preston W. Slossen, *The Great Crusade and After, 1914–1928* (New York, 1937), pp. 12–13.
21. In 1936, during the Nye Investigations, Morgan partner Thomas Lamont admitted his bias readily. "Like most of our contemporaries and friends and neighbors," he said, "we wanted the Allies to win from the outset of the war." The Morgan group was "pro-Allied by inheritance, by instinct, by opinion" and favored aid to Great Britain and France from 1914 onward. Robert Sobel, *The Origins of Interventionism* (New York, 1960), p. 28.
22. Noyes, *War Period of American Finance,* p. 177.
23. Edwards, *Evolution of Finance Capitalism,* pp. 208–209.
24. Noyes, *War Period of American Finance,* pp. 134–35.
25. *Ibid.,* pp. 181–87.
26. Cochran, *The American Business System,* p. 91.
27. Faulkner, *American Economic History,* p. 594.
28. Noyes, *War Period of American Finance,* p. 113.
29. *Ibid.,* pp. 120–21, 273–75.
30. Lundberg, *America's 60 Families,* pp. 497–98.
31. Nelson, *Merger Movements,* p. 165.
32. Neill, *Inside Story of the Stock Exchange,* p. 196.
33. Nelson, *Merger Movements,* pp. 165–66.
34. The Exchange was closed on "heatless Mondays" during the war, but this was only a minor factor in the loss of business, since Tuesdays were usually the heaviest days of the week as a result. *New York Stock Exchange Fact Book,* pp. 42–43.

35. *New York Times,* November 1–14, 1918.

36. Studenski and Krooss, *Financial History of the United States,* p. 284.

37. Noyes, *War Period of American Finance,* pp. 286–89.

38. *New York Times,* January 1, 1921.

39. *New York Stock Exchange Fact Book,* pp. 42–43.

40. The capital-surplus theory of stock dividends is no longer used by most corporations. A leading exception to this until 1964 was Commonwealth Edison, which paid to stockholders a cash dividend plus a stock dividend which equaled the undistributed surplus.

41. Noyes, *War Period of American Finance,* pp. 325–26.

42. *New York Times,* August 4, 1919.

43. Lloyd Morris, *Not So Long Ago* (New York, 1949), pp. 171–72; Watson Washburn and Edmund S. DeLong, *High and Low Financiers* (New York, 1932), pp. 268–70.

44. *New York Times,* January 3, 1921.

45. Nelson, *Merger Movements,* p. 166.

46. Sullivan, *Our Times,* Vol. VI, pp. 156–79.

47. The social dislocation of the postwar era had only tangential significance for this book. For a clear discussion of this aspect of the period, see Frederick Lewis Allen, *Only Yesterday* (New York, 1961).

48. Barron, *They Told Barron,* pp. 41–42.

49. Noyes, *War Period of American Finance,* p. 381.

50. *Ibid.,* pp. 413–14.

51. It should also be noted, however, that the banks themselves were in sounder shape in 1921 than they had been in 1893 or 1907, and that this eased the job somewhat. Lee, *Economic Fluctuations,* p. 160; Kenyon E. Poole in Williamson, *Growth of the American Economy,* p. 812.

52. George Soule, *Prosperity Decade: From War to Depression: 1917–1929* (New York, 1947), p. 101.

53. R. G. Hawtrey, *Currency and Credit* (London, 1928).

54. Cochran, *The American Business System,* p. 92.

55. Marriner S. Eccles, *Beckoning Frontiers* (New York, 1951), p. 75.

56. Soule, *Prosperity Decade,* p. 108.

57. Lee, *Economic Fluctuations,* p. 148.

58. Nelson, *Merger Movements,* p. 166.

59. Cochran and Miller, *Age of Enterprise,* pp. 314–15.

60. Soule, *Prosperity Decade,* p. 323.

61. Cochran and Miller, *Age of Enterprise,* p. 303; Slossen, *The Great Crusade and After,* p. 167.

62. Soule, *Prosperity Decade,* p. 142.

63. *Ibid.,* p. 120.

64. *Ibid.,* p. 327.

65. Cochran and Miller, *Age of Enterprise,* p. 309.

66. Slossen, *The Great Crusade and After,* p. 181; Soule, *Prosperity Decade,* p. 157.

67. Slossen, *The Great Crusade and After,* pp. 362–71.

68. Cochran, *The American Business System,* p. 41; Lee, *Economic Fluctuations,* p. 154.

69. Noyes, *The Market Place,* p. 319.

12

The Triumphant Years of the Giant Bull: 1924-1929

> In conclusion, I think you realize, as I do, that the very existence of the Federal Reserve System is a safeguard against anything like a calamity growing out of money rates. Not only have we the power to deal with such an emergency instantly by flooding the Street with money, but I think the country is well aware of this and probably places reliance upon the common sense and power of the System. In former days the psychology was different because the facts of the banking situation were different. Mob panic, and consequently mob disaster, is less likely to arise.
>
> Benjamin Strong

EARLY IN 1929, President Herbert Hoover told an audience that "our whole business system would break down in a day if there was not a high sense of moral responsibility in our business world."[1] There was a great deal of truth in this statement, unfortunately, although the President and his listeners did not realize how much.

There is no way of constructing a rascality index, but if one could be made, the highs of the Drew-Fisk-Gould era would be overshadowed by the peaks of the 1920s. If the outright plundering of the Reconstruction period were not so blatant, if the giant struggles of the Morgan-Harriman years did not capture the front pages, the amount of swindling, tax evasion, misrepresentation, incompetence, and general boondoggling was still great. The malefactors of the 1920s usually operated within the letter of the law, but they ignored or misunderstood the spirit.

The attitude of government was symbolic of this laxness. Although

Governors Al Smith and Franklin D. Roosevelt might have asked for legislation to curb the New York Stock Exchange, they remained silent. During a period when the national economy called for firm direction, Presidents Harding and Coolidge, along with their congresses, refused to act in any way to curb abuses, and President Hoover limited himself to warnings. If America was technologically entering the future with Henry Ford, it was, at the same time, returning politically to the days of Grover Cleveland, led by complacent Presidents and *laissez-faire* legislators. The politics of Cleveland—outworn even in the 1890s—provided no real response to the technology and economy of the 1920s.

This inertia was not due to ignorance, but rather was a planned abdication of responsibility by those in political power. In 1927, for example, Professor William Z. Ripley of Harvard, whose work on business problems and abuses had earned him a reputation as one of the nation's leading business economists, was invited to the White House to discuss his ideas with the President. Coolidge listened carefully to Ripley, apparently recognizing that the Professor's criticisms of corporate practices were sound, that oftentimes businesses operated contrary to the public interest, and that there was an unhealthy concentration of economic power. When Ripley was finished, Coolidge removed his cigar from between his clenched teeth, leaned forward, and asked: "Is there anything we can do down here?" Ripley answered that under existing legislation the President was powerless, and in any case, the problem should be solved through state action. Coolidge leaned back and heaved a sigh of relief.[2]

So Wall Street was left alone, and it operated unhindered by legislation during the 1920s. The reforms of the Progressives were ignored; there were no Hughes and Pujo investigations to embarrass those in power. The financiers and speculators blessed the Presidents, prayed for the health of Secretary of the Treasury Mellon, and proceeded to carve up one another in their bids for wealth and power.

The absence of outside control was only one factor in making the runaway markets of the decade so chaotic. The lack of internal discipline was of equal if not greater importance.

As has been observed, J. P. Morgan's death in 1913 and the creation of the Federal Reserve System in the same year marked the end of an era. Never again would one man dominate American finance. While Morgan lived, the Wall Street community never lacked for leadership and direction. Together with Jacob Schiff, George F. Baker,

James Stillman, and others, the House of Morgan made sure that raiders and tinhorns could not survive for long. If the district's leaders were robber barons, at least they kept order and had a sense of responsibility. Morgan's refusal to allow Gates a role in the U.S. Steel flotation was only one of many such actions the Great Man took during his reign. Whenever the market needed steadying, the sight of the Morgan contingent on the Exchange floor would calm the nerves of the smaller fry, and on more than one occasion the House of Morgan led the district out of a panic.

There were no J. P. Morgans and Jacob Schiffs in the markets of the 1920s, although their replacements, Jack Morgan and Otto Kahn, were capable men. The House of Morgan still exercised leadership in industrials, and Kuhn, Loeb led in rails, but on several occasions Wall Street did not follow them. When this happened and swift retribution did not follow, Wall Streeters realized that the Age of the Titans had passed. Some thought that Governor Benjamin Strong of the Federal Reserve Bank of New York could fill the vacuum, but Strong lacked the spark of genius and, as we shall see, might have done Wall Street more harm than good.

Taking the place of the former leaders was a plethora of syndicates. Most of the big underwritings of the decade were accomplished through from two to a dozen or more houses. Before the war an underwriting of over one million dollars was considered large, and might be carried off by a single house. The $20 million and $30 million flotations of the twenties made syndicates necessary not only in order to share risks, but also to raise the needed capital.

Although each syndicate generally acted as a temporary partnership as long as the underwriting was in progress, different types appeared during the decade. In the limited liability selling syndicate each member was responsible for distributing a set amount of securities and no more, while in an unlimited liability selling syndicate the participants sold as many securities as they could, receiving in return a percentage of the total profit. Members of a selling group were concerned only in retailing securities. A central house, usually a market leader or a banking group, directed the wholesale distribution.[3]

As the market grew more frantic and competition between houses grew in intensity, the unlimited syndicate form began to dominate. By the end of the 1920s, syndicates encouraged commission cutting, customer stealing, and "beating the gun" by trying to sell securities before the announced date of offering. These unethical practices were particularly evident from 1927 to 1929, when bonds were "undigested" during the great rise in stocks, and means of dumping them had to be found. As a result, customers were often sold bonds that had questionable value. Over 30 per cent of the bonds issued in the 1927–1929 period went into default, as against less than 15 per cent of those issued during the Morgan era.[4] The chaos brought by unregulated competition also made cooperation between investment bankers difficult. When united action was badly needed toward the end of the bull market, it was not forthcoming.

In 1936, *Fortune* published the figures for underwriting in 1927. They showed that Morgan and Kuhn, Loeb were still on the top in terms of volume, but they by no means dominated the field as they once did (see Table 12.1).

Table 12.1—Leading Underwriters, 1927

(dollars)

J. P. Morgan & Co.	520,399,000
Kuhn, Loeb, & Co.	513,014,000
Dillon, Read & Co.	409,277,000
Harris, Forbes & Co.	398,461,000
National City Co.	310,845,000

Led by Jack Morgan, but really masterminded by Thomas Lamont and others, the House of Morgan was still the greatest voice on Wall Street. Its power lay not so much in financial domination as in the good will accumulated by its founder, although the connections with banks and trust companies were still strong.

Like other Wall Street firms, Morgan solidified its position by allowing important people to buy shares at low prices prior to public offerings. These "preferred lists" included Calvin Coolidge, Bernard Baruch, John J. Raskob, Richard B. Mellon, Charles Francis Adams, Charles A. Lindbergh, and John W. Davis, among others.

Thus ran only a small part of the Morgan list. It must be remembered that each house had its own insiders, although a fortunate few were on several lists.[5] Favored customers were expected to reciprocate with political and business favors. For example, Raskob was allowed 2,000 shares of Allegheny Corporation at the offering price of $20 a share. After being on the open market for a week, the price was $33, and five months later it had reached $57. Raskob was grateful, and wrote the following note to George Whitney, a Morgan partner:[6]

Dear George:

Many thanks for your trouble and for so kindly remembering me. My check for $40,000 is enclosed herewith in payment for the Allegheny stock, which kindly have issued when ready in the name of John J. Rascob, Wilmington, Del. I appreciate deeply the courtesies shown me by you and your partners, and sincerely hope the future holds opportunity for me to reciprocate. The weather is fine and I am thoroughly enjoying golf and sunshine.

Best regards and good luck.

John

The practice of placing individuals on preferred lists was not illegal, although its morality is another matter. The fact that those listed were of both political parties was significant; Morgan and other houses wanted to assure friendly Democratic as well as Republican leadership.

Kuhn, Loeb, controlled by such able bankers as Otto Kahn, Mortimer Schiff, Felix Warburg, and later Lewis Strauss, retained its position in the rails throughout the decade, concentrating more on bonds than on stocks. Since 1902 Kuhn, Loeb had worked in harmony with Morgan, each staying in its own sphere. With the aid of smaller allied firms, these two houses tried to keep order on the Street and exclude outsiders.[7]

Dillon, Read specialized in foreign bonds, many of which were of questionable value. It was second only to Morgan in the bond field, and operated by virtue of the larger firm's sufferance. With Morgan's encouragement, Dillon, Read became banker for many non-Rockefeller oils, the most important of which was the Texas Company and Amerada Petroleum. This was not true competition, however, for it was done with Rockefeller's knowledge and assent. It was understood that the Chase National Bank, a Rockefeller controlled institution, would dominate oils and remain out of rails and industrials, and Morgan and Kuhn, Loeb would respect its position.[8] As for Dillon, Read, it was to take care of those oils which did not fit into Jersey Standard's scheme of things, and help give the industry the appearance of competition. In addition, the house would, from time to time, pull a *coup,* again with Morgan's blessings. In 1925, the firm became the banker for Dodge Brothers, and sold shares to the public in a highly successful flotation. Du Pont controlled General Motors while Ford was privately owned by a man whose contempt for Wall Street in particular and bankers in general was no secret. The Dodge flotation may be viewed as an attempt on the part of the New York Establishment to rid itself of an outsider who threatened to disturb the peace.[9]

These firms, together with the Rockefeller-controlled National City Company, dominated the Wall Street market and led most major flotations in rails, industrials, and oils. They acted in accord on general policy while attempting to keep the peace among smaller fry. There was competition on the lower levels and in the general brokerage business, but insofar as underwriting was concerned, there were powerful forces working for harmony.[10]

Unconsciously and consciously opposing the drive for an orderly market place were several forces, some internal and some external, some old and some new. The market boom, corporation needs for new capital, and the feverish excitement of the district, attracted many young men to Wall Street. As we have seen, during the 1890s farm boys and men from small towns and villages came to New York. They would often start as runners or pad-pushers and, if they were talented and had some luck, might rise to higher positions after several years.

This situation was different during the early 1920s. The investment houses began scouting college graduating classes for likely trainees; anti-intellectualism was gone from Wall Street. Selling securities to a gullible public required a certain finesse; the buyer had to believe that the salesman knew something about the shares he was retailing. During each year of the decade the Street welcomed increasing numbers of trainees who, after a few weeks of introduction to methods, were given a telephone, a desk, a list of customers, and a pat on the back. What their predecessors had taken years to attain, the salesmen of the 1920s received in weeks. While the customer's man of prewar days tended to be a social Darwinist who struggled to prevail over his fellow-brokers, and had to carefully study the market to make his way, the broker of the twenties, more often than not, lacked clear knowledge of securities and acted as part of a "team." He did not dream of rising to the top, but rather hoped for increased commissions and, in the end, perhaps a junior partnership.

In 1924 Matthew Josephson, late of Columbia University and the Paris surrealist circles, went to Wall Street and became a customer's man. Josephson admitted that he knew little of what was going on, and relied more often than not upon rumors for the advice he gave clients.

What counted for us was the business of keeping our customers trading in and out of securities, so that win or lose we gathered our broker's fees at fifteen dollars for each hundred shares . . .

During a fortnight of orientation I familiarized myself with the machinery of the securities markets, finding it complex but very neatly rationalized. Then I was put to work at the top instead of at the bottom, after receiving some tutelage from an aged partner who planned to retire soon.[11]

Josephson did well; everything was going up, and his clients were put into stocks which were swept along by the bull market. In turn, they would bring in new customers.

"You are getting *action*," one of my firm's executives said to me approvingly. "That is the main thing here, action." He meant that by turning over securities rapidly I was netting fees in good volume—a third of which was credited toward my salary. Within several weeks my salary was raised from a beginner's pay to a more comfortable sum. I was assured that I was an apt pupil. My growing confidence and zeal increased my following; as my activity expanded I became accustomed to take quick advantage of short-term movements; then my salary was raised again, so that I earned more in a week than my wife and I had sometimes lived on during three months while in Europe.[12]

Josephson continued to put his happy customers into stocks of which he had heard wild rumors, and for a while they went up. Then, after committing most of his accounts to a particular security, it fell sharply, wiping out many of his customers. Josephson realized that a more experienced customer's man would not have acted as rashly as he, but he was counseled not to feel sorry for his ruined clients.[13]

In defense of the incompetent brokers, it should be noted that there was not enough talent in the nation to provide for Wall Street's needs. By 1929, there were over 400,000 people engaged in financial pursuits in the United States, and their salaries equaled those paid in agriculture and mining combined.[14] With such a great demand for talent, and such high salaries offered even the incompetent, it was perhaps inevitable that the level of performance and morality would suffer. Many a customer's man of the period had no difficulty in swallowing the immoral practices then common on Wall Street. He was able to carry out orders that would have appalled men like Henry Clews. In 1929, for example, a large brokerage house sent the following memorandum to its sales force:

We anticipate a reasonable supply of new issues. Some of them will be easy sellers and some will be difficult, but for us to do our full duty, it is essential that we be prepared to sell any issue of securities which this company buys, regardless of whether it is hard or easy to sell.[15]

In the past, such notices could be found in bucket shops; by the late 1920s, they were not unusual in the large, conservative establishments. The giants had been replaced by the pygmies, and the pygmies were the heroes of the bull market.

During the bull market a few medium-sized brokerages specialized in areas not dominated by the giants. Blyth, Witter & Co. concentrated on the electric power and light industry flotations on the West Coast, and had its main office in San Francisco with branches in Los Angeles, Portland, Seattle, and New Orleans. Eastman Dillon & Co. was primarily interested in the Pennsylvania area, and underwrote light and medium-sized industry there as well as some utilities. Neither posed a real threat to New York, and both were allowed to grow and prosper.

A different situation existed in Chicago, where Halsey, Stuart & Co. posed a threat to Morgan's plans for a utilities holding company. The Chicago firm got a headstart by capturing Samuel Insull's business. In 1922, Insull sold $27 million in bonds through Halsey, Stuart, whose ability and interest in widespread distribution were second to none. Harold L. Stuart, the firm's head, dreamed of the day when Chicago would replace New York as the nation's financial center, with Insull as the leading American industrialist and he as its most important banker. Since utilities were the glamour securities of the decade, and since his firm was the banker to the leading American utilities magnate, such a dream, although rather far-fetched, did not seem impossible of attainment. Stuart was a capable banker, and by 1930, largely through his efforts, over a million people held shares in Insull companies.[16] At first Wall Street ignored Stuart, and then it competed with him. Morgan was planning to do for utilities what his father had done for steel. His United Corporation seemed threatened by the Insull empire. When a direct assault failed to destroy the Chicago group, Wall Street began to lay in waiting, as it had for Morse and Heinze in 1907, looking for the one false move that would be the signal for an all-out attack.

The Halsey, Stuart threat was symptomatic of a serious challenge to the Street by outsiders who were attempting to construct their own business empires. There were three major figures involved in this threat—Samuel Insull, the Van Sweringen brothers, and Ivar Kreuger—and a host of minor ones. The Giannini complex of California, centered in the huge Bank of America, posed a danger to New York's commercial banks, but Giannini never seriously thought of entering investment banking.

Samuel Insull was to his generation what Vanderbilt, Cooke, Rockefeller, and Carnegie had been to theirs: the symbol of an age and its most successful product. Insull was born in England, and worked as a stenographer before coming to America in 1881. He spent twelve years as Thomas Edison's secretary, and soon became his unofficial business manager. Insull proved to be a genius at organization as well as a highly skilled businessman; in 1884 he managed to best J. P. Morgan himself when the Great Man tried to take what Insull thought was too great an interest in the Edison Electric Light Company.[17] In 1892 he went to Chicago as head of the Chicago Edison Company, and within fifteen years had organized the Commonwealth Edison Company as one of the nation's largest utilities. Insull made several important contributions to American business ideology and practice in this period. He was the first to utilize the "open-end mortgage," by which a company could continually refinance its debt. He expanded Commonwealth's coverage greatly, bringing electricity to areas which other utilities ignored for reasons of economy. Insull believed that through rapid but careful expansion and full utilization of plant, rates could be lowered and profits increased at the same time. His successes in proving this point gave Commonwealth one of the best records in the nation.[18]

Insull's interests spread all over the Midwest during the 1920s. By the end of the decade he controlled five great systems with combined assets of $2.5 billion, which supplied 4.5 million customers with gas or electricity. In all, these companies generated one-eighth of the nation's power. They were well run and soundly financed, and were models of good business. Indeed, Insull's reputation was so great that bankers almost pleaded with him to accept their money. At a party during the late twenties, a banker approached Insull, Jr., who by then had become his father's right hand man, and said ingratiatingly, "Say, I just want you to know that if you fellows ever want to borrow more than the legal limit, all you have to do is organize a new corporation, and we'll be happy to lend you another $21,000,000."[19] Insull once remarked that "bankers will lend you umbrellas when it doesn't look like rain," but he took up many of these offers and expanded his holdings.[20]

Partially through ambition, and partially due to fears of outside raiders, Insull organized Insull Utilities Investments as a holding company in 1928. On its first day of trading the stock rose from 25 to 30, and within a half year it was selling at 150. During the same period two of I.U.I.'s constituents, Commonwealth Edison and Middle West Utilities, rose from 202 and 169 to 450 and 529 respectively. In order to prevent a takeover of I.U.I., Insull organized a second holding company, Corporation Securities of Chicago. Under a complex system of cross-financing, I.U.I. owned 28.8 per cent of Corp, while Corp owned 19.7 per cent of I.U.I.[21] "The net effect was that after September, 1929, these twin investment trusts emerged as the throne room of the Insull empire." By then, all of the Insull companies were rising rapidly at the Exchange; in the fifty days ending on August 23, 1929, these securities had appreciated at the rate of $7,000 a minute, for a total rise of over a half billion dollars.[22] On the eve of the panic of a few months later, Insull appeared impregnable.

The Van Sweringen brothers were to Cleveland what Insull was to Chicago, with two important differences: the brothers worked in harmony with Wall Street, and they were not builders, but reorganizers. Oris Paxton Van Sweringen was two years older than Mantis James Van Sweringen, but the two seemed alike in every detail. They were bachelors, lived together in the same house, and even slept in twin beds. Under their direction Shaker Heights, one of the nation's wealthiest communities, was replanned, transformed, and developed with great success. Then the brothers turned to a reorganization of Cleveland transportation, and within eight years had gained control of a rail network comprised of eight large lines. Included in their empire were the New York, Chicago, and St. Louis (commonly known as the Nickel Plate), the Erie, the Wheeling and Lake Erie, and the giant Missouri Pacific. All of this was started with an investment of $500,000 of their own money and an equal amount from friends.[23]

The Van Sweringen organization was one of the most complex the nation has ever known. It baffled the Senate investigators of 1933, and earned for the brothers praise from the master manipulator of them all, Hjalmar Schacht of the Reichsbank.

The Van Sweringens pyramided companies, controlling in this way a large amount of capital and assets through majority holdings in the top company. The brothers owned 80 per cent of the Vaness Company, which in turn owned 50 per cent of General Securities Corporation. In addition, they owned 40 per cent of General Securities outright. General Securities controlled Allegheny Corporation through a 41 per cent stock ownership, and Allegheny controlled other holding companies and operating roads, which in turn controlled still more operating roads. At the bottom levels, the Van Sweringen equity became infinitesimal, but they held control nonetheless. Thus, the brothers had less than 1 per cent of the equities in the Nickel Plate, Wheeling and Lake Erie, Pere Marquette, Erie, and Chesapeake and Ohio, but they operated the roads. In one road, the Hocking Valley, the equity worked out to .25 per cent, but the Van Sweringens controlled it as though they owned a majority of its stock.[24]

This structure was made possible through Morgan financing and large loans from Cleveland banks, which thrust funds at the brothers in much the same way that the Chicago bankers offered to help Insull. At the same time that Insull was organizing Corp and I.U.I., the Van Sweringens were the toast of Cleveland. Just as Insull beautified Chicago by constructing the Civic Opera House, the brothers led a building boom from which came modern Cleveland. And few complained if the Van Sweringens controlled large corporations with small stakes. As the leading students of the corporate form of the next decade would observe, "the stockholder in the modern corporation has surrendered a set of definite rights for a set of indefinite expectations." As long as dividends arrived regularly, as long as the stock's quotation went higher on Wall Street, the shareholders were more than willing to surrender control.[25]

In 1922 Ivar Kreuger, the Swedish match king and descendant of an admiral who had once been voted the most honest man in the nation, came to America to expand his already sizable empire. Despite a flabby appearance, clammy hands, and glassy eyes, Kreuger was able to captivate most Americans with his stories of world-wide match companies. Jack Morgan alone was unimpressed with Kreuger, telling his associates: "I don't trust that man. I want nothing to do with him." But the respected house of Lee, Higginson thought otherwise, and offered to back Kreuger, pressing funds on him, which he was more than willing to take. The eminent accounting firm of Ernst & Ernst, which kept books for Coca Cola, Firestone, and Chrysler, among others, was to audit his books. With such backing, Kreuger proceeded to organize the International Match Company, and sold

$148.5 million of its securities to the American public. Of this amount, $144 million was transferred to Kreuger interests in Europe and eventually disappeared in the complex of interrelated and pyramided companies that were under the domination of Kreuger & Toll, the match king's holding company. Little was known of Kreuger's operations—he was able to keep Ernst & Ernst away from his books most of the time—but they were apparently quite profitable. International Match's dividends were paid promptly, and Kreuger would often deposit the money for them in his New York bank before it was due. "We have so much money over here," he said airily, that "you might as well have this now." From time to time he would send a million or so extra. When the overpayment was pointed out, Kreuger would exclaim, "Oh, we simply made a mistake. We have so much money here, we just can't keep track of it."[26] No wonder the Kreuger stocks, like those of Insull and the Van Sweringens, rose steadily throughout the decade.

The old Establishment of Wall Street was barely able to hold its own, and these new men were able to sink a wedge into its once impregnable wall. Insull was honest, but in the end, naïve. The Van Sweringens were clever, and considered themselves moral as well—in the context of the 1920s, they were doing the accepted thing. Kreuger was an out-and-out fake and plunderer, who would eventually swindle the American people out of $250 million.[27] The new men were at best able and efficient managers who were out of their element in high finance, and at worst, crooks.

As previously noted, every bull market produces its share of speculators and manipulators, and the twenties was no different. Handsome, dapper Jesse Livermore was called "King of the Speculators" at that time. Before gaining his Exchange seat, he had operated a bucket shop for ten years. By the time of the young bull market he already knew every trick in the book and was busy inventing new ones. Livermore had come out of the 1907 panic with $3 million, and planned to parlay it into a billion dollars. At first, he was a failure; a bear by nature, he sold when he should have bought in 1915. He switched to a bull stance shortly thereafter, and cleaned up in 1916–1919. Then, as the war came to a close, Livermore instinctively felt a crash was coming. He sold everything, went short, and waited to reap in profits. No one knows how much money he made in the postwar crash, but it was in the millions.[28]

Livermore posed a striking contrast to the Wall Street figures of past bull markets. Unlike Little, Fisk, Gould and Gates, he remained in the background; at one time he operated from a hideaway equipped with thirty telephone lines. In 1929, visitors to the Exchange were unable to pick him out of the crowd on the floor.[29]

Livermore differed from his predecessors in his realization that the market as a whole could not be controlled, and that special situations rather than a general rise must be watched for by the speculator. He was the first to indicate what has since become a cliche—that it is a market of stocks and not a stock market. "With one thousand issues, representing every industry, listed on the Stock Exchange," he said in 1928, "there is no such thing as a trend any more." "Our market," he concluded, "is becoming more and more like the London Stock Exchange. Any attempt to fix a trend for such a variety of issues as is represented now on the Big Board is futile."[30] In describing his methods, he said:

> My principal method is to study the effect of present and future conditions on the earning power of the various companies engaged in different lines of industry. Anticipation of coming events is the whole thing. When I have my mind made up about this, I wait for the psychological moment. I do not deal promiscuously; instead, I decide how much I will trade in, and how much money I will risk on that trade, and then I buy or sell the whole quantity at once.[31]

But Livermore did not practice what he preached; at the time of the interview he was conducting several simultaneous manipulations, molding public opinion, playing upon the psychology of fears and hopes, and forcing prices up and down. "I never go into a trade unless I see at least ten points profit," he said, and he made certain that the rises came soon after his purchases.[32]

Livermore's archenemy—although more in the press than in reality—was Arthur W. Cutten, a former Chicago bookkeeper who, through shrewd deals in the grain markets, was able to arrive on Wall Street in 1925 with what many said was $25 million in profits. Paradoxically, at the same time that Cutten was leaving grain for stocks, Livermore was temporarily deserting stocks for grain; each did well in the other's specialty. By 1926 they were in the same arena, and Wall Streeters soon learned that when Cutten thought a stock would rise, Livermore would be sure to expect a fall. Both men worked hard to make their prophecies come true, Livermore by flitting in and out of a situation in a matter of hours, and Cutten by gradually accumulating shares over a period of months. There were many struggles between the two from 1926 to 1929, and when one of them began, smaller traders would gather around and buy or sell the stock involved with the same spirit as they would bet on the Dempsey-Firpo fight.[33]

In 1917 Michael J. Meehan was a theater ticket broker with offices at 71 Broadway, but the following year he moved to Wall Street, giving up tickets for stocks and bonds. By the mid-twenties he had built up one of the district's biggest Curb houses and had purchased a seat on the Exchange. Although not as powerful as Livermore or Cutten, he was far better known. Meehan loved publicity, and delighted in reading stories of his escapades. His firm, Irish to the core, included Esmonde O'Brian, John Moyland, Richard O'Brian, and J. P. McKenna. They would often enter the Exchange in a well-defined group when bulling or bearing an issue, and they operated with mathematical precision and a flair for the dramatic. When traveling by rail or ship, Meehan was never far from the stock ticker, surrounded by cronies, partners, and hangers-on. By 1927 he owned seven Exchange seats and had completed plans for a nationwide network of brokerage houses. Meehan was responsible for the introduction of branch offices on ocean liners, putting his men on the *Bremen,* the *Berengaria,* the *Leviathan,* and other luxury ships where they served customers who preferred gambling on the tape to betting in the ship's lottery.[34]

It would be impossible to discuss or even list the names of all the prominent speculators of the decade; every week produced a new plunger, a new pool, a new manipulation, and new heroes for the tape watchers. There was Louis Zimmerman, who preferred playing golf to playing the market, and still managed to make over $10 million during the 1925–1929 period. Zimmerman rarely appeared on the Street, and instead placed his orders from the clubhouses at nineteenth holes all over the country. John J. Levinson, a free-lance trader who managed pools in Celotex, Borg-Warner, and Pitney-Bowes among others, made profits of over one million dollars a year. He was on close terms with Raleigh T. Curtis, who wrote a column entitled "The Trader" for the *New York Daily News.* Levinson would buy a stock, Curtis would speak highly of it in his column, the stock would rise, Levinson would sell, and the two friends would share the profit. Each time the procedure was repeated, it was easier, for as Curtis' readers bought on his recommendations, they made them come true, and the next time they trusted him all the more. David Lion, a market manipulator, and William J. McMahon, president of the McMahon Institute of Economic Research and for a while, a widely-followed radio commentator on stock market affairs, worked a similar dodge. Lion would buy or sell stocks, and then McMahon would speak enthusiastically or disparagingly of them in the next week's broadcast or market bulletin. George Breen, a master speculator, was in the practice of buying options on stocks that he planned to "move." He then would plant rumors along the Street of mergers, higher earnings, or new managements, which would shoot the price up and add millions to his bank account. In this way he was able to salvage a small fortune for the majority stockholders of many a firm. In a typical example, Kolster Radio, a company which had earned 87 cents a share in 1927 and 20.5 cents the following year, called Breen in and told him that the firm would earn nothing in 1929. Breen was given free options on Kolster stock which enabled him to buy a given number of shares at the market closing of that day. Breen took Kolster Radio in hand, and within a month had bulled it from 70 to 95. He then sold out, making a profit of $1.3 million on no investment at all. Within another month, Kolster sold for 3. At the same time, Breen worked with Cutten, Albert Wiggin—who was chairman of the Chase National Bank—and others, in manipulating the Sinclair Consolidated Oil Corporation. The group collaborated for seven months in 1928–1929, and then cleaned up a profit of nearly $13 million.[35]

Joseph Higgins, a quiet man who preferred to work for others in the tradition of James Keene, was frequently called upon by Livermore, Cutten, and others, to direct floor raids during a cornering operation or a bull or bear move. A. Newton Plummer was often engaged to plant stories in newspapers and in radio scripts. Frank Bliss, considered the most skillful floor trader of his day, was called in from time to time to work with Higgins and others on major moves. It was said that Bliss could accumulate or sell thousands of shares without anyone being the wiser. The Fisher Brothers, who sold their coachworks to General Motors early in the decade, came to Wall Street with a fortune estimated one-half billion dollars. The slightest hint of their interest in a security would be enough to send it up, and when the Fishers sold, everybody sold. William C. Durant, out of power at General Motors, was still wealthy and very much a part of the Wall Street scene. It was said that he handled more stock than any other man during the great bull market; in 1928 he bought and sold over 11 million shares, which represented $1.25 billion. In addition, he indirectly funneled $2 billion more into the markets.[36]

Finally, there was Joseph P. Kennedy, who came to Wall Street from Boston *via* Bethlehem Steel's Fore River Yard, which he managed during the World War. Kennedy would have stood out on Wall Street during any period other than the twenties. He was bold, resourceful, and merciless; his takeover of what later became RKO was a classic tale of bluff, doubledealing, and manipulation. But in the financial world of the twenties, he was only one more shark among dozens of others.[37] One reporter, in describing the plungers of the period, wrote:

> One of them, it is reported, travels about the country in a private car, equipped as a rolling office, from which he carries on operations involving millions of shares of stock in a year. To keep in touch with the market while *en route* from one of his factories to another he is arranging now [1930] to receive stock quotations by radio. A private station in the East will, it is said, broadcast ticker prices on a short wave length just for his use. Another, operating from a small Western town, scatters his orders by wire through a score of Southern and Western brokerage houses, according to another story. By scattering his orders in such a fashion, instead of dealing direct with New York, he keeps any one from knowing what he is doing, and the world still believes him to be what he was only a few years ago; a moderately influential small town millionaire. He has traded, it is claimed, however, in $10,000,000 to $15,000,000 worth of stock in a month's time.[38]

When compared to men like these, the speculators of the previous generation appear tame indeed. Baruch was still in the market, but the once wild plunger of the 1890s was considered a wise but stodgy old man during the 1920s; he bought for cash, refused to use margins, and was cautious regarding the bull market. Harry Content remained the most respected broker on the Street, but the plungers preferred to use the Meehans and other speculative houses. As for the rest, most had either retired or had stepped into the background, leaving the center stage for the new generation.[39]

These men had several things in common. First, practically all were bulls; even Livermore was forced to convert in the face of rising values. There were no major bear raiders on the Street who might have acted to force prices down to a reasonable level. Next, they were not of the Establishment. We have already seen how Insull, the Van Sweringens, and Kreuger made their fortunes outside of the

Morgan complex, or at best, with its condescension. The Morgan-Schiff alliance, which together with the Rockefeller banks led the Establishment, represented a concord between English-American Protestants and German Jews. The new men—Zimmerman, Levinson, Meehan, Kennedy, and Breen—represented outsiders, who were east European Jews or Irish Catholics, both of whom were usually unacceptable in polite society during the twenties. The Van Sweringens, Insull, Giannini, Kreuger, Cutten, and many others who were not Irish Catholic or Jewish interlopers, came from the Midwest, Far West, and overseas. Only Livermore had the proper geneological and geographic credentials, being a New York, English-American Protestant. Significantly, he was one of the few who had made a place for himself on Wall Street before the war.

The new men were noted for their lack of interest in business power. Market manipulators of the past, such as Drew, Gould, and Gates, were often heads of corporations as well as speculators. We have seen how Drew began his leeching of the Erie only after becoming its treasurer. Livermore, Cutten, and the others lived for profits, and had little interest in running a firm. As a result, most of them knew how Wall Street operated, but few had any idea of the nature of its economic underpinning.

Finally, it should be noted that the new men had no experiences with major bear markets except that of the short postwar decline. To them the long, drawn-out panics of 1893 and 1907 were dim memories, at best. They lacked the caution that a person like Gates might have exercised. Thus, when the crash came, they were confused, frightened, and almost paralyzed. Many lost everything and left Wall Street as paupers. A few would come back and make new fortunes; some entered other aspects of business. A handful, like Livermore, would stay around Wall Street for several years and then put bullets through their heads.

The new men were heroes to millions of tape-watchers for two reasons. First, they were ideals to which the petty speculators aspired —millionaires many times over whose easy come, easy go attitude was much admired. In addition, they were credited with supporting the market and pushing it higher, thus making it possible for the little man who invested a few hundred dollars to make a small killing. This seemed perfectly legitimate to the small investor. After all, if a stock went up and was then sold, the seller made money, and the buyer would also become richer, for the price would rise again before he sold the shares. Many investors believed that if a block of stock worth $100 doubled over a year or so, the additional money had been created out of thin air, with no one the loser. It was as though a magic money machine had been invented by Wall Street and given *gratis* to the public, which felt it perfectly moral and even admirable to get something for nothing. Entranced by these notions, people entered the stock market in greater numbers and with larger amounts of money than ever before. Their purchases and sales made the gigantic Cutten and Livermore pools possible. The public thought it could not make money without the aid of manipulators; in fact, the Cuttens and Livermores could not have acted as they did without massive support from small investors.

It is difficult to say just how many people participated in the great bull market. In 1929 there were over 20 million shareholders on the books of American corporations, but many of these had shares in more than one firm, and therefore were counted several times. One estimate, based on tax returns, was that of 9 million shareholders.[40] This figure, however, ignores those who did not declare their earnings and included owners of Liberty Bonds. One informed commentator thought that there were approximately 15 million securities owners out of a population of 120 million. "Estimating a family at three to five persons and allowing one stockholder to each family, from 45,000,000 to 75,000,000 people were interested in the stock market of 1929."[41]

Perhaps the most reasonable estimate was that of Joseph McCoy, the chief actuary of the Treasury who, in 1928, said that there were some 3 million shareholders, excluding the in-and-out speculators. McCoy found that some individuals held as many as 500 different issues in a year, and thus were counted 500 times, inflating many estimates and accounting for the widely held belief that over 15 million people were in the market. He also discovered that most shareholders were city dwellers, and that those investors in rural areas usually put their money into road bonds and other municipal and state securities. The average high-salaried person, he said, owned stocks of one kind or another, often in the business in which he was engaged. Millionaires owned less than 7 per cent of the outstanding corporate stocks, but 95 per cent of the millionaires derived most of their income from dividends. There were about 200,000 widows and orphans who were solely dependent on stock dividends for their sustenance. Laborers and low-salaried workers seldom put money in stocks and bonds, McCoy concluded, using savings banks and building and loan societies for whatever surplus they might have had. It was not uncommon, however, for a worker with an income of between $2,000 and $5,000 a year to own stock. The width and breadth of ownership may be illustrated by the figures obtained by the National Industrial Conference Board for the owners of fifty shares or more of a public utility's 7 per cent preferred stock. It must be remembered that shareholders of utility preferred issues, which were usually nonspeculative, would more often than not own their shares outright. Had a similar list been compiled for some of the high-flying common stocks of the decade, a far different distribution would have been obtained. The owners of the utility preferred, by occupation, are shown in Table 12.2.

Table 12.2—Utility Preferred Stock Owners, by Occupation, 1928[42]

Housekeepers	4,029	Painters	182
Clerks	2,987	Accountants	166
Factory Workers	1,058	Metal Workers	157
Merchants	926	Barbers	155
Domestics	623	Bakers	153
Chauffeurs	601	Manufacturers	153
Electricians	582	Draftsmen	149
Engineers	558	Doctors	146
Mechanics	530	Janitors	119
Foremen	518	Mail Carriers	115
Laborers	499	Butchers	115
Machinists	499	Messengers	91
Managers	496	Artists	81
Carpenters	483	Lawyers	77
Dressmakers	372	Bankers and Brokers	65
Policemen	347	Bricklayers	65
Printers	335	Laundry Workers	65
Secretaries	314	Dentists	63
Railroad Men	312	Plasterers	60
Nurses	274	Beauty Culturists	52
Plumbers	257	Seamen	51

Most of these people bought their shares and then put them away for safekeeping; McCoy's figure of 3 million includes these shareholders along with the majority of speculators. In order to ascertain how many *active* accounts there were in 1929, we have the figure of 1,548,707 given by the member firms of twenty-nine exchanges in operation during that year. And not all of these were necessarily speculators. It was later estimated that there were only about 600,000 margin accounts during 1929.[43] Thus, although share ownership was broadly based during the twenties, participation in the market was not. It should also be noted that 51,000 individuals received half the value of the cash dividends paid by domestic corporations.

Throughout most of the decade the speculators and investors pushed prices of many old stocks to record highs, and also bought an unprecedented amount of new securities. During the same period the national income, while rising, was increasing at a far slower rate than that of stock prices. This can be seen most graphically during the second half of the decade (see Table 12.3).

Table 12.3—National Income and Stock Values, in Millions of Dollars, 1925–1929[44]

	National Income	New Securities	Value of Common Stock	Value of Preferred Stock
1925	75,600	6,200	58,987	15,947
1926	80,200	6,300	67,500	17,100
1927	78,100	7,800	74,100	17,800
1928	81,000	8,100	77,300	18,500
1929	84,100	10,200	55,100	19,700

In 1923, new issues equalled 29 per cent of the nation's annual savings; by 1929, nearly half of the savings were represented by new securities. But despite this tremendous outpouring of funds into the stock and new issues markets, consumption remained at a high level. This accomplishment seems even more fantastic when the figures for listing on the New York Stock Exchange are examined (see table 12.4). These figures lead to an obvious question: where did the money

Table 12.4—New York Stock Exchange Listings, 1924–1929[45]

	Number of Listed Issues	Number of Shares Listed	Market Value of Shares (dollars)
1924	927	433,448,561	27,072,322,192
1925	1043	491,615,837	34,489,227,125
1926	1081	585,641,222	38,376,162,138
1927	1097	654,999,126	49,736,350,946
1928	1176	757,301,677	67,478,138,151
1929	1293	1,127,683,468	64,707,878,131

come from? The answer is equally obvious: it came from borrowing.

Buying stock "on margin" was not unusual in the nineteenth century; a person, in buying a $1,000 bond, might pay $500 out of his pocket, and borrow the additional $500 from his broker, using the bond itself as collateral. If the bond paid 8 per cent, and the broker's loan cost the customer 4 per cent, then the return to the customer would be 8 per cent on his $500 investment and 4 per cent on his $500 loan, or a net return of 6 per cent. Seen as $60 per annum on an investment of $500, this works out to a 12 per cent return on the customer's investment. If the purchase had been made outright, the customer would have received $80 on a $1,000 investment.[46]

Of course, there were risks in such transactions. For example, if the bond fell from $1,000 to $400, the customer would not only be wiped out, but would have to raise an additional $100 to pay the broker. It can be seen that in buying shares on margin, the customer increased his risks as the price for a higher return. But there was a bonus for the customer, for although the losses were magnified in a bear market, profits were equally magnified in a bull market. If the bond increased at the Exchange from $1,000 to $1,500, the broker's equity remained the same ($500), while that of the customer doubled. This phenomenon, known as leverage, was a key factor in the bull rise of the twenties.

Not many people bought on margin before World War I, and only a few of those who did were speculators. In the 1920s, however, most people who opened new accounts thought in terms of margin buying. Certainly the practice of time payments for consumer goods, although quite different from margins, got small investors into the habit of paying only a portion of the price and borrowing the rest. Then too, the publicity given margin trading by the newspapers and other mass media introduced the practice to many who otherwise might never have known of it. Finally, the fantastic dreams of wealth led speculators not only to desire large fortunes, but to want to get them as soon as possible. Margin trading seemed the answer to these individuals.

The increase in margin trading posed a problem to the brokers: where would they get the money for the loans? In the past, funds had been advanced by the brokerage itself, or borrowed from banks. As time went on, however, the demand for "call money" grew, causing the rates charged customers to rise. These high rates soon attracted money from nonbanking sources, such as corporations. At the same time the Federal Reserve Banks, in answer to an appeal from English, French, and German central bankers, lowered rates in order to discourage foreigners from buying American notes and thus exporting gold from Europe to America. The low rates offered by the Federal

Reserve served to keep away the European lenders, but it also encouraged Americans to borrow at low interest charges. For example, in 1927 the rate was lowered to 3.5 per cent as part of a plan to stabilize the English gold reserve. At that time brokers' loans were bringing over 5 per cent. A member bank could borrow money from the Federal Reserve, and then turn around and lend it to the brokers, thus making upward of 1.5 per cent, with little risk. By mid-1929, brokers' loans were up to 20 per cent as a result of the demand, but even this did not dissuade speculators. Why worry about paying 20 per cent for a loan when your stock seemed sure of doubling within six months? The broker was happy; he was receiving an extremely high interest rate, and held what he thought to be excellent collateral. This collateral was then discounted at the bank, which was glad to receive the business. The next step was to discount at the Federal Reserve, and it was there that the joy ceased; beginning in 1928, the central bankers began to warn the public and its member banks of the evils of speculation, and they tried through moral suasion to curb stock purchases on margin. Their warnings went unheeded, however, even when the rates were later raised in an attempt to discourage borrowing. Brokers' loans increased phenomenally during the second half of the decade, and took off into the stratosphere in 1929. By then, the effects of nonbanking sources of loans were evident on Wall Street (see Table 12.5).

Table 12.5—Sources of Loans, 1924–1929 (Millions of Dollars)[47]

	Total Loans	By Banks	By Others
December 31, 1924	2,230	1,580	550
December 31, 1925	3,550	2,500	1,050
December 31, 1926	4,290	2,990	1,300
December 31, 1927	4,430	2,600	1,830
December 31, 1928	6,440	2,555	3,885
October 4, 1929	8,525	1,885	6,640

It can be seen that the Federal Reserve's actions in raising rates did affect bank borrowings, but the brokers and their customers found that corporations were still most anxious to lend money at 20 per cent.

The corporations had been given lower tax rates by Andrew Mellon in the hope and expectation that the additional funds would be used for investment in new plant and equipment, which in turn would be translated into more jobs and a higher standard of living. Mellon's predictions were borne out in the first half of the decade, but conditions began to change during the second half. Why invest in new plants, the corporations reasoned, if the return to be gained by entering the call money market was so much safer? A new plant might, at best, produce a return of 10 per cent *per annum,* while in 1929, call money brought what seemed to be a sure 15–20 per cent. So encouraged, the corporations entered the call money market in force. This can be seen in the fact that from 1922 to 1929, the gross national product increased 142.8 per cent and demand deposits by 125 per cent, while time deposits rose 164.4 per cent. This large supply of cash attracted Wall Street, which drew upon it for brokers' loans, as well as the banks.[48] Some of the leading companies lending money to brokers in 1929 are shown in Table 12.6.

Table 12.6—Money-Lending Companies, 1929[49]

	Peak Amount (dollars)
Electric Bond and Share	157,579,000
Bethlehem Steel Corporation	157,450,000
Standard Oil of New Jersey	97,824,000
Tri-Continental Corporation	62,150,000
Chrysler Corporation	60,150,000
Anaconda Copper Mining Corporation	32,500,000

This flow of call money helped boost stock prices to unprecedented highs, and exercised a dampening effect on the economy. It meant that instead of being used to create new jobs, capital was going into Wall Street to raise stock prices. This misuse of capital explains in large part why the market rose sharply in 1928–1929 while the economy had begun to stagnate.

The list of leading money lenders includes Tri-Continental Corporation, one of the giant investment trusts of the decade. The growth of such trusts is a significant development which helped lead to the market crash of 1929.

There had been investment trusts in Europe in the early nineteenth century, and the Massachusetts Life Insurance Company ran a trust company as early as 1823. The first modern investment company was the New York Stock Trust, formed in 1889, but prior to the twenties, there were only a few dozen, none of any real importance.[50] By the beginning of 1927, there were some 160 in existence, and this figure had doubled by early 1928. During the early months of 1929 investment trusts were being promoted at the rate of almost one a day, and the year's tally shows 265 in the "class of '29." The trusts marketed some $3 billion in new securities that year, or over one-third of all new issues. Just before the crash, the net value of all trusts reached the $8 billion mark, having increased elevenfold during a two-year period.[51]

The financial trusts were companies which held securities in other, usually operating, companies. They were attractive to investors because they offered them professional management at a fairly low fee. At their best, they enabled the novice to hire the best brains on Wall Stret and diversify his holdings. At worst, they were run by cheats and crackpots, or well-meaning but mistaken men, and they failed miserably. As one writer in the field put it:

> Every conceivable type of trust was formed: orthodox corporations with or without a pyramided capital structure . . . fixed and semi-fixed trusts with certificates of beneficial interest issued against identical units of securities; common stock trusts and trusts owning senior as well as junior securities; trusts with restrictions regarding what management could do and others with few or no restrictions; trusts that published their portfolio and others that never revealed their investments; trusts with self-liquidating features and trusts that listed their shares on some exchange; trusts that invested in foreign securities and trusts that confined themselves almost entirely to the domestic field. But most of them were corporations, most of them owned more common stocks than bonds, most of them confined themselves to domestic investments, most of them possessed great flexibility of management, most of them had a complicated capital structure. Today the vast bulk of the "trusts" of the 1920s would be classified as pyramided, closed-end investment companies and holding companies.[52]

The trusts were usually highly leveraged, that is, a great deal of their capitalization was represented by such fixed income securities as bonds and preferred stock, and only a small amount by common stock. We have already seen how, through leverage, profits are increased more rapidly in a bull market, while losses are compounded in a bear market.

There are two significant points to consider about the trusts of the 1920s. First, the purchase of trust shares on margin represented the utmost in pyramiding. The shareowner used leverage to buy shares in a leveraged company, which owned shares in other leveraged companies. The possibilities on either the bull or bear side in such a situation were indeed great, as illustrated by United States & Foreign Securities, formed by Dillon, Read, in 1924.

It had three classes of stock—first preferred, second preferred, and common. Both classes of preferred were to yield dividends limited to 6 per cent and had no voting power. The common stock, which had a minus value at the organization of the company, carried with it entire control. The bankers sold all of the first preferred to the public for about $25 million. With the shares so sold they gave as a bonus one quarter of the common stock. They themselves, with an investment of only $5 million, retained all of the second preferred and three quarters of the voting common stock. By 1928 this investment trust, after preferred dividends, had earned a cash surplus of $10 million. The price of the common stock eventually rose as high as $72 a share. Dillon, Read & Co., with an investment of about one fifth of that put into the concern by the public, eventually made between $30 million and $40 million on its own investment of $5 million.[53]

The second point to remember regarding the financial trusts is that they created no new jobs. Whereas bonds and new issues of common stock would usually lead to expansion and aid the economy, the securities of financial trusts only served to boost prices at the exchanges and over-the-counter.

The securities markets of the twenties were, on the surface, in the midst of a genuine boom, based on increased production, consumption, distribution, and so forth. Careful analysis shows, however, that installment buying, capital stagnation, faulty corporate structure, unsound banking, untried leadership, questionable financing, and greed born of fantasy led to a bull market which, at its best was a house of cards.

Notes

1. John Sears, *The New Place of the Stockholder* (New York, 1929), p. 2.

2. William Allen White, *A Puritan in Babylon* (New York, 1938), pp. 335–38.

3. *Medina,* pp. 30–32.

4. Edwards, *Evolution of Finance Capitalism,* pp. 232–34.

5. Lundberg, *America's 60 Families,* pp. 235–37; Livingston, *The American Stockholder,* p. 193.

6. United States, 74th Congress, 1st Session, Senate Committee on Banking and Currency, *Stock Exchange Practices* (Washington, 1933), pp. 173–74.

7. *Medina,* pp. 64–65.
8. Forrest McDonald, *Insull* (Chicago, 1962), p. 246.
9. Livingston, *The American Stockholder,* pp. 186–87.
10. Willard Atkins, George Edwards, and Harold Moulton, *The Regulation of the Security Markets* (Washington, 1946), pp. 34–36.
11. Matthew Josephson, *Life Among the Surrealists* (New York, 1962), pp. 276–79.
12. *Ibid.,* p. 281.
13. *Ibid.,* p. 285.
14. Soule, *Prosperity Decade,* pp. 288–89.
15. Edwards, *Evolution of Finance Capitalism,* pp. 234–35.
16. McDonald, *Insull,* pp. 204–205.
17. *Ibid.,* p. 32.
18. Insull's leading biographer gives him credit for the innovation of mass production, before Ford's introduction of the concept. *Ibid.,* p. 98.
19. *Ibid.,* p. 278.
20. *Ibid.,* p. 210.
21. *Ibid.,* p. 282; Soule, *Prosperity Decade,* p. 185.
22. McDonald, *Insull,* p. 282.
23. Allen, *Lords of Creation,* pp. 296–300.
24. Adolf A. Berle and Gardiner C. Means, *The Modern Corporation and Private Property* (New York, 1933), pp. 73–76.
25. *Ibid.,* p. 277.
26. Allen Churchill, *The Incredible Ivar Kreuger* (New York, 1957), pp. 117, 132–33, 159–62.
27. Harvey O'Connor, *Mellon's Millions* (New York, 1933), p. 345.
28. John L. Parker, *Unmasking Wall Street* (Boston, 1932), pp. 117–18.
29. Sparling, *Mystery Men of Wall Street,* pp. 62–63.
30. *Ibid.,* pp. 71–72.
31. Richard Wycoff, *Wall Street Ventures and Adventures through Forty Years* (New York, 1930), p. 254.
32. *Ibid.,* p. 255.
33. Sparling, *Mystery Men of Wall Street,* pp. 56–57.
34. *Ibid.,* pp. 145–46.
35. *Ibid.,* p. 14 ff.; Parker, *Unmasking Wall Street,* pp. 116–18.
36. Wycoff, *Wall Street Ventures,* pp. 254–55; Dies, *Behind the Wall Street Curtain,* pp. 98–99, 115–16; Rudolph Weissman, *The New Wall Street* (New York, 1939); Arthur Wickwire, *The Weeds of Wall Street* (New York, 1933), pp. 91–92.
37. *Fortune,* January, 1963, pp. 111–16.
38. Sparling, *Mystery Men of Wall Street,* pp. 192–93.
39. One of the old group, Thomas Lawson, was ill during the early bull market. Operating from his bed, he managed to participate in the market before dying in 1925. Holbrook, *Age of the Moguls,* pp. 174–75.
40. Soule, *Prosperity Decade,* pp. 293–94.
41. Sparling, *Mystery Men of Wall Street,* p. xv.
42. Sears, *New Place of the Stockholder,* pp. 35–37, 60.
43. Galbraith, *Great Crash,* pp. 82–83; Gabriel Kolko, *Wealth and Power in America* (New York, 1962), p. 50.
44. Edwards, *Evolution of Finance Capitalism,* pp. 274, 281.
45. *New York Stock Exchange Fact Book,* p. 40.
46. A good, medium grade railroad bond with an 8 per cent coupon was

not unusual before the turn of the century, while brokers' loans at 4 per cent were usual for established accounts.

47. Lester Chandler, *Benjamin Strong: Central Banker* (Washington, 1958), p. 426.

48. Lee, *Economic Fluctuations,* p. 150.

49. Lundberg, *America's 60 Families,* p. 221.

50. Hugh Bullock, *The Story of Investment Companies* (New York, 1959), pp. 1–14.

51. Galbraith, *Great Crash,* pp. 53–55.

52. Bullock, *Investment Companies,* pp. 28–29.

53. Soule, *Prosperity Decade,* p. 299; Hearings in *Stock Exchange Practice,* pp. 1566–73.

13

Death of the Giant Bull: 1925-1933

We may as well tell the truth and put the blame where it belongs. It's up to Washington now. We have stepped aside. The market is leaderless. Eventually we will take control again, but not until something is done to limit the Federal Reserve Board to the functions stated in the law that created it. Those functions are to stabilize money rates and prevent panic. It did neither. Call money jumped to twenty per cent. The country experienced the worse crash in history.

William C. Durant

THE GENEALOGY of the market boom and the causes of the 1929 collapse have been set down and analyzed in a staggering number of books, articles, and memoirs.[1] Rather than duplicate them, it would perhaps be more useful to touch upon some of the highlights of the period to see how the rise and fall of the twenties took place.

Almost everyone knows that the bull market came to a dramatic end on Black Thursday, October 24, 1929. Yet, few seem interested in knowing when the great bull market began. One reason for this state of affairs is that bear markets end and bull markets begin in undramatic fashions, with small rises which snowball into large leaps in the averages. Another is that there was not one bull market in the decade, but three large jumps separated by periods of decline and stagnation. From September, 1924 to February, 1926, the Dow-Jones industrials rose 37 per cent. Then came a two-month decline, followed by a new buying wave that lasted from April, 1926, to January, 1928, in which time the average rose 31 per cent. A three-month decline followed, and the final stage of the rise, which lasted from April, 1928 to September, 1929, took the Dow-Jones index up nearly 50 per cent.

The concept of a three-part bull market is not completely satisfactory, for a ragged but evident rise could be discerned in 1922 and 1923, and the 1926 and 1928 breaks may be considered pauses in one general advance as well as ends of separate moves. In addition, the volume and turnover rates did not rise and fall at the same times as the 1926 and 1928 drops. Finally, the price of Exchange seats, usually a good indicator of market conditions, rose steadily throughout the decade.

Perhaps it would be more accurate to say that the bull market had its genesis in the neutrality boom of 1915–1916. The markets of the twenties can then be viewed as extensions of a rise triggered by the new economic and financial position of the United States in the early twentieth century. True, there was a leveling off during American participation in the war, and a bear market did develop soon after the peace, but even then the flush of optimism did not completely die. In 1920, for example, when prices were declining, Allen A. Ryan was able to set up and execute a bull corner in Stutz Motors, a forerunner of the Livermore and Cutten operations of a few years later. Still, the market showed few signs of life during the rest of that year and throughout 1921.

It might be said that the foundation for the bull market was set down in June, 1922. At that time the New York Stock Exchange listed the shares of Piggly-Wiggly Stores, a supermarket chain in the South and West. In the early part of 1923 its president, Clarence Saunders, decided to float more stock and punish a group of bears who were trying to push down Piggly-Wiggly's price. Saunders asked Jesse Livermore, the manipulator, to start a bull pool, and thus enable Saunders to sell his new shares at a high price and, in addition, to destroy the bears. Using Frank Bliss as his floor manager, Livermore began a campaign in March which caused the stock to rise sharply. By the end of the month the corner was completed, and Piggly-Wiggly jumped fifty-two points in one day; within less than a month Livermore had engineered a rise from 40 to 120. The governors, seeing panic developing and perhaps remembering the 1914–1915 period, suspended trading in the stock—an illegal action on their part—and allowed the bears extra time to cover their commitments. Livermore, who had agreed to run the pool believing that Saunders only wanted to push the price up in order to float new stock, withdrew when he realized that punishment of the bears was also a major goal. He emerged from the debacle with an enhanced reputation, as did Bliss. Saunders was not as fortunate; instead of making $20 million as he had expected, he left Wall Street a ruined man, although he later regained a substantial part of his losses through other commitments.[2] It is fitting that the first major corner of the bull market began with a Livermore-Bliss victory, the wreck of a businessman, an avoidance of responsibility on the part of the Exchange—all this in connection with a stock named after a pig.

The Piggly-Wiggly pool took place when volume at the Exchange was usually less than a million shares a day—the average daily volume for 1923 was 860,000 shares. Just before and after the pool 500,000 share days were not uncommon. Activity picked up during the spring and summer, however, and on November 22, 1,500,000 shares were traded. In 1924 average daily volume stood at one million shares, the highest since 1919 and the second highest in the century so far. The next year volume went to 1.7 million shares, and on November 10, all previous records were eclipsed by a 3.4 million-share day. This record was surpassed in 1926, when on March 3, almost 3.9 million shares were traded. There were no days in which volume dipped below the million-share mark from the fall of 1926 to the summer of 1931. Prices of Exchange seats also rose; from a low of $76,000 in 1923, they went to 175,000 in 1926. Two years later the price reached $595,000, and in mid-1929, seats sold for $625,000, after the Exchange, doubtlessly influenced by practices of other corporations, declared a "dividend" of a quarter seat to each member, thus raising membership to 1,375.[3]

The prices of stocks began to rise immediately after the Piggly-Wiggly pool, but then fell back to April levels by year's end. An upswing developed in 1924, and the Dow-Jones averages rose more than 20 per cent. The public did not rush into the market, but it began to nibble at the edges in the fall. Up to this time the rise seemed like most previous ones, which is to say that it followed the industrial index, it was marked by sudden upward and downward movements in selected issues, and trading was generally confined to experts. In addition, the market seesawed between the lows and highs, and the narrow range of trading led most investors to believe that the 1923–1924 market was little different from those of other stagnant periods. At summer's end some market analysts began to observe that the "zigs" were going upward with greater vigor than the downward "zags," and that volume increased on rises and decreased on declines. This, they claimed, was a definite indication that the market was in a bull phase. Toward the end of the year New York newspapers began printing advertisements for market letters of a dubious nature, a sure sign that the general public had entered the arena.

Automobile sales, spurred by installment buying and good business news, began to rise sharply. So fast and unexpected was the sales increase that by the end of the year some industry leaders confided privately their fears that the market might be saturated.[4] At the Exchange, however, the price of automotive stocks pushed to new highs, leading a general advance which extended into February of 1926. In the summer of that year, when the market was in the doldrums, John J. Raskob of General Motors told reporters before leaving for a European vacation that General Motors was selling at a ridiculously low figure and should be at least 100 points higher. GM stood at 146.5 at the time; within two months it had risen to 222, and was headed still higher. This advance influenced other issues, and the automotive securities in general sparked the bull market of late 1926.

The industrial production index fell in 1927, as the effects of an English and Canadian depression hit the United States. During the year, however, stock prices rose from 157.6 to 199.6. There were two causes for this unusual phenomenon. First, the easy money policy of the Federal Reserve continued, although business did not need additional funds. The banks used some of this capital, with much foreboding, for collateral loans which helped finance the bull market. From 1925 to 1927, loans on securities increased 40 per cent while commercial loans increased 12 per cent. When Governor Strong was criticized for these practices, he responded that the easy money policy was desirable "(1) To avoid a precipitous decline in the exchanges, especially sterling, which would weaken the bank position abroad. (2) To avoid restriction upon our exports. (3) To avoid a chill to domestic business. (4) To avoid embarrassment to the smooth operation of the Dawes Plan . . ."[5] Strong felt that to raise interest rates and thus dampen the bull market, he would have to sacrifice European recovery and the English gold standard. If Europe collapsed, the United States would soon follow. Given the time, the international situation, and the stakes involved, Strong's decision to gamble that the low rates would not seriously damage the American economic and financial structure was a reasonable one.

Another bullish influence was Charles Lindbergh's flight to Paris, an event that stimulated the imagination of the public and, as far as the stock market was concerned, buoyed optimism and colored the fantastic dreams of the future. This was especially true for those stocks connected with airplanes. Wright Aeronautical, the firm which built Lindbergh's *Spirit of St. Louis,* rose from 25 to 245 in the nineteen months that followed the flight.[6] Seaboard Airlines, an Atlantic coast railroad, showed a remarkable climb as well; the new investors—who did not look into issues before buying them—thought it to be a Florida-New York airline. Toward the end of the year, Eugene Meyer, a banker of conservative instincts, expressed alarm at the wild movements of leading issues. "What will happen if they forget to bid?" he asked.[7] But not even the closing of Ford Motors during the conversion to the Model A could halt the rise for long.

Despite general talk of depression in early 1928, prolonged slumps in Europe, and a further decline in American production, the market continued to rise. Some speculators began to leave the Street at this time. Joseph Kennedy felt that prices were out of line, and Bernard Baruch began to sell stocks and buy gold from the Alaska Juneau Mines. He told friends to watch automobile sales and construction statistics; when they slipped badly, he said, a crash would be unavoidable. Whether they took his advice is unknown; in any case, bears were unpopular that season.[8] In January, Moody's Investment Service warned that stocks were too high, having "over-discounted anticipated progress." A month later the Harvard Economic Society cautioned that "business was entering upon a period of temporary readjustment." The Committee on Economic Changes warned that the evolution of the economy could lead to future difficulties, including unemployment and underproduction. Newspapers carried advertisements of investment services which asked, "Will You Overstay This Bull Market?" and "Is The Process of Deflation Under Way?" Senator La Follette introduced a resolution to limit Federal Reserve activities in brokers' loans. But the aircrafts continued their climb, and investment companies hit their stride. Atlas Corporation reached 66, triple the 1926 closing price, and others followed suit.[9]

In mid-1928, the Federal Reserve made its first attempt to halt speculation. Governor Strong, then in his last weeks of life, thought that the System could stop the fantastic rises at almost any time he chose merely by raising the bank rates and instituting a hard money policy. This might dampen the rate of economic growth, he believed, but when and if necessary, this price would be paid. Up to mid-year, Strong preferred to support Europe and the growing economy. During the summer he decided to curb Wall Street's excesses, and raised the discount rate from 3.5 per cent to 4 per cent, and then to 4.5 per cent, and finally, in December, to 5 per cent. At the same time the System began selling government bonds in the hope of withdrawing funds from the speculative stock markets. In the first half of 1928 alone more than $300 million worth of bonds were sold on the open market, with no effect. This operation left the System with only $200 million worth in reserves, and negated the possibility of further attempts at curbing the boom through open market operations.[10]

The bond sales were not enough to counter the increased flow of money into Wall Street from corporation treasuries, and brokerages did not mind paying banks 5 to 7 per cent interest when customers offered 10 per cent for margin loans. The "monster" was out of control; restraints that might have worked in 1926 were ineffectual two years later.

In February, 1929, Governor Roy Young, who had replaced the deceased Strong, issued two warnings about excessive speculation, and threatened "direct action" against banks using Federal Reserve loans to bolster the stock markets. Congress then discussed new legislation to curb the exchanges.[11] The markets began to slump, and some acute observers thought that the bull market had ended.[12] In March, Raskob set off on a new European trip and, as he had in 1926, told reporters that General Motors was selling at too low a price. It was then 187; Raskob thought it should be at 225. Within two days the stock crossed the 200 mark, continued upward, and led other issues out of the February decline.[13] The demand for margin money forced rates to 12 per cent, but even this did not deter the speculators.[14]

In May, the *Brooklyn Eagle* printed a report that Arthur Cutten, after saying farewell to Raskob, had closeted himself with the Fisher brothers and other market leaders, and decided to send prices upward. "Mr. Cutten may be said to be the leader of the largest and most influential group operating in the market today," it stated. "In Mr. Cutten's group are William C. Durant, who is playing the market by radio telephone from Europe; the seven Fisher brothers of Detroit. . . . Mike J. Meehan, of the stock exchange firm of that name, as well as several independent operators, including George Breen and Joseph Higgins. It is known that the stocks handled by this group in a single day have aggregated more than 1,000,000 shares in many recent markets."[15] Pools were formed in American Tobacco, Chrysler, National Cash Register, Montgomery Ward, Radio Corporation of America, Standard Oil of California, Union Carbide, and others. All shot upward as though jet-propelled, and the market responded with a general rise on heavy volume.[16]

President Hoover, inaugurated in March, was worried about the speculation, but most of his addresses were cheerful; there seemed to be sublime confidence in the soundness of the economy. There were, of course, some clouds on the horizon. Soon after the inauguration, a modest decline turned into a minor rout. The Federal Reserve was silent as to reserve requirements, and this was interpreted on Wall Street as a sign that the System would crack down on speculation through a new rise in the discount rate. In addition, Congress continued talking of new regulatory legislation.

At this point, Charles A. Mitchell, head of the National City Bank as well as a Class A Director of the New York Federal Reserve Bank, announced that the National City would advance $25 million to traders in order to take up the slack in Federal Reserve loans. To many it appeared as though the Age of Morgan had returned; in the future, they thought, Wall Street would look to men like Mitchell as it once did to the House of Morgan. "We feel that we have an obligation which is paramount to any Federal Reserve warning, or anything else, to avert any dangerous crisis in the money market," said Mitchell. Professor Joseph Lawrence of Princeton offered advice which backed up this stand.

> The central bank has broken faith . . . and undertaken a punitive excursion against the stock market without adequate provocation and in contravention of every principle of justice. Wall Street should patronize only banks without the system. As a community it has ample financial strength to be independent of a central bank which has demonstrated its unenlightened and militant provincialism. The state of New York will charter institutions to provide for the banking needs of the financial community. Although the provinces dominate in politics there is no reason why that dominion should extend into the field of finance. That independence may be and should be achieved without the blare of trumpets or the clash of cymbals. It is within the reach of Wall Street and should be embraced.[17]

Senator Carter Glass of Virginia spoke for the "provinces," attacking Mitchell's takeover.

He avows his superior obligation to a frantic stock market against the obligations of his oath as a director of the New York Federal Reserve Bank. . . .

Mr. Mitchell's proclamation is a challenge to the authority and the announced policy of the Federal Reserve Board. The challenge ought to be promptly met and courageously dealt with.

The Board should ask for the immediate resignation of Mr. Mitchell as a Class A director of the New York Federal Reserve Bank. . . .[18]

Congress took no action, however. Hoover said that he lacked the authority to curb Mitchell, and that only the Governor of New York, Franklin Roosevelt, could act against the Exchange. Roosevelt remained silent throughout this period. Apparently Mitchell and his supporters had won the day.

Hopes remained high that summer, despite economist Roger Babson's prediction that a crash was coming which might send prices down sixty or more points. Bernard Baruch, while selling his stocks, told reporters that a further rise was not only possible, but probable.[19] President Albert Wiggin of the Chase National Bank entered into pools to push that institution's stock upward, while at the same time selling shares short on his private account.[20] Irving Fisher said that "stock prices have reached what looks like a permanently high plateau." Joseph Lawrence agreed, and spoke of further gains after Wall Street freed itself of the fetters of the Federal Reserve. Professor Charles Dice of Ohio State University, in his *New Levels in the Stock Market,* claimed that prices were only "registering the tremendous changes that were in progress."[21]

There were some disquieting news reports. Automotive and construction figures were down. European stock exchanges were in the midst of collapses in values. In September the Clarence Hatry enterprises in Great Britain fell. An operator on the Kreuger model, Hatry had constructed an empire out of slot machines and photographic devices; his fall into bankruptcy shocked London and seemed an evil omen to the more cautious Wall Streeters.[22]

The bull market continued through September, and toward the end of the month, market analysts were telling their customers that "such and such an issue will be taken upward for five points at a specified time." The pools, led by Cutten, Livermore, and others, would then step in and, with public support, proceed to carry out the prediction.

Brokers' offices were crowded from 10 A.M. to 3 P.M. with seated or standing customers who, instead of attending to their own business, were watching the blackboard. In some customers' rooms it was difficult to get access to a spot from which the posted quotations could be seen; no one could get a chance to inspect the tape. The larger Stock Exchange firms had been forced to increase to the full capacity of office space their staff of telephone clerks, through which the outside orders, which came in an avalanche, were transmitted.[23]

The giant bull manipulations in RCA, headed by Cutten and Meehan, spread through the rest of the list, sweeping in almost all of the glamour issues of the day. When the group gained control, Radio spurted sixty-one points in four days, and Wall Street went wild.[24] Meanwhile Paul Warburg of Kuhn, Loeb, who in March had warned that prices were "quite unrelated to respective increases in plant, property, or earning power," told customers that a break would not be long in coming. President William J. Simmons of the Exchange said that "speculation in securities is not at all a bad thing in itself. . . . It is, however, necessary to recognize that we may have too much or too little security speculation." He then added that his hands were tied in dealing with the runaway market. One observer added that prices were so high that speculators were not only discounting the future, but also the hereafter.[25] Simmons merely answered in platitudes and hoped for the best.

The *Wall Street Journal,* in assessing the late summer and early fall bull market, wrote:

According to the Dow theory, this development re-establishes the major upward trend. Reassurance on this score gave fresh stimulus to bullish enthusiasm, and a long list of representative stocks surged upward to new highs. . . . The outlook for the fall months seems brighter than at any time.[26]

Baruch was stopped outside his offices by an old beggar, who told the shrewdest market figure of the time, "I have a good tip for you." Joseph Lawrence said that "the consensus of judgement of the millions whose valuations function on that admirable market, the Stock Exchange, is that stocks are not at present overvalued."

There were a few declines in late September, which market analysts interpreted as "technical corrections." Reports of worsening economic conditions were almost immediately discounted, and attacks from the Federal Reserve were met with fresh assurances from Charles Mitchell.

On October 1, Cutten denied rumors that he was liquidating his holdings, and the *Wall Street Journal* reported that "Mr. Cutten said no relaxation of the national prosperity was in sight, and expressed the opinion that the market structure could support brokers' loans of $10 billion to $12 billion." On October 6 stocks turned upward with renewed vigor, and sharp rises were recorded in RCA, Westinghouse, U.S. Steel, and American Can. On October 12, the *Journal* proclaimed:

> In the way of news developments, bulls have had much the best of it over the last week or so, and this, perhaps, is the main reason why the market has been able to score such a quick comeback. A week ago you heard all over the Street pessimistic forecasts as to the future of the market. You read in a number of newspapers . . . to the effect that we were in a major bear market. Stocks are now 10, 20, and 30 points above where they were a week ago, and optimism again prevails.

Irving Fisher announced on October 15, that he expected to see the market "a good deal higher than it is today within a few months" and Charles Mitchell said, "I see no reason for the end-of-the-year slump which some people are predicting."[27]

The market was skittish during the week that ended October 19. Optimistic reports came out of the economics departments of many universities but, on the other hand, steel production and construction figures were poor. *Time* magazine ran a cover story on Ivar Kreuger, lauding him as the wonder man of the age. At almost the same time the Swedish financier was telling a newspaperman in private that there were three secrets to his success: "One is silence, the second is more silence, while the third is still more silence."

The market developed weaknesses on Friday, October 18. U.S. Steel, General Electric, Westinghouse, and other stock leaders lost more than five points each. There had been worse days in the past, and the financial writers and the Wall Street crowd never worried about a major crash. The 1873, 1893, and 1907 crises could not recur, they said, because of strong leadership on the Street, enlightened Federal Reserve policies, the strong economic structure of the nation, and the ability to profit from lessons learned in the past. In any case, everyone knew that the great crashes were always signaled by a warning of one kind or another. In 1873 it had been the failure of Jay Cooke; several large railroads, including the Reading, had gone into receivership prior to the 1893 crash, and in 1907 the Knickerbocker Trust collapse was the panic signal. The skies seemed clear on October 18, 1929. A businessman's Administration was in Washington, the banks appeared sound, and there were no warnings of danger. Despite all this, the mid-afternoon decline of that day marked the beginning of the worst crash in American history.

The Friday losses carried into the Saturday trading, as stocks fell sharply on heavy volume. For the first time news was released of heavy margin calls, which meant that traders who had relied upon brokers' loans were being asked to either raise more collateral for their loans or be liquidated. The cry for "more margin" would echo through the Street regularly during the next two months. Although prices fell dozens of points Wall Street still did not believe that a bear market was in the making. The *Wall Street Journal* printed rumors of several giant bear pools, led by Livermore, which had driven down selected issues. It noted that Arthur Cutten, then vacationing in Atlantic City, was busy organizing such men as the Fishers and Durant into a huge bull pool to drive prices up once more. In other words, the *Journal* viewed the beginning of the crash as nothing more than a mammoth struggle between the bulls and the bears. Prices couldn't go much lower, it thought; the "big boys" wouldn't allow them to.[28]

On Monday, October 21, prices fell sharply and volume went over the 6 million mark. Professor Fisher told reporters that he wasn't concerned; the decline represented the "shaking out of the lunatic fringe." The *Journal* was cautiously optimistic.

> The market has had a very bad break, the most severe in a number of years. There may be some stocks that are still selling too high on the basis of selling price times earnings, but on the other hand there are a number of stocks that are now selling at attractive levels. . . . There is a vast amount of money awaiting investment. Thousands of traders and investors have been waiting for an opportunity to buy stocks on just such a break as has occurred over the last several weeks, and this buying, in time, will change the trend of the market.[29]

For a while, it appeared as though recovery would take place. Stocks moved upward on Tuesday morning, but by the end of trading, most had again fallen to post losses for the day. Still, the final prices showed a twenty-eight point advance in Case, followed by similar gains in Hershey, Columbian Carbon, and several other issues.

The market opened slowly on Wednesday, as speculators tried to divine whether prices would continue upward or again collapse. Then, in mid-morning, large losses were registered on a late running ticker. A total paper decline of more than $4 billion was recorded by day's end, with losses of over fifteen points in American Telephone, General Electric, Westinghouse, and Hershey. Case, which had less than 200,-000 shares outstanding and was a natural vehicle for speculation, plummeted forty-six points, and Adams Express, a soundly managed investment trust, lost ninety-six points.[30]

Brokers gathered at hotels and speakeasies that night to pass along the latest rumors. Some spoke of government intervention, and a few thought the Exchange might close until fears had been dissipated. Some, recalling the 1907 panic, predicted the worst crash in history. The most persistent rumor, however, was that the district's leaders were gathering, and had a plan to bolster prices the following morning. Old-timers told worried novices of how the legendary Morgan had called the brokers to his office in 1907, and how he had stopped the panic dead in its tracks. Irving Fisher was calm, and assured an audience of troubled bankers that "any fears that the price level of stocks might go down to where it was in 1923 or earlier are not justified by present economic conditions." Within twenty-four hours the bankers would read of the most famous day in market history: "Black Thursday."

Prices opened lower Thursday morning and never recovered. Volume picked up shortly after 10:00 A.M., and at the closing the tape was over four hours late. Almost 13 million shares were traded, as the Street was engulfed in panic. But there was still hope; Richard Whitney, the Vice-President of the Exchange and an intimate of the House of Morgan, Charles Mitchell of the National City, Albert Wiggin of Chase, George F. Baker, Jr., and other banking leaders were closeted with Thomas Lamont at a few minutes after noon. Upon emerging from the meeting, Lamont told reporters that "there has been a little distress selling on the Stock Exchange," and went on to describe the crash as being caused by the market's "technical position." Within minutes, Whitney appeared on the Exchange floor and walked briskly to the U.S. Steel post, where he bid 205 for 10,000 shares, which at the time was selling for a handful of points lower. Whitney's mission was clear: he represented a giant bankers' pool which had decided to stop the panic by bolstering the price of a key issue. Morgan had done the same thing in 1907 in supporting the Trust Company of America, and it seemed fitting that U.S. Steel should be supported in 1929 by a

Morgan partner. Whitney personally bought 200 shares and left the rest of the order with a specialist. He then went to several other posts and put in orders for some $20 million or more worth of stock.[31] This was the moment the brokers had been waiting for; they sent up a cheer and began buying. Although some selling continued, it seemed that the panic had been stemmed.[32] The market averages were down, but were far above their lows for the day, and brokers were content that the worst was over. Later evidence demonstrated that the bankers had raised prices only to sell out; when the next bear move took place, they were substantially out of the market, and would refuse aid. Baruch, who smelled a rat, refused to join the pool and sat on his gold holdings.[33] But these things were unknown the evening of October 24.

There was a minor rise on Friday, and a dip during the short Saturday session. Volume rose only slightly on the declines; there was no evidence of panic. Still, Wall Streeters went to their churches and synagogues that weekend and prayed for the health of the consortium as many once had prayed for Morgan.

The self-congratulatory spree was short-lived. Monday witnessed a near-complete collapse on heavy volume, with General Electric, Westinghouse, and American Telephone down 48, 34, and 34 points respectively. In all, the *Times* average showed a 49 point loss for the day. Once more the bankers held meetings, but Whitney and his colleagues did not appear at the Exchange to bolster prices. That evening all of the rumors were black. It was said that the bankers had sold short, and were jackals, not lions. The reputation of the banking community, so high during the summer, began to fall. Margin calls were getting dangerous, and a good deal of the day's liquidations had been by customers who could not meet their obligations. Banks and corporations, which had loaned money at from 8 to 20 per cent, were concerned; the prime stocks and bonds they held as collateral were shrinking by the hour, leaving them with huge losses. Washington and Albany were silent as to possible governmental moves and the market was leaderless.

The brokers found solace in reading Tuesday morning's *Times* and *Wall Street Journal*. The former believed "that the investor who purchases securities at this time with the discrimination that as always is a condition of prudent investing may do so with utmost confidence," and the latter noted that stocks were the same in terms of the values they represented, even though many had lost over 100 points. Those who held stocks outright had nothing to fear. "Their income is the same. They have lost a few tail feathers but in time they will grow in again, longer and more luxurious than the old ones that were lost in what the financial writers like to call the debacle."

These soothing words had no apparent effect. Tuesday was the most disastrous day in market history, eclipsing Black Thursday in terms of statistics. Over 16 million shares were traded—if the same turnover ratio of that day were to occur now, over 100 million shares would pass hands.[34] The *Times* industrial average fell forty-three points, as losses of immense magnitude were recorded from the opening bell (see Table 13.1).

Table 13.1—Stock Losses, October 29, 1929[35]

	Open	Close	Loss
Air Reduction	125⅛	120	25
Allied Chemical	205	210	35
American Can	130	120	16
American & Foreign Power	68	55	22½
American Telephone & Telegraph	225	204	28
Auburn Automobile	130	130	60
Crosley Radio	25	28	11½
Dominion Stores	22½	14	11
Electric Auto-Light	75	50	45
Fox Films	50	48	20
General Electric	245	222	28

The Governors of the Exchange met after the close to discuss a possible suspension of operations. It was decided that such an action would only worsen an already bad situation, and the bankers decided to try to restore confidence through cheery statements. The Exchange leaders exuded optimism and spoke of the bargains they planned to pick up in the next few days. President Hoover was reported as saying that "the fundamental business of the country" was sound. U.S. Steel and American Can declared extra dividends, and the latter company raised its quarterly payout as well. Some buyers were convinced that these men knew what they were talking about, and the sellers decided it was time to turn around. As a result, the market moved up strongly on Wednesday, October 30. During the day John D. Rockefeller announced that "my son and I have for some days been purchasing sound common stocks." Richard Whitney declared that the market would open at noon on Thursday and then remain closed until the following Monday, but there seemed to be no fear in this statement. Speculators welcomed the breather and said that the only reason for the closing was to allow the clerks to catch up with their paperwork.[36]

The market rose during the short Thursday session. That night the speculators and brokers agreed that although Professor Fisher was wrong in believing that stocks would remain at a high plateau, he was right in thinking that a plateau had been reached. Prices would not drop much more, they told each other, but might recover, and at worst, stabilize at present levels.[37]

On Friday came news of the failure of the Foshay enterprises of Minnesota. General Motors President Alfred Sloan said that "business is sound," and others echoed his sentiments. The Sunday *Times* predicted a rise on Monday, and offered several convincing reasons as to why prices should be higher. Only financial editor Alfred Noyes was pessimistic, but he had been predicting disaster since 1928.

Prices opened lower on Monday and continued to decline during the day, as the *Times* average sagged twenty-two points.[38] Tuesday was Election Day, and the market was closed. The Wednesday session was disastrous. One broker found it impossible to get his calls through; the telephone operator was busy talking to her broker, who had told her that he had to liquidate her account. "I'm ruined," she wailed. "All I have left in the world is my sealskin coat."[39]

The market continued lower from then on, although prices rose one trading day out of every three for the rest of the year.[40] Each decline brought optimistic statements from brokers and industrialists, a short rally, and then another fall. In early November, the *Journal* wrote cheerily: "The sun is shining again, and we will go on record as saying some good stocks are cheap. We say good stocks are cheap because John D. Rockefeller said it first. Only the foolish will combat John D.'s judgement." On November 3, the Rockefellers placed an order for one million shares of Standard Oil of New Jersey at 50 in an attempt to support the price of their key holding. But even a $50 million fund in the hands of the most respected industrial power in the nation could not stem the decline. Standard Oil, which had sold at 83 on September 16, was down to 3 by the end of 1930.[41]

By the third week in November the *Times* average stood at its lowest point since July, 1927. Thus, the entire rise of the third stage of the bull market had been wiped out. Brokers' loans, which totaled more than $8.5 billion in mid-September, were down to $4 billion, the rest being liquidated in a chorus of demands for "more margin."[42]

Toward the end of November the market staged a mild rally. Christmas shopping was heavy, and in volume exceeded the 1928 totals. The New York *Herald Tribune* wrote that "prosperity is still with us, though it is not hysterical prosperity."[43] U.S. Steel rose from 150 to 171, General Electric went from 168 to 243, and General Motors from 33 to 40. The *Times* reported that "a general price rise ends 1929 trading, with Wall Street moderately bullish for 1930."[44] Over 1.1 billion shares had been traded during the previous twelve months (a record), with the daily average volume reaching almost 4.3 million shares (another record), causing the tickers to spew forth over a million miles of tape. The turnover rate for 1929 was 119 per cent, far below the 319 per cent of 1901. But 1929 was to be the last year in which the magic 100 per cent mark would be crossed.[45]

On December 10, Charles Schwab, who well remembered the 1907 panic, said that "Never before has American business been as firmly entrenched for prosperity as it is today." John E. Edgerton, President of the National Association of Manufacturers, could "observe little on the horizon to give us undue or great concern."[46] But Pandora's box had been opened.

The analysts, looking at the crash from the vantage point of early January, claimed that prices of stocks had been too high in relation to their earnings. The correction, though severe, would doubtless serve to bring the public back to reality and, in the long run, would have a salutary effect. This analysis proved to be false. Although prices were high in relation to those of the 1922–1925 period (in price/earnings ratios), they were more reasonably priced in 1929 than they would be for most years of the next decade and the correction could have been worse (see Tables 13.2, 13.3).

A second fallacy regarding the early analysis of the crash was that

Table 13.2—Price–Earnings Ratio, 1929–1940[47]

1929	13.32
1930	15.81
1931	13.31
1932	16.80
1933	22.95
1934	19.39
1935	14.18
1936	15.44
1937	12.38
1938	15.38
1939	13.80
1940	10.24

Table 13.3—Corporate Profits Before Taxes, 1929–1933
(Billions of Dollars)[48]

1929	9.6
1930	3.3
1931	− .8
1932	−3.0
1933	.2

it would have a salutary effect on business in the long run. This was not to be, for directly or indirectly, business had a great stake in the stock market of 1929 through brokers' loans and direct investments. The "little man" may have lost all, but the brunt of the decline was born by the banks and industrial corporations, which had also gambled and lost. In addition, many corporations had to withhold new debt issues as a result of the crash. Bethlehem Steel, Continental Can, American Telephone and Telegraph, among others, were unable to gain funds for expansion, and this hindered recovery from 1929 to 1933. Beneficial mergers and acquisitions were halted. In September, for example, the National City and Corn Exchange banks had worked out terms under which the former would take over the latter through a stock exchange. For those Corn Exchange owners who didn't want National City shares, the price of $360 per share was set for their stock. By the time the deal was to have been completed, Corn Exchange shares were being quoted at $160, and needless to say, National City directors called off the deal.[49]

Even if the issues had been floated and the mergers consummated, and even if the late December recovery that ran into March had continued, there was a deeper difficulty in late 1929 that was not evident to the analysts of the day. In the past, there had always been solvent bankers in the community who would be around to pick up the pieces; in 1929, the banks were wrecked along with the stock market. This vacuum would become more evident in each succeeding month, and until it was filled, true recovery was not possible.

The economic situation in 1929 was severe, and it grew worse in 1930. As people lost jobs, their goods were repossessed, and they left the market place. New sales of consumer goods halted, and the factories that had produced automobiles, electric appliances, and other glamour items of the twenties were obliged to lay off more workers. The economy spiraled downward just as during the twenties it had shot higher and higher.

Early in 1930, Hoover began making what today seem wildly optimistic statements regarding the economy. For example, he predicted that construction that year would top the 1929 figure. In actuality, construction fell off over $2 billion from 1929's depressed figure. A pattern soon developed: Hoover would make a bright prediction, and would be proven wrong; the decline would lead the President to make more predictions, and new declines would follow. Simon D. Fess, Chairman of the Republican National Committee, was forced to admit that a remarkable correlation existed between the intensity of the President's optimism and the severity of the economic and stock market declines. "Every time the Administration gives out an optimistic statement," he complained, "the market immediately drops." Fess believed that there might be "some concerted effort on foot to discredit the Administration."[50] Actually Wall Street had lost confidence in the Great Engineer. The bankers and important brokers were still solidly Republican, but they were never great admirers of Hoover, and now they had still less reason to follow him. In June, when the market was still falling and economic activity stagnated, Hoover told a delegation of clergymen who came to ask for a public works program that their mission had been unnecessary. "You have come sixty days too late," said Hoover. "The depression is over."[51] Secretary of the Treasury Mellon declared: "I see nothing in the situation which warrants pessimism," and Secretary of Commerce Lamont predicted prosperity "in the long run."[52]

By mid-year it was evident that Hoover was either hopelessly naïve or was whistling in the dark. The *Times* stock index had dropped from 224 to 58 between November 13 and July 8.[53] In addition, Wall Street took a long, hard look at economic indicators and began to sell stocks once more (see Table 13.4).

We have seen how, in terms of price/earnings ratios, stocks were higher in 1932 than they had been in 1929. In this period, stocks declined 80 per cent, as against a 50 per cent decline in industrial activity. Although the economic falloff was one of the worst in history, the stock decline made it appear more severe than it really was. A major reason for this is the natural tendency of the stock market to exaggerate economic rises and falls. Stock prices rose at a faster rate than economic activity in 1914–1917 and from 1925–1929; from 1929–1933, prices fell in a similar fashion. Another reason for the decline was the President's "image." Despite his genuine ability and strenuous activities, Hoover was unable to win the confidence of the

**Table 13.4—Quarterly Dow-Jones Averages and
Industrial Indices, 1929–1933**[54]

	Quarter	Dow-Jones Average	Industrial Index
1929	1	308.4	58
	2	312.0	60
	3	354.3	61
	4	255.6	56
1930	1	267.1	54
	2	265.1	51
	3	227.9	47
	4	184.0	44
1931	1	176.3	42
	2	146.2	43
	3	134.5	40
	4	94.8	36
1932	1	79.5	34
	2	54.2	30
	3	61.0	29
	4	62.1	32
1933	1	58.2	30

vast majority of the American people during the depression. The crash was psychological as well as economic, and so was the depression. In many ways, it was the severest emotional jolt administered the nation since the Civil War.

Writing of his experiences from the vantage point of a more secure era, Hoover divided the depression into five phases. The first, which ran from October, 1929 to April, 1931, he blamed on domestic difficulties. The other four, covering the remaining period of his presidency, were assigned to either European collapses or political obstructionism.[55]

As might be expected, Arthur M. Schlesinger, Jr., the major Democratic historian of the period, differs with Hoover, and offers a three-phase analysis of the Republican policy. At first, he claims, Hoover favored maintenance of purchasing power through voluntary cooperation on the part of labor and management. When this proved inadequate, he returned to old-fashioned laissez-faire, "where faith in a balanced budget and the gold standard was tempered only by a commitment to protectionism." After the European collapses of 1931, Hoover supported international cooperation, and at home, sponsored a trickle down program which aided business, in the hope that recovery would then lead to more jobs and re-establish the upward spiral.

In the transformation from the second to the third stage, claims Schlesinger, Hoover was obliged to intervene directly into the economy, and in this took the first steps toward federal responsibility for business distress. More than any previous President, Hoover attempted to use the power of the office to sway the economy.

The most notable achievement of the third stage was the Reconstruction Finance Corporation of 1932, passed at a time when thousands of banks and industrial concerns were shut. The RFC was to lend them funds to enable the firms to reopen, hire back their workers, and set the economy moving once more. Hoover formed the corporation reluctantly. "The sole function of government," he said, "is to bring about a condition of affairs favorable to the beneficial development of private enterprise."[56] Had it swung into operation in 1930, it might have worked; by 1933, the economy needed stronger medicine. In addition, it was damaged by its friends and almost destroyed by its enemies. Under Chairman Eugene Meyer and President Charles G. Dawes, the RFC loaned most of the money to banks and trust companies and tended to ignore industry. Particularly subject to criticism was Dawes' loan of some $90 million to his own bank, at the same time that he was condemning relief for jobless workers. In addition, Democratic enemies of the organization, motivated both by political and ideological considerations, passed legislation making it mandatory for the RFC to publish the names of those firms receiving loans. When the public learned that a bank had been obliged to go to the RFC for funds, fears set in that it was insolvent and runs began, so that the RFC aid was usually self-canceling.[57]

Despite minor recoveries in 1930 and 1933, the general course of the economy during the Hoover years was straight down (see Table 13.5).

Table 13.5—Key Economic Indicators, 1929–1933[58]

	Gross National Income (billions of dollars)	Employee's Salaries (billions of dollars)	Unemployment (millions)	Domestic Investment as percentage of G.N.P.
1929	87.8	51.1	1.55	15.2
1930	75.7	46.8	4.34	11.2
1931	59.7	39.7	8.02	7.1
1932	42.5	31.1	12.06	1.5
1933	40.2	29.5	12.83	2.3

Hoover's pleas to labor and management to hold the line had their effects in 1930–1932, as most leading industrial corporations tried to keep dividend payments at the 1929 level. U.S. Steel, for example, saw its earnings decrease 62 per cent between 1929 and 1932, and paid dividends out of capital surplus. But common shares payments stopped after March, 1932, and a year later, the payout on preferred shares was cut from 7 to 2 per cent.[59] The brave attempt to bolster stock prices by maintaining dividends failed. As prices fell, however, the yield on common shares reached what to the speculator of the mid-twenties would have seemed astronomical heights (see Table 13.6).

Table 13.6—Dividends on Common Stock, 1929–1933[60]

	Standard & Poor's Industrial Index	Dividend Yield (per cent)
1929	21.35	3.47
1930	16.42	4.51
1931	10.51	6.15
1932	5.37	7.43
1933	7.61	4.21

The average yield in 1932 marked a high for the 1922–1965 period.

The "dividend crash" began prior to the presidential election and continued throughout the next eighteen months, during which time practically every large corporation either cut or passed payments. Some outstanding examples are shown in Table 13.7.

The loss was considerable, and took a good deal of purchasing power out of the economy. In 1929, American corporations paid out $5.8

Table 13.7—Dividend Crash, 1929–1932[61]

	1929 High	Dividend (dollars)	1932 Low	Dividend (dollars)
Air Reduction	223	5	31	4.50
Anaconda	140	7	3½	0
Bethlehem Steel	141	6	7½	0
Brooklyn Edison	375	8	6½	0
International Match Pref.	102	4	⅛	0
Western Union	272	8	13	0
Northern Pacific	119	5	10	0
U.S. Steel	262	8	21	0
Johns Manville	242	3	10	0
General Electric	400	6	13	1
American Telephone and Telegraph	310	9	71	9
Westinghouse	292	5	15	0
Fox Films	106	4	2	0

billion to their stockholders; four years later this figure stood at $2.1 billion.[62]

The psychological effects of the 1923–1929 rise were major factors in the boom, bringing optimism to shareholders and observers alike. The 1929–1933 toboggan had an opposite effect, and helped make the thirties a decade of fear. Consider, for example, the man who bought a share of Commercial Solvents, a thriving chemical company, at $15 in 1923. In the early fall of 1929 his investment had grown to $1,400, excluding dividends. How could he help but feel content with the future of both the nation and himself? By late 1932, however, the company was no longer paying dividends, and the price of the common stock had dropped to $35 a share. The investor might have reflected that he had actually more than doubled his holdings in less than a decade, but few thought of the crash in these terms; as far as he was concerned, he had lost over $1,300.

While he had been "making money on the stock market" in the twenties, the investor would have felt justified in buying goods on time, in living beyond his income, and in discounting tomorrow. The disillusioned investor of 1932 lived as frugally as was possible, turned his back on the heroes of the previous decade, lost faith in the present, and saw little hope in the future. If the upward swing took investors to the clouds, the downward turn brought many to the depths. Similar stories could be told of other investors, who took the "round trip" of 1923–1933 with other securities (see Table 13.8).

Table 13.8—Prices for Selected Stocks, 1923, 1929, and 1932[63]

	1923 Low	1929 High (adjusted for stock splits and dividends)	1932 Low
Allied Chemical & Die	59	355	42
Anaconda	32	175	3
Atcheson, Topeka, & Santa Fe	94	299	35
Du Pont	106	1617	154
General Electric	168	1612	136
General Motors	51	1075	40
New York Central	90	257	9
Radio Corporation	26	574	12
Union Carbide	51	420	46
U.S. Steel	85	366	30

During the summer of 1932, a popular game was trying to figure out how much had been lost in dollars since the crash. One group of brokers came up with the figure of $22,326,041,927 in securities shrinkages during 1931 *alone.* When this was added to the year's figures for bankruptcies ($911 million), defaulted bonds (almost $2 billion), and the loss of wages due to unemployment (approximately $18 billion), the nation's loss came to almost $43 billion.[64] A later analyst computed the securities decline on the New York Stock Exchange alone from September 1, 1929 to January 1, 1932 to have been $72 billion, a figure equal to the total gross national product in 1935.[65] With such losses, it was inevitable that a violent reaction from Wall Street should take place. The price of an Exchange seat fell from its 1929 high of $625,000 to a 1932 low of $68,000. Average daily volume declined from 4.3 million shares to 1.5 million shares in the same period.[66] It took the curb traders nearly four months in 1932 to do as much business (17.5 million shares) as they did in one record week in 1929. A seat at the Curb market (forerunner of the American Stock Exchange) cost $254,000 in 1929, and $18,500 in the summer of 1932.[67]

In the late winter of 1930, Exchange President Simmons told an audience of businessmen that "It is obvious . . . that the high level of share prices last August rendered the stock market vulnerable to a considerable price decline. . . . Every serious break in the stock market is always attributed to over-speculation. . . ."[68] Steps must be taken, he said, to correct structural weaknesses of the Exchange, get rid of malefactors, and in other ways restore public confidence in the securities markets.

During the next few years the Exchange made several attempts to clean house. In May, 1930, every broker was obliged to sign an agreement regarding ethical conduct in dealings with customers,[69] and later in the year the brokerages were asked to get rid of incompetent customers' men. In 1932 the stock of Brockway Motors was removed from trading because that company did not publish an annual report for the year, and in the following year the giant industrial firm, Allied Chemical & Dye, was removed when it did not fulfill Exchange information requirements.[70] But the Exchange disregarded Hoover's requests that it amend its rules to disallow pools and other manipulative devices. Only after being threatened by severe penalties under the Roosevelt Administration did the Board of Governors forbid the grosser forms of speculation and introduce new accounting procedures. By then it was too late to avoid outside interference.[71]

Hoover stood for economy in government and self-regulation of the exchanges during the 1932 election campaign. If Wall Street would not reform itself, however, the President was willing to accept new legislation to prevent future abuses of power. Late in 1931 he had asked Congress to undertake "the revision of our banking laws so as to safeguard the depositors." In 1932 he asked Republican congressmen to pass legislation to bring all commercial banks under the Federal Reserve, to separate investment banking from the commercial banks, and to consider other measures of a regulatory nature.[72]

As a candidate, Franklin D. Roosevelt often seemed confused. In 1932 this was interpreted by many, including Walter Lippman, as weakness, while in the following year New Deal supporters saw it as a pragmatic approach at bringing the nation out of the depression.[73] The Democratic platform of 1932 advocated the "protection of the investing public by requiring to be filed with the government and carried in advertisements of all offerings of foreign and domestic stocks and bonds true information as to bonuses, commissions, principal invested, and interests of the sellers." The platform supported regulation of the exchanges, and backed investigations of investment and commercial banking.[74] But Roosevelt soft-pedaled this part of the platform, and a large segment of the Wall Street community hoped he did not take these "radical proposals" seriously.[75]

The district was disillusioned with Hoover and unhappy about the mercurial Roosevelt. Most Wall Streeters probably voted Republican in 1932, but few did so out of a burning conviction that it was Hoover or chaos. After all, how radical could Roosevelt be, when he was supported by men like Bernard Baruch and Joseph Kennedy? During the interim between the sweeping Democratic victory and the inauguration of the new President, Hoover tried mightily to have Roosevelt commit himself to what amounted to an endorsement of the Republican platform. This effort met with no success; Roosevelt would enter the White House his own man. What this meant, however, was not clear.

During the campaign, Wall Street abuses were uncovered and a further loss of confidence set in. Congressman Fiorello LaGuardia unmasked A. Newton Plummer, a publicity man for many major pools, who had been hired to pay off some of the most respected financial writers in the nation. LaGuardia showed that Plummer had handled pools in Savage Arms, Pure Oil, Indian Motorcycle, Superior Oil, Simms Petroleum, Consolidated Laundries, and Maxwell Motors and had sent checks to leading financial analysts of the *Wall Street Journal, New York Evening Mail*, the *New York Herald Tribune*, the *New York Times,* the *New York Evening Post,* and *Financial America.*[76] During the Democratic convention several pools in liquor-related stocks were begun; it was known that practically all the leading contenders for the nomination were "wets," and it seemed that any Democratic nominee would stand an excellent chance of beating Hoover.[77] One of the manipulations was in Libby-Owens-Ford Glass, which many believed would prosper once liquor bottling began. This pool, led by Joseph Kennedy, among others, was an open secret on the Street.

By late 1931 the manipulative practices on Wall Street both before and after the crash led Congress to take action; on December 14, the Senate passed a resolution which called for the first major investigation of the securities markets since the Pujo inquiries. The impetus came from Senator Frederic C. Walcott, Republican from Connecticut, who believed that some Wall Street Democrats were planning a series of bear raids to embarrass Hoover during the 1932 campaign. The investigations, which began on April 11, 1932, found no evidence of the type that Walcott expected, but they did uncover many pools and manipulations that had existed during the twenties.

After the Roosevelt victory the committee head, Republican Senator Peter Norbeck of South Dakota, invited Ferdinand Pecora, who had supported Roosevelt in the election, to become counsel for the inquiry. Pecora accepted, and for the next two years led the senators and the nation through a maze of duplicity, fraud, and unbelievable excesses, to demonstrate that the nation's securities markets were in bad need of reforms.[78]

After the election and before the inauguration, the Pecora Committee heard evidence from many prominent Wall Streeters, including Richard Whitney, Mike Meehan, Charles Mitchell, and most of the officers of the Chase National Bank. The Committee—which was actually a subcommittee of the Senate Committee on Banking and Currency—filled over 1,200 pages with testimony of Wall Street malpractices, and the nation was given a true look at the heroes of the previous decade.

Ivar Kreuger had committed suicide in March of 1932, causing a major crash at the New York and other world exchanges. "Everybody's unloading but the cannibals in Africa," was the comment of the *New York Times* financial page.[79] An investigation showed that the Match King had forged bonds, juggled accounts, and substituted low-grade securities for high-grade ones in portfolios without bothering to tell anyone about it. Kreuger was a swindler; this much was evident. But no one knew how much he had stolen, how his thievery was accomplished, or what could be done about it. The Match King's only clear assets were around $100,000 in personal property; the rest had vanished.

The subcommittee's first witnesses included partners of Lee, Higginson, and members of Ernst & Ernst, who told of their dealings with the mysterious Swede. Donald Durant of Lee, Higginson, admitted that he had no idea of what was going on at Kreuger & Toll, even though he managed that company's accounts. For that matter, he was not sure that Kreuger was really dead.[80] George May, of the auditing firm of Price-Waterhouse & Co., admitted that his firm, which certified the books of Kreuger & Toll, had not examined many of them. He described his company's position to John Marrinan, an economic adviser to the Subcommittee:

> MR. MARRINAN: I have heard this entire Kreuger & Toll situation described or set up, rather, as a blind pool.
> MR. MAY: Well, that is a rather loose expression. I imagine that refers to the fact that Kreuger claimed that secrecy on his part was essential in regard to some of these most important transactions. Secret statements which he could not disclose without bringing disastrous consequences to the company—loss of profits. . . .
> MR. MARRINAN: I take it from your statement, Mr. May, that your firm has taken a very strong position against such set-ups as we have here, for one reason on the ground of its great secrecy?
> MR. MAY: My personal judgement on it concurs with what my partner expressed here, that if there is secrecy as to the way the money is being spent, a large part of it—there are certain amounts that you cannot get full details of, but where they assume major proportions—that it does not seem to me that that kind of security is a proper thing for the ordinary investor.[81]

The ordinary investor in the late twenties, however, did not know all this, and by the time he had found it out, Kreuger & Toll had dropped from over 120 to ½.

The next group called included businessmen connected with the Insull Empire. Insull, Jr. and Harold Stuart testified as to the pyramiding of I.U.I. and Corp, and admitted that insiders had been able to make millions of dollars from risk-free flotations during the late twenties. Pecora introduced evidence of Halsey, Stuart attempts at manipulation in Corp, which did not prevent it from falling from an April,

1930 high of 28¼ to a low of ⅛ two years later.[82] Insull, Sr. was not present at these hearings, having fled the country.[83]

Charles Mitchell appeared in late February, and tried to defend his actions during the autumn of 1929. He aggressively challenged the subcommittee to show him guilty of any legal or moral crime. Even when confronted with his own statements regarding his willingness to circumvent the Federal Reserve in making margin loans, Mitchell denied culpability, defending his actions by saying that "all banks were lending."[84] As a result of his testimony, however, Mitchell was later arrested and accused of tax evasion. Although he was acquitted, a federal civil claim for $1.1 million was upheld, and a series of appeals followed until Mitchell settled the claim in 1938.

Hugh Baker, President of the National City Company (the investment affiliate of National City Bank), was questioned by Senator Duncan Fletcher of Florida, who introduced the following "Flash" of the National City Company, into evidence:

> We are pleased to announce this morning (September 27, 1929) the beginning of one of the greatest sales contests ever held by the National City Co. There will be liberal cash prizes for a large number of men in every part of the organization and higher premium schedules.

The notice went on to list several securities, and urged the salesmen to push them on their customers. Baker was asked whether he condoned such practices, and he replied: "I doubt if that was ever looked at by anybody in our organization."[85]

The Subcommittee called Richard Whitney in early March, 1933. Whitney wandered far afield in his testimony, talking of such issues as federal budgets and deficit spending as well as Exchange practices, and probably did Wall Street more harm than any other single witness. His social and moral outlook, so admired in the bull years, seemed outmoded at a time when the nation was fighting a major depression. At one point, Whitney came out against paying bonuses to servicemen who had nonbattle-connected disabilities. Senator Smith Brookhart of Iowa tore into Whitney.

SEN. BROOKHART: You know that most of them were drafted into the war at a dollar a day, don't you?

MR. WHITNEY: Yes, sir; and a great many others were drafted during the war for nothing a day.

SEN. BROOKHART: Those dollar-a-year men who made a million or two dollars on the side in the way of profit; do you mean those?

MR. WHITNEY: I do not know anything about a million dollars on the side in profits.

SEN. BROOKHART: Those men that were drafted and paid a dollar a day, suffered economic damage at the hands of the Government, didn't they?

MR. WHITNEY: That I do not know, Senator Brookhart.

SEN. BROOKHART: You know that most of them did. You know that was not adequate pay for most of those men, don't you?

MR. WHITNEY: Well, I think they had a duty toward their country. Someone had to fight.

SEN. BROOKHART: Yes; someone had to fight in order to maintain the New York Stock Exchange, for instance.

MR. WHITNEY: No sir. The New York Stock Exchange was closed during a part of the Great War.

SEN. BROOKHART: And I am sorry it has not stayed closed ever since (*Laughter*).[86]

The Subcommittee hearings helped set the stage for the legislation regulating the money market that Congress passed during the first few months of the Roosevelt Administration.

The Wall Street community was paralyzed on March 4; as the new President took office, banks were closed, the securities markets were stagnant, and the bankers and brokers spoke seriously of the possibility of revolution. "I am not ashamed to record," wrote Joseph Kennedy three years later, "that in those days I felt and said I would be willing to part with half of what I had if I could be sure of keeping, under law and order, the other half."[87]

Wall Streeters had contradictory opinions regarding Roosevelt on that day. They feared some of the "bright young men" who surrounded the President, but they noted in many of his speeches Roosevelt had seemed as "sound" as any Democrat could be expected to be.[88] Most bankers supported legislation compelling honesty in advertising new issues, a proposal backed by Hoover as well as by Roosevelt, and some were willing to see investment and commercial banking functions separated, another point on which the incoming and outgoing Presidents agreed. The vast majority of the bankers and brokers were strongly opposed to federal regulation and supervision of the market place, however, and they hoped that Roosevelt would not take those parts of the Democratic platform which promised federal controls too seriously. They must have winced when the new President, in his Inaugural Address, spoke of how "the money changers have fled from their high seats in the temple of our civilization," and of how "we may now restore that temple to the ancient truths."[89] What this meant was not entirely clear, but it boded ill for the financial community.[90]

Notes

1. The best works are Allen's *Only Yesterday*, Galbraith's *Great Crash*, and Noyes' *Market Place*.
2. Sparling, *Mystery Men of Wall Street*, pp. 72–73, 110–11; Levinson, *Wall Street*, p. 238.
3. *New York Stock Exchange Fact Book*, pp. 38, 43.
4. Noyes, *Market Place*, pp. 318–19.
5. Chandler, *Benjamin Strong*, pp. 461–62.
6. Oscar Barck, Jr. and Nelson Blake, *Since 1900* (New York, 1959), p. 389.
7. Baruch, *Public Years*, pp. 221–22.
8. *Ibid.*, p. 222.
9. Herbert Hoover, *The Memoirs of Herbert Hoover, The Great Depression, 1929–1941* (New York, 1952), pp. 10–11; Allen, *Only Yesterday*, p. 292; Joseph S. Lawrence, *Wall Street and Washington* (Princeton, 1929), pp. 427–28.
10. Lee, *Economic Fluctuations*, p. 175.
11. Hoover, *The Great Depression*, p. 14.
12. *New York Times*, February 19, 1929.
13. Dies, *Behind the Wall Street Curtain*, p. 100.
14. Soule, *Prosperity Decade*, p. 304.
15. Sparling, *Mystery Men of Wall Street*, p. 19.
16. Dies, *Behind the Wall Street Curtain*, p. 100.
17. Lawrence, *Wall Street and Washington*, pp. 365–66.
18. Hoover, *The Great Depression*, p. 18.
19. Galbraith, *Great Crash*, p. 75.
20. Cornelius Cotter, *Government and Private Enterprise* (New York, 1960), p. 197.
21. Allen, *Only Yesterday*, p. 312.
22. W. Collins Brooke, *How the Stock Market Really Works* (London, 1930), p. 114 ff.
23. Noyes, *The Market Place*, pp. 328–29.
24. Sparling, *Mystery Men of Wall Street*, pp. 150–51.
25. *Ibid.*, pp. 84–85; Neill, *Inside Story of the Stock Exchange*, pp. 232–34; Allen, *Only Yesterday*, p. 305.
26. *Wall Street Journal*, August 23, 1929.
27. *New York Times*, October 3, 1929.
28. John Fuller, *The Money Changers* (New York, 1962), p. 149.
29. *Wall Street Journal*, October 22, 1929.
30. Galbraith, *Great Crash*, p. 103.
31. Allen, *Only Yesterday*, pp. 329–31.
32. *New York Times*, October 28, 1929.
33. Baruch, *Public Years*, p. 225.

34. *New York Stock Exchange Fact Book*, pp. 42–43.
35. *New York Times*, October 30, 1929.
36. Allen, *Only Yesterday*, p. 336.
37. *New York Times*, October 28–November 2, 1929.
38. *New York Times*, October 30, November 4, 1929.
39. Noyes, *Market Place*, p. 335.
40. Burton Crane in the *New York Times*, May 27, 1962.
41. Noyes, *Market Place*, p. 331.
42. *Ibid.*, p. 332.
43. New York *Herald Tribune*, December 3, 1929.
44. Joe Alex Morris, *What a Year!* (New York, 1956), pp. 332–33.
45. *New York Stock Exchange Fact Book*, p. 42.
46. Arthur M. Schlesinger, Jr., *The Crisis of the Old Order* (New York, 1951), pp. 162–63.
47. United States, 87th Congress, 2nd Session, Joint Economic Committee, *1962 Supplement to Economic Indicators* (Washington, 1962), p. 114.
48. *Ibid.*, p. 11.
49. Noyes, *Market Place*, p. 331.
50. Edward Angly, *Oh, Yeah!* (New York, 1930), p. 27.
51. Schlesinger, *Crisis of the Old Order*, p. 231.
52. Barck and Blake, *Since 1900*, pp. 409–10.
53. Galbraith, *Great Crash*, p. 146.
54. Nelson, *Merger Movements*, pp. 166–67.
55. Hoover, *The Great Depression*, pp. 16–18.
56. Schlesinger, *Crisis of the Old Order*, pp. 224–45.
57. Broadus Mitchell, *Depression Decade* (New York, 1947), pp. 76–81.
58. *1962 Supplement to Economic Indicators*, pp. 11, 34.
59. Noyes, *Market Place*, p. 348.
60. *1962 Supplement to Economic Indicators*, p. 114.
61. A. Newton Plummer, *The Great American Swindle* (New York, 1932), pp. 36–44.
62. *1962 Supplement to Economic Indicators*, p. 13.
63. Neill, *Inside Story of the Stock Exchange*, p. 241.
64. *Fortune*, July, 1932, p. 10.
65. Martin Mayer, *Wall Street: Men and Money* (New York, 1959), p. 235.
66. *New York Stock Exchange Fact Book*, pp. 38, 43.
67. *Fortune*, June, 1932, p. 79.
68. Neill, *Inside Story of the Stock Exchange*, p. 241.
69. Weissman, *The New Wall Street*, p. 13.
70. Livingston, *The American Stockholder*, pp. 180–82.
71. *Ibid.*, pp. 190–92.
72. Hoover, *The Great Depression*, pp. 122–23.
73. Schlesinger, *Crisis of the Old Order*, pp. 413–18.
74. Henry Steele Commager, ed., *Documents of American History* (New York, 1949), p. 418.
75. *New York Times*, January 4, 1933.
76. Wickwire, *Weeds of Wall Street*, pp. 90–91.
77. *New York Times*, August 4, 1932.
78. Black, *Watchdogs of Wall Street*, pp. 10–12.
79. Churchill, *Ivar Kreuger*, pp. 6–7.
80. United States, Senate, Committee on Banking and Currency, *Subcommittee on Banking and Currency, Stock Exchange Hearings Practices* (Washington, 1932–34), p. 1189.

81. *Ibid.*, p. 1271.

82. *Ibid.*, p. 1728.

83. Although he covers Insull's glory years fully in his biography of the utilities magnate, McDonald does not delve deeply into this period. The subcommittee did not find any gross wrongdoing in Corp and I.U.I., however.

84. *Ibid.*, p. 1816.

85. *Ibid.*, pp. 2012–14.

86. *Ibid.*, pp. 2236–37. For a report on the investigations by its leader, see Ferdinand Pecora, *Wall Street Under Oath* (New York, 1939).

87. Arthur M. Schlesinger, Jr., *The Coming of the New Deal* (New York, 1959), p. 468.

88. *New York Herald Tribune,* March 3, 1933.

89. Commager, *Documents,* p. 420.

90. *New York Times,* March 5, 1933.

14

Death and Transfiguration:
1933-1947

> The economic cost of this downswing in security values
> cannot be accurately gauged. The wholesale closing of
> banks and other financial institutions; the loss of de-
> posits and savings; the drastic curtailment of credit; the
> inability of debtors to meet their obligations; the
> growth of unemployment; the diminution of the pur-
> chasing power of the people to the point where industry
> and commerce were prostrated; and the increase in
> bankruptcy, poverty, and distress—all these conditions
> must be considered in some measure when the ultimate
> cost to the American public of speculating on the se-
> curities exchanges is computed.
>
> Senate Subcommittee on Stock Exchange Practices

THE FIRST OF the New Deal measures to affect Wall Street was the
Emergency Banking Act of March 9, 1933. Under this law the bank
holiday, in effect since March 6, was validated, and a program to reopen the institutions was initiated. As part of the bank holiday the
Exchange was closed from March 6 to March 14. By mid-month Roosevelt could report that the financial crisis was well on its way to being
solved. Bankers heaved a sigh of relief—perhaps the New Deal
wouldn't be so bad after all—and depositors looked upon the new
President as a hero.[1]

In a message to Congress on March 29, Roosevelt asked for a
law based on "the ancient truth that those who manage banks, corporations, and other agencies handling or using other people's money are
trustees acting for others." In the past, Wall Street had operated on
the principle of *caveat emptor*. Not only was this unfair in that few

investors were equipped to analyze the incomplete evidence available to them, but it was also a dangerous situation, having been a contributing element to the reckless speculation of the late twenties. Now Roosevelt proposed that "the burden of telling the whole truth (be placed) on the seller."[2] For the next two months, the nature of this new legislation was a topic of conversation in Administration circles. Although most agreed that the market place would have to be policed, the conservatives of the Brain Trust, led by Raymond Moley, would have preferred to have Wall Street oversee itself with greater vigor than it had in the past. The liberals, including Felix Frankfurter, James Landis, and Thomas Corcoran, wanted federal legislation. The liberals won most of their arguments, and the Securities Act of 1933, signed on May 27, reflected their point of view.

The Securities Act was based on the belief that if underwriters were obliged to disclose all information to customers, the shady deals and crooked flotations of the past would be impossible. Under the new law the Federal Trade Commission was granted powers to oblige underwriters to maintain certain forms and procedures in the writing of offerings literature, and they had to register issues with the FTC before they could be sold to the public. This "Truth-in-Securities Act," was accepted with little dissent by the financial community. Such a law had been discussed on Wall Street since 1918, when similar legislation had been proposed by the Capital Issues Committee and supported by Secretary of the Treasury Carter Glass.[3] In 1918 it had been viewed with horror as a flagrant interference on the part of the government; by 1933, it was considered by many conservative reformers to be a minimal program. If Wall Street resented the action at all, its discontent was centered around Roosevelt's nomination of Landis as administrator of the law. Landis was considered a radical, and was no friend of the financial world.

The Senate Subcommittee on Banking and Currency reopened its probe of Wall Street on May 23, four days before the Securities Act went into effect. During the next few months the heavyweights of Wall Street—J. P. Morgan, Jr., Thomas Lamont, Otto Kahn—made their appearances and offered explanations for what had happened in the crash, defended their positions, and, for the most part, tried to absolve themselves of any guilt while at the same time promising to reform.

After posing for photographs with a midget on his knee—perhaps to prove that he was human after all—Morgan told the Committee that "since we have no more power of knowing the future than any other man, we have made many mistakes—who has not during the past 5 years—but our mistakes have been errors of judgement and not of principle."[4] A good deal of the testimony concerned how Morgan had avoided paying income taxes, and was repeated by almost every other witness called in the following months. But looking beyond the pyrotechnics, one can see that the most important part of the testimony concerned Morgan's insistence that the financial district could do its own housecleaning, and did not need federal aid to prevent wrongdoing and punish the wicked. Thomas Lamont agreed with his partner, but voiced doubts that the Wall Street community had enough moral power to prevent breaches of ethical conduct.[5]

Otto Kahn of Kuhn, Loeb, proved to be finance capitalism's most effective and attractive spokesman at the hearings. He admitted deceptions, stupidity, selfishness, wrong-headedness, and outright fraud—on the part of the others. Reviewing the late twenties with Senator Alben Barkley, he said:

> You see, there happened from 1926 to 1929, and particularly in 1929, a perfect mania of everybody trying to buy everybody else's property, and the railroads were not excluded from that. New organizations sprung up. Money was so easy to get. The public was so eager to buy equities and pieces of paper that money was—just as it was pressed upon foreign governments, so it was pressed upon domestic corporations. . . .

Wall Street was culpable, he claimed, in going along with the mass hysteria instead of trying to curb it.

> There is nothing so strong as the determination of vast numbers of public opinion to be in the making of—no, that is not the right word —to be in when a great movement is going on. They want to be in. They do not want to sit outside and have their neighbors guess right and they guessed wrong. So they go along, and the combined power of millions of people in doing that is infinitely stronger than anything that a combination of bankers can do, and no combination of bankers can make a market such as existed in 1929 in New York. They can participate in it, and some of them did to their cost, but they cannot make it.

Kahn thought that "we might have been able to stop it earlier, but when it had taken full sway of the people there was an absolute runaway feeling throughout the country, (and) I doubt whether anyone could have stopped it before the calamity overtook us." Kahn proposed that the Federal Reserve be granted new powers over the market place, but his major hope for change lay in the belief that a change in human nature was possible after the shocks of 1929.[6]

Pecora and the senators doubted whether this change would take place; they had heard too much of irresponsible conduct on Wall Street coupled with denials of guilt. In addition, the giants of the twenties seemed amazingly ignorant of their own businesses. For example, O. P. Van Sweringen and Pecora engaged in the following exchange:

> MR. VAN SWERINGEN (*after conferring with his associates*): The statement I made about that, which I again make, was this. Chesapeake Corporation and its acquisition of securities was in fact a reorganization resulting in a mere change in the form of ownership of property. In its formation General Securities Corporation was organized as a medium for exchanging the Vaness Co. holdings of Chesapeake & Ohio stock for its stock so as to avail of the income-tax exemptions provided by Congress in connection with corporate gains in this circumstance. Just as in the formation of Allegheny, Geneva Corporation was organized as an intermediate step in the exchanges involved in that instance.
>
> MR. PECORA: Now, that answer is read from a prepared statement, is it not?
>
> MR. VAN SWERINGEN: It is.
>
> MR. PECORA: And did you prepare it?
>
> MR. VAN SWERINGEN: I did. After some little difficulty to get the details of the transaction. Perhaps I should say the intricacies of the transaction.[7]

In this and subsequent testimony, Van Sweringen indicated that he did not completely understand the structure of the railroad empire he headed.

While the investigations continued, Congress accepted and the President signed the Banking Act of 1933, more commonly known as the Glass-Steagall Act. The bill was passed quickly, but there were clashes of opinion during its framing. Henry B. Steagall of Tennessee, who was strongly anti-Wall Street, backed limitations on the large New York Banks to favor the smaller state banks. In this way, he thought, the power of Wall Street would be diffused throughout the nation. This neo-Jacksonian attitude would be prevalent among the New Deal liberals during the next seven years. Carter Glass of Virginia, one of the fathers of the Federal Reserve, was a leader of a conservative faction which favored regulation, but was unwilling to destroy the New York banking complex or decentralize American finance capitalism. Roosevelt stood somewhere between these two points of view, and his position in the matter was not made clear.

The Glass-Steagall Act represented a victory for the moderates. The Federal Deposit Insurance Corporation was established to safeguard depositors, and Federal Reserve Banks were granted more control over member banks' speculative activities. Most important, the commercial banks were obliged to give up their investment affiliates, an action which had been advocated by both political parties in 1932. Significantly, the Act did not touch upon the decentralization of power issue demanded by the liberals.

In the months that followed the large banking houses spun off investment affiliates which had been theirs for a generation. The First National Bank of Boston joined with the successors of the Chase National Bank's investment arm to form First Boston Corporation, which during the early 1930s was the largest underwriter in the nation.[8] Despite its name, First Boston was fundamentally a New York concern; its dominant position did not signify a shift of power to other cities.

J. P. Morgan & Co. elected to remain in commercial banking, and separated itself from the investment field through the creation of Morgan Stanley & Co., with Harold Stanley, a former Morgan partner, as its president. "The Philadelphia end of J. P. Morgan & Co." was organized as Drexel & Co. Edward B. Smith & Co., a firm which dated back to the 1890s, merged with the investment affiliate of the Guarantee Trust Company of New York, and eventually became Smith Barney & Co. Harriman Ripley & Co. was formed in part through the dissolution of the National City Bank's important City Company and the disaffiliation of investment functions by Brown Brothers, Harriman & Co. Similar stories could be told of most divestitures of the 1934–1935 period.[9]

Other firms were relatively unaffected by the Act. Kuhn, Loeb and the Lehmans, for example, had never been in commercial banking, and they merely continued their investment activities. Blyth & Co., a small house during the twenties, actually benefited as a result of the crash. In 1935 it merged with C. A. Mitchell & Co., a new firm organized by the former hero of the late twenties, who did his job well; within fourteen years he had increased the firm's capital over 400 per cent.[10]

In 1933, many Wall Streeters claimed that the separation of banking functions would result in a destruction of finance capitalism. This gloomy prediction proved incorrect; the separations were made with unusual ease and little fanfare. By 1936 the commercial banks were completely out of the stock markets, a further sign that a Wall Street era had passed. In 1928, the most important firms in terms of under-writings had been Morgan; Kuhn, Loeb; Dillon Read; Harris, Forbes; the National City Company; and Lee, Higginson. In 1935, the under-writing field was dominated by First Boston; Kuhn, Loeb; E. B. Smith; Lazard Freres; Field, Gore; and Blyth & Co. Some of the names might have been different, but the faces were the same. By 1936, conditions became even more normal, as Morgan Stanley (which was founded in 1935) headed the list of underwriters with Kuhn, Loeb in its customary second place. It was clear that the Establishment had weathered the early New Deal, and was still in control. In October of 1933, Roosevelt told Harold Ickes that the finance capitalists did not like one of his speeches, and that for the first time in his memory, Wall Street was not dictating federal fiscal policy.[11] Roosevelt was cor-rect in his belief that the New Deal had been able to separate the business community from the federal government, but up to that time, he had not succeeded in intruding the government effectively into Wall Street.

In December, the subcommittee finished its hearings and began to consider corrective legislation. After extensive discussions with Ad-ministration leaders, the subcommittee agreed that Wall Street needed a "policeman at the corner." On February 9, Roosevelt asked Congress for new legislation, and a strong regulatory bill was introduced in the Senate by Duncan Fletcher and in the House by Sam Rayburn. The new bill would protect investors from manipulations, misrepresenta-tions, and inside deals, and would be strongly enforced by an arm of the Federal Trade Commission.

Wall Street had accepted the Securities Act and the Glass-Steagall Act with little grumbling, and had welcomed other legislation of the early New Deal. During the first months of the National Recovery Administration, reported an insider, "it seemed as though a consider-able part of the business world had 'got religion.'" A prominent busi-nessman told another New Dealer that he considered Roosevelt to be the greatest leader since Jesus Christ, and he hoped God would forgive him for voting for Hoover.[12] The proposed regulation of the securi-ties markets was one of the Administration moves which changed the New Deal honeymoon into a bitter battle. Wall Streeters pointed to internal reforms carried out by the Exchange, and promised more in the future. The moderates said that federal regulation was unfair and unnecessary, while the conservatives predicted that FTC supervision was only the first step in the eventual Communist takeover of the United States. The district's liberals recognized that the Exchange's reforms were sound, but they argued that only federal regulation could give them any real force. In the past, they said, Wall Street had a stringent system of ethics, but the actions of the late twenties had demonstrated that the guardians of morality had been guilty of transgressions themselves. They supported New Deal moderates in asking for federal regulation, but even the most liberal of the bankers thought the Fletcher-Rayburn bill went too far.

A bitter debate followed, in which Roosevelt was accused of attempting to destroy capitalism, of being a traitor to his class, and of harboring dictatorial ambitions. Herbert Hoover called for more state regulation of exchanges, saying that the federal government was getting too powerful. Exchange President Whitney, in testifying before the House Commerce Committee, prophesied that if regulations were increased, "the security markets of the Nation will dry up." In effect, he warned the New Deal of the possibility of a "strike of capital" should it try to enter the financial district. Whitney had told the Pecora Committee that "the Exchange is a perfect institution," and now he tried to marshal the opposition.[13]

The opponents of federal regulation were unable to stop the bill, but they did succeed in changing it. The new Securities and Exchange Act was signed into law by Roosevelt on June 6, marking the beginning of the end of Wall Street's domination of finance capitalism. Symbolically, it represented the shift of economic power from the lower part of Manhattan, where it had been for over a century, to Washington. It marked the end of the era of free enterprise capitalism and the beginning of the period of controlled capitalism.[14]

The Securities and Exchange Act was an attempt to prevent securities manipulations in any form. Whereas the Securities Act dealt only with stocks and bonds prior to and during the initial offering, the new act set up a mechanism to prevent manipulations and wrongdoing at any time. With certain exceptions, all securities had to be registered with the Securities and Exchange Commission. There were provisions for the transmission and gathering of information, disclosure, and review, and investigation of securities. In addition, penalties for transgressions were instituted.[15] Yet, the law was unclear on several important points, especially those regarding liabilities, and there was no guarantee that the truth would have the purging powers the framers thought it would have. In other words, said a SEC employee, "if men wish to form a company whose avowed objective is to pitch dollars off the Empire State Building, there is nothing or little in the law to stop them so long as they tell people what they propose to do."[16]

The Securities and Exchange Act, only half-understood by Wall Street, was to be administered by the FTC until September 1, at which time a separate Securities and Exchange Commission was to be established. Landis, who was still anathema to Wall Street, was given the policing job until the new commission was ready to take power. The district assumed that Landis would become the first SEC Chairman, and would attempt to greatly reduce Wall Street's power. A later group of writers observed that "so sweeping is the control vested in the Commission that there is scarcely a single aspect of the operations of a securities exchange which is beyond the Commission's reach."[17]

Perhaps realizing that the establishment of the SEC had alienated financial leaders, Roosevelt made a characteristic gesture of compromise; he named Joseph Kennedy as Chairman in a move which stunned both Wall Street and the New Dealers. Landis protested bitterly; legislative committees had just finished examining Kennedy's manipulations in the Libby-Owens-Ford pool, and although he was not guilty of legal crimes, the morality of his actions was questionable. Ironically, the new SEC would be headed by a man who symbolized the kind of Wall Streeter the Commission was designed to curb! Secretary Ickes, whose life had been spent in fighting privilege and organizing reform movements, was dismayed. In his diary for June 30, 1934, he wrote:

> At Cabinet meeting yesterday afternoon the President talked over the appointments he had in mind on the new commissions that have been created by act of Congress. I am afraid I do not agree with him as to the chairman he is going to name for the Securities Commission. He has named Joseph P. Kennedy for that place, a former stockmarket plunger. The President has great confidence in him because he has made his pile, has invested all his money in government securities, and knows all the tricks of the trade.

Ickes wondered why the President had named Kennedy, and why Kennedy was so anxious for the post. "Apparently he is going on the assumption that Kennedy would now like to make a name for himself for the sake of his family," wrote Ickes, "but I have never known many of these cases to work out as expected."[18]

Kennedy's appointment was probably the result of Roosevelt's attempt to pay a political debt and a sign to Wall Street that the New Deal did not want to destroy finance capitalism. Kennedy did a good job in setting the new commission on its feet, and when he resigned after a year, the SEC had become a firm fixture on the Street, and was even being spoken of kindly in some financial circles. Kennedy gained the bankers' trust through his moderate interpretation of his powers, and won over some New Dealers by supporting Landis's attempts to develop the SEC's administrative law. Under his leadership, the Commission took a moderate course, prodding but not pushing the district into compliance. Even though Kennedy was succeeded by Landis it remained an essentially moderate organization, dedicated to rooting out wrongdoers from Wall Street. During its first year, the SEC recommended prosecution of 36 individuals; in 1935 177 prosecutions were recommended; and the following year the Justice Department was able to indict 368 individuals out of 379 recommendations. Still, the SEC did not gain its first criminal conviction until 1959.[19] Not until 1937, when William O. Douglas was named chairman, did it favor broad regulatory programs, and by then it was too late.

The Kennedy chairmanship eased criticism of further regulatory legislation; the Public Utility Holding Company Act of 1935 put gas and electric holding companies under the SEC; and the Malony Amendment of 1938 provided for regulation of licensing of securities salesmen. The Chandler Act of 1938 authorized the Commission to serve as advisor in reorganization proceedings. The Trust Indenture Act of 1939 limited and regulated trusteeships. The Investment Company Act and the Investment Advisors Act, both of 1940, subjected counselors to control and in other ways regulated investment firms. None of these acts received the criticism heaped on the Fletcher-Rayburn Act; indeed, by 1940 Wall Streeters talked of how the SEC had opened a new era of trust, and some brokers tried to take credit for having urged it on the Administration.

One of those investigated by the SEC was Mike Meehan. Although cleared of criminal charges, Meehan was expelled from all securities exchanges for his manipulations in the stock of Bellanca Corporation.[20] The Establishment was not displeased at seeing Meehan and his ilk under fire, but it resented outside interference in the early period and refused to cooperate with Kennedy and Landis unless absolutely necessary. Attempts on the part of the more aggressive Landis to coerce the exchanges into carrying out internal reforms came to little, and the market leaders rarely used the consulting arm of the Commission from 1934 to 1938. This is not to say that changes did not take place on Wall Street, for they did. The incompetent salesmen of the twenties were replaced by better equipped and trained personnel, and a few broker-ages began some informal training programs in 1934 and 1935. The Establishment was more self-conscious than before, and became more aware of the boundaries between shrewdness and malpractice.[21]

One of Kennedy's major accomplishments was breaking up the informal "capital strike" of 1934 and early 1935. During this period the new issues market stagnated. Then, inflationary credit policies and the essential moderation of the SEC led Swift and Co. to attempt a $43 million bond flotation—the largest since 1929—in the spring of 1935. The issue was a success, and by September, new financings rose to about $800 million.[22] Whereas the total 1934 underwritings had been less than half a billion dollars, in 1935 over $2.2 billion in new securi-ties were sold, and in 1936 this figure rose to $4.6 billion.[23] Much of this money came from individuals and corporations who had regained confidence in the economy during the early phase of the New Deal. In addition, by the end of 1935, some $5 billion of American securities were sold to Europeans, in part as a result of the devaluation of the dollar, but more because the American recovery seemed more secure than the European.[24]

The renewed activity in underwriting seemed a harbinger of better times, but in fact the bond flotations of this period reflected a more conservative assessment of the economic situation than many realized. During the late twenties, many corporations were forced to borrow money at high rates, and as a result, were in shaky condition during the depression. By 1934 borrowing rates had fallen sharply, and corpo-rations took advantage of this to conduct extensive refinancing opera-tions. For example, a firm would call in an issue of bonds that carried a 5 per cent coupon and then float a new issue at 3.5 per cent. The lower bond rates had two effects, which reinforced one another. First, they caused bond yields to fall more sharply on average than the price rise in their quotations would have indicated. From 1932 to 1939, the average price of par value bonds sold on the New York Stock Ex-change rose from 77.27 to 92.33; in the same period, yields on Moody's Aaa corporate issues fell from 5.01 to 3.01.[25] Second, demand deposits rose, because bondholders were withdrawing their funds from Wall

Street and placing them in insured institutions, which offered an interest rate comparable to those of high-grade bonds but with absolutely no risk. The banks would then invest the new money in bonds and mortgages, the yields of which would be further depressed by the comparatively plentiful funds. The net effect on the bond market was to raise prices slightly and depress yields sharply. Prices would eventually level out, but the return on bonds would never again reach the pre-1929 yields, a partial result of the effects of plentiful money in an inflationary situation. In the thirties, therefore, bonds began to lose some favor, while stocks were not trusted. The result was a general stagnation in volume throughout the decade.[26] There were few three million-share days at the Exchange after the late summer of 1933. The average daily volume for that year stood at 2.5 million, a figure which would not be surpassed until 1955, and one which was 1.7 million below that of 1929.[27]

Activity was slight during the New Deal, but prices fluctuated more than was normal. Although the stock market was no longer a center of attraction, and despite the fact that Wall Street did not dictate policies or even discuss its point of view with the Administration, it still reflected the economic recovery of Roosevelt's first term. From 1933 to 1936 the gross national product rose from $56 billion to $82 billion, salaries went from $29.5 billion to $42.9 billion, and corporate profits before taxes rose from $200 million to $5.7 billion.[28] The market responded to this news with a three-stage bull market.[29]

The first phase began with Roosevelt's inauguration and ended in July, 1933. During this period the *New York Times* Industrial Average rose from 46.85 to 98.05. Then the market began to stagnate once more. The initial flush of the Hundred Days had worn off, and the honeymoon with business had come to a halt with the passage of securities legislation. On Wall Street itself, dissension over the management policies of the Exchange and the reaction to the legislation split the ranks of the bankers. The capital strike had its effects, as did the failure of the New Deal to quickly end the depression. Finally, the Administration's monetary experimentation, especially with the gold standard and the value of the dollar, was mistrusted by bankers, brokers, and many investors. As a result, prices leveled off in 1934 and began to move in a narrow range on small volume. Whereas in 1933, 655 million shares had been traded for a turnover rate of 50 per cent, in 1934 only 324 million shares changed hands on a turnover rate of 25 per cent.[30] Uncertainty regarding the dollar led gold issues to rise to new heights; Homestake and Dome Mines rose from 65 to 544 and from 6 to 61 respectively in the 1929–1936 period.[31] During times of normal mine operations, rises in gold shares usually meant that the currency of the nation was not trusted, and such was the case in this period.

The 1934 stagnation ended in March of 1935, and once more the market moved upward, the *New York Times* Industrial Average rising from 77.92 to 116.74 by November 20. This increase reflected the continued economic recovery, which saw the gross national product leap from $49 million in 1934 to $57.1 billion in 1935.[32] In addition, the fact that earlier fears proved unjustified led to excessive optimism. The 1935 rally was the most sustained since 1929.[33] Some of the big gainers of that year are shown in Table 14.1.

Table 14.1—Selected Price Increases, 1935[34]

Common Stock	Close	Increase
American Express	175½	61
Air Reduction	169	56
American Telephone & Telegraph	155½	50¼
General Motors	56⅜	22¼
Allis-Chalmers	36	20⅛
Bethlehem Steel	51	19⅛
U.S. Steel	49⅜	9⅛
Radio Corporation of America	12	6

After a period of hesitation prior to the 1936 elections, the advance was resumed, marking the start of the third stage of the Roosevelt bull market. By late January of 1937, as the New Deal began its second term, prices had advanced 49 per cent over the 1935 lows, matching the rise of April, 1928–September, 1929.[35] In June, *Fortune* observed that between March of 1933 and April of 1937, the market valuation of all stocks listed on the Exchange had risen from $19.7 billion to $62.5 billion, and the average price of a share of stock had gone from $15.20 to $45.26.

Roosevelt began his attacks on the Supreme Court on February 5, 1937, when he sent a bill to Congress which would have changed the makeup of the tribunal. This action unsettled the nerves of many who had hoped that the President would become more conservative. In addition, Roosevelt's attempts to balance the budget, though almost successful (the federal deficit fell from $3.5 billion in 1936 to $200 million in 1937) also led to an economic decline as soon as government spending was cut. Then too, a wave of strikes unsettled the business picture. Capital spending, which had hit a post-depression peak during the first nine months of the year, slipped badly in the fall and continued downward into 1938. Finally, in August of 1937, the SEC pressed criminal charges for the first time in its history; later on, the new Chairman, William O. Douglas, reviewed market movements and accused Gerald Loeb and G. B. Cary of E. F. Hutton & Co. of having manipulated the common stock of Auburn Automobile Corporation.[36] The early 1937 rise had turned into a rout by year's end (see Table 14.2).

Table 14.2—Losses of Leading Issues, 1937[37]

Stock and Dividend	High	Low	Close	Change
American Telephone & Telegraph (9)	187	140	144½	−40⅜
Bethlehem Steel (5)	105½	41	58⅜	−17⅛
Chrysler (10)	135¼	46⅛	47⅜	−68⅛
General Electric (2.20)	64⅞	34	41⅛	−13½
General Motors (3.75)	70½	28⅝	30	−33½
U.S. Steel (1)	126½	48½	54	−24

Roosevelt moved to check the new depression in April, 1938, through the use of deficit spending and pump priming. The market came out of its nosedive and Wall Street settled down.

The Douglas attacks on Wall Street continued, however. The new Chairman demanded the Exchanges reform and warned of federal intervention unless changes were made. Some regional markets had cooperated, but most Wall Streeters, viewing Roosevelt's failure to bring prosperity as a sign of weakness, were opposed to change. The conservatives, led by Richard Whitney, strongly protested when Exchange President Charles Gay submitted a recommendation for a new constitution on January 27. A battle was shaping up within the Exchange when the district was stunned into disbelief by new disclosures of dishonesty in high places.

There had been unusual activity in the common stock of Greyhound Corporation in early January. A cursory investigation showed that Richard Whitney & Company had been engaged in heavy selling of the stock. A report of this was sent to Howland Davis, Chairman of the Exchange's Committee on Business Conduct. Whitney was investigated and quickly cleared of any malfeasance. There were, however, several irregularities uncovered in the operations of Whitney & Co., and the probing continued.[38]

During the morning of March 8, as J. P. Morgan and Thomas

Lamont were being named Knights of St. Gregory by the Pope, their close friend, Richard Whitney—five times president of the New York Stock Exchange—was suspended for insolvency. An investigation demonstrated that Whitney had used his client's securities as collateral for his speculations in the stock of Distilled Liquors Corporation. At first he had done well; Whitney's initial purchases had been at 15, and the stock rose as high as 45. But then Distilled Liquors began to decline, and Whitney borrowed more securities in order to bolster the price. By 1937 it reached 5, and Whitney was desperate. He approached Bernard Smith, a market operator who was ordinarily beneath the notice of a man of Whitney's position and pride, and asked for a loan in a manner reminiscent of Morgan's. As Smith later testified:

> He came up to see me and said he would like to get this over quickly, and told me he would like to borrow $250,000 on his face. I remarked he was putting a pretty high value on his face, so he said . . . his back was to the wall and he had to have $250,000. I told him he had a lot of nerve to ask me for $250,000 when he didn't even bid me the time of day. I told him I frankly didn't like him—that I wouldn't loan him a dime.[39]

On March 11, Wall Street learned that Whitney had been indicted for theft by New York District Attorney Thomas E. Dewey. During the trial it was shown that Whitney had negotiated 111 "loans" for almost $30 million in less than four years. He had stolen securities from the New York Yacht Club and from estates he had handled. Whitney was found guilty of grand larceny, and sentenced to from five to ten years in jail.[40] Thus ended the career of the man who, in 1933, had claimed that the Stock Exchange had no need of reform.

The district was hit with another scandal a few months later, when F. Donald Coster, head of the respected drug firm of McKesson & Robbins, was shown to have robbed his company and forged its books. McKesson & Robbins was suspended from trading in early December, and shortly thereafter Coster—really Phillip Musica, an ex-convict—committed suicide. As might have been expected, the situation at the company discredited those who claimed that Wall Street was capable of self-policing, and led to demands for still more regulation.[41]

The Whitney affair ended most of the opposition to Douglas's programs for reform. In April, the Exchange accepted a new constitution. A Board of Governors, comprised of the Exchange chairman and president, fifteen members of the Exchange, six non-member partners of

New York member firms, six partners of out-of-town member*firms, and most significantly, three representatives of the public was established. In this way, the Exchange stopped being what Douglas had called a "small private club" and began to open its doors to the public. The Board's first election showed how far the "revolution" had gone; only thirteen of the old Governing Committee were granted places on the new Board of Governors.[42]

Further reforms followed, and Douglas supervised the situation with care if not with tact. The Exchange seemed to welcome this interference. Many member firms suspected that they were fighting for their very existences, and unless they cooperated, stiffer new legislation to curb their activities might be passed. They even applauded the Malony Amendment of 1938, which organized the National Association of Securities Dealers as a watchdog group for the brokers.

In early spring it appeared that this change of heart had taken place too late; on April 29, Roosevelt asked Congress to curb the growth of concentrated economic power, and Assistant Attorney General Thurman Arnold initiated several antitrust actions. Shortly thereafter the Temporary National Economic Committee, led by Senator Joseph O'Mahoney of Wyoming with Leon Henderson serving as executive secretary, was established.

The TNEC was authorized to conduct a full-scale inquiry into the nature of the economy, and in the process try to discover how to make capitalism more efficient or, as Roosevelt put it, show how to "put idle factories and idle men to work." The investigations were far more than that, however. They followed such antibusiness inquiries as the Nye Committee's investigations of the munitions industry and the Pecora hearings.[43] When seen in conjunction with Arnold's antitrust programs, the Douglas attitude toward Wall Street, and the general Administration hostility toward the business community, the TNEC hearings emerge as a final attempt on the part of New Deal liberals to demonstrate that after five years of reform, industrial and financial concentration was as great and as dangerous as it had been during the twenties. To correct this situation, the liberals called for a return to smaller economic units and an antitrust program of merciless proportions. As part of this program, federal powers would also be broadened, in nothing less than a revamping of the economy.[44]

During the more than two years of its existence, the Committee heard 552 witnesses consume 775 hours of testimony, and published— with 3,300 technical exhibits—thirty-one volumes of hearings, six supplements, and forty-three monographs.[45] Almost every aspect of the economy was investigated in an attempt to find out how business operated. In addition, the TNEC tried to determine why recovery was not as quick as after other depressions.

The committee seemed to feel that the 1929 crash was unique in that the forces which in the past had brought the nation back to prosperity were weakened in 1929; the banks and the financial district were no longer the powers they had been in 1873, 1893, and 1907. The formative period of capitalism was over, the committee concluded, and it seemed to agree with economist Alvin Hanson that a new political and economic structure might have to be created.[46] Thus, the investigations apparently returned to the Roosevelt position of 1932.

As part of the proof for this contention, the committee tried to show that finance capitalism, so important in the earlier period, was no longer as necessary as it had been. Under normal conditions, for example, U.S. Steel was capable of financing all of its expansion internally, and the electrical industry could not only finance its own expansion, but had enough capital left over to invest in other industries. Over 70 per cent of all railroad capital came from internal sources, and similar stories were told of the aircraft and automotive industries.[47]

Having stated that finance capitalism was in its terminal stage, the committee then did a strange turnabout and tried to prove that Wall Street had too much power and would have to be further curbed. It was argued that the banking divestitures made under the Securities Act, which had resulted in the formation of the investment banks of the thirties, were only token gestures. Brown Brothers, Harriman, First Boston, Morgan Stanley, and others were still very much attached to their commercial parents. The Committee further showed that of the $10 billion in securities registered with the SEC between 1934 and 1937, 96 per cent were sold through the investment bankers, and that the top six firms—or 1 per cent of the total number of underwriters—handled 57 per cent of the flotations. In addition, the TNEC showed that the twenty leading New York firms controlled the large majority of all underwritings (see Table 14.3).

The situation in the market for quality bonds showed still greater concentration. Morgan Stanley underwrote 65 per cent of all these issues, and the entire quality bond market was in New York.[48] Other bankers acknowledged the "constructive leadership" of the Establishment, but it was also hinted that "it is desirable to have the good will of the House of Morgan" if one wanted to remain long on Wall

Table 14.3—Distribution of Underwriting (Per Cents) 1934–1939[49]

	Bonds	Preferred Stock	Common Stock	All Issues
Morgan Stanley	25.9	9.2	8.0	23.2
First Boston	12.0	5.1	—	10.7
Kuhn, Loeb	7.7	0.2	4.3	6.7
Dillon Read	7.4	10.3	1.7	7.4
Smith, Barney	4.5	9.8	5.0	5.1
Blyth & Co.	4.3	4.0	2.7	4.2
Total	61.8	38.6	21.7	57.3
Fourteen Other New York Banks	20.0	29.1	27.7	21.3
Total	81.8	67.7	49.4	78.6

Street.[50] This, after a half-decade of the New Deal, after four years of the SEC, and after the most severe depression in American history. The nation may have been nearly wrecked, but the Establishment had emerged with scarcely a bruise. Further, it was shown that the American upper class was still intact, and that egalitarian programs of the New Deal after the crash of 1929 had not seriously disturbed the structure of stock ownership in the nation. The 51,000 individuals who had received half the value of cash dividends in 1929 had risen to only 61,000 by 1937.[51]

Despite the contradictory nature of its findings regarding finance capitalism, the evidence amassed by the TNEC was impressive, and cries for reform came from Administration liberals who, after the 1937 depression, had gained power in the White House "inner circle." In 1938 Douglas asked for the establishment of strong regional capital markets, which would involve the disintegration of the Wall Street complex.[52] During the next two years, until he was named to the Supreme Court, Douglas's actions as SEC chairman were feared in the district. His successor, Jerome Frank, who took office in 1940 while the hearings were still being conducted, was more moderate, arguing that competition was ruinous, and cooperation far better than competition.[53] Still, he continued some of his predecessor's programs, although he dropped the idea of regional exchanges.

The TNEC hearings were begun during a period of peace and depression; they ended in the second year of the World War and at a time when American industry was getting back on its feet. The Committee's work was broadly based, perhaps too broadly for a concentrated attack upon America's powerful economic interests. As a result, the force of its findings was diffused and less effective than it might have been. The committee's intention was clear: it wanted new legislation to break up trusts, combinations, and control by a few. The war had already demonstrated, however, that the nation's great corporations were indispensable to the Allied and American military buildups. From the beginning they received most of the government's contracts; even after Roosevelt made a special effort to grant contracts to small businesses, the nation's largest firms executed about 70 per cent of all the orders. Thus, the war destroyed most of the committee's case. The TNEC reports and papers would provide ammunition for anti-business forces for a generation, but in terms of legislation, they were comparatively unimportant.

The market opened 1938 in the doldrums. The Whitney and McKesson & Robbins affairs had caused sharp breaks, as did the President's messages on war and peace in Europe. Perhaps forgetful of the fact that World War I had brought unprecedented prosperity to America, the stock market declined on war scares and rose when peace seemed assured. But by year's end war orders from Europe were helping put the economy back on its feet, and the market followed and to a degree anticipated the business revival, ending 1938 on an upswing (see Table 14.4).

Table 14.4—Price Fluctuations of Selected Issues, 1938[54]

Stock and Dividend	High	Low	Close	Change
American Telephone & Telegraph (9)	150¼	111	150	+ 5½
Bethlehem Steel	78⅞	39¾	78⅝	+20¼
Chrysler (2)	88½	35⅜	83	+35¾
General Electric (.96)	48	27¼	43½	+ 2⅝
General Motors (1.50)	53⅞	25½	50	+20
U.S. Steel	71¼	38	69⅛	+15⅛

The rise was on low volume; trading dropped to a daily average of one million shares from 1937's 1.5 million.[55]

Threats of war dominated the newspapers throughout 1939, replacing the New Deal as the first topic of conversation. Aided by war orders, the economy showed strength, and corporate profits before taxes reached $6.4 billion, the highest since 1929. Although there were over 9 million unemployed, recovery was being made, and it seemed clear that the jobless would soon be absorbed by the new war industries that were springing up around the country.[56]

Nonetheless, the market was uncertain early in the year, and declined. The European war scare in the late summer brought further losses, and in August the bulls and bears seemed evenly matched. On August 29 war appeared imminent, and brokers began asking whether the Exchange would close if and when the fighting began. Exchange officials confided that there was little danger of suspension, for war would not come as a surprise, as it had in 1914. In addition, the capital markets were no longer central to the economy, as they had been a generation before.

Within an hour of the September 1 opening, news of German attacks on the Polish frontier reached Wall Streeters and the market was flooded with buy orders. Within three days the Dow-Jones Average advanced twenty points. A period of decline set in, followed by a short rally, and prices then leveled off for the rest of the year. As a result, although there were wide fluctuations in prices, the key stocks showed minor variations at year's end from the 1938 closing quotations (see Table 14.5).

Table 14.5—Price Fluctuations of Selected Issues, 1939[57]

Stock and Dividend	High	Low	Close	Change
American Telephone & Telegraph (9)	171¼	148	170⅞	+20⅞
Bethlehem Steel (1.50)	100	50¼	80⅞	+ 2¼
Chrysler (5)	94⅝	53⅝	89½	+ 6½
General Electric (1.40)	44⅝	31	40⅝	− 3⅛
General Motors (3.50)	56¾	36⅜	54½	+ 4½
U. S. Steel	82¾	41⅝	66⅛	− 3

Despite the heavy volume toward the end of the year, for the first time since 1923 the trading average fell below the million-share mark, and the turnover rate for 1939 was 18 per cent, a new low.[58] There were several reasons for this stagnation. First, no one seemed to know how the war would affect the President's views regarding the TNEC hearings, or whether Roosevelt would seek a third term. Next, although the economy was recovering smartly, the depression had left scars on the national ego, and many doubted that full recovery would be possible under even the best of circumstances. Finally, while the nation had had confidence in 1914 that the Allies would win the war, there were grave doubts as to the English and French strength in 1939. Hitler seemed unstoppable, Germany had an alliance with the Soviet Union that appeared to preclude a two-front war, the Allies seemed weak, and the United States was strongly isolationist. The inability of the British to prevent a German takeover in Norway and the fall of the Netherlands and Belgium followed by the utter collapse of France depressed any confidence in a swift Allied victory.

On May 10, 1940, the British pound reached a low point in international currency transactions. Prime Minister Neville Chamberlain was replaced by Winston Churchill the following day, and within four trading sessions the Dow-Jones Industrials registered a thirty-five point decline. The British Expeditionary Force seemed trapped in France, and the market continued to slide. But the late April and May declines caused by bad war news, were balanced by the successful British evacuation at Dunkirk and good reports regarding the economy. Prices rose immediately, with raw materials and basic commodities leaping 25 per cent in September alone. By late December employment in manufacturing firms had risen 10 per cent on the year, while payrolls were up 16 per cent. On New Year's Day, industrial production exceeded the 1929 peak by 16 per cent.[59]

Despite this, 1940 was a poor year on Wall Street. Fears regarding Churchill's ability to continue the war, German successes in Europe and North Africa and Japanese threats in the Pacific added to the uncertainty of an election year led prices downward. This would be the general situation on Wall Street until the Allied victories of 1943, and the economic boom of this period seemed utterly ignored by the securities markets (see Tables 14.6, 14.7).

Table 14.6—Key Market Indicators, 1939–1943[60]

Year	Average Daily Volume	Turnover Rate (per cent)	Standard & Poor's Average
1939	954,000	18	12.06
1940	751,000	14	11.02
1941	619,000	12	9.82
1942	455,000	9	8.67
1943	1,000,000	19	11.50

Table 14.7—Economic and Market Statistics, 1929–1943[61]

Year	Gross National Product (billions of dollars)	Corporate Profits (billions of dollars) Before Taxes	Price/Earnings of Standard & Poor's Stocks Ratio
1929	104.4	9.6	13.32
1939	91.1	6.4	13.80
1940	100.6	9.3	10.24
1941	125.8	17.0	8.26
1942	159.1	20.9	8.80
1943	192.5	24.6	12.84

Thus, after a sharp recovery in 1943, the Standard & Poor's Average was still lower than it had been in 1929, despite the fact that the gross national product had almost doubled and corporate profits before taxes had risen over two and one-half times the pre-depression figures.

There were several important reasons for this strange situation, in addition to the general fear of securities which remained from the depression. The mobilization of the economy during World War II was far more complete than the World War I mobilization. By 1945, the military effort was consuming 57 per cent of the national income; in contrast, Civil War costs never rose above the 25 per cent figure, and World War I spending reached 25 per cent only after complete mobilization in 1918.[62] In all, the direct war costs to the United States were approximately $341 billion, over ten times the price for World War I.[63] This great effort required tighter controls and greater taxes than ever before in the nation's history. In 1918 there were curbs on civilian production; in 1944 the same industries were almost completely controlled. Rationing, price and wage controls, excess profits taxes, and the like, directed almost every product from shoelaces to automobiles. Unemployment ended, wages rose, and profits were at high levels. But controls, combined with a fear of a postwar depression, led many manufacturers to refuse to expand their facilities, and the government was forced to finance 84 per cent of total defense plant expenditures. This led to heavier taxes and still more controls.[64] As a result, prices of commodities did not rise as high as might ordinarily have been expected, and neither did net profits after taxes and values on the stock market.[65] Table 14.8 offers a key to an understanding of the situation.

It should be noted that although wages were higher than ever be-

Table 14.8—Selected Economic Statistics, 1929–1945[66]

Year	Unemployment (millions)	Consumer Prices (1957–59 = 100)	Defense Expenditures (billions of dollars)	Per Capita Disposable Income (dollars)	Personal Savings (billions of dollars)
1929	1.5	59.7	0.7	682	4.2
1933	12.1	45.1	0.7	364	− .6
1938	10.4	49.1	1.0	506	1.1
1939	9.5	48.4	1.1	537	2.9
1940	8.1	48.8	1.5	576	4.2
1941	5.6	51.3	6.0	697	11.1
1942	2.7	56.8	24.0	871	27.8
1943	1.1	60.3	63.2	976	33.0
1944	.7	61.3	76.8	1,061	36.9
1945	1.0	62.7	81.2	1.075	28.7

fore, the tax rate rose as well. The net budget receipts for 1939–1945 amounted to $338 billion, as against $45.6 billion for the previous seven years.[67] In part, this was the result of the new tax burden, which covered 43 per cent of war spending. In contrast, World War I taxes accounted for less than 30 per cent of the war bill (see Table 14.9).

Table 14.9—Federal Taxes (Billions of Dollars), 1938–1945[68]

Year	Total Federal Receipts	Personal Taxes	Corporate Taxes	Other Receipts
1938	6.5	1.6	.9	4.0
1939	6.7	1.2	1.3	4.2
1940	8.6	1.4	2.6	4.6
1941	15.4	2.0	7.3	6.1
1942	22.9	4.7	11.1	7.1
1943	39.3	16.5	13.6	8.2
1944	41.0	17.5	12.5	11.0
1945	42.5	19.4	10.2	12.9

If prices remained comparatively level after 1942, while employment rose and savings increased greatly, what then did the wage earners do with their money? Rationing and the halt to appliance, automobile, and housing production held down spending. Since there was a lot of surplus cash in the hands of the public, it might have been expected that some of it would find its way to Wall Street. This was not to be the case. Instead, wage earners put their money into savings banks, paid off mortgages and installments, bought insurance, and participated in Defense, War, and Victory Bond Drives. From 1940 to 1945, automobile debts fell from $2.1 billion to $500 million, personal loans from $1.2 billion to $1 billion, and total consumer debts from $8.3 billion to $5.7 billion.[69] In the same period the total of life insurance in force rose from $115.5 billion to $151.8 billion. The amount of life insurance per family unit, which had dropped during the depression, rose from $2,700 in 1940 to $3,600 in 1946.[70] The seven government bond drives brought in some $157 billion for a total of more than $185 billion in sales. Additional federal borrowing netted $201 billion. In contrast, the total bond sales of World War I—less than $22 billion—seems small.[71]

Thus, the American wage earner came out of World War II with a tremendous amount of liquid capital. In addition, the role of government, so enlarged during the New Deal and the war, seemed to assure a leveling out of the business cycle. All of the preconditions for a boom were present: savings, profits, and expectations. Still, the securities markets remained dull, the scars of the depression and fears of the postwar era still uppermost in the minds of investors. When these fears were assuaged, and individuals were pried from their savings, the bull market would commence, but not before then.

Wall Street was in the doldrums on December 5, 1941, the last trading day before the Pearl Harbor attack. War came as a shock to the district as to most Americans, but it was not wholly unexpected; through lend-lease and other arrangements, the United States had been a "belligerent neutral" for two years.

As a result, the securities markets did not witness wild gyrations. There was a minor decline on December 8, followed by a sharper one the following day. December 10 saw a slight rise, followed by another small decline. Adverse war news kept prices low for the rest of the month, and on the whole, 1941 was a bad year for the market (see Table 14.10).

Table 14.10—Selected Stocks, 1941[72]

Stock and Dividends	High	Low	Close	Change
American Telephone & Telegraph (9)	168¾	115¼	128⅞	−38⅞
Boeing Aircraft	24¾	12⅜	19⅝	+ 2⅛
Bethlehem Steel (6)	89½	51½	65	−21½
DuPont de Nemours (7)	164¼	136¼	143	−20½
General Electric (1.40)	35⅛	24¾	26⅜	− 6½
General Motors (3.75)	48½	23⅜	30¾	−17¼
U. S. Steel (4)	70¾	47	53⅜	−16¼

The sluggishness and declines carried into 1942. February was the slowest month at the Exchange since 1915. Brokers were laid off, fired, or put on part-time; the Exchange floor appeared half-deserted. There were no trends visible, as war news was uniformly bad although hopes were high. A slow rise started in December and continued through July of 1943, but then the market slipped back. Volume was very light except in low-priced issues, a sign that some gambling was taking place. Toward the end of the year there was a rally on heavier volume, and stocks had their best showing since 1936. The advances continued into 1944, with prices rising sharply in the aftermath of D-Day. The German counterattack in December cut into gains, however, and prevented 1944 from matching 1943's advance. With the resumption of the Allied attack, prices moved upward once more, and for the first time in a decade volume picked up markedly on the advances. Peace brought still heavier volume and higher prices. On balance, 1945 was almost as good a year as 1943. Some closing prices are shown in Table 14.11.

Table 14.11—Selected Stocks, 1945[73]

Stock and Dividend	High	Low	Close	Change
American Telephone & Telegraph (9)	196½	157	191	+27⅝
Boeing Aircraft	34⅜	17¼	31½	+13½
Bethlehem Steel (6)	98⅜	65	96	+30½
International Business Machines (6)	250	173½	238	+53
General Electric (1.60)	49⅝	37⅞	47¾	+ 8½
General Motors (3)	77⅞	62	75½	+11½
U.S. Steel (4)	85¾	58⅝	81⅛	+20⅞

The immediate postwar years were uncertain ones for the nation, as hopes for peace were shattered by growing difficulties with the Soviet Union. In addition, a wave of strikes in many industries, most notably rails, steels, and automobiles, led to economic disruption. Altogether, 1946 saw almost 5,000 strikes involving 15 per cent of the labor force. In order to prevent runaway inflation as the consumer returned to the market place, President Truman strongly supported wage and price controls and opposed tax cuts. Businessmen still protested that taxes were too high. Truman's Fair Deal never made any real headway, primarily due to the President's inability to get along with Congress and other pressing concerns with foreign affairs. Squabbles within the Administration gave the nation an appearance of indecision. In retrospect, it can be seen that the reconversion to a peacetime America was carried out with more efficiency than had been the case in 1919, but this was not apparent at the time. In addition, the Full Employment Bill of 1946 should have encouraged securities investments but instead, potential investors were loath to release their surplus funds. Although business expanded rapidly and employment, exclusive of strikes, was high, the prosperity was not trusted. The economic figures were available to all, but they were either ignored or disbelieved (see Table 14.12).

Table 14.12—Selected Economic Indicators, 1944–1947[74]

Year	Gross Private Investment (billions)	Gross National Product (billions)	Government Purchases (billions)	New Construction (billions)
1944	7.1	211.4	96.5	2.7
1945	10.4	213.6	82.9	3.8
1946	28.1	210.7	30.5	11.0
1947	31.5	234.3	28.4	15.0

In this same period—as private investment made up ground lost during the war and the depression—Standard & Poor's Industrial Average had a comparatively modest rise from 12.34 to 14.85. The Average rose to over 17 in 1946, but it fell sharply toward the end of the year in what now appears a strange fashion. There were two causes for this decline. First, many businessmen and investors fully expected a major crash, as had happened after World War I. More important, however, was the faith many Wall Street sophisticates had in the Dow theory.

Most market analysts writing in late August of 1946 believed that prices would rise. In fact, of the 146 market reports during the week of August 26–September 3, all but six were bullish. Of the sixty-one market letters sent out in this period, fifty-four were unqualifiedly optimistic. But some scare selling took place during the first two sessions of September, and Dow theorists warned that should the Index go below the "resistance level" of 186.02, a new bear market would be signaled. This happened during the September 3 trading: prices plummetted, and when the day's losses were computed, it was learned that over $3 billion in values had been wiped out. The market decline reinforced the fears of those who expected a depression, and these bears sold heavily in the weeks that followed. In this way, due to the unrealistic fears of some market professionals and belief in the Dow theory—which has been proven correct in its "signs" about 50 per cent of the time—the bull market was nipped in the bud.[75]

Late in 1947 the automobile industry was operating at a higher rate than that of 1929. Paperboard production, one of the most important of all economic indicators, hit new records in each successive year from 1945 to 1948.[76] The construction industry showed similar progress, with housing starts increasing every year from 1945 to 1950. There were 662,500 private nonfarm housing starts in 1946, 845,600 in 1947, and 913,500 in 1948. By 1950 there were twice as many starts as there had been in 1929.[77] Still, housing materials firms showed no progress on the stock markets. Note was taken of the baby boom, which seemed to augur well for future consumption. Inflation was a problem, but rising prices should have sent the market higher. Despite all of these bullish economic factors, quotations on the New York Stock Exchange did not rise. In 1947, stocks were selling for less than ten times earnings. Earnings were increasing rapidly, but prices stood still, as the price/earnings ratios fell to their lowest points in recent history.[78] This too was discounted by those who remembered 1929 and feared a postwar crash, as well as those who followed the Dow and other theories. The *Times* Economic Editor headlined his 1947 year-end report: "New Peacetime Record High Mark Is Reached By Times Business Index."[79]

At the time, the Wall Street situation resembled a tightly wound spring. Economic prosperity, inflation, a record level of consumption, a large backlog of savings—all were present. Most analysts agreed that if the news continued good, a bull market would have to break. The big question seemed to be, when would it happen, and how far would it go?

Notes

1. *New York Times,* March 29, 1933.
2. Schlesinger, *Coming of the New Deal,* pp. 440–41.
3. Edwards, *Evolution of Finance Capitalism,* pp. 311–12.
4. *Hearings on Stock Exchange Practices,* p. 4.
5. *Ibid.,* pp. 154, 538.
6. *Ibid.,* pp. 1005–10, 1207.
7. *Ibid.,* pp. 717–18.
8. *Medina,* pp. 88–89.
9. *Ibid.,* pp. 58–110.
10. *Ibid.,* p. 98.
11. Harold Ickes, *The Secret Diary of Harold L. Ickes: The First Thousand Days, 1933–1936* (New York, 1953), p. 113.
12. Schlesinger, *Coming of the New Deal,* p. 424.
13. *Ibid.,* pp. 461–63.
14. Ironically, the SEC main offices were tansferred to Philadelphia during World War II, and for a short time, that city was again a seat of financial power.
15. Marshall E. Dimock, *Business and Government* (New York, 1949), p. 607.
16. T. A. Wise and the Editors of *Fortune, The Insiders: A Stockholder's Guide to Wall Street* (New York, 1962), p. 188.
17. Willard E. Atkins, George W. Edwards, and Harold G. Moulton, *The Regulation of the Securities Markets* (Washington, 1946), pp. 70–71.
18. Ickes, *Secret Diary: First Thousand Days,* p. 173.
19. Miriam Ottenberg, *The Federal Investigators* (Englewood Cliffs, 1962), p. 119.
20. Weissman, *New Wall Street,* pp. 130–35.
21. *Ibid.,* pp. 9–10.
22. Schlesinger, *Coming of the New Deal,* p. 469.
23. *New York Times,* January 3, 1937.
24. Willis and Bogen, *Investment Banking,* p. 240.
25. *1962 Supplement to Economic Indicators,* p. 111; *New York Stock Exchange Fact Book,* p. 41.

26. Atkins, Edwards, and Moulton, *Regulation of Securities Markets,* pp. 37–41.

27. *New York Stock Exchange Fact Book,* p. 43.

28. *1962 Supplement to Economic Indicators,* p. 11.

29. Some would add another stage, for there was a strong recovery between the Democratic Convention and Election Day.

30. *New York Stock Exchange Fact Book,* p. 42.

31. *New York Times,* January 3, 1930, January 2, 1937.

32. *1962 Supplement to Economic Indicators,* p. 11.

33. *New York Times,* January 2, 1936.

34. *New York Times,* January 3, 1936.

35. United States, 84th Congress, 1st Session, Senate, Committee on Banking and Currency, *Factors Affecting the Stock Market* (Washington, 1955), p. 5.

36. *New York Times,* January 4, 1938.

37. *New York Times,* January 2, 1938.

38. Fuller, *The Money Changers,* pp. 112–13.

39. Galbraith, *Great Crash,* p. 169; Lundberg, *America's 60 Families,* pp. 522–33.

40. *Ibid.,* pp. 166–70; Fuller, *The Money Changers,* pp. 112–13.

41. *Ibid.,* pp. 116–19.

42. Weissman, *The New Wall Street,* pp. 95–96.

43. Sobel, *Origins of Interventionism,* pp. 26–36.

44. David Lynch, *The Concentration of Economic Power* (New York, 1946), pp. 35–71.

45. *New York Times,* July 8, 1942.

46. United States, Temporary National Economic Committee, 77th Congress, 1st Session, *Investigation of Concentration of Economic Power* (Washington, 1940), pt. 8, pp. 3837–59.

47. *Ibid.,* pt. 9, pp. 3565–5658.

48. *Ibid.,* pt. 24, p. 12993.

49. *Ibid.,* pt. 24, p. 12991.

50. *Ibid.,* pt. 22, pp. 11552, 11594.

51. Kolko, *Wealth and Power in America,* p. 50.

52. William O. Douglas, *Democracy and Finance* (New Haven, 1940), pp. 18–31.

53. Jerome Frank, *Save America First* (New York, 1938), p. 18 ff.

54. *New York Times,* January 3, 1939.

55. *New York Stock Exchange Fact Book,* pp. 42–43.

56. *1962 Supplement to Economic Indicators,* pp. 11, 34.

57. *New York Times,* January 2, 1940.

58. *New York Stock Exchange Fact Book,* pp. 42–43.

59. Mitchell, *Depression Decade,* p. 371.

60. *New York Stock Exchange Fact Book,* pp. 42–43.

61. *1962 Supplement to Economic Indicators,* pp. 7, 11, 114.

62. Cochran, *The American Business System,* pp. 134–35.

63. Bining, *Rise of American Economic Life,* p. 678.

64. Mitchell, *Depression Decade,* p. 377.

65. Faulkner, *American Economic History,* pp. 696–712.

66. *1962 Supplement to Economic Indicators,* pp. 15, 34, 88, 117.

67. Faulkner, *American Economic History,* p. 709.

68. *1962 Supplement to Economic Indicators,* p. 125.

69. *Ibid.,* p. 108.

70. Institute of Life Insurance, *Life Insurance Fact Book, 1961* (New York, 1961), pp. 8–9.

71. Bining, *Rise of American Economic Life*, p. 679.

72. *New York Times*, January 2, 1942.

73. *New York Times*, January 2, 1946.

74. *1962 Supplement to Economic Indicators*, p. 25.

75. An excellent description of this episode can be found in Fuller, *The Money Changers*, pp. 3–17.

76. *1962 Supplement to Economic Indicators*, p. 56.

77. *Ibid.*, p. 67.

78. *Ibid.*, p. 114.

15

The Tardy Boom: 1947-1960

The market is mostly a matter of psychology and emotion, and all that you find in balance sheets is what you read into them; we're all guessers to one extent or another, and when we guess wrong they say we're crooks.

Major L.L.B. Angas

THE FINANCIAL DISTRICT was a dull place during most of 1947; one-million share days were considered busy. Brokers played baseball with rolled up newspapers and crumpled quotation sheets on the Exchange floor. Forced retirements and "Scotch leaves" at half or no pay were not uncommon. In 1940 there had been 5,855 brokers, underwriters, and dealers in the district. In early 1947, there were only 4,343.[1]

Wall Street completely failed to reflect the nation's economic exuberance; stock prices did not rise with the rapidly increasing profits of listed corporations. In 1947 one could purchase such blue chip stocks as Firestone and Jones & Laughlin Steel for less than four times earnings, and Kennecott for under six times earnings. Armour, at its low, sold for a multiple of 2.7. Most quality issues were under the price/earnings ratio of ten, and many paid 8 to 12 per cent in dividends.[2]

There were few glamour issues in 1947. Even shares in automobile and appliance firms, which were doing fine business, lagged in price and volume. The new issue market was sluggish. Gloria Vanderbilt's attempt to set up a cosmetics company caused some talk, but the venture fell through. Globe Aircraft, which was to have been "the General Motors of the Air Age" was a fiasco. Odd lot transactions, a good indicator of whether the little fellow was in the market, were only 65 per cent of the 1946 volume. Indeed, the only bright spot statistically was the fact that original common stock listings on the Exchange stood at 40.4 million shares in twenty-nine newly listed corporations. Although these figures were comparatively large, they were below 1946's 50.2 million shares in fifty corporations. Stock splits, of which there had been only twenty-two in 1944, had risen to ninety-nine by 1946, and in 1947, the figure dropped back to seventy-six.[3]

Stock prices on the Exchange rose slightly toward the end of the summer, causing a few analysts to begin to speak hopefully of a new bull market. *Time* was a trifle too optimistic in its review of the year, but during the summer its forecast seemed justified.

> Wherever one looked, the U.S. was splitting its breeches. In Texas, cash farm marketings had jumped from $469 million in 1939 to $1,974 million last year. In mushrooming Houston, millionaires were so common that nobody paid them much attention. In Atlanta, Frank H. Neely, chairman of the district Federal Reserve Bank, took a look at the new industrial South and said: "I think we are more or less permanently at a higher level." . . . it was a good bet that the Street's baby bull would put on some real meat before the bull-throated roar of the U.S. economy dies down.[4]

This timid bull market ended early in 1948, and stagnation set in for the first few months of the year. Then, during the political campaigns of the summer, the rise began once more. Economic signposts were favorable, and it seemed certain that Republican Thomas E. Dewey would have no difficulty in defeating Harry Truman, who was considered unfriendly to business in general and Wall Street in particular. In May the Dow-Jones industrials pierced the 1947 high and began to show sizable gains, and by June most of the district's 1,200 market analysts were predicting a major move before Election Day. Edmund W. Tabell, then a rapidly rising market writer for Shields & Co., spoke of an ultimate topping-out area of around 260. One of the most optimistic and accurate analysts on the Street, Tabell's summer forecasts were considered foolhardy at the time. When he spoke of an ultimate high of around 400—which would put prices well above their 1929 peaks—he was considered little better than a lunatic.[5] By late summer, however, the average was above 190, and 200 seemed a reasonable objective for December 30.

Wall Street prepared for the year-end rally in late October, as volume and prices both rose. Then came the shock of the Truman victory, shattering dreams of a pro-business Administration in Washington. The next day opened with a rush of sell orders, and trading was held up as specialists tried to establish an orderly market. When sales finally appeared on the ticker, they showed prices from two to four points below previous closes. By day's end, the Dow-Jones industrials had dropped 7.3 points, the greatest decline since September of 1946, and by the end of the week, the average had fallen to 179 and had wiped out the entire pre-election rally. In this way, the 1948 bull market was brought to an abrupt end; on December 31, the average stood at 177.30, and showed a slight decline for the year.

Despite this, production and profits continued to climb; good business apparently had no politics. Inflation, which raised the prices of almost everything else, did not affect stock prices which, in the midst of the boom, were selling at their lowest price/earnings ratios since the early twenties.[6] And there seemed little hope for the future; Dow theorist Justin Barbour predicted further declines in 1949, as did John H. Lewis, one of the most bearish analysts on the Street. Glenn G. Munn of Paine, Webber, Jackson & Curtis, was more bullish, but warned in language which by then had become standard for such writers, that "business may be in a slow-motion roll-over into an old-fashioned, spiraling, chain-reaction decline."[7]

The bears proved correct in their predictions for 1949. The gross national product rose less than $900 million over the 1948 total of $336.7 billion, and corporate profits before taxes fell from $33 billion to $26.4 billion.[8] Prices declined on the market, as analysts and investors began to feel their worst fears would be realized. In June, the Dow-Jones industrials hovered around the 160 mark, and although prices leveled off during the fall and winter, a further decline was expected. Money was tight in all areas, as even the Treasury reported difficulties in selling long-term bonds. The short interest index—a compilation made from sales of borrowed stock that sellers expected to purchase at a later date at greatly reduced prices—rose sharply during this period, a clear sign of a bearish mentality. In December the index showed that 2.3 million shares were short, and this seemed a complete erosion of confidence in securities.[9] Conditions were to get worse; in March of 1950, the short interest was well over 2.5 million shares.[10] Bears concluded that this meant that prices might soon test their 1942 lows, and their expectations seemed justified. The Standard & Poor's price/earnings ratio for the year averaged out at 6.64, the lowest in the memory of most Wall Streeters.[11]

The few bulls remaining on the Street pointed out that the economy was on their side, and that in time the market would have to rise to reflect the business recovery which began in 1949. In addition, they observed, the large army of shorts would eventually have to buy back their borrowed stock. If a substantial market rise developed, the shorts might panic and rush in to cover their sales, and thus provide the impetus for a new bull market.

Stocks edged upward from their summer lows, rising to the 200 level by December 31, 1949, but this was hardly a sign of a bull market. Prescient investors might have noticed that three groups had done fairly well for the year. The gold stocks rose, and this was a bearish sign—an indication that some believed the economy was headed for a slump and were hedging in precious metals. Soft drink firms with good earnings did well; Wall Streeters attributed this to bear buying in stable food issues. The third group, however, represented the coming into being of a new kind of market: television and radio shares rose sharply, even during the bear period, and shot up strongly during the autumn and winter rises. The reason for this was obvious: in 1948 less than 3 per cent of American homes had television sets, but by the end of 1949, this figure had risen to over 10 per cent.[12] It was clear to even the most pessimistic that the television boom would not end until almost every American home had a set. Because of this, television and radio shares staged their own private bull market in 1949, and it carried into 1950. By midsummer, Admiral had gone from 7 to the equivalent of 80 in less than two years; Hoffman Radio rose from 2⅝ in mid-1949 to 23¾ a year later. During the early months of 1950, Zenith—soon to become the bellwether of the television group—rose from 31½ to the high 70s.

From television shares interest turned to other sectors, and aircrafts, appliance manufacturers, utilities, and most important, the automobiles, began to rise significantly. By spring some leading analysts were talking of a new bull market. The Dow-Jones industrials had by then risen some 10 per cent since January 1, standing at 222. Prices gave every indication of fulfilling the most optimistic prophecies, rising on most trading days during early and mid-June, and passing the 230 mark in the third week of the month. Then, on June 24, the nation learned of the North Korean attack on South Korea, and of American aid to the Rhee government. In the days that followed it became clear that the United States would be engaged in a limited war on the Asian mainland, which might turn into World War III. War scares, added to fears of new economic controls, had their effect on the Street. The market slumped, and analysts began writing of growing bear sentiment in the district.[13]

The short bear period was over by the fall, as more good earnings statements, the stabilization of conditions at the Pusan perimeter, and President Truman's refusal to impose highly restrictive economic controls had their effects. Then came news of higher dividends, stock splits, and heavy war orders. The market paused and then rallied, ending the year at a fraction below the June highs.[14]

The advance carried into 1951 and the release in January of economic and business statistics for the preceding year buoyed confidence. Stock splits had risen from fifty-seven in 1949 to 107 in 1950, and cash dividends on listed stocks from $4.2 billion to $5.4 billion.[15] The gross national product had gone from $254.1 billion to $284.6 billion, and corporate profits before taxes from $26.4 billion to $40.6 billion.[16] The economic outlook was still good, corporate earnings and dividends continued their rises, and General MacArthur appeared to have the situation in Korea under control. There were signs of a strong bullish mentality on the Street; it was noted that money was flowing out of the bond market and into stocks for the first time in a generation. Brokers on Toronto's Bay Street reported that large amounts of American money were crossing the border, to be invested in Canadian "penny stocks" to the tune of $50 million a year.[17] The preconditions for a major boom seemed to be present.

Despite this, the market slowed down in late January and leveled off in February. In April, Truman relieved MacArthur of his command and soon after, armistice talks began in Korea. It was clear that the Asian conflict would not erupt into World War III, but it was equally obvious that the United States had not been able to defeat the Red Chinese and North Koreans. For the remainder of the Truman Administration the nation seemed to stand still. The Korean War, one of the most unpopular in the nation's history, cast a pall over the market. In addition, new tax legislation in 1951, which among other things raised corporate rates from a 47 per cent to a 52 per cent maximum, frightened many investors. All in all, 1951-1952 was a standoff period; the high-low range of Dow-Jones industrials for the twenty-four months was only 53.01 points. Volume declined from 1950's daily average of almost 2 million shares to 1952's 1.3 million shares,[18] and the price of an Exchange seat fell from $54,000 in 1950 to $39,000 in 1952.[19]

The potential for expansion was present in 1951 and early 1952, but was not realized. Tighter profit margins caused corporate earnings before taxes to fall from $42.2 billion in 1951 to $36.7 billion in 1952, at the same time the gross national product rose from $329 billion to $347 billion.[20] Still, there was no sign of recession, and corporations had an easy time of it on the capital markets, where new bond and stock offerings were taken up without much difficulty. Significantly, 1951 offerings of $7.8 billion worth of new securities—a record high at the time—was made up of 30 per cent common stocks and the rest of preferred, bonds, and debentures. The ratio of common stocks to debts was also an all-time high, indicating confidence that a bull market would soon develop.[21] Investors weighed the good reports against the bad, and finding them to be about equal, refused to accept either as a complete answer. One commentator, viewing the standoff between the bulls and the bears, dubbed the situation a "horse market." The traders, he said, were "just horsing around."[22]

Bullish sentiment began to pick up in the late summer of 1952, as it appeared certain that General Eisenhower would become the next President, the first Republican to occupy the White House since 1933. Eisenhower pledged himself to end the Korean War, cut spending and taxes, lift remaining World War II controls, and encourage economic growth while at the same time preventing further inflation. All of this pleased the business community, and analysts began to issue bullish predictions regarding the coming "Eisenhower market."

Prices did rise after the Republican triumph in November, and Wall Street hailed the President-elect's selection of businessmen for key Administration posts. His early removal of wartime controls and the ending of the Korean War were also applauded. Still, the expected economic boom did not develop. Eisenhower seemed more interested in balancing the budget than in stimulating business expansion. He came out against a tax cut in 1953, claiming that to reduce revenues while the budget was unbalanced would "not be consistent with attaining the vital financial objective of a sound dollar."[23] The Federal Reserve instituted a tight money policy which was aimed at holding down inflation, but at the same time hindered business growth. With these and other deflationary efforts, the economy faltered, and in the fourth quarter of the year began to dip in the first of the Eisenhower recessions.[24] By mid-September a low point of confidence had been reached; Dow-Jones industrials were at 265.5, having fallen almost thirty points since January.[25] Colin Clark, a prominent English economist, predicted a depression for 1954, and his gloomy forecast was echoed by most American analysts. The prediction proved correct; the gross national product in 1954 was $363.1 billion as against 1953's $365.4 billion, and corporate profits before taxes fell to $34.1 billion from $38.3 billion.[26]

The stock market had not shown much vigor while the economy was expanding and was not expected to rise now that the first downturn since 1949 was in the works. Yet, in mid-September, prices leveled off, and they began to rise in October. On September 30, 1953, the Dow-Jones Industrials stood at 264.04. Exactly eight years later, the average was near its all time high, having just crossed the 700 barrier. Thus, the bull market of the fifties was born in the midst of bad business news.

The new bull market bore some surface resemblances to that of the twenties. In both there were periods during which certain glamour issues found a vogue, only to be forgotten when the next ones appeared. Colorful characters and crooks abounded, as they do in all bull periods. There were dramatic advances, and everyone seemed to be making money. But the advances of the fifties were markedly unique in some respects.

During the early months of the rise, *Fortune,* in writing of the structural nature of the district, observed:

> The market is no longer the pivotal economic institution and influence it once was. What gave the New York Stock Exchange great influence in the economy before 1939 was the part it played in the New York money market and the fact that the New York money market in turn dominated the credit structure of the United States. But now that stock trading is a cash rather than a margin proposition, the Exchange is a relatively minor force in the money market.[27]

In 1962, a government report on the nature of private capital investment, stated:

> Capital requirements were financed chiefly from internal sources during the postwar period. Retained profits from operations accounted for $139 billion and depreciation charges for $204 billion. In addition, corporations raised $145 billion, or one-fourth of total requirements, by borrowing from banks and other institution lenders and by selling securities in the capital markets. The remainder of investment funds— $76 billion—was provided by trade credits extended by other firms, and by current accruals in excess of payments. . . . As compared with

the 1920's, corporate financing in recent years featured a higher reliance on internally generated funds, a modest rise in the importance of long-term borrowing, and a sharp reduction in stock flotations.[28]

This was another way of saying that the major differences between the markets of the twenties and the fifties were the New Deal reforms and the maturation of the American economy.

There was little playing with other people's money during the fifties. Commercial and investment banking functions were separated. Margin requirements were always above the 50 per cent level, preventing great use of leverage, so common during the twenties. This barrier to speculation could be circumvented, however. One could borrow money on stock certificates by offering them as collateral at commercial banks. New securities could then be purchased with the borrowed money, and then the process could be repeated. This practice was illegal—the borrower would have to lie about the reasons for the loan—but it was used by many of the more speculative purchasers of common stocks. The sophisticated investors would "play the bond market," where some convertible bonds and debentures could be purchased on as little as 5 per cent margin.

The SEC was instrumental in keeping down excesses, especially under the leadership of Paul Windels, Jr., from 1956 to 1961. But the SEC lacked the power to step in and prevent swindles before they occurred. In addition, the vastly increased size of the new issues market—registrations rose from 496 to 1,628 during the decade—which had to be investigated by a woefully small staff made Windels' job almost impossible. As a result, several spectacular boondoggling operations took place during the bull years.[29]

Periods of speculative frenzy always draw both scoundrels and suckers to Wall Street, the way a three-alarm fire attracts curious onlookers and pickpockets. There were differences, however, between the Birrells, Gutermas, and Belles—the scoundrels of the fifties—and their predecessors. These men did not occupy the center of the stage; by mid-century, Wall Street was too well regulated for outright thievery. They had to be devious rather than direct, they were interested in money rather than power, and when discovered, they wound up in a Brazilian exile or jail instead of a suite in the Fifth Avenue Hotel. The swindlers of the fifties may have resembled individuals who in the past would have sold gold bricks or perpetual leases on the Brooklyn Bridge, but they also displayed a surprising amount of sophistication. They realized that the securities they handled were of questionable value, and they also knew that the market was loaded with money, which could be attracted by the proper bait. To them, Wall Street resembled a huge game of musical chairs, with each spectator trying to get a seat before his neighbor. Individuals who purchased their securities often realized they were of little value, but they bought them in the expectation that "another sucker" would soon be found to take them off their hands at a sizable increase in price. Such people were not so much unwitting victims as they were gullible accomplices. Many investors in the Canadian penny stocks of the early fifties and the slick manipulations of the latter part of the decade were aware of the fact that "something was being done" to the company and the equities, and they gaily went along for the ride.

In late December of 1952 and early January of 1953, the financial pages carried many advertisements from brokers regarding the fantastic profits to be made in uranium stocks. One of these read:

> No one ever made any money without taking some risk, so if you can afford to speculate and want a stock which has the best growth and profit possibilities we have seen in over twenty years of Wall Street experience—again we say, buy *Consolidated Uranium Mines* common stock now around 70 cents per share. Remember just two years ago the stock was around 15 cents—it's your guess what it will be 2 years from now.

The advertisement was signed by Tellier & Co., a small house that operated across the river in New Jersey.[30]

Walter Tellier was the central figure and, in many ways, the symbol of the Canadian stock bonanza that entranced speculators during the late forties and early fifties. Built primarily on uranium issues, the boom was strengthened by the belief that Canada faced the same type of economic boom which had transformed the United States after the Civil War. This fantasy sparked the rush to buy Canadian equities. Tellier marketed more than forty "penny stocks" of Canadian uranium mines alone from 1950 to 1955, before being indicted for violations of the Securities Act and mail fraud in December of 1955. Two years later he was in a penitentiary, serving a four and one-half year term.[31]

This period saw the emergence of several more swindlers of daring and skill. Lowell Birrell made several fortunes by manipulating the stocks of Claude Neon, United Dye & Chemical, Fidelio Breweries, Swan-Finch, and Doeskin Products, but in 1959 he was indicted for fraud. By then, however, the master manipulator was safely settled in Brazil, which has no extradition treaty with the United States. Birrel invested some of his millions in several local enterprises, and soon became an important if not a trusted member of Rio's high society.[32]

In 1953, the firm of McGrath Securities printed several maps of Mexico, showing large areas controlled by a company known as Shawano Development. The maps were published in the financial pages, along with an advertisement offering Shawano at $1.25 a share. Shawano was supposed to have vast oil reserves, and control of a "mystery fabric" known as ramie. The oil, if there was any, was never exploited, and ramie proved to be a well-known fabric of limited use. Still, the public went for Shawano Development, making its backer, Alexander Guterma, a rich man. Some 150,000 investors bought nearly 18 million shares of the almost worthless stock before the bubble burst. In 1954 Shawano reached $4 a share; four years later, after a three-for-one split, it sold for 8½ cents. Guterma bulled other stocks in the years that followed. United Dye (which had just been sucked dry by Birrell), Bon Ami, F. L. Jacobs, Micro-Moisture Controls, and Western Financial Controls all earned fortunes for the wily speculator. The SEC finally caught up with Guterma in February, 1959. Trading was suspended in Bon Ami and Jacobs, and when space was booked in Guterma's name on an Ankara flight, a warrant was issued for his arrest. "This is the biggest outrage by publicity hounds I've ever seen," he said. "This is getting a man for spitting on the sidewalk." The SEC pressed on, and despite a clever defense, Guterma was fined and imprisoned. For the first time, the SEC had successfully concluded a criminal case.[33]

Earl Belle and his associates, Murray, Edward, and Burton Talenfeld won civic awards from the small town of Saltsburg for their work in setting up a bank in town and attracting new industries to that small corner of Pennsylvania. This was in 1957; within a year, Belle and his associates had loaded the bank's portfolio with worthless securities and had sold others to unsuspecting citizens of Saltsburg. Belle's major vehicle was Cornucopia Gold Mines, from which he extracted several millions before being caught by the SEC. Cornucopia was suspended from trading on May 20, 1958. Shortly thereafter Belle and his wife were on a plane to Rio. The Talenfelds were tried and all three received fines and two went to prison. As for Belle, he sent a note to the Pittsburgh newspapers, saying:

I am deeply sorry for all the people who have been misled and for all the wrongs done and for the unwitting part I played in the deception. I wanted so much to succeed that I went along on several things I should have known better than to do. I imagine permanent exile is punishment enough for this.[34]

The Birrells, Gutermas, and Belles were colorful and imaginative, but at no time did they dominate the market. They operated on its fringes, and when discovered, were destroyed. Men like Little, Drew, Vanderbilt, Gates, and Baruch were lions; their counterparts during the fifties were little better than jackals.

If the types of speculators and manipulators of the fifties differed from those of the twenties, the manner of institutional support in the two markets was still more dissimilar. During the earlier period, undue reliance was placed on the banking community. Morgan and Mitchell had a thinly masked contempt for the public, or at best, considered them sheep. Their successors thirty years later were important men, but the New Deal reforms had blunted their powers to such an extent that no single banker or group of bankers could exercise leadership on the Street. During the fifties their places had been taken by the often faceless managers of mutual funds, trusts, pension funds, insurance portfolios, and foundations, who had to be far more solicitous of the public than the private bankers had been. In 1949, these institutions held $9.5 billion in New York Stock Exchange securities. By 1958, this figure had risen to over $44 billion, and by the end of 1960, had reached $70.5 billion. Within a decade, institutional holdings of all stocks had risen from 12.5 per cent of all equities to almost 20 per cent.[35] The men who controlled these vast resources were the new key men of Wall Street.

The largest single source of new capital came from the mutual funds, whose story is one of the most dramatic of the bull market. The oldest modern fund, the Massachusetts Investment Trust, appeared in 1924. It differed from other trusts of the time in that shareowners were able to redeem their holdings at net asset value instead of selling them at the current market quotation. In addition, MIT was purchased and sold directly from the trust, and not from another holder of its shares.

The closed-end trusts—which had a specific number of shares outstanding and were treated as any other common stock—dominated the scene during the twenties, and open-end trusts, such as MIT, were far smaller and less popular. They lacked the leverage which caused the closed-end companies to soar ever higher during the bull market, and they were not pushed by brokers, who made greater profits by keeping their accounts active. On the eve of the crash there were but nineteen closed-end trusts in operation, with aggregate assets of only $140 million, and the four largest ones had almost 30 per cent of this amount.

The crash wrecked the majority of the closed-end trusts, but the mutuals weathered the storm, and even managed to expand during the depression. In 1940 they had $500 million in assets, and were almost as large as the closed-end trusts. Within a year they were larger, and their growth continued for the next twenty years at a phenomenal rate. By 1950 net assets of mutual funds were $2.5 billion, as against less than $900 million for the trusts. A decade later, there were some 3.5 million owners of mutual funds shares, and the funds had almost $17 billion in assets.[36] By 1961 there were over 330 mutuals in operation, controlling some $22 billion in securities.[37]

The largest funds were more powerful than most banks. In 1960, MIT and Investors Mutual each had over $1.5 billion in assets, and the Wellington Fund was a billion-dollar concern. The United Funds, the Investors Stock Fund, and Fundamental Investors headed the list of mutuals with over $600 million in assets.[38] Needless to say, their impact on the market, especially in day-to-day activities, was substantial.[39]

The mutuals were popular because of their willingness to cater to small investors who, after an initial payment, could invest as little as ten dollars a month. The vigorous sales efforts made by an army of often unqualified part-time salesmen who specialized in calling on unsophisticated individuals was a significant factor in their growth. Estimates as to the number of these salesmen ran into the thousands; one authority wrote that "the only industry of a financial nature which employs substantially more aggressive merchandising methods is life insurance."[40]

Almost as important as the mutuals in supporting the market were the pension funds. From 1957 onward they invested approximately one billion dollars a year in stocks and almost $2 billion in bonds. Of the $32 billion in stock sales on all registered exchanges in 1957, the pension funds alone accounted for $1.4 billion. By the end of the decade, the funds owned over 2 per cent of all corporate stocks in the nation.[41] Some large firms, such as American Telephone & Telegraph, Sears, Roebuck, and Hershey, were substantially owned by employees through their funds. Like the mutuals, the pension funds invested the largest part of their assets in blue chip securities, in this way providing an important prop for the market and a barrier against any major bear collapse.

The large tax-exempt foundations were in a similar position, but few published their portfolio holdings and it is therefore difficult to estimate their total impact on the market. It is known, however, that the Ford Foundation, which controlled Ford Motors, had a good deal of its $2.5 billion in common stocks at the end of 1962. At that time, it held almost $8 million of Standard Oil of New Jersey, $7 million of Aluminium, Ltd., $3 million of American Telephone & Telegraph, and $3 million of International Business Machines, among its other assets.[42] The half-billion dollar Rockefeller Foundation owned over 2 per cent of Standard Oil of New Jersey.[43] The $470 million Duke Foundation was based on tobacco shares, and the Hartford Foundation, on shares of Great Atlantic and Pacific Tea Company. Similar stories could be told of most of the other large tax-free institutions.

In 1959, the total assets of American life insurance companies were almost $114 billion, of which more than $4.6 billion was in corporate stocks and $56.7 billion in United States and corporate bonds. Although the common stock holdings of life insurance firms represented only a small fraction of their total holdings, the percentage grew at a faster rate than the industry's assets as a whole. From 1949 to 1959, for example, the life companies alone acquired some $2 billion in industrial issues.[44] Like the pension funds, they held blue chips and bonds of established companies.

Stock purchase plans for employees provided another institutional change, and another source of power for stockholding groups. Although each program was different, most allowed the employee to buy a specified number of shares during a specified period for a specified price, usually 10 per cent or more below the current market quotation. In some plans the employer contributed a fixed percentage of the price for as many shares as were allowed the employee. In 1960, approximately 20 per cent of all listed firms offered purchase plans; in all, 233 companies reported a total of 248 programs. Of these, 114 were of the types described, while the others were either combination savings-investment or profit-sharing systems.[45]

Most plans permitted employees to buy only a small number of shares, and their real impact came in introducing the public to the stock market. More than 25 per cent of the new shareholders from 1956 to 1960 bought their first stock through employee purchase plans; by 1960, there were some 1,340,000 individuals investing regularly in this manner.[46]

These institutions, through which the general public participated in the market, provided the major supports for the Exchange's listed securities during the fifties. By 1961, the noninsured pension funds held $17.4 billion in listed stocks alone, while the mutual funds reported some $17.2 billion in listed shares, and the closed-end trusts added $5.6 billion. The various kinds of insurance companies, the college endowments and foundations, and the banks owned an additional $30.3 billion. In all, the financial institutions accounted for $70.5 billion of the total of $387.8 billion in Exchange valuations in 1961. To this figure must be added the wide holdings in non-Exchange stocks and bonds. In that year the institutions owned 18.2 per cent of all listed shares, and a similar amount of nonlisted securities.[47] In 1951, 61 per cent of all listed stocks were purchased by individuals; by the end of the decade, the figure had dropped to below 35 per cent.[48] But this is not to say that brokers and investment bankers were no longer important. The institutions used their services, and members of Wall Street firms were prominent on many boards of directors.

Most of the large firms of the twenties were still in business and prospering. Morgan Stanley, Lehman Brothers, Kuhn, Loeb, and Goldman, Sachs were among the more respected institutions of the district. Brokers like Bache & Co., Eastman, Dillon, and Francis I. duPont had traditions of service to generations of customers. There was, however, a major change in the securities field, which can best be illustrated by listing the largest investment bankers and brokers who were operating during the bull market of 1959 (see Table 15.1).

The name that stands out from the rest is, of course, Merrill Lynch, Pierce, Fenner & Smith, which was by far the largest brokerage and an important and growing investment banker as well. Although not of the Establishment, and often frowned upon by the older houses, Merrill Lynch—also known as "We, the People," "The Thundering Herd," and "The Bureau of Missing Persons"—has become almost as much a symbol of the Wall Street of the fifties as the House of Morgan had been of previous bull markets.

Merrill Lynch was the creation of Charles Merrill, who, along

Table 15.1—Incomes of Brokers and Investment Bankers (Millions of Dollars), 1959[49]

Brokers	Gross Income	Investment Bankers	Gross Income
Merrill Lynch, Pierce, Fenner & Smith	136	First Boston	1,042
Bache & Co.	38	Morgan Stanley	965
Francis I. duPont	31.2	Lehman Brothers	880
E. F. Hutton	30	Blyth & Co.	868
Paine, Webber, Jackson & Curtis	29.1	White, Weld	833
Dean Witter	unknown	Merrill Lynch, Pierce, Fenner & Smith	815
Walston & Co.	27.2	Kuhn, Loeb	696
Goodbody & Co.	24.8	Halsey, Stuart	650
Shearson, Hammill	24	Eastman, Dillon	456
Loeb, Rhoades	23	Stone & Webster	388

with Jay Cooke and J. P. Morgan, Sr., was one of the district's most important figures. Cooke pioneered the distribution of large issues, Morgan made the Street the center of the nation, and Merrill was able to accomplish something the New Deal attempted and could not carry through: he brought Wall Street to the nation. More than any other person, Merrill made the purchase of securities "respectable" after the lean thirties. He reintroduced the Street to the small investor, and was the best symbol of what was later called People's Capitalism. Merrill's attitude toward the securities market was graphically shown when, after the 1948 election, he responded to Truman's condemnation of "the money changers." In an advertisement which ran in several financial papers, he wrote:

> One campaign tactic did get us a little riled. That was when the moth-eaten bogey of a Wall Street tycoon was trotted out. . . . Mr. Truman knows as well as anybody that there isn't any Wall Street. That's just legend. Wall Street is Montgomery Street in San Francisco. Seventeenth Street in Denver. Marietta Street in Atlanta. Federal Street in Boston. Main Street in Waco, Texas. And it's any spot in Independence, Missouri, where thrifty people go to invest their money, to buy and sell securities.[50]

The author of this statement came to Wall Street shortly after the turn of the century. The son of an unsuccessful doctor turned part-time pharmacist, Merrill had had an undistinguished career in several colleges and was at loose ends when his fiancée's father, the treasurer of a small holding company, offered him a job as office boy. Merrill came to New York and worked through the 1907 panic, learning the ropes as had E. H. Harriman a half-century before. Although he later broke with his fiancée and left the firm, he stayed in the district, selling bonds, managing offerings, and studying the intricacies of the brokerage business. After working at George H. Burr & Co. for a while, and then for Eastman Dillon, Merrill set up his own firm, Charles E. Merrill Company, in early 1914.

Merrill had made many friends on the Street, and he prospered from the first. Within a few months he began looking for young talented brokers to staff his office and help with expansion plans. His first acquisition was Edmund Lynch, a former salesman for Liquid Carbonics, Co. who had turned to selling bonds. The two men got along fairly well at the time, and it seemed sensible to join their two lists of customers. Within a few months the firm of Merrill Lynch & Co. (the comma was omitted due to a typographical error) was a thriving concern.

The Exchange closing in 1914 almost wrecked the young firm, which was kept going by trading in the surreptitious over-the-counter market. Then, in the early twenties, Merrill Lynch prospered, due primarily to Merrill's aggressive salesmanship. He was convinced that there was a huge untapped market among the great mass of people who had never before dreamed of owning stock. He set up several modest programs for education and promotion which twenty years later would be the hallmark of his organization. It should be noted that many other brokers were engaged in similar pursuits during the twenties. It was Mike Meehan, for example, and not Charles Merrill, who must be given credit for bringing securities to the public at that time.

As the bull market started to get out of hand, Merrill worried about the state of the economy and the violence of speculation. Feeling that he might be losing his grip by having such thoughts, Merrill went to a psychiatrist to seek help. After a few sessions he left therapy, and both he and his doctor began selling their holdings. In March, 1929, he advised his customers to take strong cash positions. A trip to Washington soon after convinced Merrill that the nation was in danger of collapse. He spoke with President Coolidge, and in typical fashion offered him a post with his firm, but Silent Cal, perhaps remembering the experience of U. S. Grant, refused.

Like most brokers, Merrill issued optimistic reports after the crash and—again like most of them—he was almost completely out of the market himself. Merrill probably lost a small fortune in 1929, but he retained a larger one. In 1930, feeling the depression would last indefinitely, he sold his Exchange seat on the open market and his business to E. A. Pierce & Co. Merrill invested $5 million in Pierce, and both he and Lynch became limited partners in the firm.

During the next few years Merrill traveled, enjoyed himself, and dabbled in business affairs. He had helped in the founding of several large chain-store operations, such as McCrory, Safeway, Kresge, and Western Auto Supply and now he acted as consultant to some of them. During this period the thought of applying chain-store techniques to brokerage must have entered his mind.

From time to time Merrill would run into Lynch. The two men had several fallings out, but in 1939 they met to talk of their futures, and may have had a *rapprochement*. Lynch died soon after, however, and Merrill was on his own.

By then the firm of E. A. Pierce was slipping; it was almost dissolved in 1939. Winthrop Smith, one of the partners, asked for and received permission to invite Merrill to join the firm and revamp its top management. After consulting with several of his friends, most notably Alpheus C. Beane of the New Orleans concern of Fenner & Beane, Merrill accepted, and he joined Pierce & Co. in 1940. The firm was almost immediately reorganized under the name of Merrill Lynch, E. A. Pierce, and Cassatt—the new president insisted on keeping the name of his dead partner—and went into operation late in 1940. Shortly thereafter Alpheus Beane was invited to join the organization, which was then reorganized as Merrill Lynch, Pierce, Fenner and Beane. Beane retired in 1958, and Smith was made a full partner.[51] By then, Merrill had been two years in the grave, having seen his firm's clientele rise to just under 400,000 accounts. At the end of the decade there were some 540,000 Merrill Lynch customers, and the brokerage was doing more business than its four largest competitors combined.

The secrets of Charles Merrill's success were amazingly simple and so obvious that by the mid-fifties, almost every brokerage in the district had adopted some of them. Merrill instituted rigorous training programs for his salesmen who, during the firm's earlier days, were paid straight salaries and no commissions. He then made sure his customers were apprised of their broker's training and remuneration. In the past, Wall Street had been plagued by incompetents whose major interest was switching their customers in and out of stocks in order to make higher commissions. Because of this many customers who remembered the twenties and early thirties mistrusted the entire financial community. Merrill set out to reverse this feeling, and to a large extent, succeeded. Other brokerages either imitated Merrill's program or set up training classes along their own lines. From 1945 to 1960, for example, the rapidly expanding brokerage of Dean Witter spent $4.5 million to train 451 salesmen, of whom 295 were still with the firm by the end of the decade. Like most Wall Street houses, Dean Witter looked for men in their middle twenties, married and with family responsibilities, and holders of Masters of Business Administration degrees from first-rank universities. Should all go well, the brokerage claimed, a successful broker could expect to earn some $30,000 after ten years, while $100,000 a year was not unheard of.[52]

The brokerages of the fifties, again following Merrill's lead, backed their customer's men with large fact-finding and research organizations. If the Merrill Lynch man and his followers were accused of being parrotlike and dull—as they often were—they were at least repeating carefully considered information and opinions. During the late fifties, Merrill Lynch alone spent well over $1.5 million a year on research and market letters, which were offered free to customers and prospective customers. In the past, Wall Street discouraged the individual with only a few hundred dollars from investing—he was hardly worth the trouble of consultation, planning, and management. Merrill keyed his campaign to just such individuals, having seen from his chain-store experience how small sales to millions were worth more than a few sales to large investors. In addition, there was always the possibility that in time a small investor would become a large one. This program worked; in 1950, Merrill Lynch's gross was $45.7 million, and by 1958 it had reached $115 million.[53]

The brokerage and its personnel and philosophy were different in the fifties from any previous period, and this too was an important buttress for the Street. This is not to say that there were no crooks among some of the smaller brokerages, or that the large houses were free of incompetents and individuals of questionable morality. In general, however, the district may have lacked the talent it possessed at the turn of the century, but it was also free of most of the chicanery that was evident during the Age of Morgan.

All this was to the good, for the new customers brought to Wall Street by Merrill and his followers needed careful, responsible guidance. A week before his death, Merrill said: "I think every American would do well to invest one-twelfth of his investible funds monthly in stocks over the next five years."[54] It was his hope that responsible organizations such as his would guide the investors into safe securities. The rise of the mutual funds and the growth of the large brokerages were signs that his hopes had been fulfilled. There were, however, two major dangers on the Street. The first, the presence of sharks like Birrell, Guterma, and others, has already been discussed. The other was the ignorance of many new investors.

An Exchange survey toward the end of the fifties showed that the average annual family income of a person who purchased his first share of stock in 1959 was $8,600, while 10 per cent were making more than $15,000 a year. The new stockholder was thirty-nine years old, married, and fairly well educated. Four out of five were high school graduates, and one out of four had graduated from college. But less than half had any idea of their company's earnings, only 10 per cent knew the name of the president of any company in which they owned stock, and only 40 per cent were able to name a product made by one of their companies.[55] An earlier survey showed that only 23 per cent of the population could define common stock, and 60 per cent did not know the Exchange itself did not sell securities.[56] Such individuals needed help, and they received it if they went to the Merrill-influenced brokerages. It may have been true, as one analyst observed, that "Merrill Lynch never recognizes a market turn until it has passed."[57] At the same time, however, many of the new customers, had they followed their broker's advice, would have been spared a good deal of grief in bear declines. J. P. Morgan was once asked by a skittish investor whether the Great Man thought he should unload some of his holdings. "Sell to the sleeping point," was Morgan's reply. So it was for customers of soundly run, conservative brokerages. They may not have participated in many of the more spectacular rises, but they also avoided the sharp falls—and they were able to sleep.

The inflow of new customers, the fanfare that accompanied Merrill's promotions, and the bull market itself gave birth to the phrase "People's Capitalism," which meant that a new era had come in with the fifties—one in which most people would own "part of America's industrial plant." "Through stock ownership," wrote Professor Marcus Nadler of the Hanover Bank, "the people own the means of production." This is not really so. In fact, all evidence seems to show that a smaller proportion of the general population directly owned shares of stock in 1960 than in 1929.[58] A private survey made in 1952 estimated the number of direct owners to be 6,490,000. Every year the Exchange made new estimates. In 1956 it claimed 8.6 million owners, and by 1965, approximately 20.1 million.[59] Still, only 7.9 per cent of the population were shareholders in 1959, as against 6.6 per cent in 1937.[60] In addition, a 1951 survey showed that 2.1 per cent of the shareholders owned 58 per cent of all common stock. More than 55 per cent of families earning over $10,000 owned securities, as against less than 20 per cent for those in the $5,000–$10,000 category and 7.4 per cent for those earning from $4,000 to $5,000.[61] People's Capitalism, therefore, did not belong to as many people as was commonly thought during the fifties. Even the statement that women controlled most of the nation's wealth was deceiving. The fact that shares were in their hands was usually the result of tax or other similar considerations. In addition, only 6 per cent of all unemployed housewives owned stock, while 45 per cent of all executives were shareholders.[62]

If another interpretation of the phrase is made, however, it would seem that a new era in shareholding was indeed dawning. Most individuals during the late fifties were covered by pension funds or held life insurance policies, both of which were based in part on stocks and bonds. In 1960, for example, the Teamsters owned some $23.5 million in marketable securities, while the Hod Carriers owned $10 million, the Miners, $16.4 million, and the Machinists, $7 million.[63] Indirect ownership, then, was the true basis of People's Capitalism.

If the large funds dominated the market, and the large brokerages controlled most of the trading, the securities analysts were the key figures in guiding both types of organizations. When founded in the thirties, the New York Society of Security Analysts had only twenty members; by 1962 it boasted approximately 2,700. Total enrollment in the twenty-five regional societies comprising the National Federation of Financial Analysts was over 7,200.[64] In addition, there were at least as many more people working on analytical problems in various brokerages who were not members of the Federation. Although most claimed a degree of originality in their approaches, they could be divided into three large groups, with a few stragglers at their edges.

During the fifties the most influential analysts were "technicians," men who ignored the basic economic and business news regarding a firm and concentrated instead on the buying and selling patterns of its stock. Some of them went so far as to conduct their businesses from California or other places distant from Wall Street in order not to be influenced by too much news regarding the stocks they were watching. Although many of the technicians were devotees of the Dow Theory, most developed Dow's original ideas into something which resembled the invention of a mathematician rather than of a financial writer. Among the indicators used by such individuals were point and figure charts, confidence indices, odd-lot indices, short interest ratios, 200 day moving averages, overbought-undersold indices, volume momentum charts, and many other tools of questionable and esoteric value and meaning. A typical recommendation from a chartist, which was almost synonymous with "technician," would be: "If XYZ common goes through the resistance level of 56½ on increased volume, it would break through a triple top and should rise five to eight points to its new goal before encountering resistance." As James Dines, one of the most famous of the technicians wrote, "Technicians, using deductive logic, compute from what *is,* back to what might be happening in the company. The theory is that the price of a stock is already the total sum of every positive and negative factor anyone in a position to act knows about."[65]

A second, larger group, were the fundamentalists, who stressed business and economic considerations rather than chart action. They would study an industry or a specific firm, the economy as a whole, political factors, and the like, and then make their recommendations. Their assumption was that if earnings increased and business in general got better, the stock market would reflect the good news. As Dines observed, "Fundamentalists (using inductive logic) compute *from* earnings, dividends, and quality what the price of a stock *should* be. If this conclusion varies from the current price, the stock is then deemed to be either under or overpriced."[66]

A third group was smaller than the first two, because it required privileged information, a rare commodity in the district. It was interested in "special situations," news that a little-known, new company had some special merit, or that an old, established firm which had stagnated for years was soon to announce a bullish report. The company might be Polaroid, which had airtight patents on instant photography, or American Motors, which made a successful gamble on compact cars. Firms with net asset values far higher than their market prices, liquidation and merger candidates, and stocks on the point of being split were prime targets for the special situations analysts.

Most writers on financial affairs and others responsible for choosing stocks for customers utilized all three approaches, along with hunches. Few were willing to make unhedged predictions, since to recommend a stock which would then decline might lose customers. Hence, most analysts were either "optimistically pessimistic" or "pessimistically optimistic." The result was often a comment that the analyst was "guardedly confident" of a move upward for a certain stock sometime in the next few months or so. Such statements were fairly safe, almost useless, and quite impressive, especially to novices. One analyst would state that "investors who purchase XYZ, an interesting speculation, will see their investment turn out well in the long run." "If the stock goes down," he confided, "I tell them to wait for an upturn. If the advance materializes, I take credit for a good analysis. If it doesn't I tell them to wait some more. If they do this, and the stock still doesn't go up, they will often sell, but by then they have usually forgotten who gave them the advice in the first place."

Despite the questionable value of their predictions, the analysts became key figures during the bull market. Many surveys, however, showed their records to be rather poor. In 1933 a study concluded that forecasters' choices were 4 per cent worse than those made by random selections. In 1957, *Time,* noting there were some 30,700 market items coming out of nearly 300 Exchange firms, with a total circulation of more than 1 million, concluded from its survey that the 1933 record had not been improved upon.[67] Dr. Robert Ferber of the University of Illinois studied the effects of analysts on the 1958 market and discovered that "there is an immediate effect on most stocks when an advisory sheet touts them—sometimes lasting as long as four weeks." Then the stock slips back into its old groove, as another issue is recommended. Over a six-month period, Ferber concluded, most analysts had generally poor records.[68] Once more, we see the phenomenon of self-fulfilling prophecy.

Analyst Ragnar Naess observed: "The speculator and the general public are unimportant in shaping the trend of common stock prices. The speculator has been relegated to a minor position by legislation, and the general public is investing largely through mutual funds." The analysts, who usually determined the purchases and sales of the funds and other institutions, were the key men on the Street, and the market of the fifties was aptly called "The Age of Analysis." Men like Edmund Tabell, James Dines, Benjamin Graham, Frank Schoembs, Armand Erpf, W. Sturgis Macomber, Walter Morris, Leo Barnes were the men to watch in this period, but they were almost anonymous individuals who were known to the more sophisticated investors but could not be identified by the general public.[69] Heads of large investment trusts, such as Dwight Robinson, Joseph Fitzsimmons, Walter Morgan, and Cameron Reed, commanded more assets than Morgan did at the height of his power. Robinson, as president of Massachusetts Investors Trust, was alone responsible for over one billion dollars in assets, but was a shadowy figure outside of the district, and could walk unnoticed even there.[70]

These, then, were the men and institutions of Wall Street and their methods of operation during the bull market of the fifties. They gave the boom solid support, but at the same time their obvious power gave many investors a false sense of security. Because of the nature of the supports, a major crash such as that of 1929 was all but impossible; because of the overbought character of the boom, a crash of some kind was all but inevitable.

Notes

1. *New York Times,* January 2, 1957.
2. *Fortune,* March, 1948, pp. 77–78.
3. *New York Stock Exchange Fact Book,* p. 39.
4. *Time,* January 14, 1948, p. 92.
5. *Time,* June 14, 1948, p. 88.
6. *New York Times,* January 2, 1949.
7. *Time,* March 21, 1949, p. 96.
8. *1962 Supplement to Economic Indicators,* pp. 7, 25.
9. *New York Stock Exchange Fact Book,* p. 50.
10. *New York Times,* March 7, 1950.
11. *1962 Supplement to Economic Indicators,* p. 114.
12. Freeman, *Postwar Economic Trends in the United States,* p. 8.
13. *Time,* June 5, 1950, pp. 78–80.
14. *New York Times,* January 3, 1951.
15. *New York Stock Exchange Fact Book,* pp. 39, 47.
16. *1962 Supplement to Economic Indicators,* pp. 7, 11.
17. *Time,* October 15, 1951, p. 109.
18. *New York Stock Exchange Fact Book,* p. 43.
19. *Ibid.,* p. 38.
20. *1962 Supplement to Economic Indicators,* pp. 7, 11.
21. *Time,* March 17, 1952, p. 94.
22. *Time,* June 8, 1952, p. 95.
23. Freeman, *Postwar Economic Trends in the United States,* p. 164.
24. *New York Times,* February 2, 1954.
25. *U.S. News and World Report,* September 18, 1953, p. 82.

26. *1962 Supplement to Economic Indicators,* pp. 7, 11.

27. *Fortune,* February, 1954, p. 115.

28. United States, 87th Congress, 1st Session, Joint Economic Committee, *Variability of Private Investment in Plant and Equipment* (Washington, 1962), pp. 32, 40–41.

29. Wise, *The Insiders,* p. 199.

30. *New York Times,* January 4, 1953.

31. Black, *Watchdogs of Wall Street,* pp. 20–49.

32. Wise, *The Insiders,* pp. 119–35.

33. Black, *Watchdogs of Wall Street,* pp. 124–67.

34. *Ibid.,* pp. 168–92.

35. *New York Times,* January 4, 1960.

36. *Newsfront,* November, 1961, p. 38.

37. United States, 87th Congress, 2nd Session, Committee on Interstate and Foreign Commerce, *A Study of Mutual Funds* (Washington, 1962), pp. 4–39.

38. *Newsfront,* November, 1961, p. 41.

39. *A Study of Mutual Funds,* pp. 360–93.

40. Bullock, *Story of Investment Companies,* p. 102.

41. Paul P. Harbrecht, *Pension Funds and Economic Power* (New York, 1959), pp. 228–33.

42. *The Exchange,* February, 1963, p. 16.

43. *New York Herald Tribune,* November 4, 1962.

44. *1959 Life Insurance Fact Book,* p. 92.

45. *The Exchange,* September, 1961, p. 17.

46. The Editors of *Fortune, Markets of the Sixties* (New York, 1960), p. 208. The stock purchase plans should not be confused with stock options offered key management personnel. Under the latter system, executives receive options to purchase stock at current prices. These options would usually run for a number of years. If the stock rose in this period, the executive could buy it and, when it was sold, could declare his returns as capital gains. This device often encouraged management to work for higher market quotations for their company's issues, instead of higher profits.

47. Burton Crane, *The Sophisticated Investor* (New York, 1959), p. 202; *The Exchange,* April, 1963, p. 9.

48. *Ibid.,* p. 203.

49. Wise, *The Insiders,* p. 69.

50. Dies, *Behind the Wall Street Curtain,* pp. 118–19.

51. A good deal of the information in this section has been gained from verified interviews with brokers. There is no adequate biography of Merrill. The best source at present is Edwin P. Hoyt, *The Supersalesmen* (New York, 1962), pp. 76–103.

52. *Business Week,* April 2, 1960, p. 54.

53. The best survey of Merrill Lynch in 1962 is Wise, *The Insiders,* pp. 55–70.

54. *Time,* October 15, 1956, p. 104.

55. *New York Herald Tribune,* September 4, 1959.

56. *Time,* March 7, 1955, p. 98.

57. *Business Week,* December 13, 1958, p. 136.

58. Perlo, *Empire of High Finance,* pp. 36–37.

59. *New York Times,* February 1, 1961.

60. Kolko, *Wealth and Power in America,* pp. 50–51.

61. Livingston, *The American Stockholder,* pp. 28–29.

62. *Ibid.,* p. 32.

63. *Business Week,* June 4, 1960, p. 82.
64. *Atlantic,* April, 1962, p. 81.
65. *The Dines Letter,* March 7, 1963.
66. *Ibid.*
67. Fuller, *The Money Changers,* p. 144.
68. *Business Week,* May 31, 1958, p. 86.
69. *Business Week,* April 26, 1958, p. 156; *Fortune,* January, 1957, p. 118.
70. *Time,* June 1, 1959, pp. 77–80.

16

The New Wall Street: 1953-1965

We all know it's ridiculous. But the stock market reflects every human frailty, and the big one now is greed. Others are fear and stupidity. They'll come a little later.

Sidney Lurie

WALL STREET MARKED TIME during the first three quarters of 1953, as though to discount the economic downturn expected for the following year. Some bellwether issues fell gradually, although their earnings were undiminished. *Time* observed that "many companies listed on the New York Stock Exchange, if liquidated, would pay two and three times as much cash as the listed price of their stock." Sand and gravel magnate Henry Crown traveled the country, taking control of several firms and eventually buying the Empire State Building. Buying stocks, he said, was easier and cheaper than buying the companies they represented.[1]

Despite the fact that President Eisenhower showed every indication of being pro-business and included industrial leaders in his inner circle, the first few months of his Administration did not bring the expected bull market. Keith Funston, the new president of the Exchange, spent a good deal of time speaking to assorted groups, delivering optimistic speeches and trying to whip up enthusiasm for People's Capitalism. He ended the half-day Saturday trading and instituted the Monthly Investment Plan, through which individuals could buy stock for as little as forty dollars a month. Investment clubs, made up of people who met regularly to discuss the market and buy stocks, were also encouraged by both the New York and American Exchanges. But despite Eisenhower's pro-business statements and Funston's drumbeating, the market stood still and showed moderate declines from time to time. On September 18, *U.S. News and World Report* wrote that "stocks today, on the average, sell for about 11% less than 8 months ago. Investors, seeing prices fall in the midst of great prosperity, are mystified."

While New York's financial district remained in the doldrums, the Toronto Stock Exchange was registering the largest volume of trading in its history. First oil and gold stocks had their big plays. Then, early in 1953, came news of a huge uranium strike on Lake Athabasca in northern Saskatchewan and other metal discoveries in New Brunswick. Gunnar Gold Mines, which held uranium rights in the Athabasca region, went from 23 cents to four dollars in a month, and then climbed steadily to top thirteen dollars two months later. In the same period Chimo Gold Mines rose from 82 cents to three dollars, and New Larder Uranium from 12.5 cents to $2.82. By February, the Toronto Exchange saw several 10 million share days, and volume was still climbing.[2]

News of the great coups in Canadian "penny stocks" attracted some American investors and gamblers, a few of whom made fortunes, while most lost sizable amounts of money. By year's end the Canadian craze had begun to infect New York, and prices moved up slowly.

In January, 1954, Eisenhower promised to balance the budget and help create a beneficial business climate through tax reforms. The budget message helped spark a rally in late January, which came at the close of an autumn of moderate price rises. By the end of the month the Dow-Jones industrials had gone over 290, gaining over twenty-five points in five months and almost reaching their postwar high of 293.8. This was the resistance level for most Dow theorists, and its piercing would signal a new bull market. The penetration came in mid-February; on February 13, the Dow hit 294.03, the highest level since April of 1930. Railroad stocks and oils led the march, but every group participated. In this way, the bull market of the fifties was set into motion.[3] The Eisenhower boom began in 1954, a year during which the gross national product declined from $365.4 billion to $363.1 billion, and the Dow-Jones industrials rose 125 points.

News of the stock rises attracted increasing numbers of money-laden investors and speculators to the Street. In March, a speculative frenzy began in low-priced issues, which set off the first big drive of the bull market. Newspaper and radio commentator Walter Winchell began touting stocks on his Sunday broadcasts. When he claimed that Amurex Oil Development Co. would soon report "the biggest oil strike in North American history," the stock went from 14⅞ to 20⅞. Every week Winchell would praise another stock, which would do well for several days before dropping back to its old level. Missouri Pacific was to "make market news." The next day, "Mopac" preferred opened at 51, for a 5½ point jump over the Friday close. Universal Consolidated Oil rose six points on a Winchell tip, and then fell back ten. Similar stories could be told of American Bosch, Pantapec, Webb and Knapp, and other beneficiaries of the Sunday broadcasts. The "Winchell Market" was the clearest case of self-fulfilling prophecy the Street would know.[4] In the long run, the recommendations proved almost universally bad; Winchell was one of the poorest forecasters of the decade. In time he dropped out of the touting game, but his place was taken by others whose records were scarcely better than his. Winchell's major impact, as seen in the light of future developments, was to advertise stocks in a far more effective manner than Funston and other Wall Streeters could have done.

The bull market continued through the rest of the year, as indifferent business news was either ignored or discounted. By June the Dow had reached 330 and was still climbing; a brief July decline was followed by a strong rally. Secretary of Commerce Sinclair Weeks viewed the market's strength as a sign of "Eisenhower Prosperity." "I don't care what others think," he said. "I believe the stock market is still one of the best barometers of business this country has."[5] By early autumn some Wall Streeters began to talk of breaking the 1929 high of 381.17, a mark which had been considered impregnable. It was shattered during the first week in December, signaling a new phase of the bull market. With this, more investors began switching from bonds to stocks, money began to flow from banks and trust companies to Wall Street brokerages, and activity picked up substantially at the Exchange. The Dow-Jones industrials, which had stood as low as 279.87 earlier in the year, reached a high of 404.39 in December for the greatest percentage advance since the twenties. The price of an Exchange seat was $88,000 late in the month, an eight-year high. The turnover rate of 19 per cent was the highest since 1950, and 1954's 573 million shares represented the highest stock volume since 1931. Average daily volume exceeded 2.2 million shares, the first time the 2 million figure had been topped since 1933. Other statistics and indices were equally impressive; the bull market had apparently come to stay.[6] And the market advances were not only an American phenomenon; France, Great Britain, West Germany, and Italy also had the bull fever. Japanese stocks, after falling during much of the year, started to rise in the autumn at the rate of 10 per cent a week, and began the most spectacular bull market of the decade.[7] There was scarcely a bear on any of the world's exchanges that Christmas.

Still, some figures gave reason for pause. Cash dividends of listed firms rose from $5.9 billion in 1953 to $6.4 billion in 1954, an impressive advance but no larger than the yearly increase of 1948–1949, when there was no bull market. In addition, the median yield of the Exchange's common stocks dropped from 6.3 per cent in 1953 to 4.7 per cent in 1954—the lowest since 1945. Stock prices, then, were rising at a much faster rate than dividends.

When these figures are viewed alongside the decline in the gross national product and corporate profits in 1954, two thoughts come to mind. First, the market rise was not due to economic improvements during the year, but rather reflected the dynamic growth of the nation and inflationary pressures that had been present since the beginning of World War II. From September 15, 1953, to August 3, 1959, the market price of the *New York Times* stock average rose 162.5 per cent. In the same period, corporate earnings advanced only 35 per cent.[8] Thus, the Eisenhower bull market was solidly based on Truman prosperity.

The rise can also be explained in terms of supply and demand. After 1954 money was seeking an escape from inflation, and found it in stocks. Pension funds, mutuals, insurance companies, trusts—all had often embarrassingly large amounts of money to invest, and they too went to Wall Street to purchase stocks. Had this large demand for stocks been matched by a rapid increase in the amounts of securities available for purchase, stock prices might have remained fairly level. However, from 1953 to 1959, the total number of shares traded at the Exchange rose from 449 million to one billion. In the same period, the number of listed issues actually fell from 1,532 to 1,507. In 1954, there were some 3.2 billion shares listed for trading, by 1959, this number was only 5.8 billion.[9]

The results of this imbalance were obvious. The trusts and other large investment mediums accumulated blocks of blue chip issues and pushed their prices higher than their earnings might ordinarily have demanded. The rise in popularity of the top ten issues of 1954, and their 1954 and 1960 prices and earnings, offer an interesting study of the nature of the increased demand and its possible effect on prices (see Table 16.1).[10]

The shortage of investment quality stocks, added to the catching-up process, influenced the steep rise of this period. While it is true that

Table 16.1—Top Ten Issues, 1954–1960

	Institutions Holding Shares		High Prices		Earnings (dollars)	
	1954	1960	1954	1960	1954	1960
Standard Oil (N.J.)	506	933	37½	50½	2.98	3.18
General Electric	417	759	45½	99⅞	2.39	2.25
duPont de Nemours	393	684	170	266½	7.32	8.09
Union Carbide	391	617	89	148½	3.10	5.25
American Telephone & Telegraph	387	721	72¾	108½	3.81	5.53
General Motors	360	782	32⅞	55⅞	3.02	3.35
Gulf Oil	341	424	22½	37	2.39	3.20
Westinghouse	334	415	40⅛	65	2.39	2.22
Texaco	319	637	22	87	2.06	6.34
Kennecott	301	388	107	100⅞	7.20	7.00

1954–1960 was a prosperous era, it was not as spectacular as the bull market seemed to have indicated.

The 1954 rally carried into 1955, with the Dow crossing the 410 level in February. The advance was solid, led by blue chip industrials and a few utilities. There was little indication in the 1953–1955 period of the wildness to come. Although some low-priced issues participated in the advance and did far better than the averages, their index did not go up much faster than that of the blue chips.

The market rise in the midst of bad economic news led to a Senate investigation of Wall Street by Senator William Fulbright's Committee on Banking and Currency. When questioned as to his views on the market, Exchange President Funston testified that he had purchased stock in January and February, "and as soon as I get some more savings, I'm going to buy some more." Harvard Professor John K. Galbraith stated that the rise could become dangerous, and that the 1929 debacle could recur. Prices declined on this; a typical headline read: "Egghead Scrambles Market." Secretary of the Treasury George Humphrey's optimistic statements were key factors in one advance. Bernard Baruch's testimony soon after proved that he was still in touch with the market and that the senators had scant knowledge of its operation, and this sparked a new rally. The committee found little wrong with the market advance. "One striking characteristic of the recent boom in stock prices," it reported, "is that the increase in common stock values was unusually persistent and did not suffer from the recurring setbacks which took place during the other extended advances that have occurred since 1915."[11] Such conclusions led the market to 471.73 by July, before a mild correction was made.

The Eisenhower bull market was based in large part on confidence in the President, one of the most popular and trusted leaders in the nation's history. On September 24, Eisenhower suffered a heart attack, and the market slid sharply on the news. By then many traders had begun utilizing stop-loss orders, telling their brokers to sell their stocks should they fall to a specified price. The sharp decline set off wave upon wave of these orders, which served to reinforce the panic. As a result, the industrials plummetted 31.89 points on September 26. Trading reached a twenty-two year high, as 7.7 million shares changed hands and $12 billion in values were wiped out in one session.[12] There was some talk of the President retiring in favor of Vice President Nixon, and although journals and newspapers spoke of a possible "Nixon bull market," retirement rumors led to further declines.

Prices recovered along with the President, and bargain hunters entered the market. By the end of the year a full recovery had been made by both convalescents; Eisenhower was back on the job and the industrials closed at 488.4 on December 31, having made an 88 point advance for the year. The economic and business outlook was bright, and the market analysts were optimistic for the coming year. *Time,* reflecting the spirit of the period, named Harlowe Curtice of General Motors as its Man of the Year. The pro-business Administration in Washington was at the height of its popularity.

Two factors became evident early in 1956 which, though ignored by most Wall Streeters, should have acted as a damper for the boom. It was an election year, and whether the convalescing Eisenhower would run again was problematical. Also, the Administration's tight money policy following the slight recession of 1954 held down recovery in an attempt to halt inflation. The discount rate at the New York Federal Reserve Bank, which had been 1.5 per cent in 1954, had been steadily lifted until it reached 3 per cent in late August of 1956. This dampened the 1955–1956 boom, although the economy was operating at a record $400 billion rate during the first quarter of 1956. As the year progressed, economic activity slowed down, while commodity prices continued to rise. The Administration's program to maintain prosperity and a sound dollar had little success. In his attempt to halt the price spiral, Eisenhower had hastened a business downturn and had failed to check inflation.[13]

Political and economic problems were ignored by the Street, however. By the end of March, the industrials drove through the 500 level for the first time, and volume picked up strongly. Then a reaction set in. Domestic difficulties, an overbought market, and, in September, the British evacuation of Suez, led the market downward, causing it to hit a mid-October low of 462.35 before leveling off. Analyst Tabell wrote that "the market has lost upside momentum . . . but this is not a bear market. It is just a selective market." Tabell's view proved accurate; after the Suez War and Hungarian Rebellion in late October and early November, and Eisenhower's smashing victory over Adlai Stevenson, the market rallied. By the end of the year, the average was a shade below 500, having made a net gain for the year of eleven points.

The analysts were optimistic early in 1957, many predicting that it would be the best year in history. Some thought that the 515 level would have to be pierced before a new bull signal would be received, while others believed there might be a leveling of prices toward the third quarter. However, the tight money policy worried the Street's economists, who hoped for a change from the Federal Reserve.

Recovery had slowed up markedly by February, when Secretary Humphrey warned of "a depression which will curl your hair." Former President Hoover replied: "mine has already been curled once, and I think I can detect the signs."[14] The Administration, still more interested in a sound dollar than full employment measures, ordered curbs on spending early in the year. Secretary of Defense Charles Wilson imposed a $38 billion defense spending limit, ordered sharp cutbacks on the placement of orders, and instituted a "stretchout" in procurement. In January, Eisenhower stressed economy. "Accordingly," he said, "the Congress should continue tax rates at their present levels, and Federal expenditures should be strictly limited."[15]

The economic slowdown that continued during the summer was presaged by a market decline. In early April, the industrials had fallen below 475. A rally lifted the average over 500 late in June, but then the slide began again. At the same time, there was a switch from stocks to high grade bonds, caused by the fact that for the first time in twenty years common stock yields had fallen below those for high grade bonds.[16] By late September the average was hovering over the 450 level, and prices would decline to 420 before a recovery could be made.

The market was saved from the bears in early October by the intrusion of an external force, not by any dramatic reversal of the economy or by Eisenhower policies. On October 4, the U.S.S.R. orbited its first sputnik, and the nation was galvanized by fears of Soviet superiority in weaponry and science. By mid-October the stretch-out was forgotten, arms appropriations were being reconsidered, and the "space race" had officially begun.

Until then the entire list had declined, with the exception of such special situations as Lorillard, which had introduced a new cigarette; Magic Chef, which had switched from appliances to supermarkets; Polaroid, which had been the beneficiary of enthusiastic market letters; and a few other issues. Now a rally began, paced by space and technology issues. Between October 4 and December 16, 1957, the stocks of certain space-oriented firms showed remarkable rises, as shown in Table 16.2. The "sputnik market" led prices from their October low of 419.79 to 453.69 by the end of the year.

Table 16.2—Percentage Rise in Space Issues, October to December, 1957[17]

Aerojet-General	32.5
Douglas Aircraft	21.8
General Dynamics	24.6
Lockheed Aircraft	17.7
Marquardt Corporation	14.5
Martin Corporation	24.1
Thiokol Chemical	21.6
Reaction Motors	9.6

Congress opened its sessions in 1958 in an air of concern over space, and voted large new appropriations to the military and civilian agencies that dealt with the problem. The Administration, however, was still wedded to the idea of a balanced budget, considering a stable dollar as important as an American man on the moon. "We are not playing basketball in the stratosphere," said Defense Secretary Wilson. Although this was crudely put, it reflected the sentiments of many important Administration figures as well as those of the President himself. The bulls, taking courage from the congressional appropriations, bought stocks, while the bears, listening to Administration leaders, sold their holdings. The result was a standoff market.

Toward the summer of 1958 the important business indices began to advance, indicating that the recession was about over. The Federal Reserve was expected to raise its discount rate in order to check the boom, as it had in the past. In part because of this, most analysts thought the market would not rise much higher. Few expected a decline, but the large majority of them thought the small spring rally would soon peter out.

At this point the Treasury attempted to float a large number of long-term obligations. The bond market was swamped, and had its most abrupt collapse on record. As a result, there was a movement from bonds to equities, and the stock market took off. "At the present time," wrote chartist Alan Poole in August, "the market continues to advance in the face of high price-earnings ratios, low yields, and a very unfavorable relationship between bond and stock yields. The advance has been sparked by inflation fears, the flight from senior securities into equities and by large sums of money awaiting investment."[18] Thus, the bulls had won their wager. The combination of defense spending and Treasury management of refunding operations, along with the business recovery, led stocks into higher ground for the rest of the year. It would take a while, however, before most Wall Streeters realized that the advance was not merely a new stage of the old bull market, but rather the beginning of a new kind of market, in which glamour was more important than earnings, brainpower counted more than net assets, stock dividends were preferred to cash payouts, and price/earnings ratios of 100 to one—and more—were not unusual.

In early January of 1959, the district's leading analysts were asked for their predictions for the year ahead. Almost all expected the steel issues to be star performers, as they usually were during a period of economic recovery. Sidney Lurie of Josephthal expected ACF Industries, a manufacturer of heavy equipment, to have a good showing. James Corbett of Merrill Lynch thought the airlines showed great promise. Stanley Nabi of Schweikert liked the oils best. Standard and Poor's picked General Shoe and Melville Shoe as promising issues. Few analysts thought much of the electronics issues. Gerald M. Loeb considered IBM and General Electric overbought. L. F. Rothschild expected International Telephone and Telegraph to have a good year, and was almost alone in expressing interest in glamour stocks,[19] except for Samuel Stedman of Loeb, Rhoades, who selected Polaroid, Diner's Club, Brunswick, Zenith, and other high flyers. In the first half of the year the industrials went from 583.65 to 643.60, and Stedman's glamour portfolio rose almost 300 per cent.[20]

Much to the surprise of many, the electronics issues took Wall Street by storm. The district seemed to be talking of nothing but space travel, micro-circuits, transistors, klystron tubes, and other esoteric things. Analysts found themselves staying up late at night boning up on college mathematics and physics as well as point-and-figure charts. By March the American Stock Exchange was recording 3 million-share days with a fair degree of regularity. In May the margin requirement on the New York Exchange was raised to 90 per cent in an attempt to curb the boom. "There is no evidence of excessive use of credit in this market," said Funston, but member borrowings, which had reached a twenty-eight year peak in 1958, was still at a high level.[21] Stock splits in such glamour firms as Thiokol, Pfizer, Eastman Kodak, and a host of others helped lead the market to dizzy heights. By March the industrial index had crossed the 600 mark; three months later it was just below 650. Other markets joined in the New York advance. By mid-year the London Exchange had traveled up 58 per cent from the February lows, and other European exchanges told similar stories. "We thought it wouldn't happen here, but the whole world seemed to be caught by a frenzy of speculation," remarked a Swiss banker. "If this goes on," he concluded, "something serious is bound to happen pretty soon."[22] There was a minor dip in the autumn, but stocks came roaring back to close the year at 679.36, for an advance of almost 100 points over the previous December 31. Some issues of this spectacular first phase of the sputnik market are shown in Table 16.3.

Table 16.3—Representative Issues, 1958–1959[23]

	1958 Low	May 21, 1959 Price	1959 High	1959 Earnings
Beckman Instruments	18⅛	60¼	74¾	— .70
Hoffman Electronics	21	71⅛	86	1.31
Litton Industries	36⅞	107¼	150¾	3.08
Texas Instruments	26¾	122½	193½	3.59
Varian Associates	7⅜	38	53	.82

At mid-year a rash of new companies appeared, with such names as Astron, Dutron, Transitron, and a host of other "trons," and "electros," and they were taken up quickly by a science-crazed public. Nicholas Darvas, a professional dancer, wrote of how he made millions in the stock market through charts, and began a "Darvas Boom" which was more powerful than the Winchell market of a few years before. Again, Funston and others warned of excessive speculation—and did nothing concrete about it. Charles Schwartz, senior partner of Bache & Co., probably spoke for most brokers when he said: "It is stupid, after years of a publicity campaign to get people to buy stocks, to come out now and blow the whistle." "We have no objection to people buying into small and little known companies," he told reporters, "provided they know what they are doing."[24] But Mr. Schwartz did not say how he determined this, and most investors in glamour issues gave the appearance of not knowing what they were buying. Jack Dreyfus of Dreyfus and Co., summed up the mania when he wrote:

> Take a nice little company that's been making shoelaces for 40 years and sells at a respectable six times earnings ratio. Change the name from Shoelaces, Inc. to Electronics and Silicon Furth-Burners. In today's market, the words "electronics" and "silicon" are worth 15 times earnings. However, the real play comes from the word "furth-burners," which no one understands. A word that no one understands entitles you to double your entire score. Therefore, we have six times earnings for the shoelace business and 15 times earnings for electronic and silicon, or a total of 21 times earnings. Multiply this by two for furth-burners and we now have a score of 42 times earnings for the new company.[25]

The problem became more difficult and complex as the mania deepened. For example, an important question was how did one figure a correct price for a firm that had no earnings at all. By 1959 the traditional ten or fifteen times earnings formula had been supplanted by 100 or 200 times earnings for glamour stocks. But what of a firm like Farrington Manufacturing, a small company that made handbags and credit cards, and hoped to market a new electronics device? This firm lost money consistently, but rose rapidly on the over-the-counter market, split four for one, and reached an adjusted high of 57½ before plummetting to below two. Underwood, which had been taken over by Olivetti of Italy and had hopes of recovering its former industry position, lost a total of almost $10 a share in 1958 and 1959, and rose from 12⅞ to 30⅞ and hit 57 before slipping back to more reasonable levels in 1960. Such stories could be multiplied by dozens in 1958–1959, and they gave the bull market an uncomfortable resemblance to that of 1929.

The analysts began hedging late in 1959 and early in the following year. Loeb, Rhoades told customers "to expect a good strong rally before the end of the year, because there is money piling up in mutual funds, pension funds, and with other institutional investors." The firm warned, however, that "it will be a market of selective stocks." Tabell, who almost alone had predicted the many turns in the market since 1953, was optimistic, but also issued warnings. "We are probably now embarked on the final upward wave of the bull market," he said in April of 1959. "This is usually the most dynamic wave, with the speculative and spectacular stocks leading the way. My guess is that this phase that began in late 1957 will continue into 1961 with the Dow-Jones industrials hitting 800, possibly 850." Tabell intimated that after a climax at the 800–850 level, a major bear period would commence.[26] Economic consultant John Langam, when asked whether he expected a break in the market, replied: "There could be several months of bull market action in the stock market in the months immediately ahead. But, somewhere in the next few years, I would say we are likely to see substantially lower stock prices. We certainly won't see a further rise of consequence in price-earnings ratios."[27] Langam noted that the ratio, which had stood at 6.63 for 1950, had risen to 17.04 in 1959, an indication that prices had advanced at a rate of about 250 per cent of that of earnings. The dividend yield of common stocks had fallen from 6.57 per cent in 1950 to 3.23 per cent in 1959, the latter figure being the lowest in two generations.[28] In the same year, government bonds were yielding over 4 per cent for three- to five-year issues, a level never before reached. Many analysts, noting this, looked for a major switch from stocks to bonds in 1960.

There were other problems besides those of a technical nature. As early as November 10, 1958, *Barron's* had warned of the gold outflow resulting from the imbalance of American payments to Europe. This was not as important as many Wall Streeters seemed to think, but was a major bearish sign. Late in 1959, the gold losses caught the attention of almost all the analysts. Economist Gabriel Hauge concluded that it meant "the postwar era has ended, and a new trade era has begun." For the first time in the century, the nation was learning the meaning of a balance of payments deficit.[29]

Still, most market analysts were "guardedly confident" in mid-1959. There was some talk of recession, but more about what was dubbed "The Soaring Sixties." The giddy heights of common stocks, heavy trading at the Exchange—in 1959 daily average volume passed the 3 million mark for the first time since 1929—and a fairly satisfactory recovery from the 1958 recession seemed to augur well for the future. On the other hand, fears of automation, the expected strong competition from Common Market nations if and when a European economic union developed, what appeared to be a permanent unemployment problem, and a general economic stagnation at a high level were all bearish factors. In addition, 1960 was to be an election year, and Eisenhower, who despite his failures in stimulating business was extremely popular in the financial district, would soon step down from the White House.

On January 3, Garfield Drew, a respected technician, told his readers that there would probably be little trouble on the Exchange that year, but to expect difficulties in 1961.[30] Shortly thereafter the market began to slide. By the end of February, the industrials had fallen below 620, losing fifty points in two months. On February 29, stocks declined on heavy volume. Some analysts called it a "selling climax" and the signal for a bear market. Within two weeks the average had gone to 609, and a penetration of the 600 level seemed indicated by the charts. "I don't believe in the Dow Theory," said fundamentalist I. W. Burnham. "I don't know any rich Dow theorists."[31] But such protests smacked of the kind of cheery statements that had been made in 1929. The average fell below 600 the following week, causing William McChesney Martin of the Federal Reserve to comment, "I'm worried about the stock market. People might put it out of perspective. It's conceivable they could attach more importance to it economically than it really has, though I have no evidence of that yet."[32]

By then, the markets in western Europe and Japan had begun to slide in sympathy with New York. The Soaring Sixties had become the Slumping Sixties. Tabell, who had advised his clients to sell in January, repeated his warnings. Richard Russell, a leading technician, signaled a major bear market in mid-March, but George E. Schaefer, perhaps reading the same charts, thought the decline was merely a pause, and that the market would soon head higher. Hamilton Bolton, utilizing what was known as the "Elliott Wave Theory," told his subscribers that "we are well entranced in the fifth and final upward wave—the last in a bull market."[33]

Whether through accident or the innate superiority of his techniques, Bolton proved correct in his analysis. Prices picked up in March. The average reached the 616 level by the end of the month, and forged ahead in April. The second week in June witnessed one of the biggest rallies in stock market history, as industrials reached 654.88 on a 25.90 point rise.[34]

The summer of 1960 brought bad international news as well as the dislocation of a presidential campaign. U.N. intervention in the Congo, fighting in southeast Asia, the Berlin and Cuban problems, and fears of a new world war affected trading at the Exchange. Democratic candidate John F. Kennedy, stressing the "missile lag" and promising to "get America moving again," implied that the nation was in grave danger, and would stagnate unless drastic programs to stimulate the economy were begun. The discovery of U-2 flights over the Soviet Union and the failure of the Geneva summit meeting added to the war fears, which were reflected by falling stock prices. Analyst Gerald Colby and a few others believed the market was "currently consolidating to go through 650–655 on through its all time high by year's end," but they were in a distinct minority.

Toward the end of September, the London gold price reached $35.25½, a six-year high, and within a month gold was being quoted at forty dollars an ounce. This, the historic sign of a flight from the dollar, signaled the worse loss of confidence in America's future shown by investors since 1937. All stocks but those of gold mines dropped; by mid-September the Dow-Jones industrials were once again below the 600 level, closing the month at 580.14. Russell, consulting his charts, predicted a major decline, and Schaefer, looking at his, called for a major bull market. Tabell believed a rally was on the way, and switched his customers back into common stocks.[35]

The market broke several times in October, reaching the 560 level just before Election Day. Prices rose on news of the Kennedy victory, which investors interpreted as a sign that the new Democratic Administration would pass inflationary measures to stimulate the economy as part of the New Frontier. By the end of the year the industrials had reached 615.89, having made an impressive recovery from the November lows.

In all, 1960 had been a surprising year, in which violent fluctuations had led the industrials to trade in a 566.05–685.47 range. This was a prelude to the next phase of the bull market, which would prove to be its wildest.

The analysts were cautious in their January, 1961 reviews and previews. They had good reason for hedging; their 1960 predictions had proved disastrous. Merrill Lynch's selections of growth stocks had shown four advances to four declines, and this was one of the better records on the Street. Bache's "Intermediate Growth List" had three advances and eight declines, Hutton's "Ten Companies with New Trends" listed seven whose trends proved to be downward in 1960, and Shearson Hammill's "Moderate Price Investment Suggestions" had six declines out of eight selections.[36] The spectacular failure of the analysts in 1960 was a sign that the market had become far more erratic than it had previously been. The analysts knew this, and their early 1961 letters reflected their doubts. "As the year develops," wrote one, "the business climate may be either much better or much worse than now expected." "The economy has been undergoing a moderate readjustment but business is good in many lines," was the comment of another. "We are entering the New Year with a mixture of apprehension and anticipation" was the best one large house could say. Another, reaching the outer limits of doubletalk, told clients:

> In conclusion, we think that while near-term uncertainties exist and no one can really say the decline in stock prices has gone as far as it will, we believe we are beginning to form a base which will be both fundamentally and technically sound and from which—given the anticipated improvement in business in 1961—we could get a stock market rise of worthwhile proportions.[37]

In February, some of the analysts stuck their necks out and hoped for the best. Garfield Drew and some Dow theorists signaled the start of a new bull market, as stocks took off smartly. The Kennedy bull market, based on an initial burst of confidence in the new President, a quieting of international tensions, and a promised boom in the economy, caused jubilation on Wall Street. But unemployment had not been ended, the rate of economic growth was still low, and none of the important economic problems inherited from the Eisenhower Administration had been solved. In addition, despite appearances to the contrary, Kennedy's views on inflation and the balanced budget were strongly similar to those of his predecessor, and there were signs that he too would be willing to sacrifice economic growth for fiscal stability.

The most spectacular advances of the Kennedy bull market, like those of the post-1953 rise, were made by glamour stocks. There was an important difference, however, between the star performers of the first Eisenhower Administration and those of the early sixties. Most television, cigarette, and defense issues of the earlier era represented solid value and performance, along with the hope of future higher earnings. Many of the electronics—stocks like Litton Industries, Texas Instruments, and Fairchild Camera—were substantial companies. On the other hand, most of the glamour issues of the early sixties had few assets, meager earnings and often deficits, and questionable hopes for the future. The speculative fever of 1960–1962 was based on strange-sounding firms, esoteric commodities, shrewd promotions, and gullible customers. The key issues of this phase were low-priced electronics stocks which were usually traded over-the-counter or on the American Stock Exchange. Later, real estate issues, vending stocks, and savings and loan stocks were spotlighted. Throughout the period new issues of every description held center stage. It was the uranium boom of the early fifties all over again, but this time it seemed to affect millions of investors rather than a few thousand.

It is impossible to say when the new issue mania in low-priced stocks began, and how much it was related to the previous booms. Many writers believe it can be traced to the late fifties, when a hunger for science- and technology-based issues appeared during the first stage of the sputnik market. These stocks were often backed by little in the way of assets, but in some cases featured good management, top-flight scientists, strong patent positions, and aggressive salesmanship. Litton Industries, which had been put together by a promotional genius named Tex Thornton, and Texas Instruments, which early established a commanding position in transistors, were two examples of glamour firms of the fifties, but each had antecedents in an earlier period and in other ways was not typical of the majority of the new issues. Most of them were closer in experience to Control Data Corporation, which was underwritten in 1958. A moderately successful manufacturer of computers, Control Data had all the above-mentioned attributes in addition to a fine product. The firm issued 600,000 shares of common stock at one dollar a share. There was no public sale of the issue, most of which was taken up by friends of the founders, who knew a good thing when they saw it. Within three years the original one dollar investment had grown to over $120, and the electronics and new issue phase of the Kennedy market was past its take-off point.

In late 1960 and early 1961, there was a mad scramble of customers and orders each time a new issue was marketed. By then, almost any new stock could be counted upon to show a 20 to 50 per cent rise in price on the first day of trading, and then level off before either rising once more or falling. This was true not only for such space age issues as Nytronics, Bristol Dynamics, and Polychrome—even Mother's Cookie could count on a sizable advance. The more spectacular performers included are shown in Table 16.4.

It was little wonder that the new issue market attracted the type of investor who usually could be found at the race track, when within less than two months Datamation rose from 2 to 12½, Sealed Air Corporation from 1 to 8, and Renwell from 4 to 19.

Some brokerages began to crack down on the wild speculators in new issues. Merrill Lynch refused to deal in stocks selling for less than 2, and along with other leading houses instructed its brokers to warn customers against uninformed buying. Exchange President Funston

Table 16.4—Rises in New Issues, 1961[38]

	Issue Date	Offering Price	April 14 Price
Albee Homes	March 20	16	27¼
Alberto Culver	April 5	10	22
Bristol Dynamics	March 21	7	18
Morton Foods	April 5	12½	21
Mother's Cookie	March 8	15	24½
Nytronics	March 17	5	14
Packard Instrument	April 4	10	21¾
Polychrome	March 7	8½	19¾
Wyle Laboratories	March 7	19½	30½

spoke repeatedly about the dangers of reckless speculation, as did other financial leaders. This was to no avail, for even if the district had been able to pull all the large brokerages into line against the wildness, it could not have stemmed the speculation, because the important houses were not usually patronized by customers interested in new issues. The small electronics underwritings were most often handled by brokerages as obscure as the firms they represented. Little known and considered on the fringe of respectability by the larger houses, these brokerages represented the height of the bull market, and led customers in its wildest phase.

The typical new issue underwriter of 1960–1962 would seek out small firms engaged in scientific work, but would handle almost anything that came his way, so long as he thought it could be sold to customers on his lists. He might, for example, take 500,000 shares of XYZ Thermodynamics and try to sell it at one dollar a share. Once the details were settled with members of the firm, he would call his customers and tell them of its wonders, much like Belle, Tellier, and others of the uranium era. By 1961, however, comparatively little salesmanship was necessary: the customers were more than ready to jump on the bandwagon. The underwriter's problem was not how to sell stock, but rather how to prorate his shares. This would be done quickly, almost always before the actual offering date of the security. Thus, when the new issue hit the over-the-counter market, it was more fully subscribed.

At this point, the general public would start to bid for the issue, as would some of the insiders who had not been granted their fill of shares during the prorating period. This demand, being met by almost no supply, would shoot the stock's price upward with amazing speed. Thus, XYZ Thermodynamics, which had been offered at one dollar, might close the day at two dollars or more. The original customers would be content, since they had more than doubled their money in less than a day with little or no risk. The new purchasers, watching the stock rise, would also be satisfied, and more convinced than ever of the need to get on one or more underwriter's lists. Interestingly enough, more often than not none of these people had ever seen a copy of XYZ's prospectus, and few even knew of its business.

The most satisfied person involved in the transaction would be the underwriter. Not only did he receive his usual fee, but he probably held a sizable block of XYZ as well. In addition, many underwriters received warrants as part of their commissions. In the past many investment bankers had received warrants; Merrill Lynch in particular had made large profits through them. During the early sixties, they were used with dramatic success.

A prime example of the power of warrants was that of BBM Photocopy, a small firm underwritten by Michael A. Lomasney & Co. As part of his contract, Lomasney was granted 20,000 warrants, each to buy one share of stock offered at three dollars for the price of a penny apiece. Lomasney then underwrote 100,000 shares of BBM at three dollars a share, receiving the usual commission for his efforts. This meant that the BBM Photocopy Corporation received less than $280,-000 for its shares. Within a short time, BBM was selling for forty dollars a share, which gave the warrants a value of around $800,000. Thus, Lomasney received a little less than one million dollars for his work, while BBM's treasury was richer by less than one-third that amount.

Lomasney, who was typical of the small issue underwriters of the period, was able to make a fortune within a short period of time through such transactions. Along with Donald Marron, Michael Kletz, Stephen Fuller, and a handful of other brokers, he brought issue after issue to the over-the-counter market. For a while these men, each of whom headed a small office with no more than a secretary or two and a few salesmen, provided the spark for the Kennedy market.[39] Needless to say, this was leadership of dubious quality. Some of the houses were investigated on more than one occasion by the SEC, and one of them, Re, Re, and Sagarese, was suspended for many violations, including the distribution of more than $10 million worth of unauthorized common stock. Even the larger houses were hit by "new issue-itis." Bruns, Nordeman & Co. was disciplined for manipulations in the new issue of Gob Shops, and a few other large brokerages underwent investigations.[40]

The new issue craze gathered steam in 1960 and whipped the more speculative Wall Streeters into a frenzy by 1961. In that year each month seemed to bring forth a new glamour group. May produced the small business investment companies, which held shares in many of the new issues that later did so well on the market. Like the investment trusts of the twenties, these stocks shot upward, compounding speculation with still more speculation (see Table 16.5).

Table 16.5—Small Business Investment Issues, 1961[41]

	Issue Price	May 19 Price
Boston Capital	15	25¾
Electronics Capital	10	54
Electro-Science Investors	11	38
Growth Capital	20	35½
Techo-Fund	12½	22
Venture Capital	7½	21
Virginia Capital	10½	16½

Then came real estate firms, which paid high dividends, often out of capital, and were highly leveraged and susceptible to the slightest downward movement of the economy. Still, All State Properties rose from its low of 4⅜ to a bid in early June of 13¾, and was followed by other land-based firms.[42] Similar stories could be told of the savings and loan companies, water desalinization firms, companies engaged in services or rentals, and a host of others that were pegged as "growth industries of the future."

Although the new issues led the way, the entire list seemed to rise during 1961, a year in which the Dow-Jones industrials went from 615.89 to an all-time peak of 734.91 on December 13, before settling down to 731.13 at the end of the year. There were all the signs of extreme fantasy which precede major crashes. News of contract awards to a single plant defense firm would send its stock up over 20 per cent in a session. Bernard Baruch did not comment on the market, but spoke to his biographer of the tulip craze and other wild speculations of previous centuries, and the connection was not difficult to make. By spring the boom was the central theme of cocktail party chatter across the nation; women gave up club meetings to listen to lectures on investments. Businessmen would eschew their lunches to gather in brokerages and watch the tape. In April, the Art Market Guide &

Forecaster, writing in the jargon of the day, strongly urged the purchase of paintings in the following manner:

32 ARTISTS TO
TRIPLE IN PRICE

With the Art Market for paintings up 975% since the war—and 65% in the last year alone—you can lose immense profits by failing to keep informed of the *monetary* values of art, present and future. Among the 500 painters whose price trends are under regular study by our organization, many have gone down in price as well as up—ranging from *gains* up to 61,900% to *losses* of 87% (compared to the 975% gain for the whole market as measured by the new *AMG 500-Painters Average.*

The advertisement urged the reader to send for a copy of the latest market forecast, which included a list of thirty-two artists whose prices were expected to do better than the market as a whole.[43] All the district seemed to lack was a little boy to observe that the Emperor was in fact wearing no clothes.

There were other signals to warn the more astute investors of coming dangers. Mutual fund sales, which had declined 10 per cent in the first nine months of 1960, did not recover as well as had been expected. The Darvas craze came to the attention of New York State Attorney-General Louis Lefkowitz, who found most of the dancer's claims false. The SEC reported a record number of investigations and recommendations for indictment. Finally, Congress authorized the SEC to begin the first full-scale investigation of the securities markets since the New Deal, and under the leadership of William L. Cary, the Commission began its probe of the American Stock Exchange and the roles of specialists. This action disquieted many who had built their hopes on a giddy bull market, and who feared that any investigation would "rock the boat." Political instability contributed to these jitters. The failure of the Cuban invasion in April, the Berlin problem, and the inability of the New Frontier to show any dramatic progress dampened the initial popularity of the Kennedy Administration and added to the general insecurity on the Street. One sign of the times was a cartoon in *The New Yorker* which portrayed several businessmen discussing the market while on a commuter train. "I had the weirdest dream about my mother last night," said one. "She said I should sell all my A. T. & T. when it hits 132."[44]

In May of 1961, while the market was still on the upswing, stocks of some publishing, electronics, and vending companies began to slide.

Although 1961 ended with the Dow-Jones industrials near their all time peak, these glamour issues were well below their highs, and the situation on the American Exchange was even more bearish (see Tables 16.6 and 16.7).

Table 16.6—Representative "Glamour" Stocks, 1961

	1961 Price Range	1961 Closing
ABC Vending	17¾–27¾	21⅜
American Photocopy	29⅜–46⅜	30⅛
Ampex Corporation	17⅛–27¾	20½
Automatic Canteen	27¼–45⅝	30⅞
Bell & Howell	46¼–69⅞	48⅜
Crowell-Collier Pub.	31 –50⅞	39
Fairchild Camera	62¼–88¼	62½
McGraw-Hill Pub.	31 –43⅛	34¼
Minnesota Mining & Mfg.	66⅜–87⅝	67⅛

Table 16.7—"Glamour" Stocks on the American Exchange, 1961

	Price Range	Closing
Acme Missiles	7⅜–20	12
Apollo Industries	9⅜–35½	16
Belock Instruments	9⅝–20¼	9⅝
Circuit Foil	24 –57¾	26½
Edo Corporation	19 –40	21
I.M.C. Magnetics	7½–16⅞	7¾
Microwave Associates	32 –60⅜	36¼
Statham Instruments	16⅜–35⅝	17⅝
Teleregister Corp.	12⅛–34	13

As might have been expected, the worst situation of all maintained at the over-the-counter market (see Table 16.8). It was thought at the time that these sharp declines were only temporary setbacks, and that the glamour issues would bound back early in 1962. In reality, it was the beginning of the end for the Kennedy bull market.

Table 16.8—Over-the-Counter Issues, 1961

	Price Range	Closing
Acoustica Associates	8 –27	9¾
Baird-Atomic	9¾–26¾	10
C.E.I.R. Inc.	26 –60	30½
Cook Electric	6⅛–16	6⅛
Epsco Inc.	8½–29	9
Faradyne Electronics	7½–23½	7½
Infrared Industries	12½–25	12½
Itek Corporation	25½–61	25¾
Pocket Books, Inc.	21¾–43¼	22¼

The new year opened with a rush of optimistic reports from the analysts, who discounted recession talk and predicted new highs for 1962. William Kurtz of Paine, Webber, Jackson & Curtis expected the industrials to reach 850 sometime during the year. Tabell thought the average would hit 825 before falling off slightly. Frederick Goodrich of the U.S. Trust was "cautiously optimistic," as befitted a bank analyst, and Sidney Lurie thought, "the market will perform better."[45] "We are looking for common stocks to turn in quite a good performance in the coming year," wrote Heintz & Co. Fahnestock & Co. relied upon "a backlog of reserve purchasing power" to push prices to new highs. "After end-of-the year adjustments are out of the way," said Pershing & Co., "we would look for a tendency to give credence to the extremely favorable forecasts for the year ahead." About 45 per cent of the mutual fund managers expected the industrials to reach a new high early in 1962; only 10 per cent expected a decline by the end of the year.[46] The bears were in a distinct minority in early January of 1962.

Stocks declined in January, falling below the 700 level toward the end of the month. Investors, reading of record sales of mutual funds and cheery business forecasts, showed little fear; they sat on the side lines and waited for "buying opportunities." The more cautious investors might have noted that although sales were up, mutual funds were in an unusually liquid position; the managers were not committing all their cash to the market. The bulls thought this would mean a large spring rally, since the funds would soon have to enter the market on the buy side, but the bears interpreted it as a sign that "insiders" expected a decline. Violent fluctuations began to take place almost daily at the Exchange, and older men, remembering that a similar pattern had developed in mid-1929, began hedging on their portfolios. The small investors who had entered the market after the war continued to buy stocks; during the first four months of the year a record $1.2 billion worth of mutual fund shares were bought, an increase of 24 per cent from 1961.[47] This was an indication of the nature of leadership in the postwar market, and did not auger well for the Street in case of a sharp decline. If a crash occurred, could the small investor be counted upon to stay in the market and support prices? If he experienced a loss of confidence and sold mutual shares as easily as he bought them, the funds might have to liquidate their positions in the blue chips, thus triggering a crash that would make 1929's seem like child's play. Perhaps considering this, the Bank of New York ordered a cutback of 10 per cent in its common stock holdings, and switched pension funds from equities to bonds. Other banks followed suit, as the quiet erosion of confidence spread in January and February.

There was a slight recovery after the January falloff. In March the industrials were over the 720 mark, and many of the Street's top analysts looked for a penetration of the 734.91 record and the signal for a major bull market. This was not to be; prices fell toward the end of the month, and headed straight down. The 700 level was penetrated on the downside early in April, and after a brief consolidation, the average plunged downward once more.

There was good reason for the skittish nature of the market in April. The Kennedy crackdown on the steel companies when they tried to raise prices was considered the key to the decline, but this was only a small part of the total picture. There was a good deal of uneasiness over tax policies, which were being reconsidered by the Administration. The Kennedy trade bill, designed to enable the nation to compete and cooperate with the Common Market, was not entirely popular among investors. The SEC investigations into mutual funds and the New York Stock Exchange unnerved the Street. Many firms began to announce their capital spending plans for the year, and most were below the anticipated levels. Finally, there seemed to be two changes in investors' attitudes. Some woke up to the fact that the market could not go up indefinitely, and began to pull out before the expected crash. Next, and most important, was the dawning realization that Kennedy was a fiscal conservative who was accomplishing what had eluded Eisenhower: the throttling of inflation. Although the jobless rate was over 5 per cent, the Administration concentrated on a balanced budget instead of full employment. Kennedy succeeded in holding down the galloping dollar, but at the same time he held down the economic boom that might have developed. Tabell realized this, and told customers that "the market is selling off because we have been paying too much for stocks as a hedge against inflation." Later, Walter Lippmann analyzed the situation thusly:

> There is a loss of confidence that the Administration is fulfilling the promise to bring about something near to the full employment of capital and labor and a rising rate of economic growth. . . . It is beginning to look as if the Kennedy Administration were repeating the pattern of the Eisenhower Administration, with its three recessions brought on by the fact that each recovery was throttled down, as the only way to prevent inflation of prices, before the recovery was completed.[48]

By early May the Dow-Jones industrials had fallen below 650, and after a brief rally declined even faster than before. "I miss Ike" stickers began to appear on the bumpers of many disgruntled investors' automobiles. "Don't blame me. I voted Republican," was another slogan of the day. Few doubted by mid-month that the advance of the Kennedy market had been stemmed, although analysts differed as to whether or not a bear market was in the making.

The "selling climax" expected by many bears and anticipated by cautious investors came toward the end of the month. On Monday, May 21, there was a slight decline on slow trading. The selloff continued on Tuesday, but this time volume was heavy, with almost one million shares traded in the last half hour. Every group slipped, as the Dow fell 12.25 points for its greatest loss in more than a year. Significantly, the gold issues rose slightly, showing a growing lack of confidence in the economy. This pattern was repeated on Wednesday; the industrials fell 9.82 points to close at 626.52, the lowest level in sixteen months. Volume was high, with 5.4 million shares traded. Such glamour issues as IBM and Xerox lost 19¾ and 9⅞ points apiece, and bearishness spread throughout the list. There were 460 new lows on Wednesday and only five new highs. President Kennedy, speaking at his news conference, told the nation that the economy was strong; it was suggested that he say "the only thing we have to fear is fear itself."

There was a brief rally on Thursday morning, as the industrials rose over five points on heavy trading. But prices slipped at midday, and the bears forced them below the Wednesday close. Funston and Chairman Posner of the American Stock Exchange told reporters that there was no slump in sight, and other Exchange officials were also cheerily confident of the future. Again, this had happened just before the 1929 crash, and more bulls were "converted" to the sell side.

Friday trading was the most hectic in fourteen months, as almost 6.4 million shares were sold and the tape ran eighteen minutes late at the close. There were 695 new lows; the Dow lost 10.68 points. In this way, the Exchange ended its worst week since 1929, having lost 38.82 points. Almost $30 billion—more than the combined gross national products of Australia, Sweden, and Ireland—was wiped out. IBM lost fifty-three points on the week, while American Telephone and Telegraph declined 7⅝ and other leaders followed suit.[49]

Wall Streeters licked their wounds that weekend and wondered what to expect at the Monday opening. Most analysts agreed that the "cult of growth" had been severely shaken, perhaps destroyed. It seemed doubtful that investors would be willing to pay 100 times earnings for future new issues, but beyond this, the crystal ball was cloudy. The bears thought a major downside signal had been received, and that prices would continue their fall, perhaps to the 500 level. The bulls, considering the Friday session as a selling climax, thought the market was oversold, and expected a temporary rally at the least.

By the Monday opening, a huge volume of sell orders had accumulated, and it was difficult to maintain an orderly market from the first. Wave upon wave of massive selling hit the Exchange floor in the heaviest trading since 1929. The tape was late from the opening, and did not catch up throughout the day. The lag between sales and reported transactions on the tape ran over an hour; when trading ended on the Pacific Coast Exchange two hours after the New York closing, complete Wall Street quotes were still unavailable. The Dow-Jones industrials showed a loss of 34.95 points for the day; over $21 billion in values had been erased in a single session. American Telephone and Telegraph showed an eleven point loss, Standard Oil of New Jersey lost five, and other leaders showed similar declines. There were 1,212 declines all told, with seventy-four rises. When the final report came through late that night, it was announced that the Exchange had tabulated its first 9 million-share day since 1933.

Such a disastrous session was bound to stun the community, but unlike 1929, it had not come as a great surprise. Signs of a decline had been present for over nine months, and many investors had been prepared for a major crash. In addition, the underlying strength of the economy, and the checks—such as margin requirements and SEC regulations—which had been imposed during the New Deal had prevented a good deal of the chicanery so prevalent during the twenties. Finally, the district and the investing public had great faith in the funds, which were expected to stem the decline in short order. The 1962 collapse may have reminded some of the 1929 crash, but the resemblance was only a surface one.

Stocks opened lower on very heavy volume on Tuesday, and continued downward through the first hour. At this point—in a way which must have reminded many of J. P. Morgan in 1907—the funds and some bulls entered the arena. Prices made a rapid turnabout, and began to soar, regaining almost 65 per cent of the Monday loss by the closing bell. Once more the tape ran late; investors had to wait four hours and thirty-seven minutes to find out how their stocks did that day. The volume of trading—14.7 million shares—was the greatest since October of 1929. In 1962, however, the glowing reports from leading Exchange figures and industrialists seemed to have substance. Paradoxically, the Street seemed more optimistic in late May than it had been earlier in the month, before the crash. It was as though a dreaded event had finally taken place, and had proven not so bad after all. James Day of the Midwest Exchange in Chicago observed "I think that the investor should stop and think if his company is reporting higher earnings. It is foolish to sacrifice stocks at heavy losses." Walter Heller said what many had felt, that "the market has nothing to fear but fear itself." Walter Benedict of Investors Planning Corporation led other mutual fund managers in voicing confidence in the market, and said he was planning to pick up stocks at bargain prices. J. Paul Getty, reputedly the wealthiest man in the world, announced that he was buying heavily in oil stocks. "I don't think the slide will go on," he said. "In fact, I think there will be a rather substantial rise and very shortly."[50]

The market seesawed for the rest of the week, churning on heavy volume. By Friday's close over 40.5 million shares had been traded, smashing all post-1929 records. Unlike 1929, investors were not overly worried about margin calls and utter destruction. In point of fact, many investors seemed secretly confident of a rise, and awaited the proper moment to buy growth stocks at bargain prices. By the end of the week that moment seemed to have passed, for stocks had made a dramatic recovery from the Monday morning lows. The industrials closed Friday at 611.05, a shade lower than the previous week's close of 611.88.

With this, the post-mortems began. Administration critics blamed the crash on the steel controversy, neglecting the fact that the decline had begun before that episode. Former President Eisenhower told reporters that stocks had declined due to Kennedy's "reckless spending programs." The President replied that "the economy is rising, unemployment is down, the prospects in this month are good— I think the stock market will follow the economy." Secretary of Commerce Luther Hodges called for a tax cut to stimulate business, but this was rejected by the President and Secretary of the Treasury Dillon as unwise at the time. Dillon told a Senate committee that the crash came about because "finally the investing public just decided the prices were too high," and opined that stocks should sell around fifteen times earnings. With this, the market broke again, reaching the 560 level in mid-June, and eventually falling to 535. Then the institutions and small investors re-entered the market, and prices steadied.

The bear period lasted until late October, when the Cuban missile crisis and President Kennedy's prompt action in demanding the removal of Soviet offensive arms from the island boosted both his popularity and the stock market. The Dow-Jones industrials rose over seventy points in the fourth quarter, closing with a twelve-month loss of less than eighty points. Thus, the year that had opened with one of the worse slides in the market's history ended with one of its most spectacular recoveries. The year's trading range of 535.76–726.01 was the widest recorded.

Wall Street exuded confidence during the Christmas season of 1962. Despite the continuance of international tensions, it was believed that the tide of the Cold War had turned in favor of the West. The expected recession had never developed; instead, the automobile industry reported a banner year, and even the moribund steel makers seemed to be turning a corner. Abandoning his conservative fiscal policies, President Kennedy announced plans for a tax cut and tax reforms; he apparently decided that the risks of inflation were preferable to a stagnant economy.

The stock market of late 1962 was different from that of the pre-panic years. The bull market following the Cuban crisis lacked the wildness of the sputnik market of 1957. The May declines had awakened the dreamers, and glamour was no longer the focal point on Wall Street. The new issue market faded, and many of the fly-by-night houses of the late fifties closed their doors—it was the blue chip industrials and the rails, and not the electronics, space, and other glamour issues, which led the late 1962 advance. At year's end, the wild performers of previous years were closer to their 1962 lows than to their highs, and as in the past, the prices on the American Exchange magnified those on the Big Board (see Tables 16.9 and 16.10). The greatest losses were shown in the over-the-counter market (see Table 16.11).

By the early summer of 1963, conditions had returned to normal. The investors of the fifties were back in the market; unlike their fathers, they did not wait another generation to reappear. Like their predecessors for the past two centuries, they looked for "a sound growth stock paying over 5 per cent," and like them they could not

Table 16.9—Representative New York Exchange Stocks, 1962

	High	Low	Close
American Machine & Foundry	42½	15⅝	20½
American Photocopy	32⅛	8¼	11¾
Automatic Canteen	31¾	9¾	14¼
Brunswick Corporation	52¾	13⅛	18⅝
Cenco Instruments	68	28¼	39⅛
Fairchild Camera	70½	31	45¼
General Instrument	30	10⅛	11⅛
Hewlett-Packard	37	15¼	24⅛
International Business Machines	578½	300	390
Texas Instruments	125½	49	63½

Table 16.10—American Exchange Prices, 1962

	High	Low	Close
Acme Missiles	15⅝	3½	3¾
All-State Properties	9	2	2½
Avien Inc.	13½	3½	4
Belock Instruments	11¾	3⅝	3¾
CompuDyne Corporation	12⅞	2½	2⅞
I.M.C. Magnetics	10⅞	3⅝	4⅛
Microwave Associates	38½	8	13½
M.P.O. Vidiotronics	14⅜	5½	5¾
Robinson Technical Products	19¼	7⅝	8⅝
TelePrompter Corporation	16⅞	4¼	5¼

Table 16.11—Over-the-Counter Stocks, 1962

	High	Low	Close
Acustica Associates	10	1¾	2⅜
ALD Inc.	17⅝	3¾	4½
American Univend	18½	1	3½
Bohn Business Machines	31	4½	5½
Cove Vitamin	22	2⅞	3
Gem International	22¾	7½	7⅝
Ionics, Inc.	30	8¾	8¾
Lence Lanes	27¾	1¼	2⅛
Missile Systems	15½	2⅞	3
Wyle Laboratories	32	7	7

find one. In common with almost all investors since William Duer, they were searching for a system. Still, they were more sophisticated than their predecessors. The assassination of President Kennedy in November, 1963, did not cause a widespread slump. The market responded to the Johnson Administration with a sweeping bull market. In the 1964 presidential election both investor and broker—usually considered safely Republican, backed the President rather than take a chance with the experimentation offered by Barry Goldwater. By 1965, the market reflected both caution and hope—as it always does—but both sentiments seemed more firmly grounded in fact than ever before. The investors of the mid-sixties seemed to have reflected upon the sage advice given by the elder Morgan to a young man who asked what that master of Wall Street thought stocks would do next. Morgan never hesitated for a moment. He transfixed the neophite with his sharp glance, and replied, "They will fluctuate, young man, they will fluctuate." And so they will.

Notes

1. *Time,* January 5, 1953, p. 60.
2. *Time,* March 9, 1953, pp. 91–92.
3. *New York Times,* February 10–19, 1954.
4. *New York Times,* March 17, 1954.
5. *Time,* July 5, 1954, p. 68.
6. *New York Stock Exchange Fact Book,* pp. 38–43.
7. *Time,* January 24, 1955, p. 69.
8. Burton Crane in *New York Times,* May 27, 1962.
9. *New York Stock Exchange Fact Book,* pp. 40, 44.
10. *Time,* October 18, 1954, p. 92; Data Digests, Inc., *Monthly Stock Digest,* October, 1960; New York World Telegram and Sun, *1963 Red Book* (New York, 1963).
11. United States Government, 84th Congress, 1st Session, Committee on Banking and Currency, *Factors Affecting the Stock Market* (Washington, 1955), p. 1 ff.
12. *New York Times,* September 27, 28, 1955.
13. Freeman, *Postwar Economic Trends in the United States,* p. 81; Lee, *Economic Fluctuations,* p. 489.
14. *Business Week,* February 16, 1957, p. 56.
15. Freeman, *Postwar Economic Trends in the United States,* p. 175.
16. *Business Week,* June 22, 1957, p. 162.
17. *Business Week,* December 21, 1957, p. 109.
18. Crane, *The Sophisticated Investor,* p. 121.
19. *Business Week,* January 10, 1959, p. 98.
20. *New York Times,* January 3, 1959; *Business Week,* July 25, 1959, p. 82.
21. *Time,* May 25, 1959, p. 84.
22. *Time,* June 8, 1959, p. 97.
23. *Business Week,* May 23, 1959, p. 157; *New York World Telegram and Sun Red Book.*
24. *Time,* April 20, 1959, p. 92.
25. *Time,* July 2, 1960, p. 65.
26. *Time,* September 21, 1959, p. 92; April 27, 1959, p. 86.
27. *U.S. News and World Report,* March 21, 1960, p. 52.
28. *Business Week,* March 28, 1960.
29. *Time,* December 28, 1959, p. 52.

30. *New York Times,* January 3, 1960.
31. *Time,* March 14, 1960, p. 88.
32. *Time,* March 21, 1960, p. 88.
33. *Time,* April 4, 1960, p. 88.
34. *New York Times,* June 30, 1960.
35. *Time,* October 10, 1960, p. 104.
36. *Business Week,* January 21, 1961, p. 115.
37. Fuller, *The Money Changers,* p. 143.
38. *Business Week,* April 15, 1961, p. 129.
39. *Business Week,* September 24, 1960, pp. 147–52.
40. *Business Week,* May 6, 1961, p. 82.
41. *Business Week,* May 20, 1961, p. 135.
42. *New York Times,* June 15, 1961.
43. *New York Times,* April 8, 1962.
44. *Business Week,* October 14, 1961.
45. *Business Week,* December 9, 1961, pp. 102–103.
46. *Business Week,* February 17, 1962, p. 111; March 24, 1962, p. 120.
47. *New York Times,* June 2, 1962.
48. *New York Herald Tribune,* August 5, 1962.
49. *New York Times,* May 23–28, 1962.
50. *New York Times,* May 29–June 7, 1962.

Selected
Bibliography

Allen, Frederick Lewis. *The Great Pierpont Morgan.* New York, 1949.
———. *The Lords of Creation.* New York, 1935.
———. *Only Yesterday.* New York, 1961.
Angley, Edward. *Oh, Yeah!.* New York, 1930.
Atkins, Willard, George Edwards, and Harold Moulton. *The Regulation of the Securities Markets.* Washington, 1946.
Barbour, Violet. *Capitalism in Amsterdam in the Seventeenth Century.* Baltimore, 1950.
Barck, Oscar Jr. and Nelson Blake. *Since 1900.* New York, 1959.
Barrett, Walter. *Old Merchants of New York.* 5 volumes. New York, 1870.
Barron, Clarence. *They Told Barron.* New York, 1930.
Baruch, Bernard. *My Own Story.* New York, 1957.
———. *Baruch, The Public Years.* New York, 1960.
Beard, Miriam. *A History of the Business Man.* New York, 1938.
Berle, A. A., Jr. *Power Without Property.* New York, 1959.
———. *The Twentieth Century Capitalist Revolution.* New York, 1954.
——— and Gardner Means. *The Modern Corporation and Private Property.* New York, 1933.
Bishop, George Jr. *Charles H. Dow and the Dow Theory.* New York, 1960.
Black, Hillel. *The Watchdogs of Wall Street.* New York, 1962.
Bond, Frederic. *Stock Movements and Speculation.* New York, 1929.
Brooke, W. Collin. *How the Stock Market Really Works.* London, 1930.
Bullock, Hugh. *The Story of Investment Companies.* New York, 1959.

Burr, Anna. *The Portrait of a Banker: James Stillman, 1850–1918.* New York, 1927.

Carman, Harry and Harold Syrett. *A History of the American People.* 2 volumes. New York, 1952.

Chandler, Alfred Jr. *Henry Varnum Poor: Business Editor, Analyst and Reformer.* Cambridge, 1956.

Chandler, Lester. *Benjamin Strong, Central Banker.* Washington, 1958.

Churchill, Allen. *The Incredible Ivar Kreuger.* New York, 1957.

Clark, Victor. *History of Manufactures in the United States.* 3 volumes. New York, 1929.

Clews, Henry. *Fifty Years in Wall Street.* New York, 1908.

————. *The American Business System: A Historical Perspective.* Cambridge, 1957.

Cochran, Thomas. *Railroad Leaders, 1845–1890: The Business Mind in Action.* Cambridge, 1953.

———— and William Miller. *The Age of Enterprise: A Social History of Industrial America.* New York, 1942.

Collins, Frederick. *Money Town.* New York, 1946.

Conant, Charles. *A History of Modern Banks of Issue.* New York, 1915.

————. *Wall Street and the Country.* New York, 1904.

Corey, Lewis. *The House of Morgan.* New York, 1930.

Cotter, Cornelius. *Government and Private Enterprise.* New York, 1960.

Crane, Burton. *The Sophisticated Investor.* New York, 1959.

Davis, Joseph. *Essays in the Earlier History of American Corporations.* Cambridge, 1917.

Dayton, Abram. *Last Days of Knickerbocker Life in New York.* New York, 1880.

Diamond, Sigmund. *The Reputation of the American Businessman.* Cambridge, 1955.

Dies, Edward. *Behind the Wall Street Curtain.* Washington, 1952.

Dimock, A. W. *Wall Street and the Wilds.* New York, 1915.

Dimock, Marshall. *Business and Government.* New York, 1949.

Domett, Henry. *A History of the Bank of New York, 1784–1884.* New York, 1898.

Dos Passos, John. *A Treatise on the Law of Stock-Brokers and Stock-Exchanges.* New York, 1882.

Douglas, William O. *Democracy and Finance.* New Haven, 1940.

Eames, Francis. *The New York Stock Exchange.* New York, 1894.

Eckenrode, H. J. and Pocahontas Edmunds. *E. H. Harriman.* New York, 1930.

Edwards, George. *The Evolution of Finance Capitalism.* New York, 1938.

Ewan, C. L. *Lotteries and Sweepstakes.* London, 1932.

Ezell, John. *Fortune's Merry Wheel.* Cambridge, 1960.

Faulkner, Harold. *American Economic History.* New York, 1958.

——. *The Decline of Laissez Faire, 1897–1917*. New York, 1951.

——. *Politics, Reform, and Expansion, 1890–1900*. New York, 1959.

Fisher, Irving. *Booms and Depressions: Some First Principles*. London, 1933.

——. *The Stock Market Crash and After*. New York, 1930.

Fite, Emerson. *Social and Industrial Conditions in the North During the Civil War*. New York, 1910.

Forbes, B. C. *Men Who Are Making America*. New York, 1917.

The Editors of *Fortune*. *Markets of the Sixties*. New York, 1960.

Fowler, W. Worthington. *Ten Years in Wall Street, or Revelations of Inside Life and Experience on 'Change*. New York, 1870.

——. *Twenty Years of Inside Life in Wall Street*. New York, 1880.

Frank, Jerome. *Save America First*. New York, 1938.

Freeman, Ralph. Ed. *Postwar Economic Trends in the United States*. New York, 1960.

Fuller, John. *The Money Changers*. New York, 1962.

Galbraith, John. *The Great Crash, 1929*. Boston, 1955.

Garraty, John. *Right Hand Man*. New York, 1960.

Gras, N. S. B. *Business and Capitalism: An Introduction to Business History*. New York, 1947.

Grodinsky, Jules. *Jay Gould: His Business Career, 1867–1892*. Philadelphia, 1957.

Hammond, Bray. *Banks and Politics in America: From the Revolution to the Civil War*. Princeton, 1957.

Harbrecht, Paul. *Pension Funds and Economic Power*. New York, 1959.

Harrington, Virginia. *The New York Merchant on the Eve of the Revolution*. New York, 1935.

Harris, Charles. *Memories of Manhattan in the Sixties and Seventies*. New York, 1884.

Hawtry, R. G. *Currency and Credit*. London, 1928.

Hedges, Joseph. *Commercial Banking and the Stock Market before 1863*. Baltimore, 1938.

Hicks, Frederick. Ed. *High Finance in the Sixties: Chapters from the Early History of the Erie Railway*. New Haven, 1929.

Hidy, Ralph. *The House of Baring in American Trade and Finance, 1763–1861*. Cambridge, 1949.

Hill, Frederick. *The Story of a Street*. New York, 1908.

Hinkling, John, & Co. *Men and Idioms of Wall Street*. New York, 1875.

Hirst, Francis. *The Stock Exchange*. London, 1911.

Hofstadter, Richard. *The American Political Tradition and the Men Who Made It*. New York, 1948.

Hoggson, Noble. *Epoches in American Banking*. New York, 1929.

Holbrook, Stewart. *The Age of Moguls*. New York, 1954.

Homan, Paul and Machlup, Fritz. Eds. *Financing American Prosperity.* New York, 1945.

Hoover, Herbert. *The Memoirs of Herbert Hoover: The Great Depression, 1929–1941.* New York, 1952.

Hoyt, Edwin. *The Supersalesmen.* New York, 1962.

Hunt, Freeman. *Lives of American Merchants.* New York, 1858.

Institute of Life Insurance. *Life Insurance Fact Book, 1961.* New York, 1961.

Jenks, Leland. *The Migration of British Capital to 1875.* New York, 1938.

Josephson, Matthew. *Life Among the Surrealists.* New York, 1962.

———. *The Robber Barons.* New York, 1934.

Kimmel, Lewis. *Share Ownership in the United States.* Washington, 1952.

Kirkland, Edward. *Dream and Thought in the American Business Community, 1860–1900.* Ithaca, 1956.

———. *Industry Comes of Age: Business, Labor, and Public Policy, 1860–1897.* New York, 1961.

Kolko, Gabriel. *Wealth and Power in the United States.* New York, 1962.

Lamb, Martha and Harrison, Mrs. Burton. *History of the City of New York.* 3 volumes. New York, 1896.

Lane, Wheaton. *Commodore Vanderbilt: An Epic of the Steam Age.* New York, 1942.

Lanier, Henry. *A Century of Banking in New York, 1822–1922.* New York, 1922.

Larson, Henrietta. *Jay Cooke, Private Banker.* Cambridge, 1936.

Lawrence, Joseph. *Wall Street and Washington.* Princeton, 1929.

Lawson, Thomas. *Frenzied Finance: The Crime of Amalgamated.* London, 1906.

Lee, Maurice. *Economic Fluctuations: Growth and Stability.* Homewood, Ill., 1959.

Lefevre, Edwin. *Wall Street Stories.* New York, 1901.

Levinson, Leonard. *Wall Street: A Pictorial History.* New York, 1961.

Lightner, Otto. *The History of Business Depressions.* New York, 1922.

Livingston, J. A. *The American Stockholder.* New York, 1958.

Lundberg, Ferdinand. *America's 60 Families.* New York, 1937.

Lynch, David. *The Concentration of Economic Power.* New York, 1946.

McDonald, Forrest. *Insull.* Chicago, 1962.

Mackay, Charles. *Extraordinary Popular Delusions and the Madness of Crowds.* New York, 1932.

Martin, Joseph. *A Century of Finance.* Boston, 1898.

Mayer, Martin. *Wall Street: Men and Money.* New York, 1959.

Medbery, James. *Men and Mysteries of Wall Street.* New York, 1870.

Meeker, J. Edward. *The Work of the Stock Exchange.* New York, 1922.

Merrill, Horace. *Bourbon Leader: Grover Cleveland and the Democratic Party.* Boston, 1957.

Miller, Harry. *Banking Theories in the United States before 1860*. Cambridge, 1927.

Miller, Nathan. *The Enterprise of a Free People*. Ithaca, 1962.

Miller, William. Ed. *Men in Business*. Cambridge, 1952.

Mitchell, Broadus. *Depression Decade*. New York, 1947.

Mitchell, Wesley. *Business Cycles: The Problem and Its Setting*. New York, 1927.

Moody, John. *The Art of Wall Street Investing*. New York, 1909.

——. *The Long Road Home*. New York, 1933.

——. *The Masters of Capital*. New Haven, 1921.

Morris, Joe Alex. *What a Year!* New York, 1955.

Morris, Lloyd. *Not So Long Ago*. New York, 1949.

Myers, Margaret. *The New York Money Market*. New York, 1939.

Neill, Humphrey. *The Inside Story of the Stock Exchange*. New York, 1950.

Nelson, Ralph. *Merger Movements in American Industry: 1895–1956*. Princeton, 1959.

Nevins, Allan, Ed. *The Diary of Philip Hone, 1828–1851*. New York, 1927.

——. *Grover Cleveland: A Study in Courage*. New York, 1938.

New York Stock Exchange. *Fact Book, 1961*. New York, 1962.

Noble, H. G. S. *The New York Stock Exchange in the Crisis of 1914*. New York, 1915.

Noyes, Alexander. *Forty Years of American Finance*. New York, 1898.

——. *The Market Place*. Boston, 1938.

——. *The War Period of American Finance*. New York, 1927.

O'Connor, Harvey. *Mellon's Millions*. New York, 1933.

O'Connor, Richard. *Gould's Millions*. Garden City, 1962.

Parker, John. *Unmasking Wall Street*. Boston, 1932.

Parker, Willis H. and Jules, Bogen. *Investment Banking*. New York, 1936.

Perlo, Victor. *The Empire of High Finance*. New York, 1957.

Plummer, A. Newton. *The Great American Swindle, Inc*. New York, 1932.

Pratt, Sereno. *The Work of Wall Street*. New York, 1921.

Redlich, Fritz. *The Molding of American Banking: Men and Ideas*. 3 volumes. New York, 1951.

Ripley, William. *Main Street and Wall Street*. New York, 1927.

Robbins, Sidney and Nestor, Terleckyj. *Money Metropolis*. Cambridge, 1960.

Schlesinger, Arthur, Jr. *The Coming of the New Deal*. New York, 1959.

——. *The Crisis of the Old Order*. New York, 1957.

Schultz, Birl. *The Securities Market and How It Works*. New York, 1937.

Schwed, Fred, Jr. *Where Are the Customers' Yachts?* New York, 1955.

Sears, John. *The New Place of the Stockholder*. New York, 1929.

Slosson, Preston. *The Great Crusade and After*. New York, 1937.

Smith, Matthew. *Sunshine and Shadow in New York.* Hartford, 1893.

Smith, Walter and Cole, Arthur. *Fluctuations in American Business, 1790–1860.* Cambridge, 1935.

Sobel, Robert. *The Origins of Interventionism.* New York, 1960.

Soule, George. *Prosperity Decade.* New York, 1947.

Sparkes, Boyden and Moore, Samuel. *The Witch of Wall Street: Hetty Green.* New York, 1948.

Sparling, Earl. *Mystery Men of Wall Street.* New York, 1930.

Stedman, E. C. *The New York Stock Exchange.* New York, 1905.

Studenski, Paul and Herman Krooss. *Financial History of the United States.* New York, 1952.

Sullivan, Mark. *Our Times.* 5 volumes. New York, 1927.

Swanberg, W. A. *Jim Fisk: The Career of an Improbable Rascal.* New York, 1959.

Taylor, George. *The Transportation Revolution, 1815–1860.* New York, 1951.

Train, George. *Young America in Wall Street.* New York, 1857.

United States Government, 77th Congress, 1st Session, Temporary National Economic Committee, *Investigation of Concentration of Economic Power.* Washington, 1940.

——, 84th Congress, 1st Session, Senate Committee on Banking and Currency. *Factors Affecting the Stock Market.* Washington, 1955.

——, 84th Congress, 1st Session, Senate Committee on Banking and Currency. *Staff Report.* Washington, 1955.

——, 87th Congress, 1st Session, Joint Economic Committee. *Variability of Private Investment in Plant and Equipment.* Washington, 1962.

——, 87th Congress, 2nd Session, Joint Economic Committee. *1962 Supplement to Economic Indicators.* Washington, 1962.

——, 87th Congress, 2nd Session, Committee on Interstate and Foreign Commerce. *A Study of Mutual Funds.* Washington, 1962.

——, District Court of the United States for the Southern District of New York. *Corrected Opinion of February 4, 1954, in the case of United States vs. H. S. Morgan et al., by Harold R. Medina, U.S.C.J.* New York, 1954

Walker, James. *The Epic of American Industry.* New York, 1957.

Warshow, Robert. *Bet-a-Million Gates: The Story of a Plunger.* New York, 1932.

——. *The Story of Wall Street.* New York, 1939.

Washburn, Watson and Edmund De Long. *High and Low Financiers.* New York, 1932.

Weissman, Rudolph. *The New Wall Street.* New York, 1939.

White, Bouck. *The Book of Daniel Drew.* New York, 1937.

White, William A. *A Puritan in Babylon.* New York, 1938.

Wickwire, Arthur. *The Weeds of Wall Street.* New York, 1933.

Wilson, Rufus. *New York Old and New*. New York, 1909.

Winkler, John. *Morgan the Magnificent*. New York, 1931.

Wise, T. A. and the editors of *Fortune*. *The Insiders: A Stockholder's Guide to Wall Street*. New York, 1963.

Wycoff, Richard. *Wall Street Ventures and Adventures through Forty Years*. New York, 1930.

Index

Adams, Alvin, 53
Adams, John Quincy, 37
Alaska Juneau Mines, 266
Aldrich-Vreeland Act, 199
Alger, Horatio, 112
Allegheny Corporation, 238–39, 245
Allen, Henry, & Co., 137
Allen, Solomon, 22
Allied Chemical & Dye Co., 284
Amalgamated Copper Co., 182–83, 189, 190
Amerada Petroleum, 239
American Federation of Labor, 126
American Ice Company, 189–91
American Investment Trust, 96
American Motors Corporation, 341
American Railroad Journal, 175
American Steel & Wire Co., 156
American Stock Exchange, 199, 284, 354–55, 365
American Telegraph Company, 86
American Telephone & Telegraph Co., 111, 222
American Tin Plate Co., 156
American Tobacco Company, 199
American Tobacco Trust, 157, 185–86
Amsterdam, 6–8
Andrews, Elisha, 86
Anglo-American Telegraph Co., 82
anti-intellectualism of Wall Street, 112, 240
anti-semitism, 63–64, 109, 151
arbitrage, 80
Armstrong investigation, 185
Arnold, Thurman, 307

Arthur, Chester A., 117
Art Market Guide & Forecaster, 364–65
Astor, John Jacob, 29, 33
Atcheson, Topeka, and Santa Fe, 133, 139, 167
Atlantic Cable, 82
Atlas Corporation, 266
Auburn & Rochester Railroad, 38
Auburn Automobile Corporation, 305
Australia gold rush, 149

Babson, Roger, 269
Bache & Co., 334
Bacon, Robert, 160, 165, 168, 197
Baker, George F., 110, 164, 184, 193–94, 199
Baker, George F., Jr., 273
Baker, Hugh, 288
balance of trade (1877–78), 104
Balkan, wars of 1913, 201
Baltimore & Ohio Railroad, 37, 111
Bangs, Stetson, Tracy and MacVeigh, 136
Bankers' and Brokers' Association, 84
Banker's Magazine, 53, 104, 175
Bankers Trust Company, 182
Banking Act of 1933, 296–97
Bank of America, 243
Bank of England, 132, 187
Bank of New York, 16, 76, 98–99, 367
Bank of North America, 16–17, 190
Barbour, Justin, 323

Baring Brothers & Co., 33–34, 49, 57, 59, 132
Barker, Jacob, 40
Barkley, Alben, 295
Barnes, Leo, 342
Barney, Charles D. & Co., 111
Barney, Charles T., 192, 197
Barron, C. W., 176, 183
Barron's, 176, 357
Bartow, James, 43
Baruch, Bernard, 145, 147, 154–55, 166, 220, 266, 269, 285, 364
Bates, Joshua, 34
BBM Photocopy Corporation, 363
Beane, Alpheus C., 337
Beebe, Samuel, 30, 39–40
Beldon, William, 91, 93
Bellanca Corporation, 301
Belle, Earl, 330
Belmont, August, 63
Benedict, Walter, 371
Berney, Charles D. & Co., 154
Bethlehem Steel Company, 185, 213, 218
Biddle, Nicholas, 42, 50
Birrell, Lowell, 329–30
Black Friday, 87, 91–94
Blackstone Canal, 34
Black Thursday (1901), 166–68: (1929), 262–63, 273–76
Black Wednesday, 140
Blaine, James G., 121, 124
Bland-Allison Act, 107, 117, 125, 132, 134
Bleeker, Leonard, 30
Bliss, Frank, 249, 263
Blyth, Witter & Co., 242
Blyth & Co., 297
Board of Brokers, 30, 51
Boer War, 150, 152
Bolton, Hamilton, 358
Boston Associates, 51–52
Boston Stock Exchange, 51
Bourse, 9
Boutwell, George, 90, 92
Bowdoin, George, 128
Brain Trust, 294
Brady, "Diamond Jim," 154

Breen, George, 249, 267
Brockway Motor Company, 284
brokers' loans, 256–57
brokers of the 1870s, 109–13
Brookhart, Smith, 288–89
Brown, Alexander, 29
Brown, Alexander & Co., 36
Brown Brothers, Harriman & Co., 297
Bruns, Nordeman & Co., 363
Bryan, William Jennings, 147–49, 188, 200, 215
Budge, Schiff & Co., 110
Burnham, I. W., 358
Burns, Walter, 128
Burr, Aaron, 17, 22
Burr, George H. & Co., 336
Butterfield, Daniel, 90–92

Calahan, E. A., 86
Calhoun, John C., 35
call money, 257, 267
Calvin, John, 5
Cammack, Addison, 119, 136
Canadian Pacific Railroad, 207
Canadian "penny stocks," 329
Canadian stock boom of 1951, 325
Canadian uranium boom of 1953, 347
"canal mania," 32–38
Capital Strike of 1934–1935, 302
Carlyle, John G., 141
Carnegie, Andrew, 161–62
Carnegie Steel Co., 156
Cary, G. B., 305
Cary, William L., 365
Cassel, Ernest, 133
Catherwood, Robert, 90
Catskill Railroad, 42
Central Pacific Railroad, 82, 88
Chamberlain, Neville, 312
Chandler Act of 1938, 301
Chase, Salmon, 70, 73
Chase National Bank, 182, 239, 269, 286
Chesapeake & Delaware Canal Co., 37
Chesapeake & Ohio Canal Co., 33, 37
Chesapeake & Ohio Railroad, 144
Chestnut Street, 17, 30, 52

Chicago, Burlington, & Quincy Railroad, 163, 168
Chicago & Northwestern Railroad, 95
Chicago Edison Company, 243
Chicago fire, 93
Chimo Gold Mines, 347
Churchill, Winston, 312
Cisco, J. J. & Co., 119
City Company, 297
Civil War, 67–79
Clark, Colin, 326–27
Clark, E. W. & Co., 56
Claude Neon Corporation, 330
Clay, Henry, 42
clearing house certificates, 120, 133, 195
clergy, interest in securities, 71
Cleveland, Grover, 121, 124–26, 135–42, 148
Clews, Henry, 62, 171
closed-end trusts, 331–32
Coal Hole, 77
"coal oil johnnies," 76
Colorado Fuel & Iron Co., 158
Columbian Exposition, 139
Commercial and Financial Chronicle, 97, 109, 177, 188
Commercial Bank Building, 58
Commercial Telegraph Company, 87
Committee on Economic Changes, 266
Common Market, 357, 368
Commonwealers, 139
Commonwealth Edison Company, 243–44
Confederate States of America, 67
Consolidated Steel & Wire Company, 160
Consolidated Stock Exchange, 131
Consolidated Uranium Mines, 329
Constitution of 1817, 30–31
Constitution of 1820, 39
Content, Harry, 155, 163, 165, 250
Control Data Corporation, 361
Cooke, Jay, 56, 58, 69–71, 82, 97–98, 109, 158, 185
Cooke, Jay & Co., 97–98, 107–8
Coolidge, Calvin, 236, 236

Corbett, James, 354
Corbett, James J., 154
Corbin, Abel, 89–91
Corcoran, Thomas, 294
Corn Exchange Bank, 278
Cornucopia Gold Mines, 330
Corporation Securities of Chicago, 244
Corre's Hotel Agreement, 21
Cortelyou, George, 194
Coster, Charles H., 128, 143
Coster, F. Donald (Phillip Musica), 306
Coxey's Army, 139
Cuban Crisis, 372
curb brokers, 78
curb exchange, 199
Curtice, Harlow, 351
Curtis, Raleigh T., 248
Cutter, Arthur, 247–48, 267, 270–72

Dabney, Morgan & Co., 109
Darvas, Nicholas, 355, 365
Darwin, Charles, 112
Davis, Howland, 305
Davis, Richard Harding, 154
Davison, Henry, 199
Dawes, Charles G., 281
Dawes Plan, 265
Day, James, 371
Day and Night Bank, 192
Dean Witter & Co., 338
Delaware, Lackawanna & Western Railroad, 85, 119, 207
Delaware & Hudson Railroad, 167
Dempsey-Firpo fight, 248
Denver & Rio Grande Railroad, 144
Depew, Chauncy, 200
depressions (1819), 29; (1836), 44; (1873–78), 104–107, 116–17; (1929–37), 278–90
Dewey, Thomas E., 306, 322
Diamond Match Company, 127
Dice, Charles, 269
Dillon, Douglas, 371
Dillon, Read & Co., 239, 259
Dinamore, William, 53
Dines, James, 341–42

Dingley Tariff, 150
Distilled Liquors Corporation, 306
Distillers' and Cattle Feeders' Trust, 127
Dodge Brothers, 239
Doeskin Products, Inc., 330
Douglas, William O., 301, 305–307, 309
Dow, Charles H., 157–58, 176
Dow-Jones Service, 176
Dow theory, 317, 341, 358
Drew, Daniel, 56–57, 62, 84–85, 87, 97
Drew, Garfield, 358, 360
Drexel, Anthony J., 109
Drexel, Francis A., 109
Drexel, Harjes & Co., 109
Drexel, Morgan & Co., 109, 121, 128
Drexel & Co., 109, 297
Dreyfus, Jack, 356
Duer, William, 18–19
Duff, John R., 116
Duke Foundation, 333
Dun, R. G. and Co., 136
Duncan, Sherman & Co., 109
Dun's Review, 131
DuPont, Francis I. & Co., 334
DuPont de Nemours, E. I. & Co., 199, 215, 218
Durant, Donald, 287
Durant, William Crapo, 200, 249–50, 262, 267, 272

Eastman Dillon & Co., 242, 334
Eddy, Sykes & Co., 16
Eddy, Thomas, 16
Edgerton, John F., 277
Edison Electric Illuminating Company, 128
Edison Electric Light Company, 243
Eisenhower, Dwight D., 326, 346–47, 351, 357, 371
elections (1884), 117, 121; (1892), 135–36; (1896), 147–51; (1920), 225; (1932), 285–86; (1948), 322–23; (1964), 359
Electric Storage Battery Company, 127
Elkins Act, 184
Elliot Wave Theory, 358

Emergency Banking Act, 293
Eno, John, 119
Equitable Life Assurance Society, 183–84
Erie Canal, 26, 36, 95–96
Erie Board, *see* National Stock Exchange
Erie Railroad, 57, 85, 139, 143, 244
Erpf, Armand, 342
Euken, Rudolph, 206–207
Evening Exchange, 78

Fabbre, Egesto, 128
Fahnestock & Co., 111, 367
Fair Deal, 316
Farmer, Moses, 67
Farrington Manufacturing Corporation, 356
Federal Deposit Insurance Corporation, 297
Federal Reserve System, 199–200, 216, 223, 226–27, 255–57, 262, 266–68, 353
Federal Steel Co., 156, 160–61
Federal Trade Commission, 294, 298–300
Fenner & Beane & Co., 337
Ferber, Robert, 342
Fess, Simon D., 279
Fidelio Breweries, Inc., 330
Field, Cyrus, 65, 121
Field, Jacob, 155
Field, Stephen, 87
Fifth Avenue Hotel, 67, 78
financial writers, 341–42
First Boston Corporation, 297
First National Bank, 110, 164, 182, 194
First National Bank of Boston, 297
First Securities Company, 182–83
Fish, James D., 118
Fisher, Irving, 207, 213, 215, 271–73, 275
Fisher Brothers, 249, 267, 272
Fisk, Jim, 84, 89–96
Fisk & Hatch, 98, 111, 118–19
Fitch Brothers & Co., 36
Fitzsimmons, Joseph, 343

Fleming, John, 48
Fletcher, Duncan, 298
Fletcher-Rayburn Bill, 299, 301
Ford, Henry, 139
Ford Foundation, 333
Ford Motor Company, 200, 266
Fortune, 304, 327
Foshay enterprises, 276
Franco-Prussian War, 96
Frank, Jerome, 309
Frankfurter, Felix, 294
Frenzied Finance, 189
Frick, Henry Clay, 161, 178, 184, 191
Fry's Army, 139
Fugger, Jacob, 5
Fulbright, William, 350
Full Employment Bill of 1946, 316
Fuller, Stephen, 363
Fulton, Cutting & Co., 60
fundamentalists market, 341
Funston, Keith, 346, 355, 361–62, 369

Galbraith, John K., 350
Gallagher's Room, 78
Gardner Hill Gold & Copper, 79
Garfield, James A., 92, 116
Gary, Elbert, 160, 196–97
Gates, John W. "Bet-A-Million," 154, 160, 162, 168, 181, 197
Gay, Charles, 305
General Electric Company, 127, 218
General Motors Company, 200, 218, 265, 267
General Securities Corporation, 245
Gentil and Phipps, 78
Getty, J. Paul, 371
Gilmore, Robert & Co., 36
Gilpin's News Room, 73–76
Girard, Stephan, 25, 29
Glass, Carter, 199, 269, 294, 296
Glass-Owen Act, 199
Glass-Steagall Act, *see* Banking Act of 1933
Globe Aircraft, 321
Glyn & Co., 96
Godfrey, Charles H., 128
Godwin's Room, 77

Gold & Stock Telegraph Company, 86–87
Gold Exchange, *see* New York Gold Exchange
Gold Exchange Bank, 76, 98
Goldman, Marcus, 111
Goldman, Sachs & Co., 111, 153, 334
Gold Room, *see* New York Gold Exchange
gold rush of 1849, 54
gold speculation, 73–76
Goldwater, Barry, 374
Goluchowski, Count, 152
Gospel of Wealth, 161
Gould, George, 138
Gould, Jay, 84–85, 89–96, 115–19
Government Bond Department, 83
Graduation Act of 1854, 57
Graham, Benjamin, 342
Grant, "Buck," 118
Grant, Ulysses S., 89–90, 99, 106, 118–19
Grant & Ward, 118–19
Great Northern Railroad, 136, 163
Greeley, Horace, 58, 94
Green, Duff, 50
Green, Hetty, 114, 119
greenbacks, 73, 89, 125
Gresham's Law, 141
Greyhound Corporation, 305
Groesbeck, David, 87
Groesbeck, Ernest, 208
Guarantee Trust Company, 182, 200, 297
Gunnar Gold Mines, 347
Gunpowder Manufacturers' Association, 126
Gurney, Samuel, 34
Guterma, Alexander, 330
"guttersnipes," 78

Hall carbine affair, 109
Hallgarten & Hartzefelt, 78
Halsey, Stuart & Co., 242, 287
Hamilton, Alexander, 17, 22
Hanna, Mark, 148, 154
Hannibal & St. Joseph Railroad, 116
Hanson, Alvin, 308

Harding, Warren, 225
Harlem Railroad, 43, 59
Harriman, E. H., 112–13, 133–34, 144, 163–69, 184, 186, 190, 193, 200
Harriman Ripley & Co., 297
Harris, Forbes & Co., 154
Harris, N. W. & Co., 154
Harrison, Benjamin, 135
Hartford Foundation, 333
Harvard Economic Society, 266
Hatry, Clarence, 269
Hauge, Gabriel, 357
Hawtrey, R. G., 226
Heath, William, 86
Heintz & Co., 367
Heinze, Frederick Augustus, 189–92, 197
Heinze, Otto, & Co., 189, 191
Heller, Walter, 371
Henderson, Leon, 307
Henry, Patrick, 15
Hepburn Act, 188
Hepburn vs. Griswold, 89
Hertzfeld & Stern, 166
Hewitt, Abram, 124
Higgins, Joseph, 249, 267
Hill, James J., 133, 137, 163–65, 167, 184, 188
Hocking Valley Railroad, 245
Hodges, Luther, 371
Holmes, Oliver Wendell, 28
Hone, John, 33
Hone, Philip, 44, 47
Hoover, Herbert, 235–36, 268–69, 275, 279–82, 285–86, 289, 299, 352
Houghton, J., 175
Houseman, E. A. & Co., 145
Hudson & Mohawk Railroad, 38
Hughes, Charles Evans, 183, 188
Hughes Investigation, 198
Humphrey, George, 350, 352
Hungarian Rebellion, 352
Hunter's Daily Message, 180
Hunts' Merchants' Magazine, 175
Hyde, James Hazen, 183

Ickes, Harold, 298, 300
Illinois Central Railroad, 57

Insull, Samuel, 243–44, 250
Insull, Samuel, Jr., 287
Insull Utilities Investments, 244
International Harvester Corporation, 197
International Match Company, 245–46
International Mercantile Marine Company, 185, 193
International Silver Co., 156
Interstate Commerce Act, 127, 177
Ives, Henry, 111
Ives, Henry S. & Co., 111
Investment Advisors Act, 301
Investment Company Act, 301

Jackson, Andrew, 41–42, 44
Jefferson, Thomas, 18–19
Jerome, Addison, 79
Jerome, Leonard, 79, 113
Johnson, Lyndon, 373–74
Jonathan's coffee-house, 11
Jones, Edward D., 176
Joseph & Brothers, 48
Josephson, Matthew, 240–42

Kahn, Otto, 110, 165, 178, 237, 239, 294–96
Kansas City Gas Company, 177
Kansas-Nebraska Act, 57
Keene, James R., 115, 118, 138, 154–55, 163, 165–66, 193, 196
Kelley, William, 67
Kelly's Army, 139
Kennedy, John F., 358–59, 365, 368, 371–73
Kennedy, Joseph P., 250, 266, 285–86, 289, 300–302
Kentucky Distilleries' Association, 126
Kenyon, Cox & Co., 97
Ketchum, E. B., 76
Kidder, Peabody & Co., 111, 153–54
Kiernan News Service, 176
Kimber, Arthur, 90
King, J. G. & Sons, 50
Kletz, Michael, 363
Knickerbocker Ice Company, 192

Knickerbocker Trust Company, 192–93, 197
Knights of Labor, 126
Knox, Philander, 170
Knox vs. Lee, 89, 106
Kolster Radio Corporation, 249
Korean War, 324–26
Koster and Beal's Music Hall, 147
Kreuger, Ivar, 245–46, 250, 271, 286–87
Kreuger & Toll, Ltd., 287
Kuhn, Abraham, 110
Kuhn, Loeb & Co., 110–11, 129, 144, 153, 164–65, 183, 190, 237, 239, 297–98, 334
Kurtz, William, 367
Kyle, Alexander, 59

LaFollette, Robert, 266
LaGuardia, Fiorello, 285
Lake Superior Consolidated Iron Mining Company, 161–62
Lamb, William, 30
Lamont, Thomas, 238, 294–95, 305
Landes, Kenesaw Mountain, 184
Landis, James, 294, 300–2
Langam, John, 357
Law, John, 8–9
Lawrence, Joseph, 268–70
Lawson, Thomas W., 155, 177, 189
Lazard Fréres, 142
Lee Higginson & Co., 200, 245, 287
Lefkowitz, Louis, 365
Lehigh Valley Railroad, 143
Lehman Brothers, 111, 153, 297, 334
Levinson, John J., 248
Lewis, John H., 323
Libby-Owens-Ford Glass Corporation, 286
Liberty bonds, 216–17, 219, 223
liefhebbers, 6
Lincoln, Abraham, 74
Lincoln Trust Company, 193
Lindbergh, Charles, 265–66
Lion, David, 248
Lippman, Walter, 285, 368
Little, Jacob, 40–41, 43, 50, 60–62, 64, 72

Litton Industries, 361
Livermore, Clews & Co., 70
Livermore, Jesse, 246–47, 249–50, 263–64
Lockwood & Co., 98
Loeb, Gerald M., 305, 354
Loeb, Nina, 110
Loeb, Rhoades & Co., 356
Loeb, Solomon, 110
Lomasney, Michael A., 363
Lomasney, Michael A. & Co., 363
London, Jack, 139
London Stock Exchange, 88, 202, 208
"Long Room," 77, 85
Louisiana Company, 8
Louisville & Nashville Railroad, 82, 144
Louisville & Portland Canal Company, 37
Low, Seth, 170
Ludlow, Erza, 60
Lurie, Sidney, 346, 354
Lynch, Edmund, 336

McAllister, Ward, 113
Mac Arthur, Douglas, 325
McCall, John A., 184
McCoy, Joseph, 252–53
McEvers & Barclay, 20
McGrath Securities, 330
McKenna, J. P., 248
McKesson & Robbins Corporation, 306
McKinley, William, 147–151, **169**
McKinley Tariff, 134–35
McMahon, William J., 249
Macomb, Alexander, 18
Macomber, W. Sturgis, 342
Madison, James, 18
Magnetic Telegraph Company, 52
Mahler, Solomon, 92
Mahona, 3
Malony Amendment of 1938, 301
Manchester Guardian, 221
Manhattan Quotation Service, 87
Manual of Industrial Securities, 176
Manual of the Railroads of the United States, 175–76

Marconi, Guglielmo, 147
margin, 71
margin calls, 274
Marine National Bank, 118
Marquand & Dimock, 111
Marrinan, John, 287
Marron, Donald, 363
Martin, William McChesney, 358
Marx, Karl, 61
Massachusetts Investment Trust, 331–32
Massachusetts Life Insurance Company, 257
Maxwell, William, 17
May, George, 287
Maysville Veto, 41
Mazur, Paul M., 227
Medbury, James, 83
Meehan, Michael J., 248, 267, 270, 286, 301, 336
Mellon, Andrew, 230, 236, 279
Mercantile National Bank, 190–92
Merchants' Club of Chicago, 188
Merchants' coffee-house, 21
Merchants' Exchange Building, 39, 43, 58, 72
Merchants' Magazine, 53
Merrill, Charles, 334–39
Merrill, Charles E. & Co., 336
Merrill Lynch & Co., 336
Merrill Lynch, Pierce, Fenner & Beane, 337–38
Merrill Lynch, Pierce, Fenner & Smith, 334–35, 361, 363
Metropolitan Bank, 119
Metropolitan Street Railroad, 177–78
Metropolitan Street Railroad investigation, 188
Meyer, Eugene, 266, 281
Middle West Utilities, 244
Mining Exchange, 76
Mining Exchanges, 60, 62, 66, 68, 114
mining exchanges of 1849–53, 55
Mississippi Bubble, 8–9
Missouri, Kansas, & Texas Railroad, 97
Missouri Pacific Railroad, 244

Mitchell, C. A. & Co., 297
Mitchell, Charles A., 268–71, 273, 286, 288
Mohawk & Hudson Railroad Company, 37
Moley, Raymond, 294
Money Trust, 184–85, 199, 223
Monthly Investment Plan, 346
Moody, John, 176
Moody's Investment Service, 266
Moore, William, 161
Moore, John, 196
Moore & Schley, 196–97
Morgan, John Pierpont, 108–109, 120–21, 125, 136, 142–44, 153, 162–70, 182–85, 199–201, 236–37, 339, 374
Morgan, John Pierpont, Jr. 197, 200, 237–38, 245, 294–95, 305
Morgan, J. P. & Co., 108, 128, 143, 153, 163, 185, 237, 297
Morgan, J. S. & Co., 82, 109
Morgan, Junius Spencer, 57, 109, 121
Morgan, Walter, 343
Morgan Stanley & Co., 297–98, 308, 334
Morris, Walter, 342
Morris Canal & Banking Co., 34, 43
Morse, Anthony Wellman, 79
Morse, Charles W., 189–93, 197
Morse, Samuel F.B., 52
Morton, Levi, 111
Moyland, John, 248
Muir, William, 86
Munn, Glenn G., 323
Munsey, Frank, 179
Munsey's Magazine, 179
Murray's Wharf, 15
Musica, Phillip, 306
mutual funds, 331–33, 365
Mutual Life Insurance Company, 183–84, 200

Nabi, Stanley, 354
Nadler, Marcus, 339
Naess, Ragnar, 342
National Association of Securities Dealers, 307
National Bank of Commerce, 192

National Bank of North America, 193
National Bimetallic League, 141
National Biscuit Co., 156
National City Bank, 111, 164, 182, 194, 268–69, 278, 297
National City Company, 183, 240, 288
National Cordage Company, 137–38
National Federation of Financial Analysts, 340
National Park Bank, 150
National Recovery Act, 298
National Stock Exchange (first), 85
Neely, Frank H., 322
Nevers, B. M., 68
Nevins, R. H., 39
New Board, 51
New Deal, 285, 303–304
New Frontier, 359, 365
New Haven Railroad, 185
New Larder Uranium Mines, 347
New Street Market of 1914, 209–10, 212
New York Central Railroad, 54, 108, 118, 120
New York Chamber of Commerce, 214
New York, Chicago, and St. Louis Railroad, 244
New York Clearing House, 99, 125
New York Curb Agency, 199
New York Evening Sun, 194
New York Federal Reserve Bank, 351
New York Gas Light Company, 34
New York Gold Exchange, 75, 83, 91
New York Life Insurance Company, 183–84
New York Manufacturing Company, 24
New York Morning Herald, 53
New York and New England Railroad, 118
New York Quotation Service, 87
New York Society of Security Analysts, 340
New York Stock Exchange, 78, 83, 85–87, 98, 102–103, 114, 130–31, 140, 159–60, 171, 177, 186, 198, 202, 208–12, 254, 264, 275, 293, 298–99,

305–307, 314–15, 321; Clearing House, 99, 114, 120, 131, 191–92, 209–10; Committee on Business Conduct, 305; Law Department, 198; Unlisted Department, 198
New York Stock and Exchange Board, 30–31, 38–41, 43–44, 58–60, 67, 76
New York Stock Trust, 257
New York *Times,* 206
New York *Transcript,* 53
New York Tribune, 115
New York Warehouse and Security Company, 97
New York World, 115, 183
Niles' Weekly Register, 175
Nixon, Richard M., 351
Norbeck, Peter, 286
Norfolk & Western Railroad, 82, 144
Norris Locomotive Works, 57
North American Mines, 59
Northern Inland Lock Company, 32
Northern Pacific Railroad, 107, 118, 120, 133, 137–38, 143, 163–68, 184
Northern Securities, 170, 184
North States Gold and Copper, 79
Norton, Edward, 166
Noyes, Alexander, 179, 276
Nye Committee, 307

O'Brian, Esmonde, 248
O'Brian, Richard, 248
Ohio Life Insurance Company, 61
O'Mahoney, Joseph, 307
Open Board of Brokers (new), 114
Open Board of Stock Brokers (old), 77, 84–85
Overend, Gurney & Co., 88, 97

Pacific Mail Steamship Company, 68–69
Paine, Webber, Jackson & Curtis, 323, 367
Palmer, A. Mitchell, 225
Panama Railroad, 68
Panics (1837), 47–52; (1841), 50; (1853), 58–59; (1854), 59; (1857), 60–62, 65; (1861), 67–68; (1866),

Panics *(cont.)*
88; (1871), 94; (1873), 96–100, 106; (1877–1878), 103; (1884), 118–121; (1886), 130; (1893), 136–44; (1899), 153; (1903 Rich Man's Panic), 181–82; (1907), 188–98; (1920), 224–27; (1929), 269–79; (1962), 368–72
Payne, Oliver H., 136
Peabody, George, 36–37
Peabody & Co., 33, 109
Pecora, Ferdinand, 286, 296
Pecora Committee, 286–89, 299
Pennsylvania Company for Insurance in Lives and Granting Annuities, 29
Pennsylvania Railroad, 54, 120, 144
pension funds, 332–33
People's Capitalism, 335, 339–40, 346
Perkins, George W., 168
Pershing & Co., 367
Peto, Sir Morton, 81
Petroleum and Mining Board, 84
Petroleum Board, 76
Philadelphia Press, 82
Philadelphia & Reading Railroad, 57, 82, 137, 139
Pierce, E. A. & Co., 337
Pierpont, John, 109
Piggly-Wiggly Stores, 263–64
Pintard, John, 21
Plummer, A. Newton, 249, 285
Ponzi, Charles, 223–24
Poole, Alan, 354
pools, 127–28
Poor, Henry Varnum, 175–77
Populist Party, 126, 135
Porter, Horace, 90
Prices Current, 175
Prime, Nathaniel, 22, 30
Prime, Ward & Co., 50
Prime, Ward & Sands, 25, 33
Produce Exchange, 83, 160
Progressive movement, 184, 188
Province of Quebec bonds, 105
Public Utilities Holding Company Act, 301
Pujo, Arsené, 199

Pujo Committee, 199
Pullman strike, 139
Pure Food and Drug Act, 188
put and call options, 114–15

Raskob, John J. 238, 265, 267
Rayburn, Sam, 298
Re, Re, & Sagarese & Co., 363
Reconstruction Finance Corporation, 281
Reed, Cameron, 343
Reed, Whitelaw, 115
Resumption Act, 106
Richardson, William, 99
Rich Man's Panic, *see* Panics: 1903 *rederijii,* 6
"Red Scare" of 1920, 224–25
Richmond & West Point Terminal Company, 143
Ripley, William Z., 236
Robins, John, 33
Robinson, Dwight, 343
Rockefeller, John D., 127, 136, 161, 164, 193, 275
Rockefeller, William, 184
Rockefeller Foundation, 333
Rogers, Henry H., 177, 184
Roosevelt, Franklin D., 236, 269, 284–87, 289–90, 293, 298–305, 307, 310
Roosevelt, Theodore, 169, 184, 193–94, 197, 200
Root, Elihu, 184
Rothschild, Nathan, 10
Rothschild, N. M. & Sons, 36, 49–50, 109
Russell, Richard, 358–59
Russo-Japanese War, 186
Ryan, Allen A., 263
Ryan, Thomas Fortune, 110, 154–55, 183

Sacco-Vanzetti Case, 224
Sachs, Samuel, 111
Sage, Russell, 114, 121, 138
St. Louis Stock Exchange, 55
San Francisco earthquake, 187
San Francisco Stock Exchange, 94
Santtee Canal, 32

Satterlee, Herbert, 197, 200
Saunders, Clarence, 263–64
Schacht, Hjalmar, 244
Schaefer, George E., 358–59
Schiff, Frieda, 110
Schiff, Jacob, 110, 133, 139, 144, 151, 153, 159, 164–66, 182, 184, 187, 193
Schiff, Mortimer, 239
Schlesinger, Arthur M. Jr., 280
Schley, Grant B., 196
Schoembs, Frank, 342
Schuyler, Robert, 59
Schuyler, Walker & Co., 137
Schwab, Charles, 161–62, 165, 185, 225, 277
Schwartz, Charles, 355
Seaboard Airlines Railroad, 266
Second Bank of the United States, 29, 42
Second National Bank, 119
Securities Act of 1933, 294, 298–99
Securities and Exchange Act, 299–300
Securities and Exchange Commission, 299–302, 304–305, 308, 330, 365, 368
Seligman, J. & W. & Co., 110, 129
Senate Committee on Banking and Currency, 286, 294, 298–99
Senate Subcommittee on Stock Exchange Practices, 293
Seney, George I., 119
Seward, William, 67
Shaker Heights, 244
shareholders in 1893, 130
Shawano Development Corporation, 330
Sherman Anti-Trust, 134, 196
Sherman Silver Purchase Act, 134, 141
Shields & Co., 322
Shiloh, battle of, 69
short sales, 41
silver issue, 97, 125, 132, 148
Simmons, William J., 270, 284
Sinclair Consolidated Oil Corporation, 249
Six Per Cent Club, 18–19
Sloan, Alfred, 276

Smith, Alfred E., 236
Smith, Barney & Co., 297
Smith, Bernard, 306
Smith, Edward B. & Co., 297
Smith, Gould, Martin & Co., 95, 99
Smith, Henry N., 95, 118
Smith H. L. Co., 137
Smith, Winthrop, 337
social Darwinism, 112, 240
Solon, 2–3
South Africa gold strike, 149
Southern Pacific Railroad, 163
Southern Railroad Company, 143
South Sea Bubble, 9–10
Spanish-American War, 152
Specie Circular, 44
Spencer, Vila & Co., 70
Speyer, Albert, 91, 93, 101, 184
Speyer & Co., 36, 153, 163
Standard Oil Company, 127; of Indiana, 184; of New Jersey, 184, 190–91, 199, 276
Stanley, Harold, 297
Statist (London), 107
Steagall, Henry B., 296
Stedman, E. C., 92, 159
Stedman, Samuel, 354
Stern, Al, 166–67
Stillman, James, 111, 164, 178, 182–84, 191, 193–95
Stock and Exchange Board, *see* New York Stock and Exchange Board
stock dividends, 222
Stockholm, Anthony, 30
stock purchase plans, 333–34
stock-watering, 130
Stockwell, Alden, 81
Strauss, Lewis, 239
Strong, Benjamin, 199–200, 235, 237, 265–66
Stuart, Harold, 287
Stutz Motor Corporation, 263
Stuyvesant, Peter, 15
Suez Crisis of 1956, 352
Suffolk System, 45
Sugar Refineries Company, 127
Swan-Finch, Inc., 330
Swift & Co., 126, 302

Tabell, Edmund W., 322, 342, 352, 356–59, 368
Taft, William Howard, 199
Talenfeld Brothers, 330
Talmadge & Mawley, 60
tariffs (1816), 29; (1861), 69
Taylor, Talbot, 165
technicians, market, 341
telegraph, invention of, 52
telephone, influence of, 87, 131
Tellies, Walter, 329
Tellies & Co., 329
Temporary National Economic Committee, 307–309, 311
Tennessee Coal & Iron Co., 156, 196–97
Texas Company, 239
Texas Instruments, Inc., 361
Thomas, R. H., 194
Thompson, John, 43
Thorne, Oakleigh, 194
Thornton, Charles "Tex," 361
ticker, introduction of, 86, 131
Tilden, Samuel, 102
Tobin, John, 79
Tontine Coffee-House, 21–22, 26, 29
Toronto Stock Exchange, 347
Train, George Francis, 45, 58
transatlantic cable, 65
Tri-Continental Corporation, 257
Truman, Harry, 316, 322, 325, 335
Trust Company of America, 193–94
Trust Indenture Act of 1939, 301
"Truth in Securities Act," *see* Securities Act of 1933
tulip mania, 7
Tweed, William, 91, 94

Underwood Corporation, 356
Union Carbide Co., 156
Union Pacific Railroad, 88, 137, 139, 144, 163, 167, 177, 186, 190
Union Trust Co., 98
United Copper Co., 190–91
United Corporation, 242
United Dye & Chemical, Inc., 330
United Funds, Inc., 332
United Mexican Mining, 35

United States Commercial and Shipping Register, 175
United States Economist, 175
United States and Foreign Securities, 259
United States Rubber Co., 127
United States Steel Co., 156–57, 162–63, 167, 185, 190, 196, 199, 214, 218, 308
Untermyer, Samuel, 199

Van Buren, Martin, 48
Vanderbilt, Cornelius, 84–85, 92, 99
Vanderbilt, William, 108, 120–21
Vaness Co., 245
Van Riper, L. C., 174–75
Van Sweringen, Mantio James, 244, 250
Van Sweringen, Oris Paxton, 244, 296
Vaupell, George, 31
Veeder, Albert H., 126
Villard, Henry, 115, 118, 120, 136

Walcott, Frederic C., 286
Wald, Lillian, 139
Walker, Benjamin, 18
Wall Street, 15, 31, 47, 53, 78, 81, 113–14
Wall Street Journal, 157, 176, 270–71, 276
Wall Street National Bank, 117
Walpole, Robert, 10
Warburg, Felix M., 110, 239
Warburg, Paul, 110, 199, 270
Ward, Ferdinand, 118
Ward, Samuel, 50
Ward, Thomas, 33, 36
warrants, 363
Washington, George, 15
wash sales, 30–31, 66
Watts, John, 15
Weaver, James B., 135
Weekly Review of Trade, 136
Weeks, Sinclair, 348
Wellington Fund, Inc., 332
Western Inland Lock Navigation Company, 32

Western Union, 53, 87, 119
Westinghouse Air Brake Co., 127
Westinghouse Corporation, 192
Wheeling and Lake Erie Railroad, 244
Whiskey pool, 127
White, Horace, 187
White, S. V., 137
White, William Allen, 148
Whitney, George, 238–39
Whitney, Richard, 273–75, 286, 288–89, 299, 305–307
Whitney, Richard & Co., 305
Whitney, William C., 136
Widener, Peter A. B., 177
Wiggin, Albert, 249, 269, 273
Willing & Francis, 36
Wills, John, 70
Wilson, Charles, 352–53

Wilson, Woodrow, 215–16, 220–21
Winchell, Walter, 347–48
Windels, Paul Jr., 328
Windowglass Trust, 127
Woerishoffer, Charles, 115–16, 119, 136
Wolf, Addie, 110
Woodward, W. S., 90
World War I, 213–20
World War II, 310–16
Wright, J. Hood, 128
Wright Aeronautical Corporation, 266
Wycoff, H. I., 39

Young, Roy, 267
Young America Movement, 58

Zimmerman, Louis, 248